THIS ALL ENCOMPASSING TRIP

CHASING PEARL JAM AROUND THE WORLD

JASON LEUNG

An Infinitum Publishing Trade Paperback Original

Published in 2010 by Infinitum Publishing
a division of Infinitum Limited based in:
London, UK, Vancouver, BC, New York, NY
infinitumlimited.com

This is a work of nonfiction. Names, characters, places, and incidents are based on real facts from a true story, as viewed by the writer. The opinions of the writer are not intended to malign any religion, ethnic group, club, organization, company, gender, sexual orientation, or individual.

Book design by Sophie Kelle and Infinitum Limited

Cover sketches by Sophie Kelle
based on photographs by Jason Leung (bottom front cover photo),
Rob McVicar (top front cover photo),
and Joe Sarabia (back cover photo)

Photographs by Dana Eskelson (p 119, 236, 265, 273), Dirk Hoeppner (p 49, 56, 68),
Sophie Kelle (p 89, 112), Stefan Klopp (p 3, 10, 15, 22, 30, 33, 37, 40, 43, 44, 58, 64, 74,
76, 77, 86, 74, 76, 77, 86, 93, 94, 100, 101, 110, 111, 114, 212), Brad Laing (p 82, 391),
Monica Lopez (p 228, 248, 249), Barbara Manfredi (p 396, 398),
Annette O'Brien (p 341, 346, 352), Grethe Pin Onstad (p 281, 282, 283),
Ben Rae (p 371), Michael Spanagel (p 370, 375), Joe Sarabia (p 53, 70, 241, 253, 318),
and Jason Leung (all other photos)

Printed and bounded in the United States of America and
the United Kingdom by Lightning Source

Library of Congress Control Number: 2010914506

ISBN 978-0-578-06885-5

Please visit the website:
thisallencompassingtrip.com

For my mom and dad,
who raised me to be the person I am today.

Acknowledgements

This book would not be possible without the love and support of my parents and family. I am truly grateful for your patience and understanding throughout all of my crazy travels.

I would also like to give a huge thanks to:

The Pearl Jam family of fans, for being extraordinary people, without you guys there would be no story to write about.

Stefan and Tak, for getting this whole thing started with me.

Touring Van, European Tour Bus, and Aussie Van crews, for being unbelievable companions on the road.

All my friends in Vancouver and all over the world, for making me feel at home wherever I am.

My team of editors, Shree Bhattacharya, Rebecca Clark, Vicki Fraser, Andrew George, Kim Harrison, Randi Hethey, Sophie Kelle, Mandy Key, Janet McCullough, and Annette O'Brien, for correcting all my writing errors.

Infinitum publishing, for putting my memories into print.

Pearl Jam, for being the great rock band that they are.

Sophie, for being the inspiration to finish this book.

CONTENTS

PROLOGUE

"Are we getting something out of this all encompassing trip?" Eddie Vedder asks this question in the song *Present Tense* from Pearl Jam's 1996 release *No Code*. It's my favourite song from my favourite band and I've probably heard this song tens of thousands of times, yet, I had never really considered what the lyrics meant to me personally. That is until one summer afternoon in 2005.

As I lie on my surfboard out in the ocean off the shores of Wickannanish Beach on the West Coast of Vancouver Island, the water is calm, the sky is clear and, my back endures the intensity of the heat beaming down from the flaming sun. I patiently wait for the next set of waves that only scale about half my height. The following day I will embark on a trip across Canada with two guys from my hometown of Vancouver – two guys whom I've met only four times. We'll be picking up a bunch of complete strangers to follow Pearl Jam on tour in a van, which we had just purchased only one week prior. The plan is to drive across Canada to do their entire tour and I have no idea what I'm getting myself into. All I know is that I have always wanted to drive across and explore my home country, and Pearl Jam has given me an excuse to do so.

Am I crazy? There will be 17 concerts in total, including a warm up show at the gorgeous Gorge Amphitheater in Washington State, but I have previously seen this band quite frequently already. Do I really need to see more? Well, of course I do. This isn't just any normal band. This is Pearl Jam. This is the music that I've grown up to, it has been the soundtrack of my life, and is the reason why I have the passion that I do for music. But still, isn't this just a little excessive? I decided to do this without too much thought, and the decision was instantaneous as soon as the tour dates were announced. And although I'm usually very confident in all my decisions and stick with them through to the end, I wasn't sure why I was so confident this time around. Somehow I felt that this is something I have to do.

Sitting out in the "lineup" resting my soul and my mind, I question myself.

Meanwhile, I'm peeking over my shoulders to study the ocean, watching and trying to figure out wave patterns and deciding which one to make an attempt for takeoff. There's music running through my mind and it's usually one of the songs that have been playing in my vehicle on the way to the beach. At this moment the song is *Present Tense*. A glimpse of hope approaches. I take a peek and decide that this is the one to go for so I turn back toward the beach and paddle for my life. The wave hits the back of my board and I feel that I'm there. As I'm reassuring myself, my board begins to dive and I slowly try to pop up, but hesitate slightly and it's too late.

I fall toward the water with the wave breaking into me. While underwater, I'm taken for a spin, tumbling around like a helpless piece of clothing in a washing machine. A few seconds later, I escape but there's another wave coming down upon me. Underwater I go again and the washing machine takes me for another ride. I'm stuck in this position for another three waves before the set ends and I can escape again. After making my way back out, I'm exhausted and I take a rest, but the ocean won't allow it. I start paddling as an approaching wave sweeps me up. My board begins to dive again but, this time without any thought, I pop right up and drop smoothly in.

The wave nearly matches my height and takes me for an adventure. The power, the speed, and the excitement of 'walking on water' put me on top of the world. I feel free – I feel alive. This one wave alone makes the whole two-day surf trip worthwhile and I take it all the way to the beach, satisfied and content to end my session for the day with *Present Tense* still on my mind. "Are we getting something out of this all encompassing trip?"

As I walk from water to sand, it hits me. Life is much like surfing. The ocean is massive and unpredictable with endless possibilities. So you go out to a spot where you feel comfortable, you study its environment, you constantly evaluate and assess your position, you try to predict what's going to come toward you, and then you have to decide where you want to go from there. You can stay put and do nothing and you'll probably be safe, but do you get anything out of it? Do you gain any experience, do you learn, do you get any enjoyment? Or can you identify what you want and go for it when recognized? Patience is important as your opportunities may come infrequently but, when it does, you must grab it and make the most of it.

My whole life I've been studying and analyzing everything around me. And when the opportunity came for me to take on the trip of my life, I went for it without any hesitation at all. This is why I'm so confident. I'm ready to take chances – I'm ready to explore and put myself into unknown places and unfamiliar situations. I'm ready to learn from it all and better myself in the process. If nothing else, I will meet some new friends on a crazy road trip. I'm ready for this adventure, this all encompassing trip.

PART ONE
THE CANADA TOUR

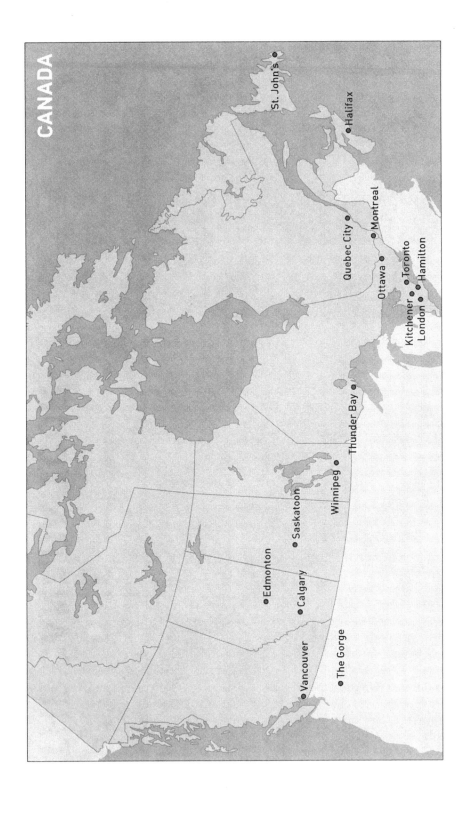

CHAPTER 1: **THE WARM UP**

September 1, 2005 » Show 1
The Gorge, Washington

ANTICIPATION HIT ME as soon as I clicked the checkout button on the goods section of Pearl Jam's website, authorizing $1743.95 to be charged on my credit card. I had just purchased tickets to every single Pearl Jam show on their tour across Canada and I've never looked more forward to anything in my life. The whole thing is still a mystery to me, but the unknown aspect of it all makes it even more exciting. I don't even know the people who I'm travelling with. But by all accounts, they seem alright.

I first came into contact with my travel mates on the Pearl Jam message forum, after writing about the possibly of travelling across my home country for this tour. Within minutes of my post, I received an enthusiastic response and was contacted about it by two fans that live in the very city where I have lived my entire life. Those two fans were Stefan and Tak.

Stefan is originally from Fauquier, a small town in the mountains of British Columbia, but lives in the trendy part of Vancouver now. After spending some time in Africa teaching computers in Uganda, he currently works as a web developer for an online car rental company. His soft spoken manner doesn't quite fit his 1.9m tall body frame, but he seems like an honest guy who can be depended on.

Tak, who lives on the east side of Vancouver, is in the restaurant and catering industry. He appears to have a good business sense and a keen interest in the marketing aspects of the music industry, so planning the tour with him has been effortless. The three of us met up on four different occasions, and a plan was hatched to drive across Canada to follow Pearl Jam.

This vacation will be a great change of pace from my daily life. My routine over the last few years had become somewhat bland. Thanks to an engineering degree, my weeks are filled with 12-hour work days as a construction coordinator/

engineer on a prominent highway construction project for the 2010 Vancouver Winter Olympics. Then in the evenings, I would endure 2 hours of boxing training three times a week and, on top of that, there would be at least one hockey game for me to sweat through in a recreational league. The weekends are the only times that I have for relaxation. I am really looking forward to a month of not having to worry about "making budget on my daily costs reports" or "keeping my hands up" when I'm sparring. I'm sure Stefan and Tak welcome the time off as well.

Anticipating the adventure that we'll take on together, we discussed the details necessary to make this work, with the biggest concern being our method of travel. We concluded that the best solution would be to buy a van and drive to each city, while offering rides along the way to help share and minimize expenses. As the tour approached, we were able to find a van and, from advertising on the message boards, passengers were signing up. Everything was coming together.

Months after the announcement of the Canadian dates, a warm up show was added at the very last minute, so we alter our plans slightly to accommodate it. This show will take place just prior to the tour at the amazing Gorge Amphitheater in George, WA, two hours east of Seattle and, going by past reviews of the venue, it's one not to be missed. Besides, what's one more show right? If anything, this mini road trip will help kick off the tour for us in grand fashion and will also give us a good indication on how our vehicle, fully loaded, might perform over the next few weeks. With this sudden development, we quickly assemble a group to fill the van for this trip, our maiden voyage.

I invite my friend Jacinta, from Melbourne, Australia, who I had met on a surf trip to Vancouver Island earlier in the year. Surfing is one of my methods of escaping the daily grind. I enjoy the calm nature of the sport and normally fit it into my active schedule once a month. On the trip where I met Jacinta, I had just finished fighting through the rough waves to get back on shore, when the Australian makes an observation. "You call that surfing?" she questions, with the thickest surfing Australian accent I've heard. We became good friends ever since and she unquestionably became my travel idol, having lived and worked in a variety of places around the world including Scotland, England, India, and now Vancouver. So it's only fitting to have her come along with me as I set forth on an exciting journey of my own. Jacinta has been a fan of the band for some time but hasn't seen them live since they toured Australia in 1998. The allure of the venue is another selling point for her.

Doubling my recruitment success, Stefan invites two of his friends along, Brad and Lester. Brad, who met Stefan one year earlier at a Pearl Jam show in Seattle at the Benaroya Hall, is from Kelowna but living in Vancouver. Sporting a goatee and dressed in a fancy Hawaiian shirt, which puts all of our dull clothing to shame, he also plans to head out east to catch some of the Ontario shows later in the tour. He claims that when he's meeting people at shows, the flashy attire is helpful for them to find him. I can't argue with that. Lester, another Vancouverite, is a concert enthusiast himself, usually attending a different local show every week including seeing Canadian artist, Matthew Good, over 30 times live. He basically attends every concert, with good taste, that comes to Vancouver.

Tak, on the other hand, has no friends to invite. He complains about how none of his friends listen to good music and keeps reminding us how refreshing it is to have found people with similar musical interests living in the same city. We feel the same way. So it's me, Stefan, Tak, Lester, Brad, and Jacinta – making up the inaugural van crew. The original six if you will.

On the day of the show, I circle around the city to pick everyone up, arriving at the Peace Arch border crossing – off Highway 99 – by noon. Traffic is heavy so Brad alertly suggests we take the truck crossing just down the road. This alternative is better but still entails what appears to be a good hour of waiting. Brad then notes that we can bypass the line and overtake the traffic through the duty free shop up ahead if we just purchase a drink or something. What a great idea! I switch lanes and fly passed the group of grumpy impatient border-crossers and head into the parking lot of the shop. We go inside for about 10 minutes, pick up a case of beer and, as we exit through the doors, we notice a long line of plastic Canadian flags fencing around the store.

"We need a flag on the van," says Tak, pulling a few off the string.

He then proceeds to stick the flags all over the van, including one on the front over top of the very American Dodge emblem. This only adds to the artistic transformation that Stefan and I had carefully performed on the van last night. Using a variety of colours of Canadian hockey tape, we spelled out *Pearl Jam Canadian Tour Van* on the front of the hood with the corresponding tour city names strategically placed along the sides. They've been laid out in chronological order of the forthcoming shows starting on the driver side, wrapping around the back, and continuing on toward the passenger side of the van. Each city is separated by an upside down red triangle resembling a yield sign, in reference to the Pearl Jam record, *Yield*. I consider myself quite artistic, but even I'm impressed with how this turned out.

"You guys should check off those yield signs as you complete each city," Brad suggests, as we add the latest piece of art to the van. Stefan and I look at each other with smiles.

"That's not a bad idea," Stefan replies. Jumping back into the van, we pull out of the lot and leap frog in front of the queue. The border patrol approaches quickly with 40 minutes saved.

"Well, what have we got here? The Pearl Jam Canadian tour van," the border official points out. "You do realize that you're leaving Canada don't you?"

"There's a concert at the Gorge today before the Canadian tour," I explain handing over all of our passports.

"When are you returning?"

"After the show tonight."

The officer takes a few minutes to examine our passports.

"Okay. Just pull over to the side here and come inside for a few minutes. We just have some paperwork to do for the Australian, then you can be on your way."

We oblige and head inside.

"Oh no, I'm going to delay you guys," Jacinta says with remorse.

"Don't worry. It shouldn't take long. So long as you have nothing to hide," I joke.

About 15 minutes, a $6 entry fee, and a search of the van later, we're free and back on the road. Traffic is much lighter south of the border and the speed limits are much higher so, heading south on the I-5 highway, I accelerate as if we had gotten away with something. The drive is filled with music provided by Brad, a mix that includes Death Cab for Cutie, Sleater-Kinney, The Supersuckers, and The White Stripes. A fine collection to drive to, however, I'm feeling a little tired so, about an hour into America, I relinquish the driving duties to Stefan. Up in the sky there are a number of dangerous looking clouds hovering around that causes a slight concern, since the venue is outdoors. But as we enter Seattle and turn onto I-90 east, the sun breaks through overpowering any chances of precipitation. Our anticipation is so intense that barely any words are spoken in the van. It's not going to be like this the whole trip, is it?

As we approach closer to the venue, we pull off the freeway at the town of North Bend. Lester and I head to the Safeway supermarket for some sandwiches and more beer for the show, leaving Stefan to fill up the tank. When we return to the van, we find Tak talking to some folks from the car beside us with such enthusiasm that you'd think he was trying to sell the van. We get back in and Stefan remains as the captain for the remaining half-hour drive.

"Those guys are going to the show too. They saw our van on the highway," says Tak, breaking the ice.

"I wonder how much notoriety you guys will receive," Jacinta asks.

"I don't know, but I just want to meet some good people and make it all the way to the other side," Stefan explains.

"Yeah, whatever we do will be fun and anything else will just be a bonus," I reply, reaching for the camcorder to try and get everyone involved.

I begin to capture some of the scenic drive toward eastern Washington on film as well as the excitement among our passengers. My experience with a video camera is even less than my experience with driving cross country, but I plan to play around with the camera I borrowed from a friend and document the trip every step of the way. Crossing the bridge over the Columbia River, a brown rectangular sign with the words "The Gorge Amphitheater Next Right" quickly approaches, resulting in a simultaneous cheer almost on cue. As we exit and follow the ramp around under the freeway, a patrol car parked at the bottom of the hill slows down our speed and our excitement level, but only momentarily. Following the vehicles in front of us, assuming they're heading in the same direction, we reach a traffic director standing in the middle of the road. He asks whether we're camping or parking and, although camping sounds like a lot of fun, we turn left for the parking lot.

With Neil Young on rotation, we enter the grassy parking lot, which seems more fitted for a game of football than a lot for vehicles. One by one we are lined up like players on the line of scrimmage to fill up the field as efficiently as possible. There are already thousands of cars parked and it's barely 4:00pm. We jump out of the van, each holding a beer, and celebrate our arrival. I feel quite content. At the venue entrance, there's a separate table in front of the box office for Ten Club tickets, the ones purchased directly through the Ten Club, Pearl Jam's fan club. These are our tickets.

"How did you do?" Stefan asks me.

"Let me see. Row 17," I reply.

"What? Me too!"

I take a look at his ticket, then a look at mine, then a look at his again.

"Dude, you're right beside me!"

"Really?"

"Yeah, look!"

Stefan glances over. "Awesome!"

The Ten Club ticketing system is based on seniority of membership: each member is assigned a membership number in sequential order of the date when the member joined. So basically, the earlier you joined the club, the lower your membership number will be. And the lower your membership number, the closer your seats will be for the show. It turns out that Stefan and my membership numbers are only a few numbers apart, a pretty amazing coincidence considering there are hundreds of thousands of members in the club.

"Where did you sit at the Vancouver show in 2003?" I ask him.

"Like the 20th row," Stefan replies.

"Ha ha. I was probably right beside you, probably even talked to you too."

"That's hilarious! It looks like we'll have four seats together for most, if not all, of the shows on this tour. That would be perfect!"

"That's if we don't get sick of each and I'm forced to start trading my tickets away," I laugh.

We get back to the van and Brad has already picked up a few posters for us. There's usually a unique poster done by a graphic artist for each show. These are immensely popular with the collectors. I've never really been into poster collecting but since I'm doing the whole tour, I thought I'll try and pick up posters for as many of the shows as I can. Gathered around the van for a few beers, we are approached by some fans coming by for a chat. A group even flew in from Georgia – Kyle, Jeff, and Kelly. We introduce ourselves and then Kyle sees my camcorder.

"Are you guys filming the trip?" Kyle asks.

"Yeah, I don't know what we're going to do with it, but we're going to film our trip and try to interview some fans. I've never used this thing before," I explain while pointing the camera toward them.

"Well, we did something similar during part of the last tour. It was a lot of fun, so hope you guys make a better one with some Canadians in it," Kyle says, as he hands over a DVD.

"Cool, we'll check it out! Canadians will definitely make it better!"

As the afternoon passes by, more and more fans continue to stop by on their way to the entrance, including a girl wearing a pair of glasses and holding a pad of paper.

"Hi, my name is Whitney and I'm writing an article for *Entertainment Weekly* magazine. May I interview you guys and take a few photos?" she asks.

"Of course," Tak replies, thrilled about the possible publicity. She tells us that she's a fan herself and has become intrigued with other Pearl Jam fans after chatting with some at a previous show.

"I was asking some fans what they thought of the show and they were like, 'It was good but, oh my god, did you go to Philly or New York?' So I was like, 'What? Who are these guys?'"

Well, these were guys like us, or who we're going to be for this tour anyway. She explains that her article will discuss whether Pearl Jam is the modern day Grateful Dead, with fans travelling from show to show until they drop. We take turns answering the questions, as she holds out her tape recorder in an upright position. A few photos are taken and then we give her our contact information and offer to keep in touch and help with whatever she needs for the article.

The original 6 in front of the van at the Gorge Amphitheater, Jacinta, me, Tak, Brad, Stefan, and Lester.

"I told you that you'll get some kind of notoriety," Jacinta explains as she grabs the camera. "Okay, what are you guys feeling right now?"

"Excited!" Lester replies.

"Anticipated!" Stefan follows.

"Anxious!" I offer. "I'm ready!"

"This is it. The first show of the tour," says Tak.

"This might be the best one," Jacinta hopes.

"It might be. But it's just the first one and every one after will only get better," I reason.

"Ok you guys ready?" asks Lester.

"Let's do it!" we bellow in chorus.

Entering through the gates, we advance toward a massive grass hill. As the horizon of the hill lowers, the sight of the blue sky grows, with the stage slowly revealing itself; and the more we see of the stage, the more we see the Columbia River running behind it within an actual gorge. When we arrive at the top of the hill, we stop and just stand frozen for a few minutes gazing down in awe. It's absolutely beautiful. Like a ski hill, the grass slopes back down before it begins to step down. This is known as the general lawn area. Below the lawn is the reserved seating area, where about 40 or 50 rows of chairs are laid out, each row wider than the last, as you go further from the stage. Behind the stage is the majestic view of the Columbia River. Stefan, Tak and Lester all stroll down to their seats, Brad is already in his front row seat, but Jacinta and I are so mesmerized by the sight from the lawn that we decide to stay up top for a little while longer. We find a spot on the grass and sit, savouring the surroundings.

"Wow this is gorgeous," Jacinta breathes.

"It really is. I've heard how lovely this place is, but this is just insane," I reply.

"Is there a supporting act?"

"I don't think so. The event says that it's an evening with Pearl Jam so I'm curious to see what that means."

With Pearl Jam having no new record to promote, this will be an unusual tour. Their two previous releases were a greatest hits album and a b-sides and rarities album, both in the same year, with their last new material being released three years ago. However, there have been rumours that a collection of new songs has been written for an upcoming album so we're hoping that they may give us a preview during this tour. As the clock strikes 6:00pm, the crowd begins to whistle and cheer and the band takes the stage. I have goosebumps all over me. Pearl Jam is going to be opening for Pearl Jam.

"Everybody in?" asks Vedder, as the other band members grab their acoustic instruments and take a seat. The first note hits and my eyes light up.

"Holy shit! *I Believe in Miracles*! A Ramones cover!" I tell Jacinta.

After the song Vedder looks around the venue.

"It's not bad, eh? Certain things in life take a long time getting there but, once you get there, it's just fucking spectacular," Vedder says, referring to the amazing backdrop of the Columbia River, which is in clear sight through the open stage. He then tells us that there's a gentleman by the name of Tom Petty in the area.

"He's going to play here tomorrow and the next night. He's staying at a hotel and can hear us right now so hello Tom. They're not going to get any sleep tonight, but we'll go easy on him for a bit," Vedder speaks over the crowd's uproar. The next few songs are played acoustically and beautifully. Then around 6:30pm, the sun begins to set, and the colours of the gorge begin to magnify. The band takes cue.

"We want to get this song to go with what's happening over there," Vedder explains pointing to the sky, before the band goes into *Lowlight*. Wow, is this for real? What great timing. The music amplifies from the gorge and fills the air. I don't think I've ever seen a performance of any kind amidst such a natural, beautiful environment. Stage effects and lighting shows are something that can be easily done with money and creativity, but this is just out of this world. The music travels perfectly up into my ears. Now *this* is what I signed up for. The set closes with a performance of *Hard to Imagine*, a song that they haven't played in a decade.

"Wow! That was amazing!" Jacinta claims.

"Yes it was! And that's just the beginning."

We head down to the seated area to locate our actual seats, which are easily found once we spot Stefan and Lester. We rave about the show and then head over to the beer garden located just to the side of the stage. The buzz is swarming around, as everyone is talking about the performance thus far. Finally reaching the front of the drink line, we grab a few beers to try and bring ourselves back down from the almost surreal experience we were a part of. Before we know it, the crowd erupts again. It's nearly dark at this point and the band is already back on stage kicking right into *Given to Fly*, a rocking song, and we're still at the beer garden feverishly trying to finish our drinks.

"Here we go," Vedder yells, just as the mellow beginning of the song picks up momentum and kicks into overdrive. Taking cue, we jump and hop toward our seats almost in synch with the drum beats being pounded out by Matt Cameron. The song is sheer energy. What a way to start the main set! Vedder finally takes a break to address the crowd three songs later.

"Hello Tom. Hey Tom, come on down," is all Vedder says before they go right back into rocking. It's rocker after rocker, including two back to back rarities from their b-sides record, *Alone* and *Sad*.

"Oh man, what's next?" I turn to Stefan who's smiling like a kid at Christmas. A few more upbeat songs later, Vedder announces that they're going to play something they've never played live before – *Undone*. We are completely blown away. Totally unexpected, and we almost don't even recognize it. What a special show this is shaping up to be. Vedder continues to tease us about Tom Petty and urges us to join him in sending a message to Mr. Petty.

"Hello Tom, come down Tom!" Vedder instructs, as the crowd of 20,000 follow. The chant is led several times throughout the show but is unsuccessful in luring the subject down to the stage. It's good fun though.

"We don't know when we'll see you again but hopefully this will last for awhile," Vedder says at the end of two encores. "Thank you all so much for coming all this way and your support over the years." Don't worry. We'll see you guys tomorrow night. "If it's alright with you, we just called up and cancelled Vancouver tomorrow night," he jokes.

The show finally comes to a close after yet another encore and the marathon has reached three and a half hours in length. If this warm up show is any indication of what's to come, we're in for one hell of a tour. At the exit gates, there's a mad scramble to get to the vehicles. Why is everyone in such a hurry? Then it becomes apparent, as the traffic jam shows exactly how thousands of vehicles attempting to enter one exiting road is supposed to look like. The idea of camping at the venue seems like a good option now. With the lot completely jammed up, we're content to stay put and wait it out. Brad twirls a drum stick, the very same one used by Matt Cameron at the show – a nice little souvenir.

"It's my third one."

"That was one of the best shows I've seen all year," Lester notes.

"I got something to donate to the van," Kyle from Georgia states as he approaches and slaps on some stickers that he had purchased at the show on the van.

"Wow, thanks man. They look great," I reply. "See you tomorrow."

We lounge around on the grassy field chatting underneath star filled black skies, all in a state of joy, waiting another hour before we even think about moving out. When back on the highway, the van is silent inside, as most begin to feel the effects of the long day. The traffic exiting the venue is still heavy and I have five hours of driving ahead of me. I begin to wear down too, so Stefan takes over for a shift just before getting back on to I-5. After an easy entry back into Canada, I jump back on the wheel.

"The van drives great, we'll be alright for the trip," Stefan reckons.

I deliver everyone back to their respective houses and finally drive myself home, through a surprising amount of traffic at this time of the night. Then I realize that I'm at the beginning of morning rush hour and the sun is rising. The time is 7:00am. I'm not going to get much rest during this trip, am I?

CHAPTER 2: **THE HOMETOWN SHOW**

September 2, 2005 » Show 2
Vancouver, British Columbia

THE FIRST CANADIAN SHOW of the tour is an exciting one. It's our hometown show and, with a great warm up from the previous night under our belt already, we're looking forward to this tour even more. I roll out of bed at around 11:00am after rolling in just three hours prior. There are a billion things that must be done before I can go on this trip. But first, I call my friend Cristin, who's coming up from Seattle to see the show with me. She's at work and thrilled about coming to Vancouver for the first time. Next, I begin to pack. Staring at my dresser, I ponder over what deems necessary for a month-long road trip, but too much time is spent procrastinating so I just randomly grab five shirts, a pair of pants, a hoodie, some socks and underwear, throw them in a big backpack, and that is it.

Still reeking of the ocean from all the sand I brought back from Vancouver Island, the van needs a big clean up. I had taken the van for a test run on a surf trip just before the Gorge and it passed. Previously owned by my friend Albert, the 1989 Dodge Ram E150 was purchased collectively by me, Stefan, and Tak. It had served as a team van for the hockey team that Albert and I played for the last few seasons, so I knew what I was getting in return. The blue painted exterior may be falling apart but the engine has been babied since the day it was purchased. When our search for the perfect van during the months leading up to the trip didn't yield much success, I continued to harass Albert about his van. He finally gave in and sold the Dodge to us with only a few weeks remaining, our trip was saved. I knew that this was the ideal vehicle even though the others were sceptical when the engine wouldn't start at their first encounter. But they trusted my judgment and gave the approval for the purchase. Putting in another thousand dollars on maintenance and repairs and the van was ready for action.

I give the van's interior a thorough cleaning and vacuuming along with a detailed washing of the outside and, before I know it, the vehicle looks as good as new, with the exception of some paint still peeling off. I examine the van for a good five minutes and think to myself, 'This is home for the next month.' A big grin creeps upon my face, which is then wiped off with a phone call around 2:00pm from Cristin.

"I've got bad news. I'm not sure if I can make it. I can't leave work yet because there's a labour happening." She works as a Spanish translator in a hospital.

"Don't worry, you'll be alright, there's still plenty of time. How long does a labour usually take?" I ask.

"It could be any length of time, a few hours or more sometimes. You never know with these things," she replies.

"It'll be fine. You'll make it."

"I hope so!"

The van nicely decorated with the tour cities running along the side.

With the exterior looking magnificent, the interior is still in need of something else. I had picked up a small 15-inch television for a bargain intending it for the van, but it needs to be installed securely. Scouring through my dad's workshop I find some pieces of lumber lying around, so I build a little table that fits just in between the front two seats. The table is further secured by nailing two additional beams at the bottom, locking into the bolted down seats. Only problem now is securing the television onto the table itself. I nail another two beams across the front and the back on the surface to prevent the television from sliding and strap it down with a couple of bungee cords. This isn't going anywhere now. To power it, I hook up a transformer adapter to the cigarette lighter, providing a power outlet for inside the van. The television is a perfect fit.

Meanwhile, Cristin calls again updating me that there's nothing to update. She's starting to get anxious about the situation and it's not in the good way. I calm her down optimistically – which she isn't at all. There's still plenty of time.

It's now 3:00pm and I've completed all that needs to be done. I call the boys to find out that they're all set and ready to rock as well, so I gather them up.

"Looking good," says Tak, as he comes inside.

"Yeah, I detailed the hell out of this machine today."

Taking the scenic route toward Stefan's place, we go through the beach and the nicer parts of town, capturing it all on our camcorder. The sun is out and the threat of rain that loomed all week has subsided. We pick up Stefan and are quickly stopped at an intersection. When the light turns green, I slowly accelerate through and notice the driver in the oncoming car squinting his eyes trying to read what it says on the front of our van. His befuddled face trying to mouth out the words suddenly lights up when he figures out what it says.

"YAAAA!" he yells out with a fist in the air followed by big thumbs up, much to our enjoyment.

On the way back to the city, Stefan suggests that we swing by the train station to pick someone up. Apparently he received a call from someone just arriving from the Gorge who wants to hang out.

"His name is Joe," Stefan mentions. "He's joining the van in Ontario."

"Oh right, I have a ticket for him tonight," I answer.

So Stefan calls Joe back informing him that we'll be there shortly.

"Don't worry, you'll know which one is the right van when we get there," Stefan explains. We pull up to the train station and are waved down by a guy with a slight goatee, corduroy pants, a blue baseball hat – worn backwards – and a good tan. I presume this is him.

"Hi, I'm Joe from Los Angeles," he introduces himself, as if we can't tell that he's from Southern California. "Man, you weren't kidding when you said I couldn't miss you guys." What he's actually thinking is, "How on earth is this van going to make it across the country?" He asks if we have any extra tickets for the show, because he was talking to a girl from Italy on the train that needs one.

"No extras but maybe there will be one at the pre-party," Tak replies.

Back on Main Street, traffic is highly congested with signs for construction up ahead, so I try to manoeuvre around the potential delay through a short cut. But as I turn into an alleyway, my progress is halted by a freight truck stopped in the middle blocking any through traffic. I calmly begin backing my way out of it, however, Joe is anything but calm in the back seat. Looking around I can see why. There are junkies injecting themselves in broad daylight at almost every corner of the alley. I count six of them along with two prostitutes just laying on the ground, and the further down the alley I drive (I need to drive down in order to turn around) the seedier it gets.

"What the fuck?!" Joe reacts in alarm.

"Ha ha. Welcome to Vancouver," Tak replies.

"This is my first time in Canada and I didn't expect to see this." Here's this guy from California, of all places, freaking out in the first five minutes he's in Vancouver. With us still being complete strangers to him, Joe is starting to second guess his decision to travel with us in the van.

"Don't worry man, this is the only bad area in the city, all the stuff pretty much just happens here and here alone," I reassure him. "Think of it as our little initiation for you." We arrive at GM Place a few minutes later to pick up our tickets and are surprised to see that I won't be sitting next to Stefan but directly opposite of him along the side of the stage instead.

"It looks like they alternate sides with the seniority once we get up into the stands," Stefan points out. With the van parked within the narrow laneways that make up Yaletown, we head into the Yaletown Brewery, where there's a pre-show party taking place. There was a fundraiser earlier, which we missed, but it's still jam-packed with fans enjoying a drink close to the venue. It has a good vibe and is also an easy place to meet up with friends. Mine are already waiting for me. With two extra pairs of tickets, I hand over one of them to my friend Sarah, who will be sharing with Joe.

"Joe, this is Sarah. Sarah, this is Joe. Here are your tickets. I'll be right back," I introduce, as I get a call from Cristin.

"I'm leaving work now. It just ended. Can I still make it?"

"Definitely. It's only 5:30 now. Depending on what the border traffic is like you should be in by 8:00 or 8:30."

I give her directions to Vancouver and she seems very relieved and happy. Back at the bar I find my other friends Charles and Randi, who are using my other extra pair.

"Hey guys, you excited?" I ask.

"Of course, I've wanted to see these guys for some time," Charles answers. We grab a table on the patio and order some food and drinks when Lester and Brad arrive on the scene.

"Back for more," Lester greets us. Brad suggests that we head to the venue if we want a poster so Stefan and Lester join him, leaving the rest of us to enjoy a few more rounds. Tak is waiting for his brother, who's on his spare ticket tonight, while I'm still waiting for Cristin to cross the border. She finally arrives in the neighbourhood around 8:30pm, after getting lost from my directions on the phone.

"Stay right there, I'll come out and get you," I inform her. I give some money to Tak to buy another round and run up a few blocks toward a car that's honking at me.

"You made it," I exclaim.

"I'm so tired," she answers. We find a parking spot and re-enter the bar where a pint of beer is waiting for us.

"Wow look at this service," Cristin remarks. We drink it fast, as time is running out, and then Tak suggests we do a shot before we leave. We oblige and speed toward the venue by foot, where Tak's brother is waiting. It's a quick introduction of everyone and then we separate again inside.

"Enjoy the show guys, see you after," I yell out.

We run to our seats, which are about 12 rows back on Stone's side, the side where guitarist Stone Gossard usually stands. And just as we drop down into our seats, we're lifted again by the roar of the crowd as the band takes the stage and opens with *Release*, one of my favourites. The gradual build toward a powerful chorus really brings the crowd into it early on. This is a sign that a good show is to come, and it does not disappoint. What follows is a show that perfectly complements the one from last night. After busting out a handful of rarities at The Gorge, the Vancouver show consists of more mainstream songs to go along with the loudest crowd I've ever heard at any event in Vancouver. After every second song, Cristin turns around in jubilation to thank me for the ticket. It's simply the best show I've ever seen in my hometown.

After the show, we meet up in front of the box office but everyone is dead tired from the night before and decides to go home. I hand the van keys over to Stefan for him to take the van back so that he can pick us up in the morning, while I go with Cristin to catch up. It has been a long day of preparation and anticipation, but the show lives up to our expectations. The Canadian tour has officially begun. Tomorrow, the drive begins.

Be it no concern
Point of no return
Go forward and reverse
Setting forth in the universe

Setting Forth

CHAPTER 3: **THE ROAD TRIP BEGINS**

September 4, 2005 » Show 3
Calgary, Alberta

ROAD TRIPS TEND TO BRING PEOPLE closer together. In our case, it's imperative that we get along otherwise it will be a miserable couple of weeks. The bonding begins with the drive to Calgary. With the morning spent viewing the gorgeous city views atop of Grouse Mountain at my backyard, I'm reminded of just how beautiful my home city is. I don't want to leave, but there's a little trip I'm about to partake in. At 3:00pm I arrive back at the house where the van is already waiting with a load of passengers, including a couple of new members to the crew. With a tall and slender build to go with his bald head, Dirk from Winnipeg is joining us for the entire tour. Mike from Albany, NY, on the other hand, is only in for the ride to Calgary. Both were at the show the night before and both seem to be good guys. I greet my newest friends and introduce myself.

"You ready?" Stefan asks, sounding anxious to get going.

"One second."

I run into the house and grab my bag along with the last addition to the interior of the van, an Xbox video game system loaded with games, music, and movies. As I come back out, Stefan is putting the finishing touches to a new piece of artwork on the exterior, the popular Pearl Jam stickman symbol resembling the tattoo sitting on my left shoulder. I say goodbye to my family and they wish me luck, cautioning me to be careful but still have fun at the same time.

"You'll be alright getting home, right?" I ask Cristin.

"I think so."

I give her Stefan's mobile number just in case, as this will be our official contact number for the trip. We say goodbye and head out in separate directions. Ten minutes later a call comes through and she's lost already. As I talk her way back on track, we arrive back into downtown Vancouver in an attempt to find our final passenger, Dan from Minnesota. He had apparently left a message on

Stefan's phone when we were at the Gorge telling us that he won't make it to that show but will be staying at the Holiday Inn in Vancouver.

"I haven't been able to get through to him all day," Stefan enlightens us.

Not knowing his full name, we aren't able to check for him at the reception, so we wait around out front, as Stefan said we would on a message he left for him the night before. Meanwhile, my friend Ben is trying to call my phone to inform me that Eddie Vedder and the entire band are sitting on the patio and drinking some beers at the restaurant bar where he works. He leaves a few voice messages at around 5:00pm, but my phone is at home and won't be with me during the trip. The bar is only two blocks away from the Holiday Inn and we have no idea what's going on. How funny would it have been if we had driven by honking and waving in the van on our way out of the city? But I never get the message and what we don't know doesn't bother us.

We continue to sit and wait in front of the Holiday Inn, still in Vancouver, late in the afternoon on the day we are supposed to begin our trip. Our progress is atrocious. Dan is supposed to be joining us for most of the trip so we don't want to blow him off but, after nearly two hours of waiting, enough is enough and we need to get back on track. With compassion, Stefan calls him again with no answer so he leaves another message informing him that we're leaving Vancouver and apologizes for things not working out. Hopefully everything is alright. We finally hit the highway by 6:00pm, where the Canadian road trip officially begins.

Calgary is just over 1000km away from Vancouver, about an 11-hour drive, and it's me, Stefan, Tak, Dirk, and Mike in the van. The plan is to drive as far as we can tonight, rest up, then finish the remainder in the morning. However, not long after hitting the road, I feel compelled to stop and pull over. Driving by the city of Chilliwack, about an hour and a half outside of Vancouver, there's a street called Vedder Road, so I conveniently make a pit stop to fill up gas. While everyone takes photos of the road sign, I add a maple leaf around the stickman with some red hockey tape to Canadianize the iconic symbol. Then, following Brad's suggestion, I insert a black checkmark inside of the yield sign next to where it says Vancouver on the van. Now that Vancouver is officially checked off, we get back to the task at hand. The engine restarts along with the stereo.

It's essential for any road trip to have good music, and being that this is an extra long one, we have plenty to choose from. The CD player in the van plays CDs as well as disks with digital mp3 music files, so Stefan pops in his disc of choice, an entire discography of Mark Lanegan. For the next few hours, the only voice heard consistently in the van is that of Lanegan's. Having just met, everyone takes turns making small talk trying to get a feel for one another but, other than the occasional conversation, the ride is quiet. We are all a little bit shy at the moment. The drive contrasts from forests to hills to valleys to farm land and then to forest on hills on top of farm lands, as the towns become smaller and smaller. It's a drive that I've done a few times before, so the lovely scenery is nothing new to me, but it's still striking to see even with limited daylight. British Columbia really has a beautiful setting and I feel blessed to call it home.

As we enter the Rocky Mountains, we begin to snake around the edges of a very rocky mountain, slowly rising in elevation. This is the major test for the van. The initial drive to the Gorge proved that the van could run smoothly on long distances for long durations, but this is what will determine whether it has enough juice to carry us up mountainous terrains. Much to our relief, the van passes with flying colours. With the most gruelling part of the drive at the start, the rest of the trip should be smooth sailing from here on, especially if Lanegan is still playing in the van. I've not heard most of his stuff but his songs are a great soundtrack for a long drive because we're listening to his entire career from beginning to end. About seven hours of Lanegan into the ride, we enter Revelstoke, one of the larger towns in eastern BC, at around 2:00am. Stefan turns Lanegan off to give the speakers a rest.

"How are you feeling?" He asks me with a bit of caution.

"Not too bad. I think I got another two or three hours in me."

Entering the town, I see a random guy wandering onto the highway approaching. He stops us in the middle of the road, so I roll down the windows and he asks if we have any rolling paper, pointing to his large plastic bag full of British Columbia's finest herbs. Not even consulting the others I tell him no, assuming that we don't. He gives me a puzzled look.

"You mean you drive a van like that and you don't got no Zig Zags?" His comment wakes us up with a good laugh, a revival of sorts, and I decide that I could continue on a little further toward the Alberta border. As we pass the town of Golden, the lack of sleep the previous few nights suddenly hits me like a ton of bricks and drowsiness has overtaken me. I suggest that we pull over and call it a night and a silent response gives me everyone's approval. A few minutes later, a sign for a national park appears so I pull in and take the dark windy road through the forest until we reach a parking lot at the end of the road.

"This is it guys. Sleep tight," I declare.

"Um, how are we going to do this?" Tak questions. Although sleeping in the van seemed like a good idea, no one has really come up with how exactly this will work yet. Examining the area, I start rearranging each luggage from the back to sit on the front two seats, opening up space on the floor in the trunk.

"I'll sleep on the floor there, two of you guys can sleep on the bed, and two can fold the captain chairs down in the middle," I suggest.

We position ourselves to our designated spots and, despite the arctic like conditions outside, we're all fast asleep within minutes. I'm sleeping in a van in the Rocky Mountains, how amazing is this? The swirling winds and chilling temperatures wake Stefan and me up early in the morning. Feeling a bit cramped up in the van, we take a walk around the park to find out that we're at the edge of a cliff towering over a powerful river 50 metres below us. It's quite a sight. Stefan and I agree that the drive is going well so we return back to the van, where no one has moved yet. Transferring the luggage back to the trunk, I get back into driving position, turn the ignition on and re-enter the highway again, with the others still half asleep. I pull over at the next town to enter the final city of the province, Field, where we wash up and fully wake ourselves up for Alberta.

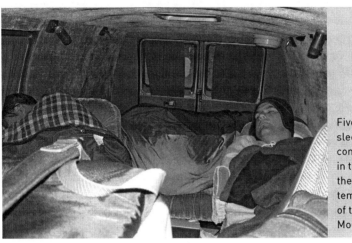

Five of us sleeping comfortably in the van in the freezing temperatures of the Rocky Mountains.

"We need a name for the van," Stefan states.

"How about the Supersucker?" Dirk suggests, as the Supersuckers are the opening band for the first half of the tour and is also playing in the CD player.

"Well the van does suck gas," Tak agrees, thinking about our gas costs.

"Supersucker it is."

An hour into Alberta, Dirk mentions that he has a friend going to the show with him who needs to be picked up in lovely Lake Louise, so I take the exit to fuel up and we check out the popular tourist attraction. Pulling into the tour bus parking section, I park next to two large coach busses, which tower over our touring machine. We spend the morning strolling around the lake. Situated in the Rocky Mountains, the main lake in Lake Louise is glacier turquoise and still enough to reflect some of the many surrounding mountains in the area – very picturesque indeed. Stefan dares me to jump into the lake.

"I'll give you $20 to jump in."

I think about it. "Give me $25 and I'll do it."

"Nope. $20 only."

I don't end up jumping in but the morning walk along the lake amongst the many photograph taking tourists is still quite refreshing. When we've had enough fresh air, we head into the small town of Lake Louise to pick up Dirk's friend. She's going to the show with him and staying in Calgary afterwards, so we are happy to help out with the ride. Inching closer toward Calgary, the highway begins to leave the mountains and the terrain becomes very flat. We know we're close. With Stefan driving, I shoot some of the scenery with the camera when, all of a sudden, a car starts honking madly at us. What's this about? I turn over my shoulders to see one of the people in the car next to us holding up something. I look again and realize that she's holding up some tickets for tonight's Pearl Jam show. We wave as she smiles and drives away from us. Guess we're not hard to spot on the road. At 1:00pm, we enter Cow-Town.

Having lived here during college, Stefan is familiar with the city and knows exactly where to find the hotels. We drive into the hotel circle and there are almost 20 hotels with plenty of vacancies all lined up next to one another for us to choose from. With nothing booked yet, we chose the cheapest option, the Super 8 Motel. Even with my rock 'n' roll dreams of sleeping in the van every night, I welcome the chance to rest on a proper bed. With our accommodations set, we head for the Calgary Saddledome and are greeted by the parking attendant.

"I'm guessing you're here for the show?"

I accept the parking ticket and pull into the first row of cars, right in front of the venue, for a great parking spot. We pick up our tickets at the box office and score four seats beside each other once again, this time in the ninth row. With excitement running through our veins, we head down a few blocks to a bar named Melrose, where the pre-show party is taking place. When we get to the entrance, Tak is greeted by some people he knows already, a couple named Kelly and Ted from Vancouver Island.

"I met these guys in lineup at the Benaroya show in Seattle last year."

After we are introduced, we enter the bar, where we've missed the fundraiser again. But there are still fans conversing, so we gladly join in and are greeted by some more people who Tak seems to be friends with.

"How do you guys know each other?" I ask.

"The van," she screams out. "We talked to you guys at the gas station on the way to the Gorge."

"I didn't see you guys," I mention.

"You were sleeping," Tak jokes.

The girls are Maria from Long Island and Lisa from Vancouver and the guy is David from Seattle, all of whom Mike seems to know as well.

"I traveled with these guys on the East Coast last year," Mike explains, "And this is my girl Barbara from Italy," as he pulls another person toward us.

"Well actually, I live in London but, yeah, I'm from Italy," Barbara reconfirms in an accent that doesn't sound Italian or English. Barbara has shoulder length brown hair and wears glasses to magnify her welcoming face.

"Are you the Italian girl that Joe met on the train from the Gorge." I ask.

"Joe? I don't know any Joe, but there's another girl from Italy here."

We go to the other Italian girl and introduce ourselves. Her name is Berenice and she did indeed meet Joe from California. We explain that Joe had mentioned that she was in need of a ticket, so we kept an eye out but never met her. Quite impressed by the international presence, we continue to meet more fans.

"Hi, I'm Genevieve from Edmonton," Another girl introduces herself, "Are you guys coming to Edmonton tomorrow?" We confirm our attendance. "I'm doing the fundraiser at the Stone House. It will be a big party," she explains.

"Oh, we'll be there, don't you worry about that," Stefan answers.

Barbara then comes over to me and asks if she can have a ride to Edmonton. Apparently, Mike had told her about the van and, although she has a Greyhound bus booked already, she'd love to ride in the van instead.

"Of course you can," I answer. "It will be fun."

I begin filming some interviews with some other fans, as the bar is lively and filled with excitement, and everyone is so friendly. Before we know it, 7:00pm hits, and it's almost time for the show. To keep to the tradition we started in Vancouver, Tak and I do a shot before heading out. This time it's tequila, giving us a little jump start for the show. As a group, we make our way to the venue. Our enthusiasm is high and we're about to see the Supersuckers, who are full of energy, exactly what you want from an opening band. The lead singer, Eddie Spaghetti, puts on a comedic performance in between songs as well, which is always a bonus. The performance pumps us up even more for the show.

Pearl Jam hasn't played Calgary in over a decade, so many of the casual fans are equally as excited as we are. As the anticipation builds, electricity courses throughout the building. When the band opens with *Oceans*, it's dynamite. With Mike taking our spare ticket and Dirk in front of us, we're all sitting together, feeding off of one another. The crowd is extremely loud, perhaps even louder than in Vancouver, and it's a volume level that's constant throughout the night. With so much energy exerted, we begin to sweat profusely. Dirk even takes off his shirt at one point.

"Put it back on man," we joke in between songs, but he remains shirtless till the end. The show leaves us a little exhausted, dehydrated and starving. With all the driving and drinking, we haven't eaten since breakfast and the only establishment open after the show seems to be Dominos takeout pizza, near the bar from earlier. The lineup is enormous, and there's only one worker inside preparing and carrying out the transactions. It's totally inefficient, but we're too hungry to pass this up. After what seems like an hour of waiting, we finally get one pizza each. They're dissolved in a flash and we return back to the hotel.

Mike has to catch an early flight back to New York, however, making it only a short weekend trip for him before heading back to work tomorrow. So after a short nap, he calls a cab for the airport and we all say goodbye to him while still half asleep. Albany Mike becomes the first casualty of the tour. His spot is immediately filled by the first random of the tour, his friend, Barbara, who we just met at the bar before the show. Things aren't always as planned.

On the edge of a know nothing town
Feeling quite superior
Deep

CHAPTER 4: **FEELING LIKE ROCK STARS**

September 5, 2005 » Show 4
Edmonton, Alberta

IT IS SAID THAT AN AVERAGE PERSON requires seven or eight hours of sleep in a night. After three nights on the tour, I have accumulated less than 10 hours combined. However, this total is almost matched in one night at the ultra comfortable Super 8 Motel. Feeling fully rejuvenated, we barely make it out before the checkout deadline of 10:00am and head back into the city to pick up our next passenger, Barbara. When Tak and I walk into her hostel, the other Italian girl, Berenice, is there on the computer. While Barbara gets her stuff ready, we find out that Berenice writes and sings in a rock band called Dedalo back home.

"Maybe you guys will open for Pearl Jam one day," Tak suggests.

"Yeah, that would be great."

We try to convince her to come to Edmonton as well, but she has a flight back to Italy booked for today.

"I'm jealous of you guys for going to the rest of the shows," she says.

But we exchange contacts, say goodbye and head back to the parking lot where Stefan and Dirk are waiting impatiently.

"What took you guys so long?" Stefan asks.

"Oh I was just trying to get another passenger," I smile. "Unsuccessful though."

Before we leave, Stefan adds a checkmark to the yield sign beside Calgary. So it's me, Stefan, Tak, Dirk, and Barbara for the ride to Edmonton, a drive that's only three hours covering 300km, much shorter than the previous one. Tak takes his turn on the wheel for this one, so I move to the back of the van and we bust out the Xbox entertainment centre, where we decide to put on the movie *Singles*. We had made it a rule of not playing any Pearl Jam music in the van so that it doesn't become overkill for us, so this is really the first Pearl Jam related content we've allowed inside our touring machine. The movie is filled with classic moments, the best of which is when Matt Dillon's character is sitting in a diner with his band Citizen Dick, played by half of the members of Pearl Jam. They're reading a review about their record, which does nothing but trash Dillon's performance. At the end of the clip, they decide to think positively.

"This negative energy just makes me stronger. We won't retreat, this band is unstoppable. This weekend we rock Portland!" Dillon proclaims.

"Tonight we rock Edmonton!" Barbara screams out.

We all laugh.

"We should put that on the van somewhere," Stefan suggests.

"That's a great idea," Tak follows. "And we could change the name for each city we get to."

When we arrive into the city centre of Edmonton, we drop Dirk off to visit another one of his friends, before making our way to the pre-party. Edmonton is a rather small town consisting of only a few main streets, and this bar is on one of these main streets. The bar is called the Stone House Pub and it's nowhere near the venue in location but, apparently, there will be a bus taking us to the show. Upon arrival, I park the van directly across the street from the bar and add the words "Tonight we rock Edmonton" on the side of the van with more hockey tape. This is the first fundraiser we've actually been able to make and it is extremely well organized by Genevieve from Edmonton.

"You guys made it," she greets us.

There are many Pearl Jam items for auction and raffle, including a few rare concert posters, a pair of tickets to the show, and even a Mike McCready autographed guitar. All the items have been donated by fans with all funds going to the Crohn's and Colitis Foundation of Canada (CCFC). This is a disease that guitarist Mike McCready has been fighting for years, and the fans have taken it upon themselves to get involved and raise some money for this cause throughout the tour. As we settle into the establishment, Tak heads to the restroom while Barbara makes her way to the bar. Stefan and I walk around and decide to sit down in a booth across from two interesting looking guys. We introduce ourselves and they reply:

"Hi I'm Jordan."

"I'm Brian. We're from Lethbridge, Alberta."

Brian is wearing a hat that features a photo of his own face on it. In the photo, he's giving a thumbs up that's almost as big as his smile. Hilarious! We instantly hit it off. Brian asks about the van as he had seen us pulling in through the window, and as I explain to them what we're doing, his eyes light up.

"Do you guys have any more room? I'm going to the next one as well, and might want to join you guys for more shows, but I have to check with work first." Could this be another random pickup? That would be great. He seems like a fun person and we have plenty of space. A few moments later we do indeed get another random pickup, but it's not Brian. Kelly from Vancouver Island finds us at the bar again and asks if there's any room in the van because she wants to go for two more shows. Her husband is flying home for work after tonight but she doesn't need to.

"Of course we do," Tak replies.

Thrilled about adding another passenger, we exchange contact info and decide to meet at their hotel room on the day we leave the city. We spend the afternoon mingling with fans and enjoying the atmosphere of the jam-packed bar that is excited to see the first Pearl Jam show in Edmonton in 12 years. This is kind of what I had in mind from the outset of the trip. There are even two guys who flew in from Brazil to see a few of these shows, one of whom is also celebrating a birthday. With the massive amount of people in attendance, the benefit seems to be highly successful. When it's show time, we all pile onto a double-decker bus that's provided by the benefit for a mere $5 donation to escort us to the venue. With nearly 100 people on board, the bus is pumping out Pearl Jam music like there's no tomorrow. But judging by the off tone yet joyful sing-a-longs while we inch closer toward Wayne Gretzky Boulevard and the Rexall Centre, it's the only music that matters at this point.

The bus drops us off directly in front of the Wayne Gretzky statue and, although this particular building was not even built when *The Great One* was playing in Edmonton, we're still in awe of the setting and pay homage to a true Canadian hero. We pick up our tickets, four seats together in row six, with our extra going to Barbara, and then Tak and I run across the street to enter a bar called Pucks for our traditional shot before the show – it's vodka tonight. The spine tingling drink is like a jolt of lightning into my system causing us to sprint back to the arena, all ready for tonight.

During the show, the song *Jeremy* is played for the first time at any show that I've been to. Like many, this is the song that first turned my attention to Pearl Jam, when it was running all over MTV 15 years ago. It's one of their most successful songs and, the fact that it has taken all these years and all these shows for me to finally see this song live – their most famous and one of the most played – is a testament to the uniqueness of their song selections for each setlist show after show. No show is ever the same, which is great, especially if you're catching an entire tour. Near the end of it, Vedder gives the floor to Mike and he takes the time to educate the audience about the fundraiser that had occurred prior to the show and even thanks Genevieve personally for organizing the event that raised over $5000. It's a job well done, but not yet finished.

After the final notes, we roam around looking for the bus, not remembering any instructions about a meeting spot. Frantically, we swim through the exiting crowd until Stefan and I finally find our ride sitting at the point of our drop off, but we've managed to lose Tak and Barbara in the process. The bus is already full and ready to leave when we board, so we assume that everyone has returned.

We attempt to climb up to the second deck and see if Tak and Barbara are up there, but the bus seems to have picked up quite a few extra passengers, leaving hardly enough breathing room. Hopefully they made it back on. It's a boisterous ride back, as the fans have enjoyed the night. Because it was a much shorter show than the previous ones, it was a somewhat disappointing effort for me. But an average show for this band is still top notch, as evident by the enthusiasm being displayed on our journey back to the bar.

Back at the bar, the after show party is rocking and right in the thick of the action is Tak and Barbara. Everyone buys a round of drinks for each other, and then random people start buying drinks for us. People are rejoicing and celebrating as if Wayne Gretzky as just won the Stanley Cup for Edmonton. When Tak and I escape the madness for a breath of fresh air outside, we are greeted by two girls having a smoke, Cindy and Sarah.

"Somebody told me that you're the guys with the van."

Tak proudly confirms their statement.

"That's awesome that you're checking off all the cities. Can we put the checkmark on for Edmonton?" they ask.

I look at Tak with confusion for a minute but then realize what they're asking.

"Of course you can, but everyone that does the checkmark has to have a photo taken with it as well."

"No problem!"

So we venture across the street to the van and perform a little ceremony for the completion of the Edmonton show. The two girls each apply a piece of hockey tape, assembling a checkmark inside the yield sign beside Edmonton. With smiles and cheers all around, even from across the street, flashes go off on our cameras and theirs. I attempt to show them the clip that was captured on our video camera but, while rewinding the tape, the machine suddenly stops. I play around with the camera for a while longer, but it seems to have locked up and isn't working anymore. Frustrated, I head back into the bar, hoping it will come back to life in the morning. My re-entrance is greeted with a drink from Barbara, and all is good again until Stefan and Tak decide to call it a night and sleep in the van. We follow them outside but, looking at Barbara, I can tell that we have a different thought on our minds. "Let's go back in for one more."

Of course one more turns into two, and two more turns into three, and three more turns into 3:30am, when the bar finally kicks us all out. Reluctantly, the remaining compatriots gather outside, everyone a little tipsy.

"I wish I could continue on with you guys," Barbara says to me. She has a bus to catch at 6:30am and then a flight from Calgary back to Italy, where she'll be attending a wedding. After that, however, she'll return and rejoin the tour, somewhere on the East Coast. I assure her that she'll be delivered to the bus station on time and that we'll definitely see her again. As we continue standing around with everyone else, most of whom are trying to figure out the taxi situation, Genevieve spots us and wanders over.

"You guys okay getting back? Where are you staying tonight?" she asks.

"Oh just across street over there," I reply, pointing to the van.

She bursts out laughing.

"That's rock 'n' roll, baby," Barbara explains.

We say goodbye and stumble across the street to our home. In the process, Barbara discovers that her glasses are missing from her face. She insists that it's okay and she'll look for them in the morning. So with her blessings, we climb into the van, where Stefan and Tak are passed out on the futon already. We sit in the middle two seats, fold them down as far as they can go without crushing our snoring van mates and, within seconds, we're asleep. I wake up a few hours later, unaware of my surroundings. I have a bit of a headache. As I slowly collect my thoughts, I see a glasses-less Barbara in the seat beside me and remember that we need to drive her to the bus station. It's 6:00am, so I manoeuvre my way up to the driver seat and my shuffling around wakes up Barbara, who's still in a daze as well. I notify her that it's time to go so she takes the more conventional approach to the front seat by using the doors. As the door slides open, a pair of glasses appears on the ground, the same ones that she mysteriously misplaced just a few short hours prior. She collects them, jumps in the passenger seat, and is ready to go.

We get to the bus station with 10 minutes to spare, just as Stefan and Tak show some signs of life. A round of goodbyes later and it's just the three of us again, feeling tired and hungry. I begin driving aimlessly, not really knowing where we're going. As we ponder about destinations, I spot a Ricky's Restaurant up ahead, and the others look at me with approval. So I pull in and we lumber into a booth. We order our food and Stefan grabs a newspaper for us to catch up on the happenings around the world. On the front page, there are headlines about a horrible hurricane hitting New Orleans. It tells us that Hurricane Katrina has left the city in ruins. So we've been on the road for just a few days and of course something huge happens. We glance through the rest of the newspaper for some more positive stories and find a review of the show from last night. As Tak reads it out load, I notice two waitresses staring at us and pointing. One of them approaches nervously.

"Did you guys perform last night?" She asks.

"Perform what?" I answer, feeling confused and tired.

"Are you guys the band? My manager was wondering if you guys are Pearl Jam."

Not understanding the question, I look at the others.

"Oh no, no, we're just fans," Stefan replies.

She smiles and walks away looking a bit embarrassed but leaving us puzzled. With the actual band not having played this city in a decade, I guess we can be mistaken for being members of Pearl Jam. But then I realize that we actually bear some resemblance to a band. We're looking a bit scruffy from the lack of sleep, we're all wearing the exact same Pearl Jam shirt, I have a semi-mohawk, and the van is parked quite visibly to the staff. At this moment, we realize what an entity the van is becoming. We were always concerned over the logistics of the trip and had never really thought about or expected the type of reactions that we've received. I'm not sure that I'm completely comfortable with the attention, but I'll roll with it. Feeling like rock stars, we chow down our breakfast as if it was the last thing we'll ever eat, savouring every bit. After giving our faces a good wash in the bathroom, we drive off.

Today is a day off for the band and a day of recovery for us. And what better way for a recovery than to relax in beautiful Jasper. A lot of driving has been done so far in the trip and while most of us have done well surviving the initial test, Tak seems to have been affected the most with life on the road. A few days on the road have taken a toll on him, and he appears exhausted. For three hours and 380km, Stefan and I take turns driving while Tak remains asleep on the futon. "You think he'll make it to the end?" Stefan worries, referring to Tak.

Sitting on bench made entirely out of hockey sticks, Tak relaxes on our day off in Jasper.

We arrive just after noon and meander around the mountainous town. After having some pizza for lunch, we decide to hike around Lake Annette. The clean air and beautiful sceneries of nature are refreshing and what seemed like a flu coming on for me is temporarily disabled. Feeling rejuvenated, we return back to Edmonton in search of some famous Alberta beef for dinner. However, after an hour of hunting for a steakhouse on the popular Whyte Street, we're unsuccessful. Instead we settle for an average steak at an Irish pub.

This is really the first time that Stefan, Tak, and I are able to spend the whole day together by ourselves. From the frantic planning of the trip at the beginning, to different passengers joining in along the ride, the three of us have yet to really get to know one another that well. And although we aren't drilling each other with questions, the slow paced day with nothing planned, has really brought each of our personalities out. Through very subtle decision making and conversations, we unknowingly are growing more comfortable with each other over the span of the day. At the pub, Tak begins to express some concern. "Do you guys realize that we're going to see *Even Flow* like 13 more times? And we have six shows in seven days starting tomorrow. Can you handle it?"

There's something about putting three guys in a vehicle that instantly creates some good male bonding. We reassure Tak that it will be fine and that he should focus more on the trip and the sites and not be too stressed out about the shows. Tak is also suffering from a case of the flu, the same one that I've fended off during the afternoon but has crept back to me this evening. Needless to say, the three of us are feeling the effects of the road trip now. It has been go-go-go before today, so everything has just built up. We're a little sick, a little tired, and have had enough overcooked steak for one meal, so we decide to make it an early night.

Driving toward the Edmonton airport, I pull into the Holiday Inn Express, where Kelly and Ted are staying. This is where we're meeting her in the morning. Stefan calls Dirk to confirm this meeting spot for the morning and then asks around a few of the surrounding hotels for prices but they're not to our liking. So without much choice, we decide to sleep in the van again, parked at the Holiday Inn Express by the airport. The rock 'n' roll life continues, only this time, we are asleep by 10:30pm.

Hear my name, take a good look
This could be the day
Porch

CHAPTER 5: **TONIGHT WE ROCK SASKATOON**

September 7, 2005 » Show 5
Saskatoon, Saskatchewan

THE CRISP FRIGID AIR sneaks in through the cracks at sunrise. As the early morning progresses, the van temperature drops continuously. Our body warmth becomes less effective until the point where we lay wide awake gazing up at the velvet blue ceilings of the refrigerator, shivering and still feeling sick. My watch tells me that it's only 7:30am, but we've had enough. Stefan calls Kelly to let her know that we're at the hotel. Surprisingly, she's up already, and invites us up for a much needed warm shower. With Tak being the last to wake up, he's also the last to come up.

While waiting for him, Stefan and I walk back down to the lobby and are greeted by the hotel staff at the front desk. They inform us about their free continental breakfast at the end of the hallway. So we oblige and feed our empty stomachs as best as we can. The television is showing the news, covering the Katrina Hurricane in New Orleans. As the hotel staff refills the breakfast portions, they approach us with a smile.

"How did you enjoy your stay here at the Holiday Inn Express?"

"Oh it was very comfortable, we really enjoyed our beds," Stefan replies.

"That's great. So what are you guys doing here in Edmonton?"

"We're driving across the country in this van and, since our stay was so good here at the Holiday Inn Express, we might just stay at all of them along the way," I insist.

"Oh how wonderful. The one in Saskatoon is very nice."

"That's nice to hear because that's our next stop."

We walk out to the van where Tak and Kelly are waiting already and I replace the words Edmonton with Saskatoon on the van, now reading "Tonight we rock Saskatoon!" Dirk arrives just minutes later and we're ready to roll. Before we leave town, however, we pick up a new passenger, Mike from Lethbridge,

Alberta – not to be confused with Mike from Albany or Brian from Lethbridge, Alberta. We don't get far before Mike realizes he's missing some money so we return to the hotel where he finds $300 in cash in an envelope still lying on the desk in his room. That's his spending money for the trip.

It's early in the day, so we have time to make one more stop on the way out of town. We need to go back to the Rexall Centre. As we reach the site of the show from last night, I pull the van up onto the sidewalk and drive right up beside the Wayne Gretzky statue for a photo shoot. Everyone takes their turn having a picture taken with Greatness and, when we are all satisfied, it's finally time to leave Edmonton.

The drive to Saskatoon brings us into the Canadian prairies, so it's a rather dull six hours, but we try to keep ourselves entertained. The van crew for this leg consists of me, Stefan, Tak, Dirk, Kelly, and Lethbridge Mike. To add some excitement to the drive, there's an abundant amount of construction along the prairie roads, keeping me awake at the wheel. Meanwhile, the Xbox is on full force in the back, with Tak and Mike having a go at some video game boxing. The competition seems fierce and there's some playful trash talking going back and forth but all is well again when they team up for the game Halo. This uneventful drive comes to a close as we arrive into Saskatoon just before 3:00pm and head straight to the venue for our tickets. I pull the van up toward the box office, park temporarily, and everyone exits the vehicle.

Me holding my 3rd row tickets for the Saskatoon show.

"Hey, nice van man," someone greets me. I turn around and it's one of the boys from the Supersuckers. He smiles and turns around to help signal and guide his own van, driven by his band mates, back up against the loading zone. This display confirms the fact that our van is definitely far superior to the Supersuckers' rental van. With a smirk on my face, I attempt to operate the video camera again, but to no avail. It's still locked down and seems to be a lost cause. Disappointed, I'm not sure what I'll do with our plans of a documentary, but that's low on the priority list as the show is more important.

We, again, have three seats together – this time in the centre of the third row, easily our best seats yet. We are stoked. Filled with extreme excitement, we drive a short distance into town for the pre-party, which is being held at the rooftop of an Irish pub called O'Shea's. There, I meet up with an old high school friend of mine, James, who's attending university in Saskatoon and who I offered my spare ticket to for tonight's show. I haven't spoken to him in years, until just a few days earlier when I called from Calgary to see if he'd be in town, and now he's seeing his first Pearl Jam concert with me. He's psyched. We catch up on the usual topics over a few bottles of local Western beer. It's always easy to lose touch with people as you become more involved in your own life, but it's also very easy to pick things right back up to where you left off with someone. We laugh and smile as if we are still in high school as he quickly makes friends with my new friends as well. It's a relaxing afternoon on the patio with a lot of familiar faces from the previous shows. Brian from Lethbridge is already in amongst the action and joins our table.

"Hey guys, I talked to my boss and it doesn't look like I can get the time off to join you guys for more shows. But we should exchange contacts anyway just in case I fly out east later on," he explains. "I definitely have to ride in that van just once though. Can we get a lift to the show tonight?"

"No problem," I reply, as Tak approaches me looking worried.

"Hey, I think there's some guy trying to break into the van downstairs."

I peek over from the balcony at our van, parked just below, and there's nothing happening. A few moments later, a man with near shoulder length hair approaches our table carrying an enormous backpack – literally twice his diminutive size – on his shoulders. He's wearing a dirty looking hoodie, which probably used to be white, and smells as if he hadn't showered in a week. This must be the homeless person that Tak is referring to.

"Hey guys, I just wanted to introduce myself. My name is Joe and I'm from Newfoundland. Somebody told me that you're the guys with that van down there," says the quirky looking fellow.

"Yup, that's our van," I respond.

"Oh that's a wicked van, man. I'm doing the whole tour myself, but I'm hitchhiking all the way," he follows, explaining his less than hygienic presentation.

We give each other a strange look but invite him to sit down for a beer, along with another guy who I recognize from Edmonton but never spoke to, Ben from Philadelphia. While Brian chats with Ben, Joe tells us that he had been hanging out in Tofino, BC a week prior to the tour and then hitchhiked to Vancouver without a ticket. He managed to get into that show and each of the shows since without any prearranged rides or tickets sorted out, and he plans on doing this all the way back to his home in St. John's, Newfoundland. It seems a little farfetched but somewhat believable. What intrigues me the most, however, is the part about him being in Tofino trying to hitchhike to Vancouver.

"I was out there at the same time with the van for a week, driving up and down the beach highway. I saw lots of hitchhikers and must have passed you on the road like 10 times," I laugh. "Do you need ride at any point of the tour?"

"Nope, just pick me up if you see me on the side of the road."

"Really?"

"Yeah, I need to do it this way."

"Okay. We'll look for you on the road and stop if we see you."

"Perfect," he says, downing his pint of beer like a true Newfoundlander.

The waitress sees what a great time we're having and brings us all a round of shots.

"Here, these are on me," she says. "Hope you guys enjoy the show." We thank her and ask if she's going to the show as well, but she isn't fortunate enough to have a ticket. Almost before she finishes her sentence, Mike announces that his spare ticket is still available and, within minutes, she's convinced to come after work. The shots are good but, being a pre-show tradition between Tak and me, they also mean it's about time for the show. So we pile into the van, all eight of us, and head back to the Credit Union Centre.

"Hey I know that girl," Stefan proclaims upon entrance of the venue. "I saw her on the last tour. I think she's from Vancouver." We head over to the short, curly haired Vancouverite, Tamara, and introduce ourselves. She recognizes Stefan so we get acquainted with each other while the Supersuckers are playing their opening set. Here we are in the middle of Canada, and we are hanging out with someone from back home. After the last notes of the opening band are played, we walk up to our seats and they're absolutely amazing. We are so close, yet still far enough back to see the entire stage. I'm greeted by another short, curly haired girl.

"Hey, aren't you the van guys?" she asks, as I give confirmation. "I've seen you guys everywhere. My name is Venassa and I live in Calgary." Our conversation seems to go all over the place but it ends with a smile and her declaration of us being her heroes for following Pearl Jam around in a van. Everyone is in good spirits as the electricity in the air intensifies. It feels more like the atmosphere of a big time boxing match than that of a concert. This buzz continues to build and even carries through after the band takes the stage.

For the first few songs, they seem somewhat tentative and the crowd is mellow. Then Vedder talks about the Katrina disaster and how the first few songs are being taped for a benefit video to help New Orleans. Maybe the band is a little nervous with the cameras rolling, but this only adds to the anticipation for the remainder of the show. When they hit *Do The Evolution*, it's like a light bulb bursting with brightness. From there, the energy just builds and the band shakes off any rust or tension they might have had before. They're back to their top notch form. By the time they play *Even Flow*, a few songs later, the rafters are shaking, as if the hurricane was in Saskatoon. And then the roof comes down, as they bust out *I Got Shit.* James is having the time of his life and constantly thanks me for the tickets throughout the show. I share the same feelings and thank him for coming with me.

For the encore, Vedder comments about Saskatoon having a magical name and they have an urge to play some campfire songs, so the pace slows down, allowing the crowd to rest from the frantic first set before the tempo picks right back up during the second half with *Betterman.* The sing-a-long song blows the roof off and leads into an unforgettable performance of *Porch.* Midway through the song, with the crowd jumping madly, Vedder approaches the source of this eruption.

"Hey it's safe here, I can come visit, right?" he asks, as he jumps off the stage and enters the crowd. Being held by his two security guards, Vedder leans into the second row to feel the energy and belts out the last verse of the song with the crowd surrounding him. He's less than a metre away from us, and we basically need to look straight up at him. Needless to say, we just about lose our minds at this point. Some in the crowd grab on to Vedder, to get a feel of the sweat that it takes to put on such a high impact show. But for the four of us, we merely just stand in awe and absorb it all in, enjoying the moment of having this living legend do his thing right above us.

The band leaves the stage after the song, allowing the crowd to recover from the powerful force that had just been laid upon us. James turns to me to thanks me one more time. The joy in his face is glaringly obvious and it's matched by everyone else in our section. With the crowd noise already at a climax, the encore begins with a cover of *Running Back to Saskatoon* by the Guess Who. Wow – way to play toward your crowd! They get about halfway through it but the crowd is so loud that they forget the second half of the song, which they probably just learned to play this morning. As the house lights come on, *Alive* finishes off the night, but we don't want to leave. Stefan and I take one look at each other and, without saying a word, we simultaneously begin chanting out loud. "ONE MORE SONG! ONE MORE SONG!"

It must have been the day of bonding we had yesterday allowing us to read each other's minds like that but, before we know it, the rest of our section joins in and then most in building follow along. "ONE MORE SONG! ONE MORE SONG!"

Vedder talks it over with the rest of the guys side stage and comes back to acknowledge the chant. "Don't know how we could leave without playing the Canadian national anthem, the world's national anthem," as they conclude with Neil Young's *Rockin' in the Free World* to end an eventful show. It's by far the most fun I've had at a show so far on the tour. With a few shows under their belt, the band has definitely warmed up and seems to be in fine form and, after a day of rest, we had enough energy to keep up with their performance. A performance that reassures us, and Tak especially, why we're on this trip. Everyone is on a high exiting the building.

I notice Dirk wearing a nice Pearl Jam hoodie that he claims he purchased at the show tonight. He tells me that it's a limited edition merchandise for this tour, which explains why I haven't seen it for sale yet. Apparently, they've been selling out within minutes of the doors opening and, because we haven't gone in early to any shows yet, we haven't had a chance to buy one. I want one.

Back at the van, I open the door to grab a bottle of water that's desperately needed to heal my throat from the punishment it was given during the previous two and half hours. As fans walk by, they cheer and comment on the van, something that's starting to become a regular thing. Two younger fans ask if they could take a photo with the van to which I agree to only if they do the checkmark for us. Happily accepting the offer, the two girls add two additional pieces of hockey tape to check off Saskatoon and then pose in front of the van for their photo. Flashes go off on their camera as well as a few of ours, making it seem like some kind of event with the press.

Still feeling the effects from the electrifying show, we chill out for another hour in the parking lot to allow the crowd to disperse and our heart rates to slow down. Goodbyes are exchanged with new and old friends until the traffic finally seems manageable enough for us to leave. After a great day, everyone is wide awake and in high spirits. The next show is 800km away in Winnipeg tomorrow night, so I get into the driver seat and begin leaving Saskatoon. Our plan is that we have no plan. We'll just drive and see what happens.

A random girl checks off Saskatoon for us after a fun show.

CHAPTER 6: **FUCKIN' UP**

September 8, 2005 » Show 6
Winnipeg, Manitoba

WHEN A GOOD FEELING overtakes me, I feel invincible and able to do anything. However, sometimes the emotions blind me and I overestimate my actual abilities. The Saskatoon show is such a high that I'm wired and feel capable of driving all night. Passing by a gas station on the way out of the city, I'm asked if we should stop and fill up the tank before hitting the highway. But with our decision of getting a head start toward Winnipeg tonight, I just want to escape the city first, so we continue on leaving Saskatoon. "I'll hit the first gas station we see on the highway."

The plan is to drive as far as we can, then pull over and camp in the prairies, before continuing on in the morning. Everyone seems to be on board as they're all still in a lively mood. It's the same crew leaving Saskatoon as it was entering: me, Stefan, Tak, Dirk, Kelly, and Mike. But what starts off as a drive full of cheerful banter, reliving the great show just witnessed, slowly turns into silence, as fatigue begins to get the best of them. The silence accentuates the nervousness running through my mind as there still has yet to be any gas stations in sight. With every town we pass, another passenger would pass out in the back, until it's just me driving and Stefan navigating who are still awake in search of a miracle gas station.

"Come on, Colonsay!" Stefan says, hoping for something in Colonsay.

"Nope!" I respond, as we exit Colonsay.

"Come on, Viscount!"

"Nope!"

"Come on, Plunkett!"

"Nope!"

As we approach each town, hope approaches us but is quickly defeated with the discovery of complete darkness and no gas station visible. I guess Highway

16 isn't exactly as serviceable as Highway 1. What will happen if we are to break down? Thoughts of pushing the van in the middle of the night cross my mind just as the empty light comes on. Oh shit! I notify Stefan and he tries to be calm about it but I can tell that he's also worried. Examining the map, he notes that the next sizable town that may have a gas station would be a town called Lanigan.

"I don't think we'll make Lanigan. It looks like another 100km away," he estimates. With the van running on empty, we continue our search. All the while, we are treated to a show of lightning storms happening around us every which way we look. Even though they appear to be striking hundreds of kilometres away from where we stand, the flatness of the plains stretch out that far and allow them to be completely visible. It's a wild display of light, taunting me about not filling up before we left. Our drive turns from looking for hope to counting down the distance to Lanigan. I start driving substantially slower in an attempt to conserve what little liquids we may still have remaining in the tank and, accordingly, the distance to Lanigan begins counting down slower as well, from 50 to 40 to 30km remaining. The silent drive is intense, but a glimmer of hope appears when we pass the final town before Lanigan, which seems to be within reach now. Half an hour later, we see the sign for Lanigan up ahead. Stefan and I celebrate silently. But as we are giving each other high fives, the van begins to sputter, and slowly comes to a complete stop, just as we hit the "Welcome to Lanigan" sign.

"What's going on?" Tak asks, as he wakes up.

"We're out of gas. But there looks like there might something just ahead."

I leave the van and continue on by foot toward the building that I see up ahead. Along the walk, I begin to wonder what everyone else is thinking back at the van. Would they be angry that we didn't fill up before we left Saskatoon? But they didn't put up much of a fight, so I don't think they really cared too much at the time. How was I supposed to know that we would drive two hours and not hit a gas station? Besides, what's a road trip across the country without running out of gas just once? I think it's great actually. And we'll be okay because I spot a well lit Esso gas station up ahead. I turn around and sprint back toward the van to inform the others. By this time, everyone is awake so we team up to push the van the remaining kilometre toward the gas station. Along the way, a car passes by and slows down as it approaches.

"Do you guys need any help?" the guy in the car asks.

"We're out of gas, but there's a gas station just up ahead."

"Okay, but we'll wait for you up there to make sure you're alright."

As we push the van into the gas station, we realize that it's not open and the pumps have been turned off. Lanigan is not big, but easily the largest town we've passed so far and it still doesn't have fuel for us. We begin to discuss our options as the other car is there waiting for us. They offer to bring us back some gas at a station 30km away that they know is open all night.

Mike, Dirk, Tak, and Kelly pushing the van to the gas station in Lanigan.

"Oh that would be great," Dirk anxiously replies.

"Well let's talk this over for a bit," I intervene.

We chat with the couple in the car who we find out are actually Pearl Jam fans on their honeymoon travelling to see a bunch of shows. They were at the show last night and are headed to Winnipeg. After a short discussion with Stefan and Tak, we conclude that our best option is to stay put and sleep in the van at the gas station, fill up the tank when it opens up again and continue our drive in the morning. The only issues are that Kelly would prefer not to sleep in the van, while Dirk seems to be on a mission to return home to Winnipeg as soon as possible. So to accommodate everyone, we ask the couple if they could take Kelly to the next hotel, where we'd pick her up the next day, and to bring back some gas only if there's a chance and it's not too far from here. With that everyone agrees and the couple sets off with Kelly. Before they leave the gas station, though, Dirk exchanges contact information with them and then proceeds to plug his phone into a power supply along the wall outside of the gas station.

"I need to charge my phone," Dirk explains. The rest of us push the van to a better parking spot and begin to setup camp.

"You know, we should just stay here even if they do come back with gas," Stefan suggests.

"Yeah, I'm pretty tired," Tak replies.

So being experts at it already, we set up our sleeping positions in the van rather quickly. All the bags are moved up to the front seats, the futon bed folded down, and our sleeping bags rolled out. Tak takes the floor, Mike takes one of the spots on the bed, and Stefan and I fold down the middle two seats, leaving an extra bed space for Dirk, but he's still playing around with his phone outside.

We are settled in and feeling rather comfortable, with Tak even falling asleep instantly, when someone starts banging on our windows.

"Guys, guys, guys, they found this gas station and are coming back with some gas for us," Dirk explains excitedly.

"I think we're just going stay here. We're all set up now," I reply.

Not satisfied with our response, Dirk remains outside of the van. No more than 15 minutes later, the car races back toward us with Dirk jumping joyfully in the air. We head out to thank the couple for their efforts and to give them some money for the gas, however, Kelly is not with them. It turns out that she had stayed behind at the gas station and is waiting for us to pick her up. Shit! We thank the couple, wish them luck on the rest of their trip, and realize that we can't leave Kelly at the other gas station. The 10-litre jerry can empties in a hurry as the rest of us transform the van from sleeping back to driving mode. We reach the gas station half an hour later, where Kelly is loitering in front.

I fill up the tank to full with the others going into the store to make use of the facilities. As I pay for the gas, I glance over at the service attendant who looks as if he hasn't slept in weeks. It must be horrible to work overnight at a 24-hour gas station that sits at the junction of Highway 6 in the middle of nowhere. Back outside, everyone is gathered around trying to figure out what the plan is. By this point it's already 3:30am and Kelly suggests that getting a hotel for her is probably a waste. So the consensus is that we've gotten this far already, we might as well keep going.

"How do you feel Jason?" Stefan asks.

"Not bad. I could probably do a few more hours. Maybe you can rest up and take over when I'm done," I reply.

"I can't sleep up front because you'll need a co-pilot to keep you up."

"I'll sit up front," Dirk volunteers.

So it's settled. We'll continue the adventure to Winnipeg. I head back into the gas station washroom to freshen up and prepare for more driving, after having already driven most of the way to Saskatoon the previous morning and the whole way up to this point after the show. But I don't feel tired yet and gladly hop back into the driver's seat. I love to drive. Almost as soon as I turn on the ignition, everyone passes out in the back, but Dirk stays true to his word and stays up in the front with me. An hour of driving and he's still up chatting along, but this doesn't last long and our once intelligent conversation turns into nonsense and mumbling. His blabbering soon becomes snoring and I'm starting to feel it too. "Hang in there Jason," I keep thinking to myself. I change the music to something a little more upbeat than Ben Harper. AC/DC is able to keep me going until I reach the town of Yorkton, where there's a gas station open. Without making the same mistake again, I pull in. The clock reads 6:00am, as I fill up the tank. The gas attendant is a lot less freaky than the previous one, so I ask him how much farther it is to Winnipeg. "I'd say another six hours."

I return to the van to relay the information back to anyone still awake, but no one is. So I figure I would do one more hour on a much narrower prairie highway, and that would be enough for me. It's been a good three hours of driving, and I haven't encountered any other traffic at all other than the couple who got us gas, so I'm feeling a bit fatigued. My eyes begin to close slightly and I start to nod away. I keep checking the clock, not liking what I see. It's only been 15 minutes since Yorkton? The drive becomes increasingly difficult and I feel like grabbing the hockey tape and taping my eyes open. The swerving of the van wakes me up momentarily. The time is now 6:30am. If I can just get through another half hour, I'll be golden and can rest up nicely in the back. I begin scratching and clawing at my face to keep myself focused. And with the prairie highway being as straight as a ruler and as dull as watching grass grow, what would seem to be a leisurely drive has turned into an intense, nerve racking battle for me.

Somehow, I will my way through it though and, at 6:45am, we approach the town of Langenburg. I see a large pullout at the entrance to the town up ahead and decide that this is it. This is where I'll make the switch. I've done well, but can't go on any further. Feeling relieved that my stressful evening will come to an end shortly, I begin to relax. The next thing I know, I hear a loud boom, and the highway drive becomes a safari ride. I had fallen asleep and drifted off the road. When I realize that it's grass in front of the van, I slam on the brakes and there seems to be a delay before the van comes to a complete stop. That's because I'm sliding into mud. Everyone is now awake and we're surrounded by weeds as high as the van.

"What the hell happened?" someone asks.

"I think I fell asleep," I reply, feeling terrible about it. "Is everyone alright?"

I look to the back and everyone is fine, so we get out of the van to find that we are in a ditch. Seeing the tire marks on the grass, we conclude that I had crossed the lane of traffic and gone off the road and then, when I slammed on the brakes, we slid into the mud. Looking at the configuration of the road, we realize that we are lucky that the ditch is shallow with a very gentle slope. Otherwise, who knows what could have happened with everyone sleeping in the back without seatbelts. Examining the van, we find no damage, so getting back on the wheel, I attempt to reverse out. But we're too deep into mud and the van is going nowhere. To make matters worse, I look up ahead and the pullout I had wanted to stop at is no more than 100m away. I double check with everyone again and we all seem to be okay. But now what?

As I look back toward where we came from, two large semi trucks approach honking at us. They're the Pearl Jam tour trucks carrying equipment to Winnipeg. We wave, but all they do is honk and drive by. We try to escape the mud once again but are unsuccessful. So our only solution is to call a tow truck to get us out. Luckily, I signed up with CAA (Canadian Automotive Association) before the trip for incidences just like this. The membership comes with a free towing. Dirk is the only one with a phone that still has battery left at this point, so he dials the number and gets through.

"Ok what's our location?" he asks.

"In a ditch," I reply, trying not to be funny. "We're like an hour east of Yorkton."

With everyone being okay, I try to find some humour in the situation so that we can relax a bit and Mike plays along, loving everyone moment of this.

"Are you guys seriously going to make it across the country?" he asks.

"Well, we expected something like this to happen, and we've all escaped without a scratch," Stefan replies, "So we should be okay."

Tak is silent. An hour later, the tow truck arrives and pulls us out and back onto even ground. We examine the van again and there are no visible damages other than a garden of weeds stuck underneath the engine. The driver tells us that the ditches are sloped the way they are because these incidents happen all the time due to how straight and boring the drive is. I feel much better after hearing this, but I'm still apologetic to everyone. We thank the tow truck driver and I hop back into the driver seat to drive for another 30 seconds toward the pullout that I had originally wanted to stop at, only it's now 9:00am. Here, I finally make the switch and move to the bed in the back.

The tow truck getting us out of the ditch in Yorkton.

Stefan takes over and the ride feels a little bumpy, with thumping noises coming through every once in a while. We conclude that it's just coming from the weeds stuck to the bottom. The annoying noises don't allow me to get any sleep. Then, as we finally enter the province of Manitoba just half an hour later, we hear an explosion and feel a giant bump. Stefan carefully pulls over and we scramble outside to find out that our rear tire has blown. At this point in the morning, it's rush hour and there's traffic of all types along the narrow single lane road. Upon exploring the situation, it turns out that the tail pipe of the muffler is bent sideways, probably from being pushed by the weeds when the van was being pulled out, and has been scraping against the sidewall of the tire ever since we got out of the ditch. This has torn the tire completely apart, so I quickly make the switch for the spare tire and bend the tail pipe as far away from the replacement tire as I can. This is the third strike for our trip to Winnipeg. What an adventure it has been.

Dirk helping me change a completely destroyed tire.

Very few words are said as we all pile back into the van and continue on with Stefan at the wheel. I'm lying down in the back for another attempt at sleeping but it's not happening. The atmosphere in the van is as a silent as it has ever been. Not a single person talking, just Neil Young singing. We're not even halfway through the trip yet and we've encountered all these problems. This is what Tak is thinking – I can see it. The others are expressionless and I still can't fall asleep. It's been more than 24 hours that I've been awake now and thoughts begin to run through my mind. How will this all play out? Will we make it all the way across the country? Will we even make it to Winnipeg? Is this my fault? The drive feels like an eternity but we're slowly making progress.

"Anyone hungry?" Stefan asks, breaking the silence.

"Yes," we all answer at once.

About two hours outside of Winnipeg, we leave Highway 16 and connect back with Highway 1. Shortly after, a Tim Horton's restaurant is spotted, so we pull in and fulfill our needs. I'm not going to sleep at this point, so I figure that a rare coffee would be good medicine for me. On the way out, we spot a middle aged woman admiring the van. She greets us with a joyful smile and compliments the van.

"Are you guys doing the whole tour?" she asks. "That's great. My daughter and I saw the first few shows and now we're driving home to Winnipeg, but I didn't know they were in Edmonton."

"Oh nice. Edmonton was three or four days ago, before Saskatoon," we answer.

"Saskatoon? They were there too? But that's not on the t-shirt either," she replies as she turns around to show us the back of her tour shirt.

We examine the dates as written on her shirt and they're strange. Vancouver on September 3, Kelowna on September 4, Calgary on September 5, and Winnipeg on September 7? Those aren't the same dates, which tour is this? When she turns back around to reveal the front of the shirt, we realize that we're not talking about the same tour. They aren't following Pearl Jam but – rather – The Backstreet Boys on tour instead. It just so happens that their Canadian tour is also coinciding with ours, with maybe a day behind or a day ahead of Pearl Jam's schedule. We clarify the confusion for her, but she's still clueless about it.

"They still exist?" Tak asks.

"Of course. This is their best tour yet."

We all have a good laugh and wish them luck on their drive home. The humorous encounter is much needed, bringing some life back into us. We remind ourselves that this is a road trip to see our favourite band on tour and that there's a show tonight in Winnipeg, we should be excited. So we begin to look on the bright side of things and think positively. We were bound to face adversity at some point during the trip and if this is all the problems that we'll face, then it's good that everything occurred at once. We didn't take control of the situation at hand so we paid for it. But amazingly, even amongst people that we don't know too well, everyone has managed to keep their composure during the whole ordeal. There hasn't been any outburst from anybody and we have all just stuck together working through the problems and, most importantly, we're all safe and none of us are hurt. So we conclude that everything will be fine and that we'll learn from this. Let's just have a good time tonight. Sporting a new attitude, we change the music from Neil Young folk music to Neil Young rock. We're heading into Neil Young's hometown of Winnipeg after all.

Before 2:00pm, we finally arrive into Winnipeg. Ironically, had we spent the night in Lanigan and drove out this morning, this would have been about the time we would have arrived into the city as well. But all is forgotten, and we're happy to be in Winnipeg. Dirk says he needs to do a boat load of chores before the show so we drop him off at his house and venture toward the city centre, where we also drop off Kelly at her pre-booked hotel. After a short discussion, it's determined that we should probably pick up a new tire, so that the spare could be stored away for future use, if needed. At the shop, we take turns pulling out as many weeds as we can, while the van is up on the hoist. The mechanic replaces the tire and inspects for damage, as we try to explain exactly what happened.

"Everything looks fine," he determines. With the good news, we're relieved and head toward the MTS Centre. After a few nights of sleeping in the van – in my case, not sleeping at all – it's determined that a hotel is in order. There will be another show tomorrow night and, although the drive isn't as long, it's still 700km away. A good night rest is essential. We find a decently priced hotel right across from the venue, check in, and then head for a few much needed pre-show drinks at a bar next door. On the way to the bar we pass a stationery store, where the idea of making some signs to tell the band about our adventure pops into my head.

"Sure. That will be fun," the others agree. At the bar, we create two signs in time for the show. As we enter the building, we see Kelly. She thanks us for the ride and the adventure and wishes us luck for the rest of the trip. We thank her for joining us and look forward to seeing her again in Montreal, which she'll be flying back for with Ted the following week. With that, we settle into our seats, which are great once again. We have four seats together in the fifth row with Mike taking our spare ticket. The band comes on and opens with a sing-a-long, *Betterman*. Then after a few upbeat songs, Vedder addresses the crowd. "Here we are. We made it to Winnipeg."

We smile at each other as Tak holds up his sign, which reads "Hey Ed, drink more wine!" referring to our belief that a drunk Vedder translates to a great show. This is based purely on his Saskatoon performance where he appeared to be sipping on more bottles than usual, so we're hoping for a repeat performance. Vedder sees the sign, smiles, and takes a big swig out of his bottle of pinot noir. Our other sign is a little more difficult to read, so I decide to wait for the house lights to come on before we hold it up. It reads "Doing whole tour, last night… ran out of gas, ran into ditch, one flat tire, but still going strong, why do I…" referring to "Why do I… keep fuckin' up" a Neil Young song that Pearl Jam sometimes covers. So after a very energetic first set, *Blood* ends the second set and the house lights come on momentarily. I hold up the sign and Vedder tries to read it. But before he can make out what it says, the lights go down. He holds one finger out saying he'll be back in a minute, so we bring it back down. Three songs into the second encore, the house lights come back on.

"Okay, here's one by Uncle Neil, it's George Bush's favourite song," Vedder introduces, as they go into *Fuckin' Up* by Neil Young. Perfect, that's the song for our sign. So when the guitar solo hits and Vedder is running around the stage, I proudly hold up the sign. This time, Vedder has a clear view and simply shrugs his shoulders smiling at us when he reads it, almost as if he's telling us that shit happens but is glad that we're safe. The acknowledgement puts a deserving smile onto our faces and reiterates just how personal the band delivers their performance to their audiences. And although a strong rumour about Neil Young showing up ends up to be false, Pearl Jam follows up with another cover song of his to end the night, *Rockin' in the Free World*.

After hitting the last notes of the song, drummer Matt Cameron stands up and tosses his two drums sticks into the air. The rest of the band waves to the crowd signalling the end and, as one of the drumsticks comes closer to landing, it also comes closer toward us. With it clear in my sight, I leap up like a wide receiver over his defenders and grab the drumstick over three guys, who wouldn't have otherwise known what was about to hit them. Pulling it down, I hold it back up in the air in victory. What a great souvenir, what a great show. It's another highly enjoyable evening, one that we definitely needed after a tough day. Feeling much better than when we entered, we leave the venue and I suggest that we grab another beer and continue the night. Why not? I haven't slept in close to 40 hours now. But for the better, the others decide against it and head back to the hotel. Rest is definitely going to be required to reach the next show in Thunder Bay, as it's going to be another long drive. Although we hope that, this time, it will be a less eventful one.

I have not been home since you left long ago
I'm thumbing my way back to heaven
Thumbing My Way

CHAPTER 7: **THE HITCHHIKER**

September 9, 2005 » Show 7
Thunder Bay, Ontario

WHAT A DIFFERENCE A GOOD night's sleep can make. A hotel bed has never felt so comfortable, perhaps too comfortable. No one remembered to set the alarm last night and we sleep well pass our intended wake up time. I peek over at the clock and read 9:00am. We had intended to leave two hours earlier but now we are frantically taking turns for the shower. Fortunately we're all quick and, by 9:30am, we're checked out and on our way out of the city, still needing to pick up Dirk at his home. Stefan calls him when we're out front but he's not ready yet. The drive to Thunder Bay is close to nine hours, but the day just began and we're already way behind schedule.

By 10:15am, Dirk is in the van but he requests to make one more stop to pick up a shirt that he had dropped off the day before. Directly beside the place where Dirk goes into, there's a Best Buy electronic store. The video camera is still not working and is basically done, so I decide to run in and see what I can get for a replacement to keep this documentary project alive. Without knowing anything about video cameras, I pick out the cheapest option, a Sony 8mm Super cam, very similar to the other one, only a slightly newer model. This will do. As I'm paying for it at the cashier, Dirk enters the store looking for me. He's now sporting a bright orange shirt with a familiar Pearl Jam Cro-Magnon logo. "I had this specially made for the tour. What do you think?"

"It looks alright!" I reply, as we leave the store. By 10:45am we're finally ready to leave Winnipeg – it's going to be tight. I take the van back onto Highway 1 and begin to gun it. No less than five minutes later, I notice someone up ahead on the side of the road.

"Hey, it's that guy!" Dirk screams emphatically, as I drive right by him.

"The hitchhiker?" I ask after a moment of thought.

"Yes!"

Picking up Newfie Joe on the side of the road, as he hitchhikes across the country for the tour.

    I slam on the brakes and pull over, put the gear in reverse, and begin backing the van up toward him along the shoulder of the highway. In the rearview mirror, I see him sprinting toward us as if we are the first vehicle to stop for him in a week, so I stop. The guys in the back slide open the door as I grab the brand new video camera for its first use. Lugging the same backpack that's nearly twice his size, the hitchhiker approaches the van quickly.

    "Wicked!" he says, with a rather large grin on his face and wearing a cleaner white hoodie.

    "What's your name and where are you from?" I ask, pointing the new video camera at him.

    "Joe Keating from Holyrood, Newfoundland, and I'm going back home to see Pearl Jam on the rock!"

    The others help him fit in the latest addition to our collection of luggage, as he gets settled into the van comfortably. Joe thanks us graciously for stopping because he had overslept in his tent and woke up later that he intended to, having only just arrived onto the highway. He was in the process of lighting his first cigarette of the day when he felt the draft of the van speeding by blow it out of his hand.

    "I'm lucky that you guys drove by when you did, because there was no way I could make this show otherwise," Joe claims, with beer in hand.

    "Well, we still have to make it ourselves," Mike replies, as I put the van into second gear.

    There's roughly 700km of driving to be done and it's 11:00am, so I drive the van faster than it has ever gone before, weaving in and out of traffic, going into oncoming traffic to overtake slower trucks, and pushing it to its limits, but also keeping safety on my mind for me and my van crew of Stefan, Tak, Dirk,

Mike and, now, Joe from Newfoundland. The drive out of Winnipeg is not as adventurous as the drive in, but it nearly matches it in intensity and excitement – at least from the driver's point of view. After two hours, we enter the province of Ontario and I pull into a gas station to fill up. The gas attendant is glowing with excitement as he tells all his customers that a rock band stopped by on a bus earlier with four other freight trucks and gave them a bunch of free stuff. Sounds like our boys.

"You know we forgot to check off Winnipeg, eh?" Stefan asks, as he turns his attention to me.

"Oh yeah! Hey Joe, you want to do it?" I ask.

"Do what?"

"We just need to add a checkmark next to Winnipeg on the van."

Joe accepts the honour and the hockey tape to officially check off Winnipeg and, while we're at it, Stefan also changes Saskatoon to Thunder Bay to show where we're going to rock tonight. With all the problems the morning before, no one ever knew that we rocked Winnipeg. When we get back on the road, Stefan takes over driving duties and I head to the back to put on a movie called *Going the Distance,* a Canadian movie about a group of people driving from Tofino to Toronto. When the movie gets too boring, we engage in a fierce competition of video boxing, which lasts until our fingers can no longer take it. My main combatant, Tak, takes over the wheel a few hours later as I ride shotgun. It appears that we've made up considerable ground and look to be very close on time for the show but Tak doesn't seem to feel we're going to make it. Impatient with the slow moving traffic in front of us on a single lane highway, he attempts to pass the truck in front of us and decides to pass the truck in front of that. Now the van may have a second gear but it certainly doesn't have a third or fourth, so the move is sketchy, especially with an oncoming semi approaching in a hurry.

"Tak, you should slow down and get behind this truck," I suggest.

"Yeah, no problem," Tak replies.

"Tak?"

"It's under control!"

"TAK!" we all scream, seeing nothing but the glare of the oncoming headlights.

Just as we see our lives flash before us, Tak manages to handle the van, as if it was a video game on the Xbox, and squeeze in just ahead of the honking truck in front of us and seconds before the oncoming honking semi causes any fatalities. We all let out a giant sigh of relief and continue on. "No more passing okay?"

Stefan's phone rings at around 7:00pm to break the monotone of the driving noise. It's Joe from California, who was in Vancouver with us and is now joining the van for the ride through Ontario. He's already at the venue and is wondering where we are. Stefan informs him that our estimated time of arrival will be another half hour and, sure enough, we pull up to the Fort William Gardens at 7:30pm sharp. There's a large crowd in front of the venue, a venue that doesn't appear capable of holding the amount of people in that crowd.

"Start honking the horn," Tak suggests. As soon as I blow the horn, the crowd erupts.

"THUNDER BAY ROCKS!" we yell out, while driving by a roaring cheer.

Around the corner, we find street parking and Stefan calls Joe to let him know we've arrived. Apparently I had driven right by him in front of the venue, but he was lost amongst all the people in the crowd screaming at us. He arrives a minute later carrying only a small suitcase, a guitar case on his back and, wearing similar clothing as the last time we saw him – corduroy pants, a green collared shirt, and a blue baseball hat worn backwards. Travelling light and wearing the same uniform might be the result of his US Naval training from the past. This is sort of a mini reunion and we're all excited to see Joe again. During his introductions to everyone else, we suddenly realize that there's a minor issue: there are now two Joes with us. We've had two Mikes in the van before, but at separate times. So to avoid any confusion, we simply give Joe from California the name Cali Joe and give Joe from Newfoundland the name Newfie Joe. No more problems now, except for the fact that neither Joe has a ticket for the show. Fortunately for them, however, we have our extra ticket available for Cali Joe, and Dirk has his extra available for Newfie Joe so we're all settled.

We pick up our tickets and they're four consecutive seats again, this time in the eighth row. Dirk and Newfie Joe are only a few rows in front of us, and Mike has a ticket behind the stage. The lineup entering the building is quite slow, as security seems to be fairly tight and, judging by the fact that most of the locals are dressed up nicely, this might be the biggest event to hit Thunder Bay in some time. Upon entrance, I attempt to explore the venue but I don't get very far in this tiny building. At around 4000 capacity, this is easily the smallest venue of the tour and it seems more like a high school gymnasium than it does a hockey arena. There isn't any beer for sale inside and the only things you can purchase other than the Pearl Jam merchandise are hot dogs, french fries, and soda pop from a machine. We walk onto the tiny floor and toward our seats and are hit with a strong heat wave.

The Supersuckers are playing their final show of the tour so Vedder joins them on stage for their final song. By the end of their performance, the arena is toasty, and it's evident that air conditioning doesn't exist in the building. I feel as sticky as if I were on the beach without the ocean breeze. This is going to be brutal. But once Pearl Jam hits the stage, the stickiness doesn't seem to bother me as much anymore. With every jump, every note sung, and every cheer, I'm now working up the sweat instead. Even Vedder makes a comment about the sauna-like conditions in the arena.

"We'll remember you as being very, very kind, and incredibly hot up on stage. It's the hottest," Vedder says, after a great first set and an equally solid but mellow second set. He then compares the arena to a small theatre and climbs up into the crowd behind the stage.

"I always wanted to see what it looks like from back here," Vedder announces, as he proceeds to sing *Last Kiss* in the middle of the crowd behind the stage. Upon closer look, Mike appears to be sitting not too far from where all the action is taking place. So behind the stage tickets aren't that bad after all. For the closing song of the evening, the Supersuckers join in to end another solid show and their own tour. When the band walks off stage, the sweat dripping down my neck is starting to bother me again, so we exit as quickly as we can. Once outside, we're able to breathe normally again, except for Mike, who confirms that he was, in fact, sitting behind the stage right where Vedder sat to sing *Last Kiss*. He's lost for words but the grin on his face is priceless, a feeling all of us share with him. As I start the van, Tak insist that we drive around the venue a couple of times and honk the horn at fans. I oblige, and we receive cheers all around.

"So what are we doing for accommodations tonight?" Cali Joe asks.

"Hmm, not sure, we haven't thought about it," I answer.

"Let's just get a hotel room," Dirk follows. "My mom said she'll pay for it."

We drive a few blocks away from the venue, pull into a Super 8 Motel, and are welcomed by some fans that were obviously at the show. Dirk runs in to get a room, while the rest of us chat with the fans. "I had a great night," they keep screaming. Tak begins to film away and one girl starts posing for the camera. We ask her if she wants to do the checkmark on the van and, without any questions asked, she knows exactly what to say, what to do, and how to do it. "Wooo! Tonight we rock Thunder Bay!" she screams as the checkmark is applied. "Best show ever! Best night ever! Thank you guys!"

Dirk returns with the keys to the room during the media circus surrounding the checkmark and, satisfied with everything, we decide to finally eat our first meal of the day. The only place still open is Boston Pizza, where we order a couple of pizzas and two giant team pitchers of beer. Cali Joe is mesmerized at the sight, as he has never seen any jug of beer quite that large before. While we all contribute to finishing the jugs, Dirk decides to order a pink coloured drink as bright as the orange is on his shirt. Maybe he's trying to be funny. In any case, it certainly brings a smile to our faces.

The night is festive and the mood is joyful. We are now, distance-wise, over halfway through the tour and we've survived arguably the toughest stretch of driving that we'll face. It's still a long way to go but we feel like celebrating tonight, for it is the first time we have felt relaxed. With the arrivals of both Joes, it's like an injection of new life into this tour for us. Back at the parking lot, Stefan notices something odd about Tak's name on his driver's license so we begin to playfully tease him about his name being something else. He insists on being called Tak Man.

After having to settle for Tak or Tak Man, we leave him alone. Before heading back to our hotel, we drop off Mike at a hotel he had booked ahead of time. He's flying home early in the morning and wants to get some decent sleep before takeoff. Back at our hotel, everyone crams into the double room, while I sleep alone in the van. Tomorrow we have a day off but a long drive ahead of us. The next show is in Kitchener, *only* 1500km away. I thought we had completed the toughest drives already.

Cali Joe getting ready for a Boston Pizza team pitcher.

CHAPTER 8: **LET THE TAILGATING BEGIN**

September 11, 2005 » Show 8
Kitchener, Ontario

"WE'LL BE READY IN A MINUTE," Newfie Joe answers, as I bang on door to the hotel room where everyone else spent the night. Having slept alone in the van, I'm able to wake up bright and early in the morning. By 9:00am, we are checked out and on our way out of town. The drive from Thunder Bay to Kitchener will be the longest straight drive of the tour, spanning 1500km and an estimated 18 hours of nonstop driving. There's a short cut by taking a ferry across Lake Superior and then another one across Lake Huron, but we're sceptical about how much faster this could actually be, especially if we miss a ferry. We do have a day off from the tour today, so we decide to go at it the conventional way and snake around the great lakes instead.

Before leaving the city, we visit the supermarket to buy some bread and other sandwich supplies for lunch and also some snacks and drinks for the long drive. Returning to the parking lot, we see Dirk standing locked outside of the van, holding a tube of Preparation H.

"What's that?" I ask with a smirk.

"Oh, I just picked it up inside," he answers.

I pull out of the lot and begin to drive.

"WHAT THE FUCK ARE YOU DOING?" I hear moments later, and in the mirror I see Dirk's bare ass hanging out for everyone to see.

"I need to apply this cream, because I'm getting a minor case of the haemorrhoids for sitting in the van so long!" he replies.

"Here, go in that booth and do it in there," I suggest, as I pull the van back into the parking lot. Once he finishes his business and returns, we burst out laughing.

"Dirk, you're a character!"

"Thank you."

As we paid respect to one Canadian hero while leaving Edmonton, we decide to do the same for another before leaving Thunder Bay by visiting the Terry Fox monument. His heroic run across Canada started in St. John's and went in the opposite direction that we're going in, but it ended sadly in Thunder Bay due to cancer. Back on the road, Stefan decides he wants to drive so I don't argue. I sit in the back with Tak, while the Joes team up for a game of Halo on the Xbox. For three hours, it's a relaxing drive through the beautiful sceneries of Lake Superior until we approach a town called Marathon. Just outside of it, we pull into a scenic lookout and national park with picnic tables.

One by one we peel ourselves off the cushioned seats of the van for a stretch and a sandwich. Cali Joe grabs his guitar and reveals why he brought it along with him – he can play. Strumming through a great version of *Don't Be Shy* by Cats Stevens, Cali Joe changes the lyrics from "Love is where we all belong" to "Canada is where we all belong." He's quickly becoming our new adopted Canadian. The music must have traveled all the way back to the highway, as other drivers start pulling into the park, one of whom is wearing a Pearl Jam shirt.

"Hey do you guys have any weed?" he asks.

Why does everyone ask us this? I guess it's the British Columbia license plates, or probably it's the van. He introduces himself as Gregg from New Jersey. He was in Thunder Bay and is now on his way to Kitchener and some of the other shows in Ontario, driving by himself. After a short conversation, it's time to hit the road again. Stefan is still going strong at the wheel, while I stay at the back to find out more about Newfie Joe. It turns out that he has a degree in English and has just finished a few years of teaching in Japan and Korea, coming back specifically to hitchhike his way home for the tour. He has traveled the world, mostly by hitchhiking, and has a library full of stories to share. He's truly an interesting fellow indeed.

"Man, I'm glad you guys picked me up when you did, cause I wouldn't have made that trip to Thunder Bay in time if you didn't," Newfie Joe says, as he swallows some liquid from an aluminum can labelled Molson Canadian, "and this stretch would have been the toughest to hitchhike. There's this town coming up called Wawa, and you don't want to end up here if you're hitchhiking. It's the death spot for hitchhikers." He's an intelligent man with a wealth of hitchhiking experience around the world, and he knows how to tell stories. An hour later, a sign informs us that Wawa is 50km away.

"Do you want to be let off here?" I jokingly ask Newfie Joe.

"NO!" he answers seriously.

A few moments later, we actually do see a man standing on the side of the road, but we're not sure if he's hitchhiking. The man has his back to the road and looks like he's writing something. As Stefan blows right pass him, the man turns around holding a sign.

"Guys, it says Pearl Jam Kitchener on it!" Dirk says, looking behind him.

Stefan turns the van around and approaches the hitchhiker. I get the video camera ready for his introduction, while Dirk starts snapping photos of him holding his sign. It's a rock star entrance for the man into the van. His name is Paul from Tofino, BC on Vancouver Island, but he grew up in another town on called Nanaimo, the same town as Tak did and we also find out that he even lived on the same street as Tak at one point in time. Tak is almost overenthusiastic about the coincidence.

"I didn't think anyone would stop," he claims, "So I made this sign."

Picking up our second hitchhiker in as many days, Paul from Tofino, BC.

So it's me, Stefan, Tak, Dirk, Newfie Joe, Cali Joe, and now Paul on our way to Kitchener. The van is fully loaded. To celebrate the addition of our second hitchhiker, we decide to make a stop in beloved Wawa. There, we fill up gas and pay a visit to the beer store where we load up on some delicious local Red Maple, Bohemian, and Waterloo Dark. As we exit the store, there are some kids on bikes admiring the van.

"Are you guys a band or something?" they ask.

"Yes, we're on our way to Kitchener for a show. This is Joe and Joe. They're the guitarists, Dirk is the drummer, and I'm the singer," I respond.

"Awesome. Can we take a photo with you guys?"

"Sure."

We snap a photo and then I jump into the driver seat and start pulling out.

"Man, you're the lead singer *and* you have to drive that piece of shit?" one of the kids laughs. I smile at them and drive out of Wawa. In the process of getting beer, Dirk also picks up a pack of beer store playing cards, so the boys in the back start to play some Texas Hold'em poker using pieces of gum from a giant tub of Double Bubble to bet with. This creative concept lasts only until they begin chewing on their chips. With the sun beginning to set, we dip down in elevation and Lake Superior suddenly appears in sight, so I make a proposal.

"Anyone want to jump in the lake with me?" I ask.

"Do I ever?" Stefan responds instantly.

At the bottom of the hill, I pull into the first accessible entrance and we create our own path through the woods onto the beach. Cali Joe joins and also changes into his swim trunks, while the others think we're crazy for jumping into a lake in Ontario in September just as the sun begins to set. The first touch feels like an ice bath, but then becomes tolerable and the fresh water is actually relatively warm – at least compared to the freezing conditions I'm used to with the salty waters of Vancouver Island.

"Fuck it! I'm jumping in," Newfie Joe says to the others. Without any shorts, he merely strips down to his underwear to get wet in. What an amazing way to watch the sky transform colours. I'm able to stretch my body out and let the minimum amount of waves carry me out, and then wash me back toward the pebbly shore. I haven't felt this free and relaxed since the tour began, and I can see that it's a similar feeling with Stefan and Cali Joe. By the time we're out of the lake, it's nearly dark.

Three more hours of driving in pitch darkness and it's time to call it a night, so we find a park just outside of Sudbury and setup camp. I've always enjoyed camping as a kid and, although this isn't normal camping, sleeping in a van in the middle of nowhere still puts me in touch with nature. It has been a nice relaxing day of driving covering almost 12 out of the 18 hours to our destination, excellent progress. The remaining 6 hours of driving is blitzed through in the morning and there's a feeling of excitement amongst the silent tiredness of our passengers. We enter the city of Kitchener just after 1:00pm.

As Stefan pulls the van into the parking lot of the venue, we immediately notice a different vibe. It's still rather early but there are already fans hanging out in the parking lot with numerous alcoholic drinks in hand. They're even being supervised by Waterloo Patrol. Being close to the border, it looks like the Americans have come up for this show and they've brought their tailgating traditions with them. We drop off the two hitchhikers and pick up our tickets and, judging by our seats, there are definitely more Pearl Jam fans out East. We're no longer sitting four together, and are now up onto the side stage on opposite ends. At the box office, we bump into a familiar face, Brad from Kelowna, who rode in the van to the Gorge with us. Wearing another Hawaiian shirt, Brad is already with our next passenger Tatiana, who we've been looking for around the venue. She has flown all the way from Sao Paulo, Brazil just to join us in the van for the next few shows.

"This is my first Pearl Jam show ever, and I'm really excited," she says. "I've waited 15 years for this moment." Tatiana had given up waiting for Pearl Jam to come to Brazil for a tour, and booked this trip to Canada for the chance to finally see them in concert. However, soon after the start of the Canadian tour, the band announced their first ever tour of South America to follow, including five shows in Brazil. She laughs at the irony but is happy to have both opportunities to be exposed to her favourite band. Driving out of the parking lot, we manage to find a Subway amongst all of the donut shops in the area, but the sandwich shop has somehow run out of bread. So instead, we're forced to eat at Tim Horton's, which appears to be on every other corner in this city.

We make a brief appearance at the pre-show party at a bar called the Rum Runner but, not being in a bar mood today, we decide to head back to the venue and check out the tailgating action instead. Exiting the bar, we see a group of people taking photos of the van. Most of them are from Mexico and one from Belgium, but all are dedicated fans travelling a long way for these shows. Back at the Kitchener Memorial Auditorium, we get our first taste of tailgating. I pull back into the parking lot, which is now almost full, find a spot near the end and, the second I step out of the van, I'm immediately handed a beer. Beside us is a group of 20 to 30 fans just drinking away, playing games, and enjoying themselves. And right in the middle of this action is Newfie Joe.

A warm reception from the tailgaters in Kitchener.

The group is made up of people from all over, including a few Americans, but mainly people from Ontario. And although we've run out of supplies from the drive into town, our new friends have plenty of food and drinks readily available to share. One guy even pours half a bottle of rye into a cup for me to consume. With games being played, meat being grilled, and beer being drunk, the scene is more like a college football game than a concert. The festive mood is enjoyable, and we get right into the action. Cali Joe brings out his guitar, and thus commences a collaborative performance of *In My Tree* where everyone in the area sings along and drums away on the van. As we near show time, we begin heading into the venue despite all of the fun we're enjoying outside of the building.

This is the first show for which Sleater-Kinney is the opening band, but we miss their performance. We don't miss the main band though, as they open, fittingly, with *Long Road*. I can see Tatiana cheering frantically just one section over. The crowd looks much larger than the 7000 capacity – which it claims to hold – but it may just be because the crowd is so loud that it sounds larger than it is. After a different first set and a longer than usual second set, the band comes back out to play us *In My Tree* to start the last encore. It's a fun show and another solid performance, as we hit the middle part of the tour.

After the show, we gather around the van to capture immediate reactions on film. Tatiana is ecstatic and just glowing with joy. The show is even better than she had ever hoped, and then she gets the honour of checking off Kitchener on the van. During the media frenzy of the ceremony, Paul comes by and thanks us for getting him to Kitchener and says he should be okay from here on his own. With Brad and Newfie Joe hanging around as well, we play some guitar and some street hockey, while waiting for the traffic to die down. The tailgating group from before slowly disappears, but not before one of them donates a box full of food to us. Once clear, we drive back to the Rum Runner bar for a proper drink.

At the bar, we see our Mexican friends again, who apparently Newfie Joe has already met and talked to about arranging rides with for the next few shows. In the group now is another guy from Mexico City who was not with them earlier, Carlos. He's travelling alone for the tour but has now met some new friends from his home country and a few Canadians as well. As we leave Newfie Joe with the Mexicans, we return to the van and realize that finding a hotel in the area seems almost pointless, so we decide to drive on to the next city for an early start tomorrow. Gone are the days of the all day drives. Our next destination is London, Ontario, just over an hour away, and the van now consists of me, Stefan, Tak, Dirk, Cali Joe, and Tatiana.

I pull onto Highway 401 to begin this journey. Five minutes later I'm passed by a semi truck, one of the tour trucks. He gives me a friendly honk driving by so I try to accelerate and catch up with him. But the van only reaches a maximum of 130km/hr and the truck is way beyond that, so I give up. It's probably the same truck that left us for dead in the ditch back in Saskatchewan, I think to myself. An hour into the drive, we easily find a hotel just outside of the city. The long road to Kitchener has been conquered, as well as the short road to London.

Don't it make you smile
When the sun don't shine
Don't it make you smile?

Smile

CHAPTER 9: **DON'T IT MAKE YOU SMILE?**

September 12, 2005 » Show 9
London, Ontario

MY BODY HASN'T FELT SO RECHARGED since I left home. Maybe because it knows that we don't need to drive any distance today. Or maybe the first proper bed of the tour for me has something to do with it. With the close proximity of these southern Ontario cities, we are finally given some time to relax and enjoy our trip outside of the van more. We're also starting to fill up the van with passengers and making new friends every minute. In the morning, we meet our newest passenger, Josh from Washington DC, who will be joining us until Montreal. Already in the city, we casually stroll down the street toward the venue and grab lunch from a nearby market. Josh begins to express his environmental political views to us over a beef dip sandwich. He's an interesting fellow with some idealistic things to say. After lunch, we pick up our tickets at the box office, which puts us back together for four seats 20 rows back. We then leave the passengers to roam around town, while Stefan, Tak, and I take advantage of the extra time we have to do a few chores.

First on the list is laundry. A week's worth of road trip clothing must be cleaned for the final stretch of the tour, so we look for a laundry mat not too far from the venue. We drop Stefan off with our dirty clothes and promise him we'd be back in less than an hour, while Tak and I attend to task number two – van maintenance. With about 8000km driven on the trip already, it's time to change the oil and do an inspection to make sure our machine remains running smoothly. Everything checks out okay, and we are finished earlier than expected.

"What do we do now?" Tak asks

"I'm going to do my hair," I reply, pointing to the hair salon beside Speedy Auto Mechanics.

"What are you going to get?" he wonders.

"The McCready!"

We enter First Choice Haircutters and ask how long it would lake to colour my hair red, and they estimate 30 to 40 minutes. Okay, we might be a little late getting back to Stefan, but maybe he'll fold our clothes while he waits for us. So I sit down and they restyle my miniature mohawk before applying a purplish red dye onto my pitch black hair. For the next 20 minutes, I sit with a plastic cap over my hair underneath the heat of a hair dryer, not looking very rock-n-roll-like at all. Meanwhile Tak is filming away with the hairdressers laughing at my situation. They check on the progress and decide that more colour is needed, ignoring the fact that I probably need some bleach first for the colour to stay properly. So another 30 minutes of colouring and drying is done. Tired of waiting around, Tak goes for a walk. When he returns, I'm again getting more colour applied. By this point, I tell them it's probably good enough, and that I'm late meeting a friend. Removing the cap, my hair is revealed and it actually turns out alright, so I thank them and rush back into the van. Two hours after we left Stefan, we return back to the laundry mat.

"What the hell took so long?" he asks angrily.

"Sorry," I apologize, "it took longer than expected. But the van is good now and I got some colour in my hair."

"What colour?" he questions analyzing my hair.

My hair has always been short – crew-cut short. For this tour, I decided to play around with it and leave the middle section longer than the rest, in an attempt to form a rocking Mohawk. It's very subtle and apparently so is the colour that I've just added to it.

As we had hoped, Stefan has folded all of our clothing and has been waiting for over an hour, eager to return to the venue. Apparently Brad had called him during his waiting around and offered to give his spare ticket to Stefan for tonight's show. Brad has a very low Ten Club membership number, which results in tickets in the front row most nights. So Stefan accepts the generous offer and has been itching to return to the venue. We pick up the others by 6:00pm over at Josh's hotel and head directly to the John Labatt Centre. Everyone is pumped for the show. Pulling into the parking lot, we notice a rather long lineup at the entrance, so Stefan decides to jump out early, as he needs to meet Brad. I pull into a spot, within the tightly congested lot located directly across from the venue and, while Dirk and Tatiana run to the venue followed by Josh soon after, the rest of us continue our newfound love of tailgating. The first person to greet us when we step out of the van is of course our hitchhiker, Newfie Joe.

"Hey how was the drive guys?" he asks. "I was talking to the guy who organized the pre-party in Kitchener last night after you guys left, and he gave me some contacts with the CCFC. St. John's, Newfoundland has no pre-party, so I'm going to make a few phone calls. Let's make it happen."

"Sounds good. We'll spread the word."

"Hey, do you know if there are any spare tickets around?" he wonders.

"Yes. We have one because Stefan isn't using his now. Do you want it?" I ask.

"Hell yeah!"

"Good. So it's you, me, Tak, and Cali Joe."

"Wicked!"

Our tailgating party continues as more fans begin to gather around the van, one of whom is from Australia.

"Hi, I'm Annette from Melbourne, Australia," she introduces herself.

She tells us about Vedder coming out into the parking lot earlier to meet with fans and how she was in amongst the crowd snapping away with the camera. So I turn on my camera and begin filming her story about meeting Eddie Vedder. Apparently, he was holding a pen and paper in hand, asking fans what songs they wanted on the setlist tonight.

"What did you request?" I ask.

"I said Sleight of Hand but I don't know if he wrote that down."

"Did you see what he wrote down at all?" Cali Joe asks.

"Yeah, but I was too busy staring at him so I don't know."

My camera then turns to Cali Joe telling his stories of meeting Stone Gossard and Mike McCready and how they're very down to earth, normal people.

"It's like talking to anyone of you guys. So you could be from Vancouver, from Australia, from Los Angeles, from Brazil…"

"Where are you guys from?" I quickly ask some people walking by.

"We're from Sarnia, Ontario," they answer. "It's not that interesting."

"…so they will take their time to talk to you and thank you for coming to the shows. They really do give back to the fans," Cali Joe continues. Feeling inspired by Annette's story, Tak and I begin roaming the parking lot with the video camera to ask fans what they want to hear tonight. Near the end, we come upon a group of fans chilling close to the van – Alana from Vancouver, and Christine, Brett, and Spencer from Hamilton. I recognize Alana, as she confirms that she's working with the merchandise on the tour but has a day off today. She's wearing one of the limited tour hoodies that I want but has been selling out within minutes at every show. I ask her about it and she promises to save one for me if I see her inside. Changing the subject, we ask for their requests for tonight.

"I'm looking for *State of Love and Trust* and *In Hiding*," Spencer says.

"I missed *Rearviewmirror* last night, so I want that tonight," Brett follows.

"And for me? *Smile*, but they won't play that," Christine says with a smile.

At 8:00pm, we enter the arena full of energy from beer. As we walk through the curtains onto the floor, we are hit with the roar from the crowd, and the show hasn't even started yet. It's such an enthusiastic crowd that they're able to maintain the Mexican wave all the way around for a good 10 minutes. When the band steps onto the stage, the roof almost collapses. *Oceans* is the opener and it's loud – the crowd that is. The first set is amazing, including the rarity *Black Red Yellow*, our van favourite *In My Tree*, and a Dead Kennedy's cover of *Bleed For Me* that is just killer. Sitting with Cali Joe and Newfie Joe is a real treat as well. Midway through, there's a chant for Stone Gossard to sing, probably led by Stefan and Brad, who are literally standing underneath him in the front row. But Stone says he wants to dance instead and proceeds to shake his plaid-pants-wearing behind in Stefan's face. The set ends with Brett's request, the best version of *Rearviewmirror* I've ever heard. During the encore Tak takes one of his earplugs out and turns to me.

"Is this really as loud as I think it is?" he asks.

"Yes!" I scream, nodding my head just in case he doesn't hear.

An equally amazing first encore follows before starting the second encore with *Go*. What the fuck? Are they starting the show all over again? This is normally one of the first few songs they play to get the crowd going. But we're not complaining and throw every ounce of our remaining energy into rocking out. Spencer's request, *State of Love and Trust*, is played a few songs later and then Vedder addresses the crowd.

"Alright! I met some of you out in the parking lot earlier. I just want to say hello to all those folks. They were kind, and they gave us some song requests and I hope you're all happy!" he announces as the band goes into Christine's request of *Smile*. This is always a favourite of mine, but despite the fun nature and positive lyrics, it's rarely played. During the song, Vedder brings a little girl from crowd up onto the stage and dances around with her. What a great moment that must be for her and what a great show it is for all of us. Cemented in our nightly high, we venture back into the parking lot, where Christine runs up to me with a big smile on her face.

"Did you guys have something to do with that? They played my song. They played all of our songs," she screams joyfully. I neither confirm nor deny it, but tell her that we're happy that it happened. Around the van, we drown ourselves with water and, even though not everyone knows where the van is parked, they manage to locate us fairly quickly as a small crowd slowly forms around what has become an entity on its own. As the parking lot begins to empty, a woman comes by and asks if she and her daughter can take photos with the van – it's the little girl who Vedder brought on stage. Travelling from Ohio, she's now holding a tambourine signed by Vedder as well as the setlist from the show. It's her first concert ever and she probably doesn't even know what happened.

"Who gave you that tambourine?" I ask her.

"Eddie!" she replies happily.

We head to the bar where the after party is being held and order some much needed food. The usual suspects on hand and, with the van parked just outside, I drag Annette out of the bar to check off London, while everyone else cheers on from across the street. As we finish, I look up and one of the tour busses drives by and we clearly see bassist Jeff Ament looking out the window over at us. We give him a wave and he responds by giving the hang loose sign and a big smile, which brings a big smile to our faces. Not long after, we drop Josh back to his hotel with his fellow American, Cali Joe, sneaking up with him, despite the air tight security monitoring with cameras at every corner. The rest of us drive out of the city centre and check into a hotel of our own, where I'm able to sleep on a bed again. My comfortable back brings a big smile to face, as it has just been a day filled with smiles all around.

Stefan with a smiling little girl who was given a signed tambourine from Eddie Vedder at her first concert.

It might be your guile
It could be your mind
It might be the way you take your time

U

CHAPTER 10: THE ASSHOLE OF CANADA

September 13, 2005 » Show 10
Hamilton, Ontario

THIS HOTEL BUSINESS is starting to get a little too comfortable for me. I wake up late at 11:00am, but everyone is still in a deep trance. It's time to check out of the Howard Johnson, so I start flicking the lights on and off madly and yelling at everyone. They respond, slowly. I check out at reception, while everyone is getting ready and, surprisingly, the Tak man is first out and ready to roll, so I ask him to help clean out the van with me. We rid ourselves of all unnecessary plastic bags, empty cans, and miscellaneous pieces of rubbish accumulated over the last few days of tailgating. Luckily for us, there's a giant dumpster in the lot, where we dispose of our garbage.

When everyone is ready, they jump into the spotlessly clean van and we pick up our American passengers, who are right on the ball and ready to go. On the way out, Cali Joe notices something missing. Apparently, we still have a full bottle of vodka unopened in the van somewhere. Upon further review, we conclude that it was probably lost during our morning cleanup of the van.

"Actually, I think I threw out something in a paper bag that was kind of heavy," Tak confesses.

"That's it," Cali Joe points out.

Not wanting to waste such a prized possession, we make a detour back to the Howard Johnson and, before I could even park properly, Cali Joe is out the door and into the dumpster. I grab the video camera in anticipation of a good moment and it doesn't disappoint. Cali Joe is neck high inside, rummaging through various pieces of articles, before finally pulling out the familiar brown paper bag. He peeks inside and pulls out the prize.

"YES! YES! WE FOUND THE VODKA! I love my fucking vodka, man," he announces as we all applaud and cheer in jubilation. With that piece of business taken care of, we drive out toward Hamilton, just over an hour away. The van crew for this leg includes me, Stefan, Tak, Dirk, Cali Joe, Tatiana, and Josh. On the way there, we stop in for a visit of Niagara Falls. I pull into the parking lot just before 2:00pm and quickly dash out to relieve myself on one of the many trees, while Stefan snaps paparazzi-like photos of my unlawful actions. When I return, Cali Joe is making good use of that precious bottle of vodka by pouring out drinks for everyone.

"So we've got vodka coke, vodka sprite, and vodka ginger ale. What will it be?" he asks while putting on his bartender hat.

"How about a vodka on the rocks?" I request.

"Done! Straight out of the dumpster," he confirms as he fills up my cup with ice. "By the way, the bottle of vodka, straight out of the dumpster, was sitting in the same ice that I just put into this cup, so hopefully there's nothing too foul in that dumpster."

"Ha ha!"

"So who's driving back?" Stefan asks, as Cali Joe hands me my drink.

"Do you want to?" I answer.

"Well, I guess I have no choice," he laughs.

With our drink situation sorted, we head inside to see the top tourist attraction in Canada. Everyone is impressed and snapping photos away.

"It's beautiful man. Look at the power. It's like Pearl Jam power!" Josh points out.

Soon, I turn on the camera and ask everyone for their thoughts midway through the tour. Stefan can't narrow down a single highlight, but points out that he has really enjoyed the performances of *Blood*, *In My Tree*, and *Hard to Imagine*. "I've been waiting for that song forever, and now it's like three times," he refers to the latter.

"How has the Canadian crowd been?" I ask Cali Joe.

"They're a better crowd than back in the States, I'll say that," he answers. "Last night was one of the loudest shows I've ever seen. I think the highlight is the Canadian tour, the van, and the boys from Vancouver."

"Not me," Dirk jokes.

"And the Dirk man from Winnipeg," he adds with a laugh. "And the perpetual orange shirt," Cali Joe continues.

"Didn't you wear that yesterday?" I ask, about the orange shirt he made.

"I think it's the eighth day in a row now," Stefan offers.

"I've been wearing this shirt since Winnipeg and now we're in Niagara Falls. It's getting some good PJ mileage, I'll say that much."

"What about you Tak?"

"I think the highlight was last night, when I was throwing up in the parking lot, and none of you were able to capture it on camera," Tak responds.

"What? I didn't see this?"

"That's why it's a highlight!" He laughs.

"Ha ha! The Tak man!"

"The Yak Man!" Cali Joe corrects.

The afternoon is well spent, enjoying the sites and relaxing, before we head into town toward historic Copps Coliseum, the site of the 1987 Canada Cup of hockey, where Mario Lemieux scored the goal to beat the Russians to create a truly special moment in Canadian history. This was what got me into hockey as a young Canadian, so I can't wait to arrive. However, our entry into the city isn't pleasant, with traffic weaving in and out, cars honking repeatedly at each other, and drivers cursing out through their windows, even at the innocent van. On top of that, there's a cloud of smoke hovering over the city, taking away from the beautiful skyline that might have been, or maybe it's done on purpose to hide the lack of a skyline. Guess this is why they call Hamilton the steel town of Canada. Cali Joe thinks he's back home in Los Angeles.

"What's wrong with this place?" says Stefan as we go the through traffic.

"It's a dump," I respond.

We pull into the parking lot across from the venue and decide to walk around the town. The scenery doesn't get any better. A few minutes into our walk, the smog and heat gets to Cali Joe and he decides to cool off by dipping his feet into a fountain but, as he enters, the spout goes off from above and he's now receiving a full on shower. Already completely soaked, he dashes across the fountain to exit from the other side. We show up at the pre-show party hungry and wet. There are quite a few fans here but we don't bother socializing too much, except for Tak and Dirk, who take turns answering questions from a newspaper journalist.

With an easy relaxed day, we decide to enter the show early to catch a preset acoustic song that Vedder has been doing just before the opening band throughout the tour. Our seats today are on opposite sides again, just like the show in Kitchener, with Tatiana taking my extra ticket. Within seconds of us sitting down, Vedder comes out and plays a solo version of *Throw You Arms Around Me* that leaves a tingling feeling running through my body. When finished, Vedder introduces their friends from Portland, Sleater-Kinney. Their performance is very enjoyable and filled with as much energy as three women can exert on stage. When Pearl Jam comes on, they surprise us again with *Porch* as the opener. The first set is long, well over an hour and a half which, for a lot of bands, is the length of their entire show. But not Pearl Jam.

For the encore, the band comes on stage wearing tuxedos. A few songs in, Vedder explains that his friend Jack is having a wedding tonight, and then jokingly blames the city of Hamilton for not allowing him to attend. He instead sends them a toast and dedicates a cover song of *Harvest Moon* by Neil Young to them. This is followed by an even longer second encore, as the band busts out another seven songs to end the show. The end of the marathon-like show ends a stretch of six shows in seven nights for us and, just when you think that the band can't get any better, they do. This show was simply amazing.

Back at the van, we're greeted by some local friends that we made at the previous show. I ask Christine from Hamilton to check off her hometown on the van, which is located along the crack of the back door.

"Since Hamilton is the asshole of Canada, we get the crack of the van," she laughs, just prior to placing the hockey tape in checkmark formation. For the next hour and a half we continue to hang around the van, playing guitar, and attempting to make a plan for tonight, while other fans stop on by to say hi. Paul the hitchhiker makes his way over during Cali Joe's mellow jam session and hangs out for a drink, as does Newfie Joe. But they both need to leave early to join up with the rides they've arranged separately for the next city. By the time the parking lot is completely empty, we've formed a circle around a local girl, Shannon Briggs, who's playing some of her original songs for our listening pleasure. We're impressed and give her a warm applause. She expresses how sitting on a cold pavement ground has never been so enjoyable.

Local musician Shannon Briggs performs for us at the parking lot after the show.

There's a day off tomorrow and the next show is in Montreal. After a short discussion, we decide to drive out of Hamilton to find a hotel closer to Toronto tonight, and then stop in Ottawa tomorrow night on the way to Montreal. So we set off toward Toronto, and begin searching for hotels. We try four or five but they claim that there is nothing available in Toronto or its surrounding suburbs. Apparently, we're in the middle of the Toronto film festival and U2 are playing Toronto all week, the reason why the next show for us is in Montreal and not Toronto. Frustrated from an hour of driving around for hotels, I drive back toward Hamilton and find a Motel 6 in the town of Burlington. Five pack into the room, while I sleep in the van and Dirk, for some reason, decides to sleep outside on the patch of grass in front of the van. He snuggles into a sleeping bag on top of his mattress just metres away from highway 403.

CHAPTER 11: **VIVE LA PEARL JAM**

September 15, 2005 » Show 11
Montreal, Quebec

THE SUN, SO BRIGHT, filters through the windshield in the morning, cooking me inside of the van as if it were an oven. I can only imagine how Dirk felt when he's first hit with the early morning rays, sleeping on the grass by the highway. Spending the night in Hamilton was not our first choice, but it does allow us to pick up the morning newspaper and read the interview that Tak and Dirk gave to the reporter before the show yesterday. When asked about the comparison of Pearl Jam to U2, Dirk says that "U2 is boring." He then blames them for our tour schedule having to make a detour around Toronto, while U2 performs there all week, before we can come back to see Pearl Jam play in the same city. It's a funny read and we all laugh at the writer's lame review of last night's show. The discussion makes the short drive up to Toronto seem even shorter.

The plan is to have lunch in Toronto, drop Tatiana off because she has a flight booked from Toronto to Montreal, and then head up to Ottawa for the night. Once in the city centre, we stroll down Yonge Street, where we separate to do different things. A few of us find an internet café to check our email for the first time in over a week. On the Pearl Jam sites, I'm surprised to see stories from people talking about their encounters with us and the van.

Meanwhile, Stefan and Cali Joe wander off by themselves and come across the headquarters of 102.1 The Edge, the top rock radio station in Toronto. On the door of building is a sign that says "Come on in." Following the instructions, they enter the radio station and run into a girl just stepping out of the broadcast room. After showing her some photos of our van, she seems rather impressed and asks if they want to go on the air real quickly. It turns out that she's the DJ and her name is Josie. So Stefan and Cali Joe answer her questions about our trip in an interview on the radio and then are asked to request a song to be played on air. Of the songs that they ask for, none are on their rotation, so they pick *Crazy*

Mary by default, before taking a few photos of the excitement.

As the clock strikes 3:00pm, we all meet up back at the van. While Tatiana stays behind for her flight to Montreal, we take off on the road. As I pull out of the city, the first rain drops of the tour are seen. Minus one passenger, it's now back to being just the guys on this leg – me, Stefan, Tak, Dirk, Cali Joe, and Josh.

Stefan talks about our trip on Toronto radio station 102.1 The Edge.

To take advantage of our freedom, the boys plan to play hard tonight. A few hours up Highway 401, we make a stop in Kingston to load up at the liquor store with vodka, whiskey, and beer for tonight. Feeling inspired about heading toward the French part of Canada, Cali Joe grabs the hockey tape and adds a "Vive La Pearl Jam" on the side, while I add a map of Canada on the other side, tracing out our route for the tour. With our supplies all set, Stefan takes over driving duties as I navigate. The drive to Ottawa is another three hours and, half an hour into the drive, we are all just glancing over at the box full of liquor that was just purchased, eagerly anticipating our arrival to Ottawa.

"I think they're cold now," Josh suggests. "I'm just going to have one beer, anyone want to join me?"

"I'll have one too," we all instantly answer in unison.

One turns into two, two turns into three, and three turns into the end of our beer supply, and there's still a good two hours of driving remaining. With the boys out back feeling a little buzzed, they decide to go against our rule of no Pearl Jam music in the van and start mixing some Pearl Jam rarities in until it becomes a Pearl Jam only playlist. With our favourite songs pumping in the van, we hit the vodka next. I like mine strong and so does the bartender, so Cali Joe pours a couple of extra stiff vodka cokes for me, himself and an extra one as well. With Josh content with his organic beers and Dirk happily drinking his coolers, Tak is handed the extra cup of vodka coke. He takes a sip of his drink and quickly adds more ice into it. Meanwhile, the responsible one, Stefan, is sober and driving and probably hating all of us at this point.

"We skipped Montreal to go to Ottawa tonight, so it better be good," Josh proclaims.

"If it doesn't go off, I'll make it go off!" Cali Joe responds, as Tak continues to dump handfuls of ice into his drink. "Ottawa will go off tonight!"

For the second round of the vodka, the bartender is forced to make our drinks a little weaker this time, trying to conserve our supplies. He hands over another drink to me and is about to make one for Tak until he notices that the first one is still being watering down with more ice being added every couple of sips. This prompts Cali Joe to declare Tak as "The Ice Man."

"What are talking about man?" Tak asks.

"I'm talking about how weak you are," he laughs. "You're fucking drowning that drink with ice like there's no tomorrow."

"Ice man! Ice man! Ice man!" we chant boisterously, as our sober driver, Stefan, takes us through an intense rain storm. We are all completely hammered entering Ottawa, as the rain becomes stronger and our sense of direction becomes foggier. We become completely lost looking for our hostel that we had booked earlier in the day, so Stefan pulls over in front of a pharmacy. Dirk quickly jumps out of the van and runs in to buy some shaving cream. When he returns, he instructs Stefan to follow the man in the car in front of us. "He knows where the hostel is."

"So we're following a complete stranger?" Cali Joe asks. "This is kind of sketchy, but not as bad as that fucking place in Vancouver that Jason took us," referring to the alley way of junkies and crack whores that I drove him through. Our new leader takes us back through some familiar roads that we came in on, until we are delivered right at the doorsteps of our hostel just as the rain stops.

"This is it?" Tak asks.

"Yep!"

"But this looks like a jail."

"It is. Well it was a jail, but now it's a hostel. It's the jail hostel." I answer.

"Awesome!" Josh comments.

During check in, Tak, still completely hammered, manages to find a piece of chalk from somewhere and begins to write "Pearl Jam Sept 16" all over the doors and walls of the entrance, referring to the show in Ottawa that we'll come back for. This is the first time I've seen him this drunk, ice or no ice. Exploring the hostel, we find the jail cells downstairs with its gates opened for us to visit. The cells are even smaller than the inside of the van and, being surrounded by cold brick walls, it's definitely less cozy. Further down the hall there's a noose hanging from the ceiling and then a few larger cells. Needless to say, this isn't a place where you'd want to stay for too long but, fortunately for us, we have a dorm room all to ourselves to sleep in instead of a cell. On the way out, the girl at reception gives a few recommendations of bars to check out on a slow

Wednesday night in this college town. With that advice, we venture out into our nation's capital, except for Dirk, who has some kind of shaving accident and decides to stay in.

Along the way, we make a quick food stop at the Pita Pit to soak in all the alcohol that we've already put in our bodies. The night is young but most of the crowd in the first bar we enter is not. So we try another area just on the edge of the University and are successful in finding a bar called Zaphod. Spinning a selection of indie music, it's the only one with any kind of atmosphere that suits us rockers. Sensing a good vibe, Josh immediately buys everyone two rounds of Jagermeister shots and a beer each. I feel like a University student again – going to the bar for drinks on a Friday night after a long week of studying. Our buzz continues to rise with many more drinks being purchased at this little rock bar and, with Arcade Fire pumping loudly from the speakers, we socialize with the local students. I tease one girl, Megan, about how she resembles Corin Tucker, the singer from Sleater-Kinney.

"Thanks, I love Sleater-Kinney! I'm going to see them next week with Pearl Jam," she proclaims.

"Oh really? We're going too," I answer.

"Nice. You guys should come over for a keg party after the show."

The night is fun as we are definitely making Ottawa go off tonight. When the bar closes at 2:00am sharp, we hear rumours of people walking another 15 minutes across the river into the city of Hull and the province of Quebec, where bars apparently are open for another hour. However, taking a look at our conditions, we decide that it's best to go back and rest up for tomorrow. But before the information can be relayed to Cali Joe, he's gone. Assuming that he's trying to find the river and will return on his own later, we return to the hostel.

When we enter our dorm room, Dirk is quietly snoring away. We join him within seconds. About three hours later, we're all woken up by the snoring of a grizzly bear named Cali Joe. He's back and is fully amplifying his breathing in the bed underneath me. For the next hour, we take turns throwing our pillows at him, in an attempt to turn down his volume. When it appears that silence is finally achieved and we are able to peacefully go back to our sleep, the alarm on his phone starts going off. In the end, none of us get much rest and it's as if we have spent a rough night in jail.

In the morning, we casually check out of jail and continue on our way. Before we leave, the manager of the hostel comes out and complains about our graffiti on the walls, so we apologize. Tak has no recollection of the incident. On the way out of town, we drive by the Parliament Building and I stop the van in the middle of the road for a quick photo. After a few nasty honks from rush hour drivers, I pull away and drive in the direction of Montreal, about three hours away. The drive is mellow, but an excitement slowly builds as we enter the culture capital of Canada.

"Crown me king of Montreal!" Josh proclaims. With everyone having different agendas, we're slightly disorganized entering the city, but it's early. Josh is meeting up with some friends and will be travelling with them to the next show, so we pull up to the venue to park and say our goodbyes. We then immediately go after our first order of business in Montreal – eating a genuine poutine. Cali Joe has no idea what we're referring to, but he goes with the flow anyway. The first restaurant we see is a place called La Belle Province and it definitely has this delicious French Canadian snack, consisting of fries, gravy, and cheese curds.

"Oh my god, this is the best thing I've ever tasted!" Cali Joe claims. With our cravings fulfilled, we head to the box office to pick up our tickets and meet up with a new passenger who will be joining us, Tom from Wisconsin. Walking toward the front of the Bell Centre, we see a familiar face a small distance ahead. It's Newfie Joe. The hitchhiker has beaten us to the venue. Brad is also hanging out and has already been offered $1000 for his front row tickets, but he told the scalper to fuck off. We catch up as we wait for Tom, who's easily spotted wearing a Milwaukee Brewers baseball cap, as well as Tatiana, who arrived safely from Toronto last night. When the group is all together, we begin to look for accommodations. Tom recommends the hostel that he stayed at the previous night but it's fully booked. However, the receptionist helps us book into another hostel, just one metro stop away. Using public transit for the first time on the trip, we arrive at our hostel and check in.

I call my friend Catherine, who lived in Vancouver briefly, to let her know that I'm in town, so we decide to meet up for a drink in the city. We catch up and of course the topic comes up as to what I am doing in Montreal, so I fill her in on the tour and trip. Still with a spare ticket for tonight's show, I ask if she wants to come. "Oui," she replies ecstatically. "I don't know many songs from them, but I'd love to go."

We arrive at the venue and head right to our seats on the side stage, opposite Stefan's seats. Catherine is excited for her first time seeing Pearl Jam and explains that she has friends at the show sitting in the upper deck of a crowd that's a little bit different than the others. Not nearly as loud as some but louder than most, the audience seems to really enjoy clapping their hands with the beat and participating in sing-a-longs. It's very festive. During the encore, they start off with their radio hit *Last Kiss*.

"Oh, I love this song," Catherine says turning to me. "I didn't know it was Pearl Jam."

I smile as she seems to be thoroughly enjoying the show. Afterwards, everyone meets up at the van where Catherine is given the honour of checking off Montreal with the photography out in full force. As usual, we hang around the parking lot until the crowd dies down and then drive off to the hostel, parking the van on the streets. At the corner of the hostel, we're greeted by four random girls holding a suitcase. We say hi and then one opens the suitcase and it contains various types of mushrooms. They ask what we're doing tonight and inquire if we wanted to go to an underground club with them. Stefan, Cali Joe, Dirk, and Tom tag along while Tak, Tatiana, Catherine, and I decide to find our own events for the night. Back in the centre of town, we're having a few drinks at a bar when Tak suddenly disappears. Tatiana tries to find him. Minutes later, she returns and says that Tak is throwing up behind a plant in the corner. Again we miss the elusive opportunity to capture it on camera.

From here, Tatiana heads back to her friend's place, where she's spending the night, and Tak decides to pass out in the van. Catherine and I sit outside of the hostel to talk some more but it's 2:00am at this point and she has school in the morning. So when Tom and Dirk return shortly after, we say goodbye and she thanks me for taking her to the show. While Dirk goes back up to the room, Tom tells me that Stefan and Cali Joe are still at the bar, so I drag him back out there. At the bar, Cali Joe is shivering and showing visual affects of the mushrooms. None of the girls from before are still around.

"You should have seen him, man," Stefan says. "He ran through another fountain and got totally soaked."

"I had to go back to the hostel and change again," Cali Joe follows.

As the bar closes, we walk back toward our hostel. We pass by the infamous fountain on the way, and Cali Joe reiterates his love for fountains. However, stretching out to the extents of the park that it's in, this fountain looks more like a mini lake. No wonder he got drenched. We return to the hostel where Cali Joe passes out instantly, thinking about poutine and fountains.

Mon amie, Catherine, does the checkmark for her hometown show, Montreal.

Now that you're gone
All the troubles suddenly explained
infinitum
Parachutes

CHAPTER 12: **ED'S SHIRT**

September 16, 2005 » Show 12
Ottawa, Ontario

THERE'S SOME KIND OF STENCH creeping into my nose. I can't make out what it is and I can't even make out where I am, until the familiar sounds of Cali Joe's snoring reminds me that I'm sharing a room with seven others. Somebody in the room has smelly feet but the chances of narrowing it down to whom is slim. Feeling surprisingly well rested, I decide to get up, a notion that's followed by the others as well. The snoring even stops, as Cali Joe rises to his feet. They all seem to have been lying in bed bothered by the smell too, so it must be coming from one of the other two randoms in the dorm room. I head out to check on the van and Tak is already awake reading a newspaper. He runs into the hostel to borrow a quick shower, and then we're able to check out at the bright and early time of 9:00am – a new record. So it's me, Stefan, Tak, Dirk, Cali Joe, Tom, and Tatiana, who we pick up in the city, doing the dull three-hour drive backtracking toward Ottawa.

"Do they have poutine in here?" Cali Joe asks as we enter the capital city. I park the van and, as we walk into the city centre, we spot a chip truck – a mobile poutine catering truck – so everyone orders a jumbo poutine each for brunch, including our vegetarian from Winnipeg. And much like Cali Joe's reaction, our newest American passenger, Tom, is pleasantly surprised with the first taste of this newfound love. Together we sit in a line on a bench much like a construction crew having lunch on the job site. The silence speaks loudly about how much we're enjoying it.

"How is the poutine, guys?" Tak asks.

"Phenomenal!" Cali Joe responds instantly. "I want to swim in a big tub of poutine!"

After a brief walk around town, we visit the Parliament Building, taking a tour of the government house, much to the excitement of our American friends. At the entrance, our tour guide hands out an information sheet and then proceeds to show us around the place where Canada's political actions take place. Our favourite room is the one where the senate meetings take place, which is decked out in red carpet, red benches, and red tables. The tour is very informative, full of facts that we've learned once upon a time in school, so the tour guide quizzes us on our knowledge.

Stefan, me, Dirk, Tom, Tatiana, and Cali Joe all eating our new favourite snack, poutine.

"Does anyone know when Canada achieved confederation?" the tour guide asks.

"1867," answers a voice from behind.

"Correct!" The voice sounds rather familiar.

"The Parliament is made up of three partners. Can anyone tell me who they are?" the tour guide quizzes.

"The Governor General, The elected House of Commons and the appointed Senate," the same voice responds.

"That's right! And how many members are in the House of Commons and the Senate?"

"301 and 104."

Amazed by the quick responses, we turn around to identify the genius. It's Cali Joe. What the fuck? The tour guide continues on with her quiz and, every time we turn to Cali Joe, he comes up with the right answers. We're completely shocked with his vast knowledge of the Canadian political system. He's actually qualified to be our adopted Canadian, but how does he know so much?

"Well, I kind of cheated. I was reading the information sheet that was handed out at the beginning. And I had it out in front of me," Cali Joe laughs. No wonder. We're all impressed nonetheless. However, Tak isn't as interested as we catch him leaning against a pillar half asleep. At the end of the tour, we ask the tour guide if she knows if the guys in Pearl Jam have ever taken a tour of Parliament. She's not sure who we're talking about but does mention that Kelly

Clarkson came through last week. This response puts an end to our conversation and also an end to the educational start to our afternoon. With the show tonight being in a town called Kanata, about 45 minutes outside of Ottawa, we check into our hotel, The Embassy, and head out toward the Corel Centre before rush hour hits.

The van in front of the Parliament Building.

Back on the highway, the rain begins to fall causing the traffic to build up and the drive to take longer than expected, but we still arrive at the venue relatively early. Picking up our tickets, we notice a lineup of fans being let into the entrance of the building already. It seems like they are about to start selling merchandise. Perfect. This will be my opportunity to grab one of those limited edition hoodies. I join the crowd and when I get to the front I ask for a poster and a hoodie. The merchandise dealer hands me a poster but tells me that they just sold the last hoodie.

"What? But you just opened up."

"Yeah, but we had less than 20 at this table. They've been going very fast."

"I know. I've been to every show."

Feeling gutted, I walk away from the merchandise booth in disbelief and head back to the van. Before leaving the hallway in the building, I notice a couple of girls and their mom trying on what appears to be two hoodies each. Unbelievable. How are they able to get that many, when I can't even get one for myself? Granted, I haven't made an effort to buy them at every show, but I've been to all of them. As I head dangerously close to that feeling of entitlement, I pull myself back and am reminded that it's just a hoodie and not that important. Besides, I'll have the rest of the tour to try again.

Back at the van, the tailgating has already begun, however, we're the only ones. But with Cali Joe strumming on the ukulele and Tom pounding away on a bottle of Johnny Walker whiskey, others begin to join us. Two guys approach the van with huge grins on their face. They introduce themselves as Bowman from Seattle and Dolan from Cleveland.

"We just wanted to come meet you guys," Dolan says. "Seen your van at all the shows…"

"Sexy!" Bowman adds.

"… and we've done quite a few shows ourselves, and thought your van was pretty cool."

It turns out that in 2003 these two fans did the entire Riot Act tour, taking them to Australia, Japan, and all over North America.

"So this is how many shows for you guys?" Tak asks.

"I don't even keep track anymore, but its well over 100," Dolan answers.

"So you've seen the band back in the day and kind of watch the progression over the years. It's got to be quite different, you see them age, and have a kid…" Cali Joe points out.

"I think they're playing better now," Bowman comments.

"This is the best I think I've heard them play," Cali Joe agrees.

"So what are you guys looking for when you come to a show now?" Tom asks.

"I just look to have a good time," Dolan answers.

"Do you guys still get the same feel at the shows?" Tak wonders.

"I look for it in different ways now, like enjoying the crowd," Bowman responds.

"So how would you compare the crowds in Canada so far?" Cali Joe asks.

"Oh they've been fantastic," Dolan claims.

"Crowds in Canada are better," Bowman says.

"Way better," Dolan follows.

"Is there a song you want to hear tonight?" Tak asks.

"I'd love to hear *Don't Give Me No Lip*," they answer simultaneously.

As we let them go on their way, Newfie Joe shows up with Carlos from Mexico. We hand them both a drink. Soon after that, Brad turns up with a friend, Matt from New Hampshire, who decides to give Brad's spare ticket back to him so that he could give Tatiana an opportunity to sit in the front row. When she's informed of this news, she insists on entering the building immediately to take full advantage of her nice upgrade in seats. Her ticket now goes to Newfie Joe while our spare goes to Josh, who has just arrived with some of his friends, finding the van fairly easily. Everybody wins.

Still wanting to try for one of the limited hoodies, I decide to go in early, but again they're sold out and I'm not allowed back outside of the venue where everyone else is. What am I going to do inside the venue for such a long time? Luckily, Alana spots me and calls out, but she's not at the merchandise table. She's carrying posters instead and selling them around the building. She informs me that the next show will be the last for her on the tour, so we hang out while she works. I help her carry around some of the posters, even managing to sell three of them. When it's time for Sleater-Kinney to take the stage, we say goodbye and I take my seat, where Stefan, Tak, and Josh are already at. We are all together in row 20 on the floor tonight with the show fittingly opening with the rarity *Wash*.

The boys are on tonight. As the show progresses, we hear a good mixture of songs that hasn't been played too often this tour along with a few old favourites. Each song is played with every bit of passion as they can be and their timing is near flawless. We're probably the furthest back from the stage that we've been all tour, but it's still amazing. Midway through the first set, Stone Gossard acknowledges an ongoing chant that started in London, a chant calling for him to sing. But this time instead of choosing to dance, he grabs the microphone and sings *Don't Give Me No Lip* for the first time ever. Judging by the performance, I don't know why he hasn't sung this one before as it's such a fun song. All four of us are jumping wildly up and down, screaming out the words while Stone looks down at his lyric sheet to remind him of the words to his own song. This high energy performance is followed soon after by perhaps the best live version of *Black* I've ever seen, and the emotions that are involved with the song always makes it special for me to hear.

The long first set is followed by two long encores, each consisting of a variety of songs that we haven't heard much of so far. After a good but fairly standard show in Montreal, the boys really pulled together for this show, one of the best this tour. As the band comes back on stage for the final encore, I notice a yellow piece of clothing hanging from the back pocket of Vedder's pants. A few songs later, he pulls it out and drapes it over one of the speakers. It's Tatiana's Brazilian soccer jersey. She must have thrown it up on stage during the first encore.

After the final notes are played, we wait patiently at our seats for Tatiana to find us. Josh says goodbye and thanks us for the rides, as this is his last show and he needs to find the friends that he came with. So the three of us are left to discuss how great the show was and how much of a joy it was to see that Brazilian jersey up on stage. Then, the Hawaiian shirt wearing Brad suddenly appears in front of us, shielding a joyful Brazilian girl. She's speechless and can't find her words as she's visibly in shock and happiness at the same time.

"Did you get your Brazilian jersey back?" Stefan asks.

"No, she got something better," Brad answers for Tatiana, who still can't talk. "She got Ed's shirt!"

"Vedder?" we all ask together.

"Yep. But we should go, in case they ask for it back," Brad laughs.

On the walk out, Brad tells us that Tatiana's shirt was still on the stage at the end of the show and some fans were asking the security guard for it. Brad then explains to the security that it was Tatiana's shirt and she should have it if they were giving it back. Amongst all the confusion, the security guard just randomly hands Tatiana a different shirt that was lying on the ground. She told Brad that it wasn't her shirt and Brad, upon a quick glance, realized it was Vedder's shirt and decides that they don't need Tatiana's shirt back and both vacate the front area of the arena quickly. We are all quite impressed with her souvenir. Out front, we meet up with Matt from New Hampshire, who sat up in the stands to allow Tatiana to sit up front. She gives him a huge hug as the rain begins to come down hard again. We decide to meet up back at the hotel, so we run back to the van, where a couple is standing admiring our van while getting soaked.

"You guys want to come in?" I offer.

"Yeah, for sure."

Dirk hasn't returned yet, so we waited in the van for him with our new friends from Ottawa. As the rain dies out, I ask one of them to do the checkmark for Ottawa just as Dirk arrives back at the van. After the abbreviated ceremony, we follow the traffic out of the parking lot and head back to Ottawa, giving the couple a lift in the process. On the highway, a car honks at us repeatedly. It's Matt's car and Tatiana begins waving her new shirt out the window at us. After dropping the couple off in the middle of town, we return to our hotel, where the others are waiting. With a case of beer and numerous pizzas ordered, we spend the rest of the evening relaxing and calming down from an exciting show. This is the last show for Brad on the tour, so we thank him for everything when he and Matt leave for their hotel at 3:00am. Our second trip back to Ottawa is a rewarding and memorable one. Tomorrow is a day off and we've already decided to go back to Montreal for more poutine.

CHAPTER 13: CALI JOE'S LAST STAND

September 19, 2005 » Show 13
Toronto, Ontario

BEING FULLY IN MID-TOUR FORM, things are starting to become routine. We wake up, drive to the next city, head to the pre-show party, go to the show, have a drink afterwards, then it all starts all over again the next day. The problem we've found while doing this tour is that everything is happening at such a fast pace that we don't really get any time to relax. We're constantly on the move and, while it keeps things exciting, we haven't really had much of a chance to fully take in everything. With the drives in between cities being a lot shorter lately, things have calmed down somewhat. And after the Ottawa show, we finally get a rest. With U2 still finishing up their week-long worth of shows in our next city, we have two full days off before Pearl Jam is scheduled to play Toronto. To fill the void, we decide to head back to Montreal with a van crew that includes me, Stefan, Tak, Cali Joe, Tatiana, and Tom. Dirk, on the other hand, is flying to Toronto right away and will meet us at the show.

With a late start in the morning, we arrive into Montreal in time for a late lunch. Stefan has a brother living in Montreal, who he didn't have time to visit the other day, so we pick him up from his condoplex and he guides us around the city. Rain begins to pour again but our stomachs are making noises, so lining up in front of the famous Swartz restaurant for a delicious smoked meat sandwich is almost torture. Montreal is known for its smoked meat and, after a half hour wait, this does not disappoint. The tender beef brisket is marinated for 10 days, slow cooked to perfection, and then thinly sliced before being stacked three inches high in between two pieces of rye bread. Served with mustard and a side of pickle, it's mouth watering delicious. At the very least, it's a break from eating poutine the last few days. With our appetite more than fully satisfied, we leave Stefan behind with his brother and check into the Quality Inn in the centre of the city.

Matt, Tatiana, and Brad posing with Ed's shirt, which Tatiana got from the Ottawa show.

Stocked with bagels, beer, and wine, we chill out in the hotel room playing around with Tatiana's Ed shirt, which reeks of sweat that only such a hard working rock star could exert. We take turns wearing it, drinking wine with it and, of course, taking photos with it. Cali Joe turns on the television and everything is in French. Flipping through the channels, he comes across a game from the Canadian Football League and is intrigued. We explain the rules to him and Tom, who are more used to a different game south of the border, and both quickly catch on, thoroughly enjoying the rest of their first CFL game. Shortly after, Stefan arrives at the hotel to find us having gotten a good start on the alcohol for the night. And as quickly as he arrives, we all leave to explore the nightlife of Montreal on rue Saint Laurent. Two bars and two drinks later, Cali Joe darts into a tattoo parlour.

"I need to re-pierce my tongue," he says. We wait patiently as he opens up the hole in his tongue that was once pierced before. Stefan and I look at tattoo artwork, while Tom and Tatiana look for food, and Tak poses with a motorcycle that's on display. Fifteen gruelling minutes later, Cali Joe comes out and shows us his newest piece of jewellery. It looks pretty hardcore. Continuing on with our pub crawl, we soon arrive onto rue Saint Catherine and we're reminded that Club Super Sex, a famous strip club, is on this street. "Ou est le Sex Supere?" we would jokingly ask each other, while walking down the street. Not more than 20 minutes later, while Stefan and Tom are checking out a jazz bar, we look up and there, in front of us, is Club Super Sex.

"Should we go in?" Tak asks.

"Umm, yeah, I guess," I respond.

After paying a small cover charge, which Tatiana didn't have to pay, we're escorted to a table and given a complimentary jug of beer. Without much action happening, we aren't impressed, so we leave after our drinks are finished. Stefan and Tom are outside waiting for us. Even though we didn't tell them where we were going, they just somehow knew where we were at. Further down the road we arrive at the main centre of arts, and at the top of it is a series of fountains. Cali Joe can't resist. He goes into the water and comes out looking as if a rain cloud had followed him around all day. By 2:00am, the only thing left to do is to get our daily fix of poutine. Cali Joe and I are keen, but the others are in desperate need of a bed. After visiting another La Belle Province, we wash it down with a final drink, before stumbling back to our hotel at 4:00am. Cali Joe goes straight to the hotel room, while I go to the van to grab my sleeping bag and, in the process, end up falling asleep on the futon in the van.

The next morning is slow to get going. Our check out time isn't until noon so we manage to make the most of it and get out 15 minutes after. Everyone is dead tired and hungry, so while most go for some of the remaining bagels from yesterday, Cali Joe and I go for one last poutine, and we hit the king of all poutine at a place called Fritz. Topped with steak, onions, and mushrooms, this poutine is a little taste of heaven, and both of us scarf it down as if we haven't eaten in days. This is the proper way to say au revoir to Montreal.

Today is another day off, but most of it will be spent driving back to Toronto, which is six hours away. I do some of the early driving, but can't last more than an hour before letting Stefan take over. I move to the back with Cali Joe, who's already passed out on the futon, which Tak has warmed up for us nicely during the drive earlier. Four hours later, I wake up to the noise of honking horns and rush hour traffic. We are entering the greater Toronto area. We check into a Super 8 Motel in North York, on the outskirts of the city, and drive into the centre. At a restaurant in little Italy, we have our first proper dinner of the trip before retiring for the night.

On the drive back toward the city the next morning, Cali Joe tells me that he knows someone that might need a ride to the next show. On the day before the Gorge show, he met a guy at his hostel who mentioned that he might be doing these next few shows.

"His name is Ben from Australia and he has no transportation sorted out. I told him about you guys, so he might need a ride."

"Okay. Just point him out if you see him."

We get into the city early and I pull into the parking lot across from the venue to park for the day. $30 later and we have the prime parking spot in front of the Air Canada Centre. As we exit the vehicle, Cali Joe points to some guy sitting on a bench not too far from us.

"That's him, that's Ben, the guy that I was telling you about."

That was easy. I introduce myself and he confirms his need for a ride, so I advise him to meet us at the van after the show. With that issue sorted, we pick up our tickets at the box office, while Tak waits nervously outside. Tak had previously done an internship with the promoter who just happens to be working on this tour, so for the Toronto show he has been invited backstage for a lunch. His legs are shaking, so we all drill him with questions and play around with him, capturing it all on camera.

"What's going on today Tak?" I ask.

"Oh we got nice weather. But I think it's time for you guys to go," he answers avoiding the subject.

"I don't think I've had anyone try to get rid of me as much as Tak is right now," Cali Joe laughs.

"She got Eddie's shirt," Tak points to Tatiana.

"That's old news."

"I think the last time you had this camera on, he said that today would be his favourite part of the tour," Tom adds.

"My birthday is coming up," Tak responds.

"That's next week. What's happening today?"

"We're rocking Toronto, go explore the city," he further evades the subject.

"What are you going to do while we explore?"

"I'm having lunch. You guys should go find some poutine," he laughs.

Ten minutes of intensive interviewing later, we've had our fun and leave him alone to explore the largest city in Canada. Directly across from the Air Canada Centre is the CN Tower. We walk by, but the lineup to get in is far too long so we continue on. This is Cali Joe's final show of the tour, but he has an itch to do more shows. At an internet café, he begins searching for flights to St. John's, Newfoundland for the tour finale, but prices are close to $1000 and it doesn't look good. He also looks for a hostel for the night, as we plan to drive out of the city after the show.

While he does his thing, Tatiana meets up with a friend for lunch, and Stefan, Tom and I pay a visit to the Hockey Hall of Fame. Inside, we have the opportunity to see our holy grail and every Canadian's dream, the Stanley Cup. An exhilarating feeling runs through me, as I touch the trophy that I see get awarded to the champion every year on television. After two hours of indulging ourselves with hockey history, we head up the CN Tower. At the top of the tallest standing structure in the world, we can view the entire city including the venue and the van parked in front of it. Having done enough sightseeing for one day, we take the elevator down 500m back to the ground level at a speed of roughly 20km/hr

At a nearby bar, The Loose Moose, we grab a drink and attend our first pre-party since Hamilton, and Newfie Joe is there sitting with a jug of beer ready to share with us. He tells us some stories from the road while we wait for Tak to arrive. Sporting a recycled backstage working pass from the last show in Ottawa, Tak shows up with a huge smile on his face. He describes how he was eating the crew's food, helping setup some chairs, met the tour manager, and even met their yoga instructor for the tour, Natasha, who Jacinta works with and had told us to look out for. Basically, he claims to have met everyone except for the band, but he's satisfied.

Back at the van, the rest of the crew is waiting around, including Dirk, who's ready for more van action. Cali Joe confirms that he'll not be able to fly to St. John's because the flights are just too expensive. We're disappointed and refuse to let him leave. In fact, I begin hockey taping him to the van to keep him with us, but he breaks free from the super adhesive just in time for the show.

Tonight we are back to sitting on opposite sides, with Stefan and Tatiana on Stone's side, and Tak and I on Mike's side. But being only six rows back, we have a fantastic view. The show is very standard overall. The first set goes by and we have no reaction. Maybe our expectations were too high for this one, maybe we've just seen too many in a row, but we're not feeling it as much as we have at all of the other shows. Perhaps we're just feeding from the band's energy, which appear to be low as well, even with the two days of rest in between shows. When they come back for the encore, we notice a few more bodies standing at the side of the stage.

"Hey isn't that U2 there?" Tak asks. Taking a closer look, we conclude that Bono, the Edge, and Larry Mullen Jr, have come out for a closer view of the concert. By the time they get to the end of the second encore, most of the crowd has noticed the extra audience members. Vedder even acknowledges them, thanking U2 for opening all week for Pearl Jam. He then sheds some light onto why they might be in the poor conditions that they're in tonight. Apparently Bono has been buying them $1500 bottles of vodka all weekend and they have been partying late the last few nights in Toronto, including after an appearance by Vedder at the last U2 show.

For *Rockin' In The Free World*, the band is joined on stage by Bono, singing along with Vedder. I'm not the biggest U2 fan, but it's intriguing to see the two iconic front men standing side by side on the same stage. Although Dirk might have been bored to death. After the unbelievable show we saw in Ottawa, Toronto does not even come close. But once again, an average show from this band is far superior to most shows from other bands, so we still leave in satisfaction.

Everyone gathers around the van after the show, including Newfie Joe, who makes a last ditch effort to lure Cali Joe back to his hometown for the final shows of the tour. It's unsuccessful. We continue greeting random fans as they come by the van including one guy who had heard Cali Joe and Stefan talking about our trip on the radio a few days earlier. After signing an autograph on the guy's Pearl Jam ticket, Cali Joe approaches the van and I hand him the hockey tape for the Toronto checkmark. Chants of Joe surround this media circus of a ceremony, as photographs are flashing left, right, and centre. It's a bit sad to have someone leave, especially someone who has grown to be a very good friend in such a small amount of time. But something tells me that we'll be seeing him again.

While the traffic is still clearing out, we play some street hockey and even some basketball with a mini hoop set up on the side of the van to kill time. The next show is in Quebec City tomorrow night, 10 hours away, so we decide to get a head start on the drive.

Cali Joe not wanting to leave.

An hour into the drive, Stefan takes over to do his part. About three hours outside of Toronto, we drive past Kingston and see a sign for a campsite. At this point, Stefan is getting as tired as everyone else in the van, so we decide to call it a night and find this campsite. Taking the exit, we begin following the signs, which appear to be leading us to nowhere. Our restless state of mind doesn't allow us to work through the problem at hand and, after half an hour of aimlessly searching for the campsite, we stumble upon a flat patch of grass. This will do. Stefan pulls over and we set up camp for the night, with four sleeping in a tent and three in the van. This is the last stretch of the tour and thus marks the return of the long distance drives between shows. It has been far too relaxing and fun this past week, but the hardcore travelling is now back – and this time we're ready for it.

CHAPTER 14: **ARE WE STILL IN CANADA?**

September 20, 2005 » Show 14
Quebec City, Quebec

CAMPING ALWAYS BRINGS EARLY RISERS and, even though we're not in our sleeping bags until after 3:00am, everyone is up at the crack of dawn despite the noise of a train passing by every hour. And what was merely just a patch of grass in the middle of the night turns out to be a lovely park overlooking a watershed. Stefan and I spend 10 minutes exploring the historic site at the head of Lake Ontario and return to find everything packed away and ready to go. A good head start from last night leaves only six hours remaining on our drive. With a van crew that includes me, Stefan, Tak, Dirk, Tatiana, Tom, and Ben, I pull into a gas station to fill up and freshen up before we continue on.

"Do we look like we illegally camped out last night?" Tom jokes. "If I hang out with you guys any longer, I'd just look like I'm completely homeless."

"Illegally?"

"I went to get gas, and she was like, 'wow, you had a rough night huh?'"

"That's the rock 'n' roll life!" I respond, while Tak is still asleep in the back.

Halfway to our destination, Stefan takes over and drives the remaining distance to Quebec City. It's a rather dull drive, with the exception of a few mountainous areas as we come closer, so we try to entertain our passengers. In the back, I spend some time chatting with Ben to find out his story. Apparently he was at the Green Tortoise hostel in Seattle the day before the show at the Gorge, and he was just playing away on the guitar in his room when he heard someone else playing Pearl Jam down the hallway. He knocked on the door and Cali Joe answered. From there, they proceeded to jam together in front of the space needle for the rest of the day. He's a young fellow who has decided to just go see shows in North America and Europe because bands don't come to Australia as often as he'd liked. And contrary to our opinion, he thoroughly enjoyed the Toronto show. He's a soft spoken guy but I like him. When we're not talking, Dirk and I decide to introduce our American and Australian friends to some good Canadian television by playing episodes from the *Trailer Park Boys*. It doesn't take long for Tom to be hooked, and we nearly manage to get through all of season one before closing in on our destination.

We arrive in Quebec City to a downpour of rain with some kind of weird dark German techno music being played in the van. I'm not sure why this is on. We've made good time and arrive early in the afternoon, so when we're lost again driving past the exit for the city, we decide to keep going and explore the region. Not too far out, we stumble upon a waterfall, which is flowing quite nicely. After a short excursion around the waterfall, we drive directly to the venue, to pick up our tickets. I can hear someone calling out to us. It's Matt from New Hampshire and he introduces us to his friend Mike from Charlotte, who Stefan seems to know already.

"I've got an extra front row ticket if any of you want it," Mike asks. "I'm just asking for face value." We politely decline. Ben has his ticket already, Dirk and Tom both have an extra that they need to get rid of, and we have four great seats together in the fifth row. This will be the last show for Tatiana and Tom and we wanted to sit together. However, upon returning to the van and telling Tak about the offer, he decides to jump all over it. We give him shit for his decision.

"Hey, how often do you get to sit front row?" he rationalizes. Needing to sell three extra tickets now, we drive back into the city, where Tatiana has a hostel booked. The original plan was to do what we did last night and drive out after the show for some camping outside of the city but, after driving through the city and walking around a bit, the allure and beauty of the old town persuades us to spend the night and further explore inside the castle walls in the morning. Tom, Ben, and Dirk also book a room at the hostel, while Stefan, Tak and I decide the van is good enough for us. When our accommodations are all figured out, we move on to tickets. Dirk wants to head straight back to the venue, so we shuffle them around, handing over Tom's tickets to sell along with Dirk's extra. It will now be Tom and Tatiana sitting with me and Stefan, just what we wanted. Dirk and Ben bus back to the venue, while the rest of us explore Quebec City.

"Wow, this is so cool," Stefan remarks. "It's almost like Europe." The stone roads, grassy hills, and castle-like buildings definitely give the city a different look than anything we've seen so far in the country. At times we question each other whether it's even part of Canada. I've always wanted to visit Europe, so I guess this is the closest I'll ever get to it, culturally. Over the hills, we stroll down onto a wooden walkway alongside of the St. Lawrence River. At the end of the path, we cut back into the town and find a place for a nice dinner at a French restaurant. I order a French onion soup and we enjoy some last drinks with our leaving passengers. It's a more mellow day and less eventful than what we have become accustomed to in the past week, but it's nice to have the change in pace. We tease Tak some more about ditching us for his front row seat.

"Do you want to wear my Eddie t-shirt tonight?" Tatiana asks him.

"Ha ha! Yeah, I should eh?"

We head back to le Colisee Pepsi Arena feeling relaxed and ready to rock. As we enter, I head straight to the merchandise stand to look for my hoodie. The first one has nothing but the second one has one still hanging on the wall, so I get excited and quickly snatch it up. Sporting my new limited edition Pearl Jam hoodie, I walk through the curtains and onto the floor. Just as I step onto the floor, I see Carlos from Mexico and greet him.

"Hey have you seen Newfie Joe?" he asks.

"No. I thought he was with you guys."

"No he wasn't. I'm not sure if he made it or not."

"Oh, I think he'll find a way to get here."

Carlos tells me that it's his last show but it was a pleasure to be in my beautiful country. I tell him that it was great to have foreigners come and enjoy Canada, and I hope we get another opportunity to meet again. We say goodbye and head to our seats. Everyone is there already. Dirk wasn't able to sell our extra tickets, but it doesn't matter – we are sitting together close to the stage and that is all that really matters. Early on, we're quickly treated to intense performances of *Not For You* and *Blood* that sets the tone for a great show that does not disappoint. In the encore, Tatiana gets the song she has been hoping for all tour, *Footsteps*, and it's played beautifully for her final show. Feeling fully content with the show, we head back into the city, where we park the van at the hostel's underground lot and begin wondering the streets.

"Hey, come check this out." Tak yells at us glancing into a store window. We peek inside to see a sign that reads "Gas, Grass, or Ass. Nobody rides for free."

"Ha ha, that should be the slogan of the van."

Entrance into Old Quebec.

After one quick drink, most of us are beat already, so we decide to the end the mellow night. On our way out of the bar, Tom grabs the Pearl Jam poster taped to the wall as a souvenir. The mood is somewhat sombre, as we know that we must say goodbye soon. Outside the hostel there's a group of familiar faces we've seen over the past few shows hanging out. We gather them around the van and I hand Tom the hockey tape, which he uses to apply a perfect checkmark next to Quebec City. We thank Tom for coming along and he's very appreciative.

"I'd like to say one word," Tom announces with my video camera in his face. "Honestly guys, I've had a blast. And thank you for letting me be a part of this experience."

"It's been great having you with us."

"I'd also like to say that it's fucking cool that you guys did this because guys talk about doing this all the time, like get in a car, drive across the country and see all these shows. But no one ever fucking does this man. People talk, talk, talk, but the fact that you guys did it is inspiring, you know. It's totally inspiring. So thank you!"

A group hug ensues after a bittersweet moment. We have made some close friends with a lot of new people in a very short amount of time during this trip and bodies are beginning to fall now. The tour is coming to a close shortly and we're feeling a little sad. We thank Tom and Tatiana for coming along and, like Cali Joe, I don't think we've seen the last of them. While everyone retreats back to their hostel room, the three of us wander back to the parking lot for another night in the van, our shelter, our warmth, our home.

I scream in affirmation
Of connecting dislocations
And exceeding limitations
Be achieving levitation

Big Wave

CHAPTER 15: SURFING THE ATLANTIC

September 22, 2005 » Show 15
Halifax, Nova Scotia

MOTHER NATURE HAS, for the most part, cooperated with us during this trip. However, with the showers being more frequent as of late, including the one threatening to hit us overnight, we're a bit sceptical of whether it was a good idea to spend the night in Quebec City. But as we wake up and stumble out of the van, Stefan and I peek outside of the dark parking lot to find nothing but bright sunshine. With Tak still asleep, we venture out to explore the beautiful city. When we return, Dirk and Ben are already waiting at the van. I open up to let them in and find Tak still asleep. Nevertheless, we pull out and start our drive toward the next city. For the 12-hour trip to Halifax, we now have a depleted van crew of me, Stefan, Tak, Dirk, and Ben.

The drive is quiet, almost as if no one knows one another, similar to our first drive out of Vancouver. Fatigue from a couple of weeks on the road has set in and most of us in the van are completely passed out, while Stefan and I are driving and navigating up front. Three hours later, I pull into the town just before the New Brunswick border to answer our growling stomachs. The town is small but there are a few options. I park the van on the streets and, as soon as the van stops, everyone wakes up.

"What's going on?' Tak asks.

"Where are we?" Dirk wonders.

"I don't know where we are but we're getting some food. Want to come?"

After a few minutes of contemplating, we settle for a Chinese buffet that's just screaming out at us. The food isn't as bad as I thought it would be, so we end up eating a tour's worth of food all in one sitting. During the meal we discuss our plans for the day. I suggest we go to PEI (Prince Edward Island) and camp there for the night before driving to Halifax in the morning. It's the only province without a show because it's a little out of the way, but I really wanted to see all of the provinces. The others have no real opinion, so we leave it open.

Back on the highway, Stefan takes the wheel and as we hit sunset we detour off the main highway to drive up the scenic route along the Bay of Funday in New Brunswick. By 7:00pm, it's pitch black and we never really get to see the beauties that this region has to offer. Driving through the small town of Saint John, New Brunswick – not to be confused with St. John's, Newfoundland – we decide to grab a slice of pizza at a takeout place and talk about our plans for the evening. The lady taking our order is on the phone the entire time, even talking about us to her husband on the other end. It's pretty comical to listen to. But the food is decent and our discussion is conclusive. With Halifax about four hours away, a two-hour detour to spend the night in PEI is voted against by Dirk and Tak. Ben and Stefan are indecisive, so the majority wins and we go directly to Halifax. I guess I'll have to visit PEI next time I'm driving on the other side of the country.

The night drive takes us into Halifax by midnight, but not before we are forced to pay 25 cents for a toll bridge. Tak is well rested from a full day of sleeping, so I pull over to let him take control of the wheel leading us into the city. Trying to find accommodations, we conclude that the hotels are either booked or too expensive, so we would need to find a hostel. Just at the end of the city, there's a hostel but they don't allow any check-ins until 7:00am. Tak drives around the area for a little longer and then pulls into a parking spot and we decide to just crash out in the van parked on the street. Dirk leaves and returns 10 minutes later.

"Guys, I found the perfect place to sleep," he claims. "I'm going to grab my stuff and go there."

"Wait, where are you going?" I ask.

"The cemetery."

"What? You're nuts," Stefan responds.

"I'll see you in the morning."

The rest of us cozy up in the van after a full day of driving. With the heat of the sun beaming down upon us the next morning, we're slow to respond. I'm sleeping on the ground in the trunk, so I open the back door and roll out of the van still in my sleeping bag. It's broad daylight. I rub my eyes to wake myself up and see a girl smiling at me while she walks by. I look around and there are people everywhere, and lots of beautiful young girls, all dressed nicely and wearing a grin on their face. I guess I do look a bit scruffy, being shirtless, still in my sleeping bag, and barely awake. I retreat back into the van to put on some pants and a shirt. When I exit our vehicle for the second time I realize where we are.

"Guys, we're parked on the streets right in front of Dalhousie University," I inform the others. "There are students walking around everywhere." After freshening up, we wander down the street to find the cemetery but Dirk is nowhere to be found. I try the hostel on the next block and, sure enough, there's Dirk passed out on the couch.

"Do you know this guy?" the receptionist asks.

"Yeah, he wants to check in I think."

We wake Dirk up and he decides to get a room to sleep in during the morning. He'll meet up with us later as we plan to do some exploring. After three weeks of driving across land, we've finally reached the ocean again. Excited with our new surroundings, I suggest we go for a surf and relax on the beach. Not interested in things he can do back home, Ben decides to stay behind as well, as we find a rental shop for surfing equipment. "Who knows, maybe you'll see Eddie Vedder surfing out there," the shop owner comments, as he helps carry the boards out of the store for us.

Me and Stefan getting ready to hit the ocean.

Following the suggestion we received from the shop, we drive out an hour along the coast to Martinique Beach to catch some waves. The swell is low today but it doesn't matter, we just want to be in the ocean. And while Stefan and I fight through the crashing waves, Tak is chilling on white sand taking photos and video of us. Just before the start of the tour, I was surfing in the Pacific Ocean and now I'm surfing the Atlantic. It's pretty amazing and my feeling is one of total relaxation. The schedule along the way has been fairly strict but the ocean has a way of relaxing my mind and soothing my soul, allowing me to forget everything that's going on. There are no schedules out here. The morning is fun and relaxing. Afterwards, we decide to try some of the famous Atlantic Ocean lobster at a nearby lobster shack. This is by far the best meal we've had all tour. The lobster is so tasty and fresh, that the $30 price tag is well worth it.

As we drive back through town, we drop off our surfboards, pick up Dirk and Ben at the hostel, and head toward the venue. Finding a parking spot on the street just a few blocks from the venue, we head toward the Split Crow Pub where the pre-party is taking place. As we spot the bar, we also spot Newfie Joe out front. He confirms that he did indeed make it to Quebec City. Inside we see another old friend, Barbara, who's back after a week absent from the tour and wearing glasses again. She's there with her friend Vanessa, who just moved to Halifax a few weeks earlier. "It was tough to be away, but I'm ready to rock the East Coast!" Barbara indicates.

Tak at Martinique Beach.

The rest of the afternoon is spent enjoying ourselves at the pub on the patio, talking to familiar faces and meeting some new people. For the fundraiser, we all buy an arm's length worth of raffle tickets in the hope of winning some valuable Pearl Jam memorabilia from the draw. This is the last organized pre-party of the tour, but we're trying to help Newfie Joe set up a last minute one in St. John's and he seems like he has some leads on it already.

"I have to go meet the band's PR chick to get something sorted for St. John's," he tells me.

"Who? Nicole?"

"Yeah, I called the people at CCFC and she has some stuff for me to pick up. You want to come?"

"Sure. Do you have a place to hold the party yet?"

"Nope. I'll need to make some calls when I get home. You've got van space for me right?"

"Of course."

So the two of us walk to the Metro Centre and hang out around the back where security escorts us into the venue. It's very systematic, as one car arrives after another, containing people involved with the show. Each group is led by security until they're in the building. A few moments later, Nicole arrives and Newfie Joe approaches her. She seems to be extremely busy, so I stay behind and wait. Twenty minutes later, Newfie Joe returns with a box and some poster tubes. "Oh, I got some good stuff here. Can I put them in the van?"

I help Newfie Joe carry the auction items as he lugs his gigantic backpack toward van for storage. Back at the pub, we arrive just in time for the raffle draw, where Barbara is fortunate enough to win a poster autographed by Mike McCready. I store another poster tube in the van and then we are off to the show. Tonight we have four seats together in the sixth row with our extra ticket going to Ben. Walking in, we catch the tail end of Sleater-Kinney's performance, their last show of the tour. In St. John's, it will only be Pearl Jam. When the lights come up, we run into Matt and Mike, who are up in the front row again. Mike asks me what we're going to do with the van after the tour.

"I'm not sure," I respond. "We haven't figured that out yet. We're flying back, so I don't know."

"If you want, I know some of the people at Ten Club. I could ask if they could tow it at the back of one of their trucks or something," Mike suggests.

"I'd rather have someone drive it back and I've been talking to this girl about it, so we'll see what happens in St. John's."

The dimming lights end our conversation and I retreat back to my seats. *Hard to Imagine* opens up the show and, if that's the only song they play, I can still leave happy. A few more rockers later comes *Breath*, a rarity which they play maybe once a tour, if at all. What a treat. Vedder stumbles on a few of the lyrics, but everyone is rocking so hard by this point that no one really cares. When finished, Vedder jokes about his mess up and asks for a bottle of beer, a bottle of the locally brewed Alexander Keith's.

"I said fuck Heineken, give me a Keith's!"

When they come back on for the encore, Vedder complains that he still hasn't gotten his requested beer yet and demands for one to be brought to him before they continue. "If someone gets us a god damn Keith's, we'll play all night."

There is still no beer by the time the second encore comes. Finally at the end of *Alive*, a stage person runs out with a can in his hand and the crowd erupts as Vedder is presented with a can of locally brewed Alexander Keith's. He smiles to the crowd. "If it's the worst beer we've ever had, you're all in big fucking trouble," Vedder laughs. "It says eight pack. What the fuck is that? We must be in Canada."

A sip is taken and immediately spat out as a joke, before he takes a huge chug of the Nova Scotian beer and gives us his approval. "It's not bad, it's not bad. Bring me the other seven."

Vedder then places the half drunken can on top of his head and balances it as if it was a surfer and his head was a surf board. The can amazingly stays motionless for the song *Down*, but I guess surfers have good balance.

"Okay, our strategy has now changed. We're not going to stop playing until we finish the Keith's," Vedder now proclaims.

Rejuvenated from the beer, the band continues on and plays nearly 10 more songs for the second encore, including *Bushleaguer* for the first time this tour, to end a spectacular show, the final one for mainland Canada. We exit the arena feeling great and thirsty for a can of Keith's. Meeting up on the streets in front of the van after the show, Barbara and her friend Vanessa are given the honours of checking off Halifax. The applause and cheering attracts locals walking by as well, including one guy who wants to give the van the Halifax dent. He claims that you haven't truly been to Halifax until a local rams their head into your vehicle. But as much as we want to see this drunk local hurt himself, we politely decline. After all the commotion, we head to the bar for a drink, where Mike buys us all a round of beer. It's a generous gesture and well appreciated.

Stefan tries calling someone that has been inquiring about a ride to Newfoundland but, after a short conversation, Bobby from Providence decides to book a flight instead of roughing it with us for the long trip. No worries, it will mean more room for us. At around 2:00am, the bar closes and our hunger opens up. It always seems to be the same time of the night. Entering a nearby Pita Pit, a couple of familiar faces, who are enjoying a late meal of their own, greet us. Malland and Matt from London, Ontario approach the cashier and ask to pay for all of our subs without even talking to us. We're pleasantly surprised at yet another great gesture by Pearl Jam fans and thank them for it. They'll be flying to St. John's the next day, so we'll see them again.

The next show is in Newfoundland, a province off the mainland of Canada, meaning a ferry is required to reach our final destination. However, the terminal is another four hours north in Sydney, Nova Scotia. After demolishing our sandwiches, we gather up the crew and drive out of the city. An hour into the drive, Tak takes over, as he has become our designated extra late night driver. With everyone passed out in the van except for Tak and Stefan up front, our driver fearlessly leads us on an overnight excursion. Making good time, Tak delivers us to the terminal by 6:00am – an hour and a half to spare for the first ferry of the day – and joins the lineup of cars. Glancing over top of the vehicles in front, we see the mammoth ferry towering over us and realize that the final trip of the tour is going to be the longest yet.

I know I was born
And I know that I'll die
The in between is mine

I Am Mine

CHAPTER 16: **THE ROCK**

September 24 – 25, 2005 » Show 16 & 17
St. John's, Newfoundland

ONE BY ONE, the cars are lined up like animals entering Noah's ark and, as the time approaches closer to departure, the vehicles increase exponentially. The wait for the ferry is slow and gruelling. People watching becomes the source of entertainment. A few lanes over, Pearl Jam's tour trucks are all sitting in pole position with all the other over-sized vehicles but the band, themselves, are most definitely flying. No way would they be enduring the lengthy ride 110km across the Cabot Strait. Tak claims that we beat the trucks to the ferry terminal and is proud of his achievement.

Beside us is another van of similar size. It's towing a trailer which, judging be the low suspensions on its wheels, is carrying a lot of heavy gear that we can't see, but we do see at least five passengers inside. I make eye contact with the driver and we give each other a nod in acknowledgement of our vehicles. They look like a band but, then again, we also look like a band. They smile at us when the horn goes off from the ferry, signalling the start of boarding. I pull the van onto the ferry and our initial step for entering Newfoundland has begun. Our final van crew includes me, Stefan, Tak, Dirk, Newfie Joe, and Ben. When boarded, we leave the van and head up to the ferry deck.

It's only 7:30am when the ferry departs but, as Newfie Joe states, once we're on the ferry, we're already in Newfoundland and the bar is open all the time. Heeding his words of wisdom, we settle in at the bar where Newfie Joe insists we try a Newfoundland beer called Black Horse. Some of the tour truck drivers are also at the bar so we ask them how their drive has been. They seem to have enjoyed their time trucking around our country and one of them even admitted honking at us in the prairies when we were in the ditch. He wanted to help, but they had strict deadlines to meet and thought we'd be okay.

Also joining us for a drink at the bar are two guys we've seen on and off throughout the tour. They're both named Nathan from Philadelphia and they've driven the whole tour as well, sleeping in their car every night. We share road stories and enjoy a nice morning beer to start the six-hour ferry ride. With two beers in my system before 9:00am, I exit the bar and find a seat to pass out in. Some of the others also join me for a much needed nap, trying to recuperate from the little amount of sleep we had last night. When I wake up, Stefan is talking with one of the guys from the other van and I'm lured into the conversation. It's fairly one sided with them mainly asking about us and what the story about the van is. We give them a little information, but not too much.

I look at my watch and it's not even 10:00am yet and, after the six-hour ferry ride, there's still another 11 hours of driving before we'll reach our destination. Add in the four-hour drive from Halifax to the terminal and the total travel time for this leg will be over 20 hours, easily the longest connection of the tour. If we hadn't driven to the terminal after last night's show, however, we would have had to wake up early this morning to catch the ferry at noon. And if we missed that, the next scheduled departure would have been midnight and we wouldn't be able to make it to St. John's in time. Is the band trying to make it impossible to follow them? But I love the challenge of it all and have come to realize that the journey to these cities is half the fun.

Up on the deck of the ferry, we peak back to where we had come from, but it's no longer in sight. All I see is blue, from the water to the sky. Around the front of the ferry, we slowly close in on Newfoundland, which is also known as "The Rock" because the island is actually a large rock. It also happens to be International Talk Like A Pirate Day, as the ship approaches land, so we obey the rules and make every *rrrr* pirate references as best we can.

At 2:00pm, the ferry docks, and we are welcomed by a huge rain storm as the van steps onto the island. A typical Newfie welcome apparently. It's so wet, that I have the windshield wipers on full and still can't see a thing. Our wipers are useless. I knew there was still some maintenance I needed to take care of on the van. I carefully steer the beast through the roads, following only the red brake lights of the vehicle driving in front. Hopefully he knows where he's going. Soon it lightens up and I'm able to see clearly again. The drive is another mellow one, as it has become a recurring theme for passengers to fall asleep in the comfortable van. The rain drowns out the voices talking in the van, so I put on some Nine Inch Nails to balance out the sounds.

The sky turns dark before 6:00pm and it's still raining. I switch over driving duties to Stefan and he goes for another two hours until we hit the town of Gander to fill up gas. There is a bar and hotel around the corner, at which Stefan suggests we just stay for the night, since it's dark and the weather is miserable. We all agree and a few of us head into the hotel to check in. As I exit the van, I notice that the other van from the ferry is gassing up beside us as well.

"Hey, how's the drive going?" I ask.

"Wet, but good. We're going your way too," the tall bearded van driver responds.

"Oh, you're going to the show," I presume.

"You bet."

"We're going to call it a night here, you guys continuing on?" Stefan asks.

"Yeah, we have to get there tonight," he responds. "Maybe you'll see us in St. John's."

"For sure. Good luck!"

Everyone crashes out in the room right away, except for Newfie Joe and me, as we hang out by the van with a drink. Newfie Joe enlightens me on some more road stories from this tour and mentions that he had found something on the highway the other day. He reaches into his bag and pulls out a plastic bag, wrapped carefully in newspapers. Unravelling it, he reveals a whole ounce of marijuana. Finally, there's weed in this van. We have a good laugh, we smoke a good joint, we have a better laugh, and then we crash out in the van.

A knock on the back door wakes us up in the morning. It's Dirk and he informs us that there's free breakfast for the hotel guests, so we load up on bread and fruit before continuing on with the task at hand. It's been a long ride and a long trip, but we're almost there. Three and a half weeks seem to have gone by faster than one of the marathon Pearl Jam shows. And even though there's still another three or four hours of driving remaining, I can already feel the electricity inside the van. This is the last city, two back to back shows in St. John's, Newfie Joe's hometown. He, himself, has successfully hitchhiked across the country keeping up with the tour. Of course I can just let him off on the side of the road right now and he'll probably find a way to continue, but I don't, because he has become one of the many good friends that we've made in the process.

To add to the excitement, today is also Tak's birthday. When we pull into one of the gas stations, Newfie Joe purchases a bright orange hat and insists that he wears it in St. John's for the special day. Tak obliges and the drive just got a whole lot brighter. He explains that the orange hat is a moose hunting hat worn by hunters to stand out in the woods and not get shot. No one will ever miss you in one of these. With an hour left to go, we pass by a turn off on the highway with a sign pointing to a city curiously named Dildo. We can't pass up a photo opportunity like this. I turn around at the next exit and backtrack to get the money shot before getting back on track. By this point, the rain from last night has cleared up and the sun is poking through. Today is going to be a good day.

As we enter St. John's, I start to get a similar small town feeling as I did in Thunder Bay. Off the highway, the venue is already within sight and driving by we get many waves and cheers from fans standing by. Newfie Joe leaves us at this point to make his phone calls in preparation for the hopeful party. We pick up our tickets at the box office and, as I open up my envelope, I see seats in the fifth row right beside Stefan's.

Tak and Stefan wishing we were going to Dildo, Newfoundland.

"Hey, you guys are in the van right?" a fan asks us. "I'm Mitch and I've a got spare front row ticket tonight if you know anyone that deserves it."

"Maybe Newfie Joe. This is his hometown show," I reply. "He just left us but we'll find him at the bar later."

"Okay, I'll look for him then."

We check into our hotel, the Quality Inn, and then drop everyone off in the city centre except for the original three of us. Tak is super excited about the prospects of the day, and has his head out the window like a dog, barking at all the locals walking by. His hat falls off and I need to pull over so he can go fetch it. As he retrieves his hat, Stefan spots the band's keyboardist Boom, standing in front of a hemp shop directly beside where the hat is. We yell out "Boom" and he acknowledges us in response. Tak picks up his hat and runs back to the van, totally unaware of who was standing there.

"What are you guys so happy about?" Tak asks coming back into the van. To show him, I drive back around the block again but this time he's gone, however, driving back up the hill, Tak's hat falls out of the window again. Did Newfie Joe buy him a bad luck hat or something? I pull over and Tak fetches his lost item. When he returns, walking up the hill behind him is the band's base player Jeff Ament. He looks over at the van with a smile and walks toward us.

"So the Dodge Ram made it!" Jeff greets us.

We shake hands and he thanks us for the support and asks if we want him to autograph the van, an idea that has never even crossed my mind. Agreeing to his suggestion, we hand over a black sharpie for him to write "St. John's or Bust!" with his signature. Maybe the orange hat is a good luck charm after all. This is the first band member I've met and, like everyone has mentioned, it was as casual as meeting up with an old friend. Jeff is polite and spends a good 10 minutes talking with us. How cool is that?

We let him go on his way and head out toward Cape Spear, the eastern most point in Canada. The views and scenery of waves crashing against the rocks are just an amazing sight. Looking far out into the open waters and, knowing that the next piece of land is Europe, blows my mind and confirms the fact that we've made it all the way across the country. I've always wanted to visit Europe, I guess this is the closest I'll get to it, geographically. We make the most of every second – taking lots of photos, running up and down the hill, and just enjoying the moment realizing that our tour is near the end. The afternoon is a nice way to unwind and loosen up from the long journey from Halifax so that we can be ready for the show. Back in town, we drive by the venue again and there are some fans waiting around, including Barbara.

"How was the drive?" she asks.

"Long. How was the flight?"

"Short."

A fan then comes up to us and says she has a pair of second row tickets if we want it. Barbara gives me a look, and I look at the others.

"Go for it," Stefan urges.

"Okay, let's do it," I tell the fan, and she hands us over the tickets.

We pile back into the van and drive down a few blocks to park on Water Street. Up one block is George Street, this is where Newfie Joe told us to go. No more than five minutes on George Street, we bump into him. He had made some calls but it's too late to get a pre-party organized for today, but everything is all set for tomorrow. Amazing. He actually pulled it off, organizing a fundraiser within a matter of hours. To celebrate Tak's birthday, he takes us into the first building we see, a bar, and inside we bump into Mike from Charlotte. Mitch is also there, so we introduce Newfie Joe to him and, an hour later, he gives him his front row ticket. Overjoyed with everything, Newfie Joe buys a round of White Russians. Tak, feeling a little tipsy at this point, is itching to make a sign for the show to request a song for his birthday. After much thought, the indecisive birthday boy finally chooses the song *Light Years* as his request and Mike marks it down on a florescent poster paper. We buy Tak another few drinks and, with the camera rolling, we're about to sing happy birthday to him. But Tak wants to make it big.

Stefan, me, Barbara, and Tak enjoying George Street in St. John's, Newfoundland.

"Let's get a huge crowd going," he insists, "and some girls too!" Tak and I wander on to the next bar and with the camera in hand we start greeting people. Near the back of the bar, a blonde girl compliments Tak's orange hat. We tell her that it's Tak's birthday and ask if she and her friends would like to sing happy birthday to him. Without hesitation, they follow us out into the streets where the others are already at, so we decide to sing on the streets.

I grab a chair and place it in the middle of George Street for Tak to sit on like a king on his throne, set up the camera pointing toward us, and on three, the group begins singing *Happy Birthday* in unison. Tak is loving the attention. Enjoying our company, the blonde girl, Lisa, suggests that we meet them after the show and they can show us around George St. I think the after party is going to be pretty wild. This is, apparently, the biggest band to ever come to St. John's and the entire town is going to be at the show and then spill onto George Street afterwards. There's definitely a buzz in the air already.

Tonight's show was originally billed as "An Evening with Pearl Jam," similar to the first show of this adventure at The Gorge. With this label, no opening bands were expected to be on stage, but then rumours started circulating reporting the contrary and that a supporting act has been added last minute. Amongst all of the confusion, we decide to enter Mile One Stadium early at 7:00pm in case something special happens.

The arena is moderate in size, 7000 seat capacity, and normally used for a minor hockey team in the AHL. Barbara and I walk up to our seats in the second row directly behind Mitch, but Newfie Joe isn't with him. He's still at the bar. We look back to get a perspective of the arena, and it looks a lot smaller than 7000 seats. As we start to get cozy, the band walks onto the stage, but it's not Pearl Jam. So the rumours are correct and there's a surprise opening act.

"Good evening. We are Wintersleep," the tall bearded singer announces. I take a closer look at him and the rest of the band members and they look oddly familiar, but I can't quite point it out. I look at Barbara and ask if she knows these guys but she doesn't. A few songs later, they announce that they were a last minute addition to the show and that they're from Halifax. I look back at Stefan and he's mouthing something to me that I can't make out. Then he motions his hands as if he's driving. I examine the band members again and then it dawns on me. These are the guys in the other van on the ferry, who said we might see them in St. John's. What a coincidence. I tell Barbara this and she laughs.

Wintersleep puts on a great performance and I'm standing there watching them in disbelief that, at this time yesterday, we were chatting with these guys at a gas station and now they're in front of me up on stage, the same stage that Pearl Jam will take to in a moment. I'm thinking how much of a thrill it is for me to watch them on stage, and then I'm thinking how much of a thrill it is for them to be on this stage opening up for Pearl Jam, and it doesn't even compare. Good for Wintersleep. Their hard rocking indie style set lasts about 45 minutes and they're well received. But then it's time for the main event, the reason why the entire town has turned out tonight.

When Pearl Jam arrives on stage, they open with *Can't Keep*. A few songs later, Newfie Joe stumbles into the front row directly in front of me. He glances back and a big smile overcomes his face. Seeing him up front for his hometown show puts a warm feeling into me, as no one is as deserving of that seat than he is. Every other song, he turns around shaking his head at me in disbelief of what's happening, before focusing back on the stage. Near the end of the first set there's another performance of Stone's *Don't Give Me No Lip*, this time Stone peeks down at his lyric sheet only twice. He's getting better at this song.

"Jase man, I can't believe these seats. I don't deserve this," Newfie tells me during the encore break. "I'm used to sitting up in the stands. This is unbelievable!"

For the beginning of the encore, the band fittingly launches into *Thumbing My Way*, and Newfie Joe just stands motionless with his eyes closed and takes it all in. It's as if the song is sung for him. When the band goes into *Alive* near the end of the show, it seems the feelings have built up so much for him that he can't even look at the stage anymore. With his eyes closed and his body fully turned away from his inspiration for this trip, he belts out the words "I'm still alive" along with Vedder and the rest of crowd. It's something to see. When the show concludes, he backs off and takes a seat in his chair, speechless. I try to pat him on the back, but he insists on having a moment on his own. Five minutes of self meditation, and then he stands up and walks back up to the rail, where the security guard hands him a piece of paper. He opens it up, and it's the lyrics sheet for *Don't Give Me No Lip*.

"Let's do George Street proper," he tells me after depositing this rare souvenir into his pocket. We gather up the boys and Newfie Joe brings us to an upstairs bar, just off of George Street, where we are to be screeched in. The screech in is a Newfoundland tradition where they sing a song, kiss a frozen cod fish, and drink a shot of Screech rum – the official rum of Newfoundland – and after this, you are formally welcomed into Newfoundland. It seems a bit odd to me, but we go along with it anyway. The place is completely packed but Newfie Joe knows the owner of the place and gets us on the list for the ceremony. Apparently this is also the place that screeched in some members of Pearl Jam the night before. After a round of drinks, a man dressed in a fisherman outfit enters the bar and calls us out one by one. It's me, Stefan, Tak, Barbara, and a few other Americans here for the show.

"Hey you're Jason with the van right?" one of them asks me. "I'm Jason from Philly. You emailed me about our RV trip." Before the tour began and we were finding ways to travel for this tour, I came across this RV that Jason and a few others were planning to drive for the tour. It went to all the shows as well but, for some funny reason, we never saw it nor did we bump into anyone from the

RV until now. We are about to swap road stories when the fisherman begins the ceremony with the introductions. He starts off by reading from a scroll about the screech in and then sings what sounds like drinking songs, in the most Newfie accent possible, an accent similar to Irish but completely different at the same time. Following his lead, we sing along while he dances. Finally, he pulls a frozen cod fish out of a plastic garbage bag and we're meant to kiss it. It's an odd ceremony indeed. After kissing the fish, we're given shots of Newfoundland screech rum, which is basically bottom of the barrel Jamaican rum that didn't make it to Jamaica and was bottled for Newfoundland. When the shot is finished, the fisherman officially pronounces us Newfoundlanders. There's even a certificate that we can buy, stating that we've been officially screeched in.

Now that we are official Newfoundlanders, we meet up with Lisa and her friends and they take us on a pub crawl like no other. Walking onto George Street there's a feeling of celebration, it's very festive, as if we are at Mardi Gras. The pedestrian-only street is packed full of music, food vendors, and people, who have probably just come out from the concert. Just about every direction you look, you see a bar. The street is merely three or four blocks in length, but there must be over 50 bars on it. Some places have bars on top of bars on top of bars. It's quite the scene indeed. With so many options to choose from, the local girls guide us to where all the hot spots are. I begin filming but after a few shots, decided that I shouldn't be handling the camera anymore and ask Ben if he wants to help out, since he's the sober one. He happily accepts the role of cameraman, so I hand over the camera for his filming pleasure.

For the next two hours, we hop in and out of nearly 10 bars for cheap White Russian cocktails, and we haven't even scratched the surface of the street yet. Since it is Tak's birthday, he ends up drinking two for every one we drink. Needless to say, he's enjoying the night. And with all the distractions happening on the street, we eventually lose our cameraman at one point, but Ben is able to find us again – I'm sure we're not hard to miss in a small area. With so much going on, we're able to meet many people and spread the word about the pre-party for tomorrow's show, seeing that most of them will be going again. The local girls show us an exceptional time.

Back on the streets, Newfie Joe tracks us down and he has brought familiar faces along with him, the Nathans from Philly. We celebrate the reunion with a round of White Russians. We're definitely rocking St. John's tonight. This trip has been so unbelievable and, after tomorrow, it will be over. It's a little bit sad because we know this is coming, but at the same time we're giving it our all tonight. It's the celebration for a great tour, a great trip, with some great people.

"So what are you going to do with the van?" one of the Nathans ask.

"Well, I've been talking to this girl Amanda, who is from here and has expressed interest in driving it back across to Vancouver at some point," I answer.

"She'll take care of it for me either way and, if she doesn't drive it back, maybe we'll auction it off and donate it to a charity."

"Have you called that girl yet?" Stefan asks.

"No, I have to do that. But let's worry about that tomorrow, it'll be fine. Tonight we rock St. John's!"

With another round of liquor in us we decide it's a good idea to video tape a message and send it to Cali Joe, who was trying desperately to make it out here to join us but couldn't in the end. Gathering around in a group with the street party happening in the background, we wait for Ben to switch on the record button.

"We're sending a message to Mr. California Joe," Stefan starts out.

"You have missed out on the biggest party in Canada," I follow.

"Cali Joe, look what you're missing," Tak adds, as he pulls in Lisa.

"Thanks for the van space Joe," Ben says turning to the camera.

"I don't know California Joe, but he sucks," Nathan comments.

"Yeah, whoever he is, he missed a fucking lot," The other Nathan says.

"Goodnight Joe!" Ben finishes, turning off the camera for the night.

It's after 2:00am and hunger is hitting me hard after eating nothing since the free breakfast at the hotel in Gander. Newfie Joe is hungry as well, so the two of us get our usual late night snack. Down the street we find a subway that looks relatively busy. We walk in. Standing at the back of the long lineup, we begin reflecting on the tour.

"Jase man, this has been crazy," Newfie Joe says. "I can't thank you enough for everything, if I didn't meet you guys I might not have made it to some of the shows. That Thunder Bay one was cutting it tight. And riding the van back home was perfect."

"No worries man. It's been a pleasure," I reply. "I just can't believe it's almost over."

"What are you going to do with the van man? I don't have much money, but I can try to buy it off you and drive it back across the country. Or I can take care of it for you as well."

"I'm supposed to call this girl, Amanda. She said she would look after it for me."

"Hey are you Jason?" a girl in front of Newfie Joe turns around to ask me.

"Yes."

"I'm Amanda."

"Holy shit! Amanda, how are you? How did you enjoy the show?"

"Good and good."

"Talk about coincidences."

We chat for while and almost forget to order a sandwich when it comes to our turn. Basically she tells me that there's nothing to worry about, she'll take care of the van, and hopefully be able to drive it back across the country when they do the trip. If not, she'll look around for people that would be interested in driving it across country. "There are always people here that want to do that drive, so it shouldn't be a problem."

I tell her about the pre-show party that we're putting on tomorrow, and then she tells me about the post-show party that she'll be going to where we can meet to drop off the van. Everything appears to have worked out. I knew that there was nothing to worry about. With that all sorted, Newfie Joe follows me back to Water Street, where the van is still parked, and we head back to the hotel for our last sleep of the tour. I pull the van into the parking lot and head up to the room, where everyone is passed out. There's some bed space left for Newfie Joe, but I retreat back outside to sleep in the van one last time.

The next morning I wake up feeling numb. Not just from the massive amount of alcohol and little amount of food consumed yesterday, but from the feeling that today is the end. This is the last time I'll wake up in the van. It has arrived. This day was going to come sooner or later, but I try to convince myself not to feel sad and just enjoy the day – our last of the tour. I head up to the room, where half of the boys are awake and the other half are out cold. It takes some time to get everyone on their feet but, once up, we slowly clean out the van and pack up all of our gear so that we don't have to worry about it later. After we partied our asses off last night, there's a sombre feeling amongst everyone this morning and we clearly don't want to go home.

Ben is staying one more night in St. John's before he flies overseas and he wants to have a good night's sleep. We drive by the venue and he suggests that we pull into the Delta Hotel, directly across from the venue and where the band is staying. There's no parking on the street, so I pull the van directly up to the entrance.

"I thought you have no money Ben. How are you going to afford this?" I ask.

"I'll just put it on my credit card and worry about it later."

Stepping out of the van, there's a group of girls staring at us with giant smiles on their faces. I look over their shoulders and see a sign about a beauty school convention happening at the hotel. One of them walks over and says hi. I ask if they were part of the beauty school convention and she confirms. She then asks for my autograph.

"Autograph? What do you want me to sign?"

"How about this?" she says holding out the program for the convention.

I look over at the others with confusion, I look back at her, and then at the van. She must think that we are Pearl Jam. I smile back and, just then I spot Jeff Ament walking behind her toward the hotel. He notices, gives us a hang loose and we acknowledge him back. She begins waving the black sharpie at me, so before we further deceive her, I break the news to her.

"No, no, no, we're not the band. He's the band right there," I tell her pointing at Ament.

She looks over at Ament, looks back at us, then at the van.

"Really? Umm, can you sign it anyway?" she asks hesitantly.

"Ok if you want."

With a black sharpie pen, I put my autograph on a clear spot near the middle of the program. She passes it around to the others and we all give her our signature, and then she asks if we could take a photo with her. We agree. She asks one of the other girls to handle the camera. She thanks us and we thank her. I think we just made her day. Inside the hotel, while Ben is checking in, Newfie Joe goes to the restaurant for some breakfast and the rest of us hang out in the lobby by the elevators. When the first elevator door opens, Mike McCready walks out of it and sees us.

"Hey guys, how's it going?" he greets us knowing that we're fans.

We tell him about our van and our trip, and his face just lights up.

"That's hardcore man. I couldn't handle touring in a van anymore. I guess I'm getting old," he laughs.

We ask one of the hotel staff to take a photo of us with McCready and then we let him go on about his business. What a great moment. But before we can talk about it with each other, Newfie Joe comes running up toward us.

"Guys, I just ran into Stone," he announces.

Apparently he was looking for a seat at the restaurant, and somebody pointed him in the direction where Stone Gossard was sitting. He was going to leave him alone but, as he was walking toward him, a piece of paper fell out of his pocket. He looked down and it's the lyric sheet for *Don't Give Me No Lip* from last night. So he knew that he had to go over and show it to him.

"Excuse me, Stone. I don't mean to bother you but I thought this was pretty funny," Newfie Joe said handing over the folded piece of paper.

Stone opened it up and closed it immediately.

"Where did you get this?" he asked with an embarrassing smile.

"Man, you don't even know the words to your one song?" Newfie Joe laughed.

Stone signed the lyric sheet for him, while the friends sitting around him joined in on the humour. As he concludes his story, Ben comes over and informs us that he's all checked in. We fill him in on our recent events and he just laughs, "Man, I miss out on all the good stuff."

We pile all of our luggage into Ben's room to store for the day and then leave him alone to rest. Newfie Joe needs to setup the pre-party, leaving the three of us alone again. We head out for a last drive in the van to run a few errands. After grabbing a late breakfast, we head to Wal-Mart and decide to develop some of our photos from the tour, which we plan to give to the band at the show somehow. We haven't figured out how yet, but maybe we'll just put it in a bag and throw it on stage. With a stack of tour memories in hand, we return back into town and find a parking spot on Water Street again. It's a tight spot and, when I begin to back in, my angle is way off. I pull out and start all over again. As I back in the second time, a girl runs out of the restaurant we're parking in front of and starts directing me into the spot like an airplane director.

"Don't people from BC know how to park?" she jokes as we come out. "I'm Ginny and this is my sister Rachel. Welcome to Newfoundland."

We get a good conversation going and the topic about driving the van back to Vancouver comes up and Ginny quickly points at Rachel, who says that she's always up for a trip and could possibly do it in the future. She gives me her contact information and we allow the girls to get back to work. Walking toward the pre-party we bump into Matt and Malland, who bought us sandwiches at the Pita Pit in Halifax. They follow us to Normies for the fundraiser that Newfie Joe has miraculously put together, where Barbara, Dirk, and Ben are already sitting in amongst a small group of fans. The turnout is good but the vibe is even better.

Up for raffle today is a couple of posters signed by the band, a "Free Newfoundland" shirt signed by the band, and also some local wine from Rodrigues Winery, a friend of Newfie Joe's. We all buy a bunch of raffle tickets and hang out for a chilled out afternoon. I brought the developed photos in with me and begin writing descriptions of the people and places on the back of them, and then I write a letter to go along with the package:

> To the band,
>
> We wanted to share with you some of the experiences and memories we had on this amazing trip across our home country. This started out with three guys from Vancouver dreaming of one day following our favourite band on tour. Thanks for choosing our great country and we hope you've enjoyed your time here. None of us knew each other before this tour and now we're good friends and have met many others along the way. We organized a carpool picking up fans doing multiple shows along the way including a few hitchhikers, one of whom hitchhiked to every show all the way back to his home in Newfoundland. Enclosed are a few photos of our trip. Thanks for a September to remember and see you on the next tour. DVD to come.
>
> PJ Tour Van 2005
> Jason, Stefan, Tak
> From Vancouver

I finish writing just in time for the raffle draw where a girl from Michigan wins all three posters. For the next prize I watch each one of the digits on my ticket be called, so I claim my prize of three bottles of Rodrigues wine, perfect.

I give one to Stefan and one to Tak and we immediately crack them open for a taste. The same girl wins the signed Newfoundland shirt as well, so she decides to donate one of the posters back to the raffle. All in all it's a fun party. Sipping on a glass of my new wine, I wrap the letter around the photos and head out the door to put them safely back in the van. Just outside, Newfie Joe is having a smoke and he introduces me to Lino Rodrigues from Rodrigues Wines. I turn on the camera to ask him a few questions while Newfie Joe commentates.

"Our good friend here is the wine master for Rodrigues Wine. We gave him a call and he donated a case of Newfoundland wine."

"It would be great if Eddie Vedder started drinking a bottle on stage," Rodrigues states.

My attention then turns to a couple walking toward us. They wave.

"Here is our man that we're holding the benefit for, Mr. Mike McCready, rocking and rolling in St. John's Newfoundland," Newfie Joe introduces.

"How's it going?" I greet Mike.

"Right on," he answers.

"This is our CCFC fundraiser," Newfie Joe tells him, and he thanks us for the great effort. Remembering me from earlier in the day, he asks if the van is around and I merely point across the street.

"Do you want to see it?" I ask. "Do you want to autograph it?"

"Sure," he agrees.

Newfie Joe runs in to grab Stefan and Tak, while I take McCready and his wife Ashley across the street to the van.

"Wow! That's wicked. And you've got all the cities there too," he observes.

"Yeah, it's hockey tape. We've checked them off as we go," I laugh.

I open the van to get the same black sharpie which I used to autograph the beauty school girl's program, while Stefan and Tak arrive. I hand McCready the pen as he admires what has been our home for the past month.

"So you guys went to all the shows?" Ashley asks. "How do you guys do it? What do you guys do for a living?"

"We just took a month holiday from work. It wasn't too hard to pull off," Stefan answers.

"What was it? 14,000km?" Newfie Joe asks.

"Wow!" McCready remarks, "Are you guys driving back?"

"Nope flying."

"What's going to happen to the van?" Ashley asks.

"Not sure, we were thinking about having it driven back by someone, or maybe even auctioning it off for a charity," I answer. "Are there any touring plans coming up next year?"

"Yes, as a matter of fact. We'll start in Toronto, I think, and then work our way down the East Coast of the US," McCready replies.

"Oh okay. Maybe we'll drive it back during that tour," I smile.

We chat for another 20 minutes, a very casual conversation. It feels surreal but very normal at the same time.

"Shall I do this?" McCready asks pointing the pen toward the van.

With the video camera rolling and photography cameras flashing, McCready signs, "The Coolest Van in the World. Thanks! Mike McCready" and then draws a picture of himself beside it. As I shake hands with him, I realize that I'm still holding the stack of photos in my hand with the letter, so I give it directly to McCready and we thank him for everything. He tells us that he's going to be late for the soundcheck, but he stays and continues our conversation. Ashley thanks us for the photos and the support and asks us to write down our contact information for her and then she gives us hers. While this is all happening, a few people come by and walk up to me.

"Do you mind if we take photos of the van?" they ask.

"Of course not," I reply, as McCready, who was completely ignored, smiles.

We give them a final thank you before allowing them to get back to soundcheck. The moment lasts about 30 minutes, but it definitely went by much faster in our minds. There was really no desire for us to meet the band during this tour, as we were merely interested in just going to the shows and meeting fans, but the events of today have been pretty cool, making it a perfect last day of the tour. Meeting Mike and Jeff has further embedded into our minds just how great this band is. We head back into the bar feeling pretty good about ourselves.

Pearl Jam guitarist, Mike McCready, signing the van in St. John's.

"Where were you guys?" Ben asks.

"Outside with Mike McCready. Why didn't you come out?"

"What? Again? I don't have any luck."

With the clock closing in on show time, we wrap up the party, which raises about $600, and head to the venue. Newfie Joe needs to return some of the items to Nicole, the band's PR person, while we pick up our tickets at the box office. Today we have tickets bought from the Ticketmaster public sale, because there was no Ten Club tickets available for this show, so accordingly, we have our worst seats of the tour. We do, however, have three seats together near the top of the stand and it will be fun.

Mike McCready's signature on the van.

Our location is far back but, being in a small building, it's not that far. Someone calls our names from behind, and it's the two Nathans from Philly. There's a whole row of empty seats beside them, so we decide to move back and sit with them for Wintersleep, who we're excited for again. They don't disappoint. As their set closes, Newfie Joe somehow finds us and sits in one the seats beside us.

"Hey guys, I just talked to Nicole and she loves those photos you guys gave them," he tells us. "She said Ed especially likes the one of the surfboards and the van. She asked if they could use it for something in the future, so I gave her your contact."

"Oh really? Thanks."

"What did you write on the back of that one?" Stefan asks me.

"Just the location, Martinique Beach in Halifax, and that we tried to surf but the waves weren't very big," I explain.

We stick around in our new seats to chat it up with our fellow road trippers and, before we know it, the lights go dark and the show begins. It hits us unexpectedly, and so does the rest of the show. The feeling is sort of anti-climatic, knowing that this is the last show of the tour, and we'll be flying home afterwards. It does feel like a bit of a downer, but being able to sit together with a bunch of friends certainly helps keep the energy level flowing – and we rock out as hard as we can. Near the end of the first set, they play *In My Tree*, which has kind of become the theme song for this tour. "Wave to all my friends," Vedder sings. The encore is shorter than usual, and then they open the second encore with Tak's request from last night's show, ~~Light Years.~~

The second encore is again shorter than normal but, joined on stage by all the members of Wintersleep, they end it with a great performance of *Rockin' in the Free World*. When the final notes are played, we can't and won't stop cheering. Overall, the tour finale isn't the marathon show that we expected but, after having travelled across this enormous country, we certainly understand how much of a toll it has taken out of them. It certainly has taken something out of us. Vedder thanks the crowd, thanks Canada and then makes what we believe is a reference to us.

"Good luck to all you surfers out there, I hear the waves are coming, be safe, thank you."

"He must be referring to our photo," Stefan suggests.

Outside the venue I run into Rachel and ask her to join us for a drink. She has to wait for her sister but tells me to call her later to meet up. Not too long after, everyone magically appears and is gathered around but, before we head directly to George Street, we need to take care of the van first. Meeting Amanda at her post-show party, we all head toward the van. When we arrive, there are a couple of girls, who we've seen before, hovering around the van like groupies around a band. They ask if they can take a photo with it, so we grant them their wish. We watch as one of them climbs on top to lie on the roof of the van for the photo. One of the girls starts asking me questions about the van but, needing to quickly hand it over to Amanda, our conversation is cut short. Stefan, Tak, and I don't even catch her name. We pay our final respects to the van as I give the keys to Amanda. Whatever happens, it has been a great ride and it has served us well. Not wanting the dream to end, we refuse to check off St. John's. We walk away from our home and find the others at the bar.

Me looking on as three van groupies pose for a photo.

Being a Sunday night, the intensity of the street crowd isn't the same as the night before but we've gathered a good group of people together that just wants to enjoy the night, so it will be a good one for us. The discussion among us is mainly about how great this tour has been. Tak claims it to be the best month of his life, Stefan has very fond memories of everything that has occurred, and I've fulfilled my dream of driving across the country. We come to the conclusion that it has been the fans that we've met who has really made this trip for us. It's the passengers that joined us in the van and have now become very good friends, as well as the fans that we keep running into in various cities who bought us drinks, food, and even gas.

When our thirst is fulfilled, our hunger needs some attention, so Newfie Joe brings us to a restaurant style bar where he insist we try the Newfoundland version of poutine, consisting of fries, dressing (which is Stove-Top stuffing), and gravy. Stefan and I are all over this and, with each mouth watering bite, it becomes more and more tasty, but still does not beat the delicious poutine.

With the whole group sitting around the table laughing and smiling, I start to reflect on each one of them. The two Nathans, who drove the entire tour as well, rocked the show with us tonight. Beside them are Lisa and her friends, who took us around George Street and showed us a great time on both nights. It's much appreciated. Then there's Dirk, a real character who has entertained us from beginning to end. He has been a delight to have on board. Next to him is Ben, who didn't really say much but, when he did, it was often funny. He's a great cameraman, great guitar player, a really great guy and I'm glad Cali Joe remembered him. As for Barbara, who threw away her bus ticket to join us in the van, then made a triumphant return in the Atlantic East Coast, she hasn't stopped smiling since I met her and has really rocked out hard with us. Matt and Malland, who we seem to see everywhere, bought us food in Halifax, a great gesture from them. To his side is Mitch, who was kind enough to give his extra front row ticket to Newfie Joe. Of course there's Newfie Joe, who has been an inspiration to us all. I'm not sure if I'll ever see him again, but it has been a pleasure. And at the end of the table is Sarah from Toronto, who I didn't actually meet, but she's sitting at our table.

The night is a little emotional and, as festive as everything is on this final night of celebration, I needed to get away for a few moments for myself. I walk down the street to clear my mind and into another bar where Amanda is. To my relief, she shows me that she still has the keys to our baby. I buy her a drink and we chat for some time, because I haven't actually talked to this girl and now I'm leaving her with the van. She almost has no voice remaining after the two shows, but we're still able to communicate quite effectively. She seems like a good person, so I have faith and a good feeling that this will work out somehow, just not sure how yet. I thank her in advance and return to the restaurant bar that I had left from earlier, but nobody is there anymore. It's nearly 2:00am, so

I wander back onto George Street to do my own thing.

By 3:00am I walk back toward the Delta hotel where our bags are waiting. Approaching the Mile One Centre I see Stefan, Tak, Ben and Barbara walk up the street – what great timing. We head back up to Ben's room to grab our stuff and say goodbye to our two international van passengers. And even though they're from overseas, I get the feeling that I'll be seeing Ben and Barbara again at some point. Taking a taxi, we arrive at the airport with plenty of time to spare. Another great night of partying has worn us out. This whole tour has worn us out. We were basically running on adrenaline for the final week. Waiting at our gate, we're the only ones there. Tak lies down for a nap. We sit there drained and speechless, when someone else finally enters the airport and walks toward us.

"Hey you're the van guys right?" he asks. "I'm Bobby from Providence. I was supposed to ride with you guys from Halifax, but cancelled last minute."

"Oh hey. How's it going? Enjoy St. John's?"

"Oh yeah. It was a blast."

"I agree. Maybe see you on the next tour."

"Definitely!"

We board the plane and Tak passes out like a log, but I'm having trouble sleeping. The chairs aren't comfortable, the leg room is awful, and the elbow space is tight. I feel so locked in here. I miss the van already.

Me surfing the van at Cape Spear, the most Eastern point of North America.

CANADA TOUR **BY THE NUMBERS**

25 days on the road
17 Pearl Jam shows
471 total live songs
95 unique songs
13,986km driven
18 total van passengers
Longest Drive – Thunder Bay to Kitchener 1500km
Longest Show – The Gorge
Most played song – Corduroy 17 times

EXPENSES (US Dollars)
$3,519.90 TOTAL EXPENSE
$870.04 for van purchase, maintenance, insurance (total for everyone was $2,650.13)
$375.00 for new video camera purchase
$2274.86 tour expenses ($90.99 per day)
    $298.61 for flights
    $240.58 for gas (total for everyone was $1,443.33)
    $143.16 for accommodations (total for everyone was $737.33)
    $358.00 for food
    $892.50 for concert tickets
    $342.00 for merchandise and souvenirs

VAN CHECKMARKS
The Gorge – Jason from Vancouver
Vancouver – Jason from Vancouver
Calgary – Stefan from Vancouver
Edmonton – two random girls from Calgary
Saskatoon – two random girls from Saskatoon
Winnipeg – Newfie Joe from St John's
Thunder Bay – Nancy from Winnipeg
Kitchener – Tatiana from Brazil
London – Annette from Australia
Hamilton – Christine from Hamilton
Montreal – Catherine from Montreal
Ottawa – random girl from Ottawa
Toronto – Cali Joe from Los Angeles
Quebec City – Tom from Wisconsin
Halifax – Barbara from Italy
St John's – Nobody

I'm ahead, I'm advanced
I'm the first mammal to make plans
Do The Evolution

CHAPTER 17: **REFLECTION**

September 2005 – May 2006
Vancouver, British Columbia

WHEN YOUR DREAMS have been fulfilled, what's the next step? Do you go back to the way you were and live happily or do you let your dreams sweep you away to achieve bigger and better things? How do you top it? The Pearl Jam Canadian tour allowed me to drive coast to coast through my home country, which has always been a dream of mine. In general, people tend to travel other countries before they really get to know their own. I wanted to see Canada before I go anywhere else. On top of that, we were treated to the best rock concerts of our lives and met some amazing people along the way. It truly was the trip of a lifetime.

Our flight leaves St. John's at 6:00am, bringing us back home just before noon. The journey lasts just over 10 hours for what took nearly a month to drive. Upon arriving in Vancouver, we decide to take a limousine into town because it's actually cheaper than a cab. It's not quite the van, however. At home, my family is happy to see me well and alive, but I'm too tired to talk and go straight to bed.

When I wake up a few hours later, it seems like a different day but it's still the same day. On my desk is a ticket for tonight's Nine Inch Nails concert in Vancouver. Happy to continue the month of rock 'n' roll, I pick up Stefan and some other friends in my car, and we're off to another show. Our friends are curious about how our trip was, but the only thing we can tell them is that it was great. How do you even begin to explain everything? I would need an entire book. The concert is amazing and I let loose all of my remaining energy into the highly intensive general admission crowd, but it's very different from the previous shows I saw this month. There's no talking, no encores, no breaks in between songs, just pure energy for two straight hours. It's fantastic and painful at the same time. Afterwards, everyone goes home because they have to work tomorrow, including me.

In the morning I go into the office feeling weak and sick. Everyone welcomes me back with open arms, but everything appears to be the same as it was when I left one month ago. Nothing has really changed much, and being back at work almost feels like being in prison for me. It's difficult and it gets worse day after day. I'm back in the grind, working twelve hours a day, with very little spare time for anything else. Is this what living is about?

As I start looking through photos and video footage from the tour, the memories bring a smile to my face. Stefan sets up a website, calling us the Touring Van, and I begin researching video editing techniques and work through our video footage during any spare time I have. Over the course of the next few months, through trial and a lot of error, I'm able to eventually put together a video that roughly documents our trip onto a DVD. And having kept in contact with everyone else, getting the DVD out there is not hard at all. It is well received.

Back at work, things are no different. And although the context of my work may vary from day to day, it's more or less the same stuff. I'm starting to get antsy and feel a need for another vacation. With the DVD completed, I fall back into my regular routine of work, boxing and hockey, even bringing Stefan onto my hockey team in the process. Weekends are for friends and recovery. The benefit from this cycle of events is that I am able to save a lot, adding to the large amount of money that I have put away over the years. But what good is money if it's not eventually used?

Through hockey and local concerts, Stefan and I have become very close friends. I also still keep in contact with everyone from the tour, with Cali Joe even coming up for a visit during the CFL's Grey Cup weekend. But the one question that's always asked is, "How's the van doing?" It's evident that the van has touched so many, including its owners. And with the possibility of Amanda driving it back for us becoming less likely month after month, I conclude that the only method is to take matters into our own hands and get the van back ourselves. Remembering what McCready mentioned about starting their next tour in the East Coast of the US, I propose the idea of flying back to St. John's to retrieve the van and do some shows along the way back home. Stefan and Tak are open to the idea, as none of us have been to that side of the US before. So with that goal in mind, we continue to save our money.

In early March, almost six months after the conclusion of the Canadian tour, Pearl Jam announces the first leg of their World Tour, and it involves the North East of the US, just like McCready had said. But the lack of information for other dates discourages us from making any firm plans. When the next leg of the tour is revealed a few weeks later, showing a clear path back home through the West Coast, my mind is made up and I'm going to get the van back. The main issue, of course, is getting time off of work. So in a meeting with my boss,

I express my desires to take an extended vacation to do some more travelling and confess that my focus at work has been diminishing since returning. His initial reaction is one of surprise but, after listening to my reasoning, he actually encourages me and believes that I'm making the right decision. He then proceeds to tell me about his travels in between semesters during university and gives me his blessings to take as much time off as I require. I inform him that I have no idea how long I'll need, but he says that we can sort out work when I'm ready to come back. So I send in my month's notice and officially quit my job.

Stefan and Tak, on the other hand, are only able to take a certain amount of time off, forcing them to choose between the East Coast and the West Coast. They chose the coast closer to home. So going at it by myself now, I'd need at least one person to drive the van with me from St. John's to make this all happen. Other fans seem keen on joining the van out east, but there isn't anyone interested in coming to Newfoundland with me. Then, I realize that the people most likely to drive with me from Newfoundland are Newfoundlanders, so I try calling Newfie Joe but, not surprisingly, he's not home. Amanda has no desire to do it, so I call my one remaining contact in St. John's, Rachel. After a few minutes of catching up, I jump right in and ask her if she wants to come to Boston with me in the Touring Van. Without hesitation, she says yes, putting the wheels in motion. Pearl Jam releases their much anticipated new self titled record on May 2, 2006. A few weeks later, the Touring Van will be invading America, and I now have all the time in the world.

PART TWO
THE US TOUR

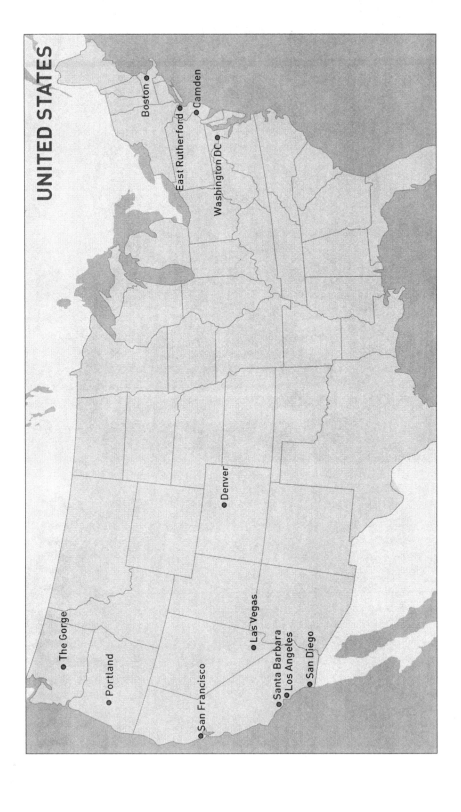

I am lost, I'm no guide
but I'm by your side
I am right by your side

Leash

CHAPTER 18: **INVADING AMERICA**

May 24 – 25, 2006 » Show 18 & 19
Boston, Massachusetts

THIS IS THE START OF THE JOURNEY, another journey, but this time I venture out by myself. I wake up early to start packing for more than two months on the road. It takes me about an hour to get everything together, stuffing only the bare minimum I need into one giant hockey bag. There isn't much going through my mind right now, other than the feeling of delight that I'm not at work today. At check-in, my hockey bag is over the weight limit, so I remove some clothing and deposit it into a giant clear plastic bag. Air Canada allows me to check in two pieces of luggage, so I'm okay. I wait patiently at the gate and find it a bit different than the last time. I'm excited, but it's not the same type of excitement. Maybe it's because I'm in an airport and have no control of my initial voyage.

The stopover in Toronto is a complete gong show, as my connecting flight is delayed. It's late at night and there's no update as to when the flight will go ahead because, apparently, there was a storm earlier in Toronto and all flights have been pushed back. I sit on the ground in the corner of a jam-packed Pearson Airport, with nothing to do except to watch people. Not too far from me, there's a man in a business suit talking feverishly on his mobile phone, probably bringing his work to the airport with him. Beside him are parents hectically trying to calm their restless children, but they're the ones that need to be settled. Further down the row are a couple of seniors sitting around and looking confused, trying to decipher the announcements being made. And in front of me is a young couple, the girl lying down for a nap while the guy reads a book. I sit watching all of these people and wonder where they're going and what they'll be doing there. Surely, none are going to Newfoundland. Over three hours after the scheduled time, I'm finally able to board my flight at 1:00am. The flight is half empty and I have an entire row to myself, so I lie down to rest for what will be an early start tomorrow morning.

CAUGHT THESE SHOWS WITH MY FRIEND WHO WENT TO HALIFAX WITH ME. HAD 2ND ROW OFF THE FLOOR ON MIKE'S SIDE

GREAT SHOWS AND THEY LOVE PLAYING BOSTON ! HZTM

My sleep is peaceful but, as we approach Newfoundland, we hit massive turbulence and I awake abruptly. The plane begins to dip and dive, unexpectedly, like a rollercoaster. I hold my breath, scared for my life, while screams and cries begin to circulate through the cabin. My trip that hasn't even commenced yet, could end right here. After a few anxious moments, the plane finally pulls through and calmly positions itself for landing again. And what was only a few minutes of extreme flying felt more like an eternity. People are silent and appear nervous as the plane descends toward the runway. When the wheels hit the pavement for a rough landing, a big sigh of relief is felt throughout the plane from both passengers and crew members, followed by cheers and clapping of celebration. It's an adventure to start my adventure.

The flight arrives in St. John's at 5:00am. Looking at the arrivals screen reveals that the flight into St. John's before our flight was redirected to Halifax and didn't actually land here. I guess we're lucky to have endured the heavy winds and turbulence to get us to our destination. I'm glad, because another delay would make it much more difficult for me to carry out everything I need to do in preparation for the trip. At 7:30am, I hop into a taxi and direct him to C and C Cycles in Mount Pearl, the garage where the van is being stored.

"First time in Newfoundland?" the driver asks.

"No. I've been here before. It's beautiful."

He drops me off at the address I give him, and it's a motorcycle shop. Is this the right one? I open the door and approach the shop. Peeking inside I see a bunch of motorcycles and motorcycle parts. But looking through the fence into the yard next to the shop, I see the van sitting all by its lonesome. I grab my stuff, pay the taxi fare of $40, and return to the front door. It's locked and not yet open. I walk back to the fence and look out at my blue machine. Oh, how I've missed it!

"Can I help you?" a voice behind me asks.

"Yes, I'm here to pick up my van."

"Oh right, I'll just be a few minutes opening up."

"No problem, I've got all the time in the world."

I leave my bags in the store and walk through the fence, as he opens the door, to close in on the beast. Circling it, I notice that two of the tires are completely flat, there are frost marks on the sides (probably from the Newfoundland winter) and the most of the hockey tape is either peeling off or fading away. The two signatures from McCready and Ament are very faint now, almost nonexistent. It's definitely not looking as sharp as I remember it. Back in the store, I settle my bill for the seven months of storage, and then the guy fills up my tires. I put the keys into the ignition and give it a go but nothing happens. I try again and still nothing. The battery must be drained. With his pickup truck, the guy gives me a jump start, and the van is alive again. I throw my bags into the back, still pristine and clean, thank the shop for taking care of it, and head out on my way. A few blocks away from the shop, I pull into a gas station to fill up the almost certainly dry tank. It costs nearly $100. I hop back in and start the van again. Nothing happens. I wasn't thinking and probably should have kept the van running to charge it fully because the battery is dead again. Looking down the road on the left I see a sign for Mount Pearl Auto King, so I put the van in neutral and push it from the inside of the driver's door with my left hand, while steering with my right. In the middle of the empty streets, I walk the van toward the mechanic shop.

"Hi, are you guys busy?" I ask.

"Yeah we're swamped. What do you need?" the mechanic answers.

"I think my battery is gone. Can I get a charge?"

"Sure, that can be done."

While the battery is charging, I also charge my mobile phone, and grab some food at the gas station down the road. Two hours and $60 for an hour's labour later, the van is back on the road. Mount Pearl is about half an hour outside of St. John's, so I'm forced to take the highway toward the city. It brings back memories of the open road with the freedom to roam. I miss this life. I put on one of the many CDs I brought with me and turn the music up loud. One of the speakers cuts in and out, but I sing at the top of my lungs to compensate for it. I'm going back to St. John's, the site of Touring Van's last stand. I'm excited to see this lovely city again.

Pulling into the city centre, I park across from the Mile One Centre and take some moments to reminisce. The building is just as I remember it, and I can picture us standing outside after the final show about to head down the block for a night of celebration. I try to call Rachel, but my phone isn't working and I don't know why, so I enter a pool hall and use their pay phone. She tells me that she's at work and gives me the address, so I write it down and tell her that I'll be over tomorrow to meet up. I then call Amanda, who had arranged an appointment with a mechanic to do a full check-up for me. She gives me her home address and invites me over for the afternoon. Tired from the exhausting flight, I pull into a park, unpack my sleeping bag and pull out my pillow to take a nap. Within minutes I'm passed out asleep once again in the van and loving it.

When I wake up it's nearly 5:00pm, so I head on over to Amanda's. Once there, I'm greeted with a friendly hug and a cheerful smile. She tells me that there hasn't been much happening since last September. The shows that I saw were apparently some of the biggest events for the city, and I felt privileged to have been a part of it. She declares that it was a pleasure to take care of the van and said she even used it to move some furniture into her new place. I thank her for all her help and then she hands over a piece of paper with the address of the mechanic on it. An appointment has been set for tomorrow morning. I thank her again and she wishes me luck.

Fully awake now, I drive back to the city and park on the familiar Water Street, in front of the Blue on Water restaurant, where I met Rachel and where McCready signed the van. Walking back along George Street, it feels like a ghost town. There isn't a single person around and some of the bars are closed, but I can still picture Tak sitting on the chair in the middle of the street as we sing "Happy Birthday" to him. At the end of the road, I hear some music coming from a Mexican bar called Zapatas, so I investigate. The place is empty but I sit down for a drink anyway. Where is everyone? Is this place always this dead when Pearl Jam isn't around? I figure I might as well try calling Newfie Joe, even though the chances are he won't be around, but my phone is still not working.

"What's the matter?" the bartender asks, noticing my frustration.

"There's no service on my phone and I don't know why. I just upgraded to a North American plan a few days ago. This is garbage!" I explain.

"If you want, you can use our phone."

"Thanks!"

I pull out the piece of napkin with Newfie Joe's number written on it from eight months ago and dial. It rings four or five times before someone picks up.

"Hello?" an unfamiliar voice answers.

"Hi, I'm looking for Joe. Would he be around by any chance?"

"Joe Senior or Joe Junior?"

"Umm, Junior."

"No, he's not here."

"Can you tell him that Jason from Vancouver is in town for the weekend?"

"Will do."

It's just as I thought. He might even be out of the country or hitchhiking overseas right now and he hasn't answered any of my emails, but at least I gave it a try. I finish my beer, thank the bartender, and wander back to Water Street, where I notice a restaurant advertising "Fresh Fish Today!" I walk in and order the most Newfie dish you can get – pan-fried cod fish with chips, gravy, and dressing. It's delicious and I wonder why I didn't try this the last time I was here. I guess we were too busy to actually eat. I finish up, and start heading back toward the van. It's around 9:00pm and there isn't much more to do tonight, so I decide to call it a night. Crossing the street within a block from the van, I change my mind and decide to check out the harbour. I'm only in St. John's for a few days so I might as well see everything I missed last time, and after a heavy meal, the walk will probably do me good. The streets are abandoned except for someone walking on the opposite side in the distance. As I close in on the guy, he calls out to me. "Hey!"

I ignore him but he calls out again – even louder this time – so I look over. Who the hell *is* this? Do I know him? I try to get a better look as he calls out again, this time crossing the street. I answer, though still clueless of his identity.

When he's close enough to extend his hand toward me, I realize who it is – It's Newfie Joe, only he's sporting a shorter haircut and a full beard. I pull him in for a hug in excitement.

"How's it going brother?" he asks with a joyful laugh.

"Good. Did you know I was here?"

"Not really. I got a message from my folks about an hour ago saying that you were in town, so I thought I'd just come down here and look for you."

"Crazy!" I laugh. "Want to go for a drink?"

"Of course, you're in Newfoundland now, man."

We walk up to George Street and Newfie Joe explains that because it's the first long weekend holiday of the summer so everyone deserts the place to go camping. He also says that the September weekend we were in St. John's was insane and not normal. We walk to a familiar bar but there's no one inside – not even the bartender – so we go next door to an almost equally empty bar. Joe buys me a drink and we chat.

"So, what's up? What are you doing here?" he asks curiously, even though he knows the answer.

"What do you think? I'm picking up the van and doing the tour," I answer.

"Where are the rest of the boys?"

"They're working but will join me out west, so I'm doing this leg alone."

He takes a sip from his pint. "What shows are you hitting up?"

"I'm starting out in Boston, then I go to Philly, DC, Jersey, New York, and then I have a few weeks off before the West Coast."

"You're driving down to Boston from here by yourself?"

"Nope. This girl I met last time, Rachel, she's going to be driving down with me. So there's lots of room remaining."

He thinks for a second. "Did I meet her?"

"I'm not sure but she was around when Mike was signing the van."

"Hmmm, probably not then. Let's get another drink at another bar," he suggests. "What's the deal with your shirt?"

"Oh, it's a shirt that Brad made. It has Mike's guitar pick on it. What do you think?" I ask, while turning around for him to see the back as well.

"Looks rad man!" he approves, as we walk into the next bar. "So when's the Boston show?"

"It's on Wednesday the 24th, but we are leaving St. John's on Sunday," I reply. "That's three days from now."

We sit and he downs his beer in one go. "Okay, I'm in!" he announces.

"Really?"

"I think so. Just for the East Coast though. I need to sort out a few things, but in a day or two I should be good to go."

"Excellent!"

We grab another drink to celebrate our unexpected encounter and then walk back to the van, where Newfie Joe's face is all smiles. I drop him off at the house where he's staying at and he tells me that he'll call when it's all sorted and confirmed, so I give him Rachel's number, since my phone is still not working. Driving back down the road, I pull into a parking lot, jump into the back where the sleeping bag is already setup, and call it a night.

The next morning, I get up early and decide to check out a tourist site that we missed last time, Signal Hill. The old fort is located near the end of the city and overlooks most of St. John's and out into the harbour. It's beautiful. The weather is also friendlier today so the sights are clear and panoramic. I sit on the edge beside a cannon and watch as a small number of tourists wander around. When it's time for my appointment, I head to the mechanic. His shop setup is at his own house and there are about five other cars parked on his driveway, on which he appears to be working. I walk in and there are three or four people there watching him install a set of brake callipers on yet another car. The mechanic slides out from underneath and greets me.

"How can I help you sir?"

"Hi, I've got the van that needs to be checked up on."

"I'm pretty busy today. Why don't you come back tomorrow."

"Oh? I thought I had an appointment for today."

"Really? Let me check."

He runs into his house and looks through his calendar and then returns.

"Nope. I don't have anything here, but I'll try my best to help you out. What do you need done?"

"I just need an overall maintenance check. The van has been in storage for eight months and I'm going to be driving it across country for the next three months, so I just want to make sure everything is okay."

"Okay, I'll try to squeeze you in. Come back in about two hours or you can wait here." I decide to wait.

I head back to the van trying to figure out something to do in the meantime. Going through my bag, I see the multiple rolls of hockey tape that I brought with me, so I decide to strip off all the old fading decorations on the van. It takes me a good hour to fully clean out the exterior and when it's done, the van looks as bare as it did the day it was purchased, aside from a little more rust. I wait inside while the mechanic is finishing up work on the car. Then he comes toward me and asks where the van is.

I lead him outside and he jumps in the driver seat to take it for a test drive. Rounding the block, he pulls it into his garage and lifts up the hood to test the compression on the engine. After further inspection he gives me the thumbs up.

"Looks fine. Engine is good. Brakes are good. You might want to change that tail pipe but it's not a big deal," he recommends, referring to the hole in the muffler caused by my accident from the Saskatoon ditch. "You need to change all you fluids and then it should be good to go. I don't have time for that now but you can go anywhere to do it. And take this belt. Your steering is a little stiff, so you might need to replace the belt at some point."

I thank him and give him $20 for the quick check, and then head down the road to a Canadian Tire store that I saw earlier to get all of the fluids changed. It is another $120 for a complete flush out and new fluids, but it will be worth it in the end. While waiting for my service, I buy a cooler for the van, which will be important for tailgating. Once everything is all said and done, I drive back to the city, with a smoother running vehicle, to meet up with Rachel. As I pull into a spot in front of her work, Rachel spots me from inside and comes out to watch me do a better job of parking than the last time she observed me. When I back up into the spot, the steering suddenly becomes very stiff and starts squealing. That must be the belt the mechanic was referring to. In front of Basho Japanese restaurant, Rachel greets me with a smile, a hug, and a kiss. She's stoked.

"It's good to see you!" she says.

"Are you excited?"

"Definitely, I can't wait. I'm still working for another few hours but my sister's coming down very soon. You can have a drink with her."

I follow her up to her office, where she's arranging schedules for the staff, and highlighting the week she has taken off to come with me. About 10 minutes later, her sister Ginny comes in. Rachel pours us a drink and I tell them of my encounter with Newfie Joe and that he's also considering coming down with us.

"Oh that's great. We've watched your DVD a few times and Newfie Joe is a character. I've always wondered what happened to him. It'll definitely be a lot easier with the three of you driving down as opposed to just two," Ginny notes.

"Where are you staying in St. John's?" Rachel asks.

"In the van," I laugh.

"Oh no, you should have told me earlier! Come stay with us!"

We stay for a few more drinks and wait until Rachel is off work. After grabbing some food, we head to the house with Rachel directing me in the van. By the time we arrive it's late, so we go straight to sleep. In the morning, we plan for a big feast before our voyage begins, so we load up on groceries including steaks, potatoes, salads, and vegetables. I meet Rachel's brother, Adam, in the morning and he grabs his guitar and plays me songs from his band, Hey Rosetta!, as the girls are preparing the food. The tunes sound great and I tell him that they have a bright future. Later in the afternoon, Rachel's parents return home from a trip.

"Mom, Dad, this is Jason. He's the touring van guy that Rachel's going with down to the states," says Ginny, introducing me.

"Pleasure to meet you," I say extending my hand.

"Yes, we've heard lots about you. Please make yourself at home."

Everything is pretty much ready to go on the van. The last remaining task is to decorate the van with hockey tape, so I head outside for two hours and carefully redesign the entire exterior of the van. Not forgetting about the Canadian tour, I leave the Canadian map on one side along with the corresponding checked off Canadian cities crammed together. On the other side, I place the matching American cities along with a new map of the US with my newly acquired blue hockey tape. After redoing the front to say "Pearl Jam Tour – Canada 2005/US 2006 Touring Van", the van is looking sharp once again.

"Wow, I can't believe you had the patience to do all of that. I would have given up after 10 minutes," Rachel comments, as I come back inside. "Looking good! Dinner is almost ready." Rachel brings out a big bowl of olives and hands it to me. I tell her that I don't like olives and she's in disbelief. "You don't like olives? Oh man, they're the best!"

The van newly decorated for the US tour.

She continues to tease me with the olives until dinner is served. The meal is more than we can handle, with almost half of the food still remaining when we finish. Completely stuffed, I head outside with Rachel's dad to build a bonfire. Soon Rachel runs out and tells me I have a phone call. It's Newfie Joe. He tells me that he just quit his job so he's definitely in, but he has to get back to his parents' place tonight to get his stuff and we can pick him up from there. I offer him a ride back, but he says he'll be fine hitchhiking. Back at the bonfire, Adam entertains us with more Hey Rosetta! songs and, before we know it, we're all ready for bed.

Early Sunday morning, we're up and ready to go. I thank Rachel's family and the van is on the road by 7:00am. Stopping only for coffee, we arrive into Holyrood by 8:00am and I pull onto Keating's Lane. I get out of the van and walk around to the back where there's a suitcase sitting outside. The door is wide open and I see Newfie Joe walking out toward me.

"Man, I just got home like two hours ago."

"What happened?" I ask.

"It took longer than I thought to sort shit out in the city and, by the time I got to the highway, it was nearly 2:00am. I waited over an hour for a ride and said fuck it, so I called a cab. It cost me over $100 but I'm here. Let's hit the road!"

Carrying a suitcase this time, rather than the familiar backpack, Newfie Joe organizes the trunk to fit everything around my gigantic hockey bag. I introduce him to Rachel, and then pull out the video camera to ask our returning passenger what his thoughts are.

"It's Newfie Joe back with the van!" he announces. "I was walking along George street and who do I see? Jason. He asked me to come, so I definitely had to jump in this van one more time and do it up proper. So here we are. We're getting the heck out of here and hitting Pearl Jam in the States."

With my two Newfoundlanders on board, the van is ready for its first destination. Boston was chosen as the starting point for this tour because it's the closest city to St. John's. However, the drive to get there will be the longest trip ever for the van. A total of 2400km of driving in addition to a six-hour ferry ride is required but, since it's just May 21, I've given us three days to work with. It shouldn't be a problem. For the first few hours of driving, Newfie Joe is sprawled out on the bed sleeping like a log, while Rachel and I chat up front. We discuss ideas of what we could do on the days off during the tour. She really wants to see New York and has booked her flight home from there. I haven't been to New York either, so we could possibly spend the day roaming around Manhattan. Our anticipation brings excitement, as none of us have ever been to the eastern side of America before.

When we arrive in Gander, I stop to fill up at the same gas station we stopped at last time, only driving the opposite direction. Rachel asks if I want her to drive for a while, so I accept. She's understandably excited to be the first female Touring Van driver ever and promptly calls her family and friends and, in doing so, also becomes the first to talk on the cell phone while driving the van at the same time. After half an hour with the phone glued to her ears, she complains about the stiff steering and I tell her about the extra belt I brought in case the problem gets worse. We make good time and arrive in Corner Brook just after 6:00pm in time for some food at Mary Browns Fried Chicken.

"What are you expecting from this tour?" Newfie Joe asks me.

"I don't know. It's going to be different," I answer. "I know a few people coming out for the shows, but we don't have too many passengers signed up for the van yet. Everyone is feeling the West Coast instead."

Newfie Joe, the hitchhiker, driving the Touring Van.

"Fuck that! We're going to rock the East Coast. They're not going to know what hit them," Newfie Joe replies.

"For sure. I think I've convinced Cali Joe to come out for some of these shows though, but I'm not sure. I'll have to call him about it."

After filling ourselves with grease, we pick up a case of beer and drive the remaining few hours to the Port Aux Basques ferry terminal. Our ferry departs at midnight and we arrive with an hour and a half to spare, so we crack open the case to celebrate reaching our first milestone of the drive. We share stories from the previous tour, laughing and relaxing in the van until we are able to board the vessel. Once on, we set up camp and, although it's not permitted for us to stay in the vehicles due to safety reasons, we sleep in the van for the entire ferry ride. Without any hassles during the night, we dock around 6:00am and get an early start out of the gates.

The drive in the morning is quite mellow with the only sounds coming from the stereo speakers, which are starting to blow. Approaching Moncton, New Brunswick, I suggest that we make a detour to Prince Edward Island because I missed it last time, but the idea is flatly rejected again. Later on, with Rachel asleep, I ask Newfie Joe if he wants to give me a break and drive for a bit. He agrees to give it a try, and the hitchhiker has taken over the van.

"This thing is freaky, man," he comments. "I haven't driven in years either."

"Just watch out for the power steering."

A few hours down the road we arrive in Fredericton, where we stop to get gas and to make sandwiches for lunch. We buy some snacks and fruit at the supermarket and head toward the American border. Just in front of it, I pull into the duty-free shop to pick up some last minute Canadian items and to make sure we're all set. Newfie Joe gets all excited after seeing an entire section of alcohol from Newfoundland, so we purchase a flat of Black Horse beer and a bottle of our favourite Screech rum to bring down south with us.

"You have your passports and everything?" I ask.

"I'm good," Rachel answers.

"Any drugs or illegal narcotics on us?"

"Oh shit! Thanks for the reminder. I've got a pill somewhere," Newfie Joe says, scrambling around in the van. "I just have to find it."

"Pop it or get rid of it!"

"It's here somewhere. It's been sitting around for the last few months. Ah, there it is," Newfie Joe says as he deposits it in the garbage bin.

Once we're set, I pull back onto the highway and approach the border toward Houlton, Maine. It's about 3:00pm on a Monday afternoon and there isn't a single car crossing the border with us. This could get interesting.

"What are your citizenships and where are you off to?" border patrol asks.

"We're all Canadian and we're heading down to Boston," I answer handing our passports over.

"You drove all the way from Columbia?" he asks, referring to British Columbia.

"Yes sir."

"How many of you in there?"

"Three."

"Purpose of your trip?"

"We're seeing a bunch of rock concerts along the Northeast. And then I'm driving back west."

"How long is your trip?"

"Well, Rachel is going back after a week, Joe is leaving after two or three weeks, and I'm staying for three months."

He pauses, looks at me for a minute, and then tells me to pull over to come inside for further questioning. I oblige and we head into the building. At the counter, I'm asked to hand over the van keys and they're given to the other border patrol agents. I give them permission to search the van, and they proceed to do so with the aid of two full-sized dogs. Another agent grabs our passports and walks back to his desk to check us out on the computer.

"Okay let me get this straight. You guys are going down to Boston and a bunch of other places to see some concerts?" he questions.

"Yes sir," I answer.

"What's your itinerary and how long is everyone staying again?"

"We go to Boston for a few days, then to Philadelphia for a few days, and then to New York, where Rachel will be flying home from."

"Do you have your flight info with you?" he asks Rachel.

"Yes I do," Rachel answers handing over her confirmation printout.

"And then what's happening after New York?"

"We head to Washington DC, then up to East Rutherford for a few days, and then Joe returns home."

"How are you getting home sir?" he asks Newfie Joe.

"I'm going to take a bus."

"Do you have a ticket for it yet?"

"Not yet."

"Okay and what about you?" he continues with me.

"I'll be driving across to the West Coast and back home from there."

"And how long are you here for?"

"Close to three months."

"What do you do for work?"

"I'm a Civil Engineer and Construction Manager."

"And they let just let take three months off like that?"

"Yes sir."

"Okay, why don't you guys have a seat."

We sit down on the only three chairs they have in the office and after a minute he starts calling us up individually for more questions. I'm the last to be called. Back up again, he tells me that if I have anything I'm hiding that I don't want the others to know, it's okay to tell him. Then I'm asked to explain my story again and to produce proof of my occupation. I open up my wallet and hand over my Professional Engineering Association member's card and a former boss's business card. Just then, one of the patrol agents searching the van comes in and asks about all the DVDs in the van. I had brought along the remaining 25 Touring Van DVDs from the Canadian tour that I had leftover to give away at the shows. I said they're just fun travel videos I've made for friends.

"Do they contain copyrighted music?"

"No, I've got approval for everything in there."

"Okay so you're going to be down in the US for three months, what are you going to do about money? Are you going to work?"

"No, I have enough money saved up."

"How much cash do you have on you?"

"About $500."

"Is that going to be enough?"

"I have my bank cards and credit cards too."

"Okay you may sit down now."

I'm rather calm throughout the whole process but the criminal style interrogation is getting to be a bit intimidating, as their questions are certainly designed to rattle us and play with our nerves. This is Rachel's first border experience and she's not enjoying the moment at all. She's not sweating much but I can tell she's anxious to be released. Sitting silently together, I can feel their eyes watching our every move from a camera. We wait for another half hour, while the entire office is trying to find something on us but when they can't, our keys are returned along with our passports.

"Welcome to America," he says handing them over.

Back in the van, we make sure everything is still intact but we notice paw marks on some of our luggage and half our bananas were eaten by the dogs. A little frustrated with the whole process, we drive down the I-95. The next hour is spent bitching about the border experience, but the Touring Van has officially invaded America and we are well on our way to Boston, six hours away. Driving through Maine we spot a couple of moose on the side of the road, so I keep a look out for others on the road. A few moments later, I see one dart out across the road, but it crosses the street completely.

"Wow that can be dangerous. How's the steering now?" Rachel asks. Just as I tell her it's fine, the steering suddenly tightens up again. I try turning the wheel to change lanes but it's a struggle. Slowly, I'm able to manoeuvre the van onto the shoulder and bring it out of harm's way. We get out and I pop the hood to check out the power steering belt, and it's almost about to snap. I grab the extra belt and begin taking out the old one when I hear Rachel scream.

"What happened?"

"Another moose just ran across the highway, less than 10 metres from us," she explains.

Unfazed by the incident, I'm able to replace the belt but, without the tools, I'm not able to tighten it properly. We get back in the van and begin driving slowly but we can hear the loose belt making a cluster of noises in front of us.

"That doesn't sound good. We should just take it to a mechanic," Rachel suggests. "I don't want to take any chances with moose running around."

Since we have plenty of time on our hands, I agree and pull out at the next exit into the town of Bangor. Crawling like a snail around the city, I find a VIP Auto Center but it's closed. It's around 6:00pm. Across the street there's a Days Inn Hotel and after one night in the van, Rachel is itching for a shower, so we check into the hotel for the night. Saving our Newfoundland beer for the shows, we buy a case of cheap American beer and a bottle of wine to entertain us for the night, with the three of us crammed into a small room. The next morning, we drive across the street back to the shop, where they change and tighten up two belts for us. And with the purchase of new windshield wipers and a car air freshener, another $150 is spent on maintenance but it will be all worth it. The van is completely healthy again, ready for the road.

The rest of the drive is easy but getting into Boston is a challenge. As I enter what appears to be the exit for the city centre, we approach a tunnel instead. Further down the tunnel are more exits, with no useful information for us to get our bearings straight. I take what looks like the most logical direction from what I saw outside of the tunnel, but this loops us back in the opposite direction. I can see the downtown area in my rearview mirror and can't seem to figure out which exit to take to get there. We end up driving in circles three or four times before hitting the right entrance for the city by mid-afternoon. What a mess of a highway system.

Our first order of business in Boston is to see Fenway Park. The Red Sox are playing the Yankees tonight, *the* marquee matchup in all of American sports. I pull the van into a parking spot in the centre of town and, after adding a few more decorations to the van, we walk through the city toward the ball park. The frenzy of fans roaming around Fenway is like no sporting event seen in Canada. There are families with their Red Sox shirts and hats on ready for an evening of hot dogs, peanuts, and cheering. There are college kids ready for a night of boozing and heckling. And there are also businessmen rushing in after work to relieve some stress with a relaxing night of America's favourite pastime. We wander around the stadium snapping photos and inquiring about tickets but decide that it's too expensive to attend this sold-out game. Instead, we grab a drink at a number of the bars across from the stadium to experience the atmosphere. Halfway through the game, we grow restless and decide to take a walk through the city.

"So what's up with Cali Joe? Is he joining us or what?" Newfie Joe asks.

"I'll call him right now and ask. I won't tell him you're here so he'll be surprised," I answer.

On the phone, Cali Joe informs me that he won't be able to make it out for the next shows in Philadelphia, but will try for the East Rutherford shows at the end of the first leg. I relay this information to the others as we wander through a park, and then I call Melissa, who lives in Boston and will be catching a ride with us to the next city. She gives me her address and invites us to spend the night. When our legs become tired from walking, we return to the van and follow the directions to Melissa's place. Instead of taking the chaotic highways that we experienced earlier, I decide to drive through the city and the suburbs instead. This proves to be equally as challenging, with many of the streets not having visible street signs at all. Furthermore, I should know better than to let the hitchhiker navigate us around a foreign city. Finally, I give up and call Melissa for exact directions, arriving late at night.

Melissa greets us with a smile. We chat for a few minutes but it's late, so she offers us some floor space to sleep on. Preferring to be in our van instead, Newfie Joe and I rough it like old times, while Rachel sleeps inside the house with the cats. As we settle in for the night, we have a few drinks in the van and I turn on my laptop hunting for a free wireless network. When connected, I fire over an email to everyone for an update on the trip attached with photos of the newly decorated van. As soon as I turn off the computer, I slip into my sleeping bag. Newfie Joe is passed out already.

The next morning, we're up early and the jam-packed street of eight hours ago is now half empty. I knock on the house door and Rachel answers. Melissa has left for work already. We clean up and make our move to what was formally known as the Fleet Center, now called the TD Banknorth Garden. I pull the van into the small parking lot beside the venue but it looks more like an alleyway than a parking lot and is a little seedy-looking. We finish decorating the van and, even though it's already noon, Rachel and I decide to get some breakfast while Newfie Joe guards our home. After satisfying our stomachs with some grease, we go back to the van to prepare for the pre-show events.

"Is our van going to be safe?" I ask the others jokingly.

"I don't think so," Rachel answers.

"If anything happens, we'll all just hitchhike," Newfie Joe happily suggests.

"Are you prepared to do that?" I ask Rachel.

"Not a chance. Well... maybe."

With that vote of confidence, we walk across the street to the Harp Bar, one of the many bars lined up facing the arena. It's mellow inside but I see one familiar face, Bobby from Rhode Island, who I met at the St. John's airport at the end of the Canadian tour. He's also with a Newfie friend, Ryan, so we let the Newfoundlanders get acquainted with one another. Having decided to do this tour at the last minute, I didn't buy any tickets at the time of sale and instead, I have found tickets for many of the first leg shows through the various Pearl Jam message boards. Today I'm meeting a fan named John for a pair of tickets to both Boston shows. After our transaction, I thank him and head to the box office to see if there are any extra tickets, as Newfie Joe still needs one. There not too many people around but I run into Brad's friends Matt from New Hampshire and Brian from DC. They're standing over a box full of orange t-shirts.

"What are you guys up to?" I ask.

"Oh, these are the Stone guitar pick shirts that Brian and Brad made, like the Mike shirt you've got on," Matt explains, as he hands over a shirt to me.

"Oh nice. I thought you guys were just making these for friends."

"We were, but then we decided that it would be great to get the charities involved too," Brian tells me, as he hands over a piece of paper with donation instructions on it.

So the idea is that the Stone and Mike guitar pick shirts will be given away for free, with the understanding that the recipient donates any amount of money to the Crohn's and Colitis Foundation of America (CCFA), similar to the CCFC fundraising that was part of the Canadian tour. Matt then informs me that Brad will be arriving soon and that he has an extra ticket for me if I need it. I tell them where to find us and return to give Newfie Joe the good news about the ticket. With Back Seat Lover, a Pearl Jam cover band, now performing on stage, Harp's has filled up and is now hopping. I buy a round of Jagerbombs for our table and Bobby confesses that it will be his 50th time seeing Pearl Jam tonight. He's excited.

Brad comes by and tells us that the shirt operation has been shut down. "The Ten Club thought we were selling the shirts but, when we explained what we were doing, they suggested that we do it a little more discreetly off venue property," he explains. "They also kept the box of shirts, but I've got more coming tomorrow. I may need a ride to Philly with the shirts."

"Yeah, no problem. We can help get the shirts out there for you guys as well if you want," I answer.

With our tickets sorted for tonight, it's show time. On the way back to the venue, there are a few people that recognize me from our Canadian tour DVD. Oscar from Boston knows who I am right away, while Chris from New Jersey and Mic from Wisconsin also say hi. The latter two are doing the entire first leg by car. It looks like I'm not the only crazy one out there. Inside the venue, Rachel and I find our seats and they're up a ways back near the corner. We're not particularly close to the stage, but it doesn't really matter. My Morning Jacket is the opening band and having enjoyed listening to their CD, I'm excited to see them. However, their mellow, slow paced music doesn't quite do it for me as a warm up band. The performance that follows is a different story.

With a mixture of songs from the new album, old classics, and a few rare ones including *Rats*, the show matches the energy of the boisterous crowd. From where we're sitting, we can see the crowd in full and can hear everyone singing at the top of their lungs. The show is dynamic and it's a real treat to hear the new songs live for the first time. As the first encore comes to a close, Brian, who's up in the front row, throws one of his orange Stone shirts on stage. It gets picked up by someone and when the band comes back out for the second encore, Jeff Ament is wearing it! The band must have been told about these shirts with the box being confiscated. A few songs later, Vedder points to the guy next to Brian, Rick, who proceeds to take off his Stone shirt and throws it on stage. Vedder grabs it, pulls it over his head, and starts modeling it across the stage. At the end of the song, he returns the shirt back to Rick. Brad and Brian are probably going mental at this point. Showing his appreciation for the effort, Vedder throws a tambourine out to Brian during the final song of the night.

After the show, we all gather around the van, where Brian shows us his newly obtained tambourine and Newfie Joe explains how Brad went ape shit after seeing the shirts on stage. Even though there's still another show in Boston tomorrow night, I hand Rachel the hockey tape to check off Boston with a little added Newfie twist, where she takes a drink from the bottle of Screech rum afterwards. We drive back to Melissa's place – this time with Melissa directing us inside the van – still high on excitement from our first show of the tour, Newfie Joe and I have a few drinks in the van before sleeping. Not even halfway through our beer, we notice some flashing lights outside. Police lights! A few seconds later, there's a knock on our window, so we open the door.

"How's it going guys? What's going on here?" the police officer asks.

"Oh, we're just calling it a night. Our friend lives right there," I answer pointing to Melissa's house.

"So you guys are driving around the country or something?" he asks after examining the decorations on the van.

"Yeah, we drove this van across Canada last year, and now we're taking it across the US," Newfie Joe responds.

"Are you guys going to the Pearl Jam show here in Boston?"

"Yeah, we're following them around the country."

"Oh that's cool. My brother is going tomorrow night, he's very excited," he explains. "Well, I can't charge you guys for following Pearl Jam on tour. So have a safe trip."

What potentially could have been a problematic situation turns into an enjoyable conversation. Newfie Joe and I have a laugh and decide to do one more drink before wrapping ourselves into our sleeping bags.

The warm temperature in the van wakes us up the next morning and we're starting to get used to this van business again. Melissa has the day off from work today, so she rides into town with us and, instead of paying to park in the shady parking lot again, we drive up a block from the venue and park on the street for free, directly in front of Hooters. Trying to save some money, Newfie Joe stays in the van to drink instead of at the bars. Melissa goes off to meet some of her friends, while Rachel and I wander in and out of the many bars warming up for another epic show tonight. Every place is playing nonstop Pearl Jam music, and one is playing nonstop Pearl Jam DVDs on their screens. The town is really pumped for the show. We head back to Harp's bar, where we run into Bobby and Ryan again, so I interview Bobby with my new video camera.

There's a slight buzz going around about the band soundchecking *Leash*, a song that hasn't been played in over a decade. On the David Letterman show a month earlier, the entire crowd held up signs requesting *Leash* to be played, only to have Vedder bring out a sign of his own specifically noting that "*Leash* won't be played tonight."

"What better place to play it than in Boston, the last place they played it." Bobby says.

I next turn the camera toward Chris and Mic, and Mic claims that hearing *Rats* last night might have been the highlight of his life. They're doing about 20 shows each this tour, driving through the entire first leg, and a few more on the second leg including all the way out west to The Gorge. "There's nothing else to do this summer," Chris explains.

I thank them for the interview and then return to the van to drop off my camera and check up on Newfie Joe. He's not there but Brad is, and he's holding a box full of Mike shirts freshly delivered this morning. He hands me a bunch of shirts along with a stack of paper with the donation information on it for me to give away with at the bar, while he'll do the same near the venue. Right then, Newfie Joe comes out through the doors of Hooters.

"Dude, I just talked to the manager at Hooters and he said he wants to get all the Hooters girls out later and take a photo with the van," he informs me.

"Oh really? Awesome. You still staying here?"

"Just for a bit but I still need a ticket. I'll probably pop out to the bar later, but let me know if you hear anything."

With a sack of shirts and a stack of papers, I head back to Harp's and, for the next hour, Rachel and I wander around the bar handing out shirts to random fans. A few moments later, Newfie Joe enters the bar and tells me that someone has been looking for us and wants to ride in the van. "He's writing a magazine article but I thought I'd clear it with you first." I tell him it would be fine.

So Newfie Joe returns with the guy who is wearing a taxi driver style hat. He introduces himself as Tim and explains that he's writing an article about Pearl Jam on the road for *Relix* magazine and, instead of having everything set up for him, he wants to travel around with fans to do it the way the fans do it. Apparently, when asked about fans he could travel with, the Ten Club advised him to find the Canadians and the van.

"I came to Boston with nothing sorted in terms of transportation in the hopes that I'd find you guys. Had no luck yesterday, but then I met Brad doing his t-shirt thing today and he brought me to the van," he explains.

"Well, welcome on board. We'd be glad to have you in the van. Do you want a drink?" I ask, as we receive our Jagerbombs from our waitress. I offer him one, but he turns it down. "How far do you need to ride with us for?" I ask.

"Probably right to the end of the first leg, but I'm not sure at this point."

"So you came here with the only goal of finding us?"

"Yes," he reconfirms.

"You're lucky because this is our first show of the tour."

"I had a feeling about Boston," he smiles. "Where are you guys staying?"

"Just in the van parked outside of someone's house," I laugh.

"I got a suite just a block from here, where you guys are more than welcome to stay," he offers.

We accept the offer and designate the van as the meeting spot after the show. Rachel and I continue handing out the shirts, while at the same time asking people if they have any extra tickets for Newfie Joe. When we run out of shirts, people start coming up to us and asking where we got the shirts. I direct them to visit the CCFA website, and promise them that more will be available at the next shows. As for the ticket situation, it's starting to look grim, and Newfie Joe takes a run to the box office for a final check. He returns a little later without any luck and buys a raffle from the pre-party hoping to win the pair of tickets that's available. The draw comes and goes but he doesn't win. But upon collecting his tickets, the winner of the tickets approaches us and gives Newfie Joe his spare, knowing that he has been looking. Grateful for the generosity, Newfie Joe begins buying rounds of drinks. My Morning Jacket is about to hit the stage, but we decide to skip them today and just enjoy our time at the bar.

When it's time for the show, we've accumulated a good buzz and our energy level is through the roof. The band comes out on fire with a rocking first set. There's certainly a buzz in the air, with fans anticipating, or rather, hoping for a performance of *Leash*. After a mellow but lengthy first encore, they come out for the second encore and Boom, the keyboardist, is wearing one of the Mike shirts. I look up front for Brian and assume he's the one jumping higher than anyone else in the front row.

With the surprising but welcome inclusions of *Smile* and *Indifference* following, the show seems to be near the end but, then, silence hits. The crowd is hushed, listening to what might come next. And without a word said, the band goes right into it – *Leash!!* The crowd suddenly erupts to an even higher level, while Rachel and I are jumping out of our row going crazy. I think I momentarily lose my voice. The song sounds a little rusty and their timing is off but, hey, they haven't played it in forever so the crowd gives their appreciation for it. Theo Epstein, the general manager of the Boston Red Sox, joins the band onstage for a brief performance, before *Yellow Ledbetter* closes a memorable show.

Back at the van after the show, everyone is talking about *Leash*, almost forgetting how great the rest of the show was. Rick got the setlist afterwards and points out *Leash* on it. I try to interview Rachel's reaction of the show, but she's at a loss for words and so very happy about seeing what we just witnessed. And with the van being parked in a more visible location this time, everyone walking by us stops to say hi. Some of them have seen the van before on the internet, some ask for a DVD from the last tour, and many ask for one of the Stone or Mike shirts. The demand for the shirts is so high now that Brad and Brian call in for another order to be shipped to the next city. A few Canadian fans also walk by and tell me that they remember the van from Montreal and ask if we have a Canadian flag with us, which we don't. "Well you do now!" he says throwing his flag to me.

I let Melissa know that we're staying in town tonight and will pick her up in the morning, so she grabs a ride home with her friend. Just then, Tim shows up at the van and reveals that he's staying at the hotel just half a block down from Hooters. We allow the crowd to die out around the van, and then grab our stuff for the night. Newfie Joe insists on guarding the van by sleeping in it, so Rachel and I head up to Tim's hotel, where we are given a sofa bed to sleep on. The day was exciting and exhausting, so with Tim quietly typing away notes on his laptop, our eyes quickly shut.

No need to be void
or save up on life
You got to spend it all

Light Years

CHAPTER 19: **TAILGATING MANIA**

May 27 – 28, 2006 » Show 20 & 21
Camden, New Jersey

THE NEXT TWO SHOWS are going to be in Camden, NJ, just across the river from Philadelphia, PA where we'll be staying. Driving out of Boston is where the Touring Van experience really begins. As we wake up, Tim is still typing away on his laptop, as if he had never gone to sleep. Rachel and I are a little bit out of it after a full day of partying but, after a quick shower, we're fresh and ready to go. In the van, Newfie Joe is still rolling around but is quick to get ready. I drive up the street to Brad's hotel, where he loads up more Stone and Mike shirts than his own personal luggage. We pick up Melissa at her house – she's already outside waiting for us – and from there, Tim directs me the rest of the way. So the first Touring Van crew for the trip consists of me, Rachel, Newfie Joe, Melissa, Brad, and Tim.

Our drive out of Boston seems to last forever, as getting out is just as chaotic as getting in but, with the help of my new co-pilot, our route is much more efficient. As we enter Connecticut, the skies open up and rain begins to fall, much to the relief of our new American passenger, who was sweating profusely after discovering the lack of air conditioning in the van. To avoid the traffic in New York, Tim suggests we drive onto the New Jersey Turnpike, where the paying of highway tolls begin and so does the Memorial Day weekend traffic. With the downtime, Tim is able take notes and interviews me while I'm driving. The one question he really wants to know is why I'm doing this, so I discuss how Pearl Jam's music has always been a large part of who I am, and that after completing the Canadian tour and meeting many others who share that connection, I got a taste of life on the road and travelling and I wanted more. So I decided to quit my job and continue the travels to see where it takes me.

"Pearl Jam has really changed my life and, after that tour, my perspective on life has become different," I explain. "It's such a positive atmosphere at these shows, and the people I've met are some of the best people ever."

He wonders how I justify leaving a good career, going in a totally different direction. "Well, through travelling you see a lot and learn a lot about the world and yourself. I've realized how much richer my life can be by meeting so many different interesting people, and these Pearl Jam tours have allowed me to do this," I clarify. "This is a part of my life that I'll never have again. I'm young and I've done nothing but work hard at school and then at work. I have a lot of money saved up and my career will always be there if I choose to go back, so why not invest in my life rather than in property or something like that? Besides, this is too much fun and work isn't. I don't have any responsibilities holding me back from this, so why not?"

"Why not?" Tim laughs. "I love it!"

We continue the interview for another half an hour, before the tunes are pumped back up again. Tim is a little surprised that we don't really listen to Pearl Jam in the vehicle, choosing a variety of other bands instead. He commends us and says it's refreshing, unlike the dry heat he's barely surviving. Crossing over the Ben Franklin Bridge, we enter Philadelphia late in the afternoon. I drop off Melissa at her hotel, drop off Tim at his, and then we head toward Brad's hotel, the Marriott. After several failed calls to find a cheap hotel of our own, Brad invites us to just crash with him.

"Brian's already paid for the room but he's not coming anymore, so why don't you guys stay here?" he suggests. "There's an extra bed, so we can make it work." Accepting the offer, I run out to the van and move it from street parking to the hotel valet parking. This is the first time the van will be valet parked and it's quite exciting. I pull up to the entrance, where the valet attendant takes down the room number and then grabs the keys from me. Brad and I unload what we need from the van and head back up to the room where he proceeds to sort through nearly hundreds of Mike and Stone shirts. Once we're settled in, we wander down Market Street to meet up with Tim, who's having dinner with a friend. We let him know about our plan to find some Philly cheesesteaks for dinner but he opts for an early night instead.

Swimming in a pile of Mike and Stone shirts that were designed by Brian and Brad.

So without our navigator, we wander aimlessly around the streets of Philadelphia, quickly noticing that there are as many Dunkin' Donuts restaurants here as there are Tim Horton's in Kitchener, Ontario. We manage to find our way toward the Liberty Bell, but further exploration proves that the six-hour drive earlier in the day has taken a toll on us. Returning to the hotel, I notice the van parked on the streets, one spot ahead of where I had moved it from earlier to get it valet parked. I guess it doesn't fit in the underground lot or something. There's also a note on it from another Pearl Jam fan from Vancouver, Brandon, who knows about the van and wants to meet up at the show. I try calling the room number written on the note, and he answers but is too tired to talk. Feeling similarly tired, we retire for the night.

When I wake up the next morning, Brad is up already and looks as if he's getting ready for a marathon or something. Without his usual Hawaiian shirt on, he's now sporting a pair of shorts and a headband. I almost don't recognize him. I ask the track star what he's dressed for and he confirms that he is, in fact, going out for a morning run and asks if I want to come. Knowing that I'll be consuming nothing but cheesesteaks and beer over the next few days, I join him. We let the others know that we're jogging through the blistering heat toward Benjamin Franklin Parkway. Running underneath all of the flags along this street and passing by many fountains and statues reminds me of something – oh right – Rocky! At the end of the road is the entrance to the park along the river and the Art Museum, scene of the famous Rocky steps in the movie. An hour into our run, we approach a bridge. But instead of crossing the river, we decide it's far enough and jog back. At the Art Museum again, I mimic the Rocky run up the steps – celebrating at the top – while Brad films me on camera. By the time we get back to the hotel, we've probably covered close to 15km in an hour and a half of solid running, which is a great way to start the day.

With my exercise for the tour all complete, we round up the two Newfoundlanders and head to South Philly for some cheesesteaks. Consulting Tim last night, we decide that we can't search for the best cheesesteak in Philly without going to the two most famous ones, Geno's and Pat's. Today we opt for Geno's for lunch. Parking the van in front of a schoolyard, we have to walk a block to the restaurant, which has a line up around the block anyway. The rival across the street has a similar crowd of people waiting for their chance to order some of Philly's finest. The service is efficient, so the line moves quickly. As we get closer to the front, we see the inside decorated with photos of the so-called celebrities who have eaten at Geno's, none of which Rachel recognizes. As we reach the counter, I notice a sign instructing how to properly order a cheesesteak. You must say the type of cheese first and then "with" if you want fried onions, or "without" if you don't want fried onions. When my turn comes up, I order an "American with" and Rachel does the same. The transaction is quick, and within a minute, I receive my hoagie.

"How long have you guys been in business?" Newfie Joe asks.

"Since 1966."

"Are you guys better than Pat's?" I follow, holding the camera in his face.

"Excuse me?"

"Are you guys better than Pat's?" I repeat.

"Of course we're better than Pat's," he answers. "Why would you be eating here if we weren't better than Pat's?"

In anticipation of the experience, we find a table along the edge of the sidewalk. Brad orders one without the bread because he's allergic to flour, and Newfie Joe doesn't order one at all because he has cut off all meat since the Canadian tour, so they're curious about our opinions on our first genuine "chilly pheese steak," as Newfie keeps mistakenly calling them.

"I think I should have gotten the cheesier whizzy, extra cheese or something. It's kind of bland," Rachel describes.

"Tastes pretty healthy actually," I joke. "The blandness keeps it healthy."

Overall, it's somewhat disappointing. Perhaps we've hyped it too much, but it won't stop us from trying it again. Full on bland cheesesteaks, we attempt to pick up some supplies for the show, but it appears to be difficult to buy beer in this city. There are no stores that really sell beer – not even grocery stores, corner stores, or even wine and spirit stores have it in stock. Asking around, we're told that most pubs sell beer to go but, needing a large quantity we're directed to a beer depot to load up on beer, wine, and ice. With all the necessities, we head to Camden for what's expected to be the tailgate party to end all tailgate parties.

Crossing over the river, we can see the Camden Tweeter Centre down below, and with it is the massive number of cars already parked in the lots. It's barely after noon, but it's a Saturday on Memorial Day weekend so the fans have come out early and in full force. I pull the van into lot 2 but it has been closed off, because it's completely full and so are lots 1 and 3. I explain to the parking attendant that there's a fundraiser happening in lot 2, which we've brought items for, so we need to be there. She claims that there's no space available at all. However, she can get us into lot 1 and won't charge us the $15 parking fee. Done. Brad hops out to deliver the box of shirts to the fundraiser and we drive up to lot 1. Each lot is separated by a chain link fence, with the entrances closed off by a chain. As the parking attendant gets the okay to let us in via radio, he unhooks the gate and I roll the van into the parking lot to a bunch of cheers and smiles. "I can't believe it. The van is here!" someone yells out.

I pull into a parking space and a crowd immediately greets us, some of whom have no idea what the van is all about, while others already know who we are. Digging into our stash of beer, I see Brad returning to the van calling me over. As I approach him, it looks like he's trying to hide something or someone behind him. Peeking over his shoulder, I do a double take at the guy holding a video camera of his own, wearing a familiar backwards blue hat. I've seen a ghost, it's Cali Joe.

"Fuck! You made it!" I scream.

"Surprise!" he announces.

"What a big surprise. But I've got a good one for you too," I reply, guiding him toward the van where the others are.

"What the fuck? Newfie Joe?!!" he says, shocked.

"Since you didn't make it over to Newfoundland, we thought we'd bring Newfoundland to you," Newfie Joe replies, handing over a Black Horse Newfoundland beer.

"Man, I was banking on this big surprise and I get it right back with Newfie Joe being here. I never thought I'd see the guy again."

"So you lied to me on the phone the other night?" I ask.

"No, I wasn't going to come when I talked to you. But then I got the pictures of the van all nicely redecorated and I saw the Boston 2 setlist so the reunion couldn't wait any longer," Cali Joe answers. "I decided about noon yesterday to fly out, and here we are in Philly."

"The two Joes rolling in the van again," I announced.

"Who would have thought," Newfie Joe follows.

Cali Joe and Newfie Joe back with the van again in Camden, NJ.

Earlier in the day, Cali Joe even found a pair of tickets for the show, so he has a spare for Newfie Joe. Brad gives us all Stone shirts to wear, including a special blue one, which I put on, and then I meet up with Justin, the fan I'm buying a spare ticket from for these shows. He gives me a third row ticket, which I hand over to an exhilarated Rachel. She takes a full swig from her bottle of wine, celebrating the fact that this will be the closest she has ever been to the stage, before joining me in exploring the rest of the tailgating action.

The scene is pretty wild. It's similar to the tailgating experience we had in Kitchener, except for the fact that *everyone* is participating and contributing to the madness and it's ten times as big, filling up four parking lots. Walking past each group of people feels like walking down a strip of nightclubs, each pumping out different music. Once we've gotten close enough to the next group, the previous group's music is drowned out by the current group's music. It's all different music but it's all Pearl Jam, just different songs from different live recordings. Some are playing drinking games, throwing footballs, grilling burgers, and most are just chilling out and chatting over a burger or a beer or both. It definitely seems like everyone is simply enjoying their time and forgetting about the rest of the world.

We manage to find the fundraiser tent in lot 2, run by Laura from Chicago, who started up The Wishlist Foundation, a fan run organization that helps put on fundraisers during these Pearl Jam pre-show parties. It was started up mainly due to the success of the fan-run fundraisers that occurred throughout Canada, when they realized how much money could be raised by just gathering a group of Pearl Jam fans together. I've not met Laura before but we know of each other through the Pearl Jam world.

"Hey Jason," she greets me, as I film her reaction. "Oh no, the camera!"

With the help of a number of other fans, Laura is managing a table full of items for sale with all money going toward the charity of choice, CCFA. This includes bootleg CDs from various concerts, posters, raffle tickets, and the familiar Touring Van DVD from the Canadian tour. Missing from the table, however, are the Stone and Mike shirts, which arrived too late and will be available tomorrow. In the area of the tent are a few familiar faces – Chris and Mic.

"How was your trip down?" Chris asks as he leads me to their vehicle.

"This is the touring car," Mic proclaims it, "and this is the touring bag."

"I've already put over 2000 miles on this," Chris reveals.

Wandering around some more, I find Kyle from Atlanta, who I met at the Gorge last year and with who I'll be staying with during the time between the first and second legs of the tour. He brings me to his group of friends, filled with familiar faces. Mike from Charlotte, who we met at Quebec City, is there, along with Jason from Philly, who got screeched in with us in St. John's. Jason is also celebrating his birthday so, accordingly, there's a large group of friends within the surrounding area.

"It's my 74th show and it's my birthday. This is the first time they're playing on my birthday, and they're playing my hometown. You got to appreciate that," he announces with a Burger King crown on his head. "Everybody came. Jason from Vancouver is here."

"We have Vancouver, Florida, Georgia, North Carolina, Texas, Philly, and Germany," Kyle introduces.

In addition to Jason, the group also includes a number of fans who drove in the RV during the Canadian tour, a group that we didn't meet until the end. Nicole from Asheville is one of these RV people, and she has a spare ticket to tonight's show for me after Tak, who it was originally for, didn't make it out East. I also meet Katrina from Atlanta, who put together a touring fans website to help fans track their fan club tickets for each show.

"It's a pretty insane tailgate," Kyle confesses. "I've got to give it up to the Philadelphians, because they know how to do it right. There are lots of flip cup tables, beer pong tables, lots of little games where you throw things." Before the tour, Kyle and I had talked about putting together a documentary on Pearl Jam fans in general, so we take the camera and start randomly interviewing fans in the parking lot. Some give interesting answers and some sing instead. I run into Oscar from Boston and begin interviewing him and his friends.

"What's this for?" his friend asks.

"I'm being interviewed for a documentary," Oscar explains.

"Oh, Touring Van! Touring Van! I watched it on YouTube. It brought tears to my eyes," she cries. "It was a beautiful thing. Well done documentation. Where's the van?"

"In lot 1."

"We're going to go pay homage to the van. Well done."

In addition to people recognizing the camera, many are asking about my Stone shirt and where I got it. Back at the van, the crowd is dying down, but we continue with a few more drinks to cool us down from the afternoon heat. I ask Cali Joe what his plans are and how long he'll be with us.

"Well, I fly home Monday and I go to work Tuesday and Wednesday. Then I take a red-eye out Wednesday night to catch the East Rutherford shows and fly out on Sunday morning. I'm starting to get a little carried away," he laughs, "but it's great."

With the venue being in an outdoor amphitheatre, we can hear My Morning Jacket starting their set, but we're not interested. When they're done, we head to our seats. The show is another solid one. Maybe it's without the surprises and rarities of the previous shows in Boston – except for another performance of *Leash* – but it definitely has the same energy and perhaps an even louder audience cheering them on. When the show ends, Rachel comes stumbling out of the pit up front, having had the time of her life. I thank Nicole for my ticket and she returns to find her ride, while Rachel and I look for the Joes back at the parking lot, where there seems to be a mad rush for everyone to get the hell out of the mayhem.

Feeling a bit dehydrated from the heat and the wine, Rachel decides to rest in the van, while we try to cool down from the show's intensity. To soothe our souls, Cali Joe strums away on his guitar, much like on the Canadian tour.

"How's it like to be back in the van?" I ask.

"It's like home."

"What has brought you back? What makes these moments so special?"

"It's the experience. It's all of it. It's the music. It's the people. It's the camaraderie. It's just something, without doing it yourself, I don't know if you can really tell someone else what it's like," Cali Joe explains, while wearing his orange Stone shirt. "And to be here with the boys again and the van... there's no other place I'd rather be."

"That's some honest shit right there," Newfie Joe offers, also wearing an orange Stone shirt. "I understand because it's a similar feeling I'm having."

"It was my first show with Newfie Joe tonight," Cali Joe proclaims, as he puts his arm around him. "We were matching. We were rocking out together. We kept each other going. I could not have asked for a fucking better show."

"If you ask for some crazy fucking sex, I'm out." Newfie Joe laughs.

"If the van's a rocking..." Cali Joe jokes.

Before he can finish the sentence I receive a call from Tim. Apparently the lineup to the ferry going across the river was packed and he missed the last ferry back to Philly, so he's wondering if we're still around. I let him know where we are and, with the lot now about half empty, it's not hard to find us. There are cups and plastic and even glass all over the road, making the environment look more like a garbage dump. It's filthy. I begin picking up some beer cans to add them to our recycling bag, but there's just too many so I give up. Using a hockey stick left in the van from last tour, I start to clear the glass out of the way of our driving path.

"You can take Jason out of Canada but you can't take Canada out of Jason," Cali Joe observes.

By now, the lots have nearly cleared out, except for three or four vehicles, which are each stalled with dead batteries stemming from all of the music they were playing earlier in the day. With the road now a little freer of debris, I pull the van up to help jump-start their vehicles until they're good to go. As these vehicles leave, a police car races toward us.

"If I were you, I'd get out of here now," warns the officer.

Camden does have a reputation for being one of the roughest neighbourhoods in the country, boasting one of the highest murder rates per capita in the nation. And what seemed to be a friendly, clean, and safe area earlier in the day now resembles a filthy dark alley way with no telling what could happen. Needless to say, the officer looks to be as hard as they come, with a rugged face, arms the size of my thighs, and the body of a tank. Tim echoes his words and suggests that we leave while the police are still around. But intrigued by being in the presence of perhaps the toughest forces in the country, Newfie Joe has other ideas.

"Can we interview you on video?" he asks.

"No, and it's not safe here. It could get ugly soon," the officer replies.

"How about just a photo?" Newfie insists.

The officer looks at us as if we're crazy, and then examines the van.

"You guys travelling around to see Pearl Jam or something?" he asks

"Yes, we came from Canada," Newfie answers and explains the whole story to him while Tim grows a little more restless.

"All right, just one photo, and then get the hell out of here," says the officer cracking half a smile.

Newfie Joe leans into the police car and I snap the photo of him with one of Camden's finest. The cop tells us there are other officers out on the streets to direct us out of Camden, and that we should follow their directions. Heeding his words, we pile back into the van and leave. Sure enough, immediately after turning onto the streets, there's a lineup of police cars pointing us in the safe direction. We make it safely onto the bridge and arrive back in Philadelphia, where we drop off Tim and then park on the street near our hotel without using valet parking this time. Rachel, still not feeling well, returns to the room, while us boys head out for a second try of cheesesteak as per Cali Joe's request. Down the road we find Sonny's Famous Steaks still open, so we pop in and order a "whiz with" each, Brad without the buns.

Newfie Joe gets a smile from one of Camden's finest.

"So poutine or cheesesteak?" I ask Cali Joe as he digs deep.

"Well it's still poutine," he answers after a long thought about it, "but this is pretty damn good!"

"And now we have the vegetarian eating a cheesesteak," I announce as Newfie Joe prepares for a bite.

"I don't know about this man. I lasted six months but you're in Philly only once," he explains. "I got to get the real shit."

"So what does the Newfster think about it?" I ask as he slowly chews up the meat.

"Wow! Not bad at all."

The cheesesteaks are better than the ones from earlier in the day, and have now won our taste buds back again. We take the scenic route back to the hotel to walk off our midnight snacks before joining Rachel in the room and passing out for the night.

With most of us sprawled out on the floor, the next morning is a little slow getting going. Brad jokingly asks me if I want to go for another run and I politely decline but, to his credit, he goes out again. When he returns not much later, we're up and ready to go. We do a little bit of sightseeing and photography, driving through the city, snapping away at statues, flags, and the Rocky steps at the Art Museum. Each person then takes their turn posing on top of the van for a photo and then Cali Joe spots the giant fountain behind the van. Trying to conserve battery power in my digital camera, I begin using my video camera to snap away at photos. Standing at the fountain, I notice the Canadian flag hanging near the end of the roundabout amongst the line of flags on Ben Franklin Parkway. So I leave my video camera at the fountain and run over to the van to park underneath the Canadian Flag for a photo opportunity.

Fifteen minutes later, the others return to the van to give me some bad news. The video camera had somehow gotten swept into the fountain and is completely soaked. It does not seem functional anymore, so I leave it to dry in the heat. Another tour and another video camera breaks down. I don't have any luck with these things. Luckily Cali Joe has his video camera with him to film the progress of his surprise visit, so he offers to lend me his camera for the rest of the tour. Getting all of the sightseeing out of our system, we head back to South Philly for some more cheesesteak. However, being close to noon on a Sunday, the lineup is more than twice as long as last time, so we head to a Mexican restaurant around the corner instead.

Next, we reload on beer and ice and arrive at the Tweeter Centre before 1:00pm. With an earlier arrival, we're able to find a spot in lot 2, which looks like a polar opposite to the state it was in last night. The piles of trash and broken bottles have been swiftly cleaned up, just in time for another full day of filth to come. With the Canadian flag draped over the windshield, the van is ready for the party, and the hoards of people begin flocking over to say hi. Many are familiar faces and even more are new faces.

"Oh my god, I love your van," one girl squeals.

"Thanks. I'm Jason."

"I'm Holly. I've got two cases of beer that I need to get rid of, so you guys can totally have it."

"Sure, just bring it over whenever. We'll be here."

Sporting new Mike shirts, Newfie Joe and I begin to roam around the parking lot to meet people and show off the shirts and direct them to the CCFA tent. Back at the van, a rather large group begins to form. The younger group of kids parked beside the van looks a bit intimidated, but we soon intermix with their group with our guitars and begin jamming away together. After a few songs, they seem more comfortable and even offer us beer and hot dogs. I take another loop around the parking lot, this time with Cali Joe. When we make it to the CCFA tent, Laura says that the shirts have sold and are a big hit.

Good thing Brad still has some saved for the other shows. I notice Holly looking through the auction items and the Touring Van DVD in particular.

"Holly, what happened to the beer?" I joke.

"Oh right, I'll get it now. Is that the van?"

"Yup."

She takes us back to her vehicle where she hands over not one but two cases of beer to Cali Joe and me. "Are you sure you really want to give this away?" we ask. She confirms and says she'll help drink it with us as well. Grateful for the generosity, I tell her we've got something for her in return. She follows us back to the van and I hand over my Stone shirt as well as a Touring Van DVD.

"Oh wow, that's awesome. Can you guys sign it as well?"

Surprised by the request, Cali Joe, Newfie Joe, and I sign the DVD.

"Are you guys coming to DC?" she asks.

"Yes."

"I live like 20 minutes outside of DC. You should totally stay at my place. We've got lots of space. It's like a party house."

We exchange phone numbers and begin working on our new supply of alcohol. For the rest of the afternoon, we remain at the van, as more and more people come by to visit and more and more people end up hanging around near the van. It gets to the point where, most of the people in lot 2 are just going back and forth between the CCFA tent and the van. Among the people that stop by for a drink are Ben from Philly who was the first person that Newfie Joe met on the Canadian tour, Brandon from Vancouver who left the note on the van at the Marriott, Karol from Fort Lauderdale, Karen from Ontario, Gregg from New Jersey who asked us for weed at the scenic lookout during our drive out of Thunder Bay, and a character known as "Jimmy Da Kid". After finishing his interview with My Morning Jacket, Tim also comes out to join in the fun. Having a ball of a time, I only film a few interviews with Cali Joe's camera and suggest to Kyle that I would do more at the next show.

By the time the scorching sun begins to set on another epic tailgate party, we get our tickets organized. I give Justin's ticket, third row again, to Newfie Joe, Cali Joe and I share a pair of tickets, and Brad surprises Rachel with his spare front row for her last show with us. She's shocked and now even more excited about the show. Before heading in, I remind everyone to come back to the van after the show for a checkmark ceremony. We "hot box" the van with some random fans and then enter the venue.

The show starts with *Wash,* a song that prays for rain to cool off the heat wave we've experienced during the past few days. Over two and a half hours of pure rock 'n' roll later, the last notes of *Yellow Ledbetter* end an epic marathon show. The energy of the crowd for this show surpasses even the level of the last show and leaves no doubt in my mind that Philly fans rock harder than Boston fans – but not by much.

Rachel is happy about her front row ticket from Brad.

After the show, we run up to the front where our two Newfie friends are with Brad as well as Bobby and Ryan. It turns out that they were in the fourth row, so there was a Newfie in front row, a Newfie in the third row, and a Newfie in the fourth row.

"Newfoundland rocked the ghetto baby! And we fucking rocked the front tonight!" Newfie Joe proclaims at the van after the show.

Rachel's smile does not leave her face for the remainder of the night, thanks to Brad for the hook up. I thank her and Newfie Joe for helping me get the van down from Newfoundland to start the tour, and Cali Joe echoes my thanks for helping make this happen. To continue with the Newfoundland theme, Newfie Joe pulls out the bottle of Screech rum for Cali Joe to try.

"This will put hairs on your chest," Newfie Joe says handing it over.

"I could use some of that," Cali Joe replies before taking a big swig.

"Screech? What's that stuff?" an onlooker asks.

"Is it like *Saved By The Bell* Screech?" another wonders.

We all follow with a swig of our own, toasting Newfoundland.

"Where's that stuff from?" the same onlooker asks.

"That's fucking straight from Newfoundland baby," Newfie Joe answers. "We had a fucking great show. Did we have a great show? Wooo!"

Everyone joins in on the cheer that leads perfectly into our checkmark ceremony, done by Jason from Philly after seeing his 75th show.

"Once he's done the checkmark, of course, we have to break out the Screech!" Newfie Joe says reeking of Screech himself.

As the checkmark is applied to numerous cheers, I hand him the bottle of Screech and he takes a big swig out of it.

"That's so foul man," he claims, handing the bottle back to me.

With the ceremony complete, we say goodbye to the small crowd and roll out of the parking lot but there are no police to guide us through the streets of Camden tonight. I make a turn and immediately realize that it's the wrong direction. But still in a good mood, everyone is calm and begin to joke about our potentially dangerous situation.

"Tonight the Touring Van gets rocked in Philly," Brad laughs.

Eventually I backtrack my way back onto the main road, which takes us onto the bridge out of Camden. Disappointed with our lack of cheesesteak for lunch, we drive back out to South Philly. And even past midnight, the line for Pat's is even longer than it was during the daytime. It takes roughly 20 minutes for our turn to come up. As I order, a half drunk Newfie Joe has a hold of the video camera. "So yesterday we were eating at Geno's and they said they make the best cheesesteak…"

"Go back to Geno's then. Don't start any shit with us. If you want a cheesesteak, go to the back of the line," the guy at the counter interrupts.

Newfie Joe decides against lining up again and chooses, rather, to watch us devour our third cheesesteak in as many days. Our fix for the day is successful and delicious. Eating the best cheesesteak of the trip is the only way to close out our time in Philly.

CHAPTER 20: **I BELIEVE IN MIRACLES**

May 30, 2006 » Show 22
Washington, DC

I CAN STILL FEEL THE CHEESESTEAK inside my stomach. What a tasty one it was too. With Cali Joe flying out early, we're up by 6:00am to deliver him to the airport. It's not as an emotional goodbye as last time, because we know he'll be returning in a few days. Brad stays behind, as he's going straight to the nation's capital, the site of the next show tomorrow night. Brian lives in the area, so I presume they're scheming up some dreams with their t-shirts. Our plan is to drive up to New York for the day off and visit the Big Apple since Rachel has a flight out of there tomorrow morning. As we're driving out of the city, I receive a call from Tim. He's wondering what our plans are and then suggests we head to his house on the Jersey shore and spend the day on the beach. After a short deliberation we return to the city to pick up Tim.

Taking the Jersey Turnpike, the drive is less than two hours but the heat has intensified from the past few days, a fact that assures us that the beach is the right place to be. In the van, everyone is still recovering from the big weekend we had, so it's quiet. Pulling onto I-195, I stop for gas at a station called Wawa. Newfie Joe cracks up seeing the sign bearing the name of the same small town in Ontario, which he claims is where all hitchhikers don't want to get stuck. After pondering leaving Newfie Joe at the Wawa gas station, I decide against it and continue on to Seaside Heights. When we reach the beach, Tim brings us to his little beach bungalow, a half block away from the ocean.

However, upon entering his yard, he finds a mess. There are beer cans everywhere, garbage on the ground, and even an inflatable pool filled with water. It's similar to the carnage on display at the parking lot of Camden on a much smaller scale. Some kids, who rented the house beside his for Memorial Day, are still there, so Tim gives them shit and we help clean the yard. Today is a day to recover, and Newfie Joe and I decide not to consume any alcohol. We clear out the van of all rubbish, including two large garbage bags full of empty aluminum beer cans, which we dump in the recycling bin out front. But as soon as we finish cleaning up Tim's yard and the van, we notice a case of beer remaining in our cooler. Newfie Joe gives me a look. "Well we want to clean everything out of the van right?" I laugh as I hand him a beer.

We thank Tim again for inviting us and he's appreciative of us coming. "You get to see the real Jersey. I didn't want you guys to get the impression of New Jersey from Camden and the parking lot of the Meadowlands arena."

After a few relaxing drinks, we make our way down to the beach and, being a holiday, it's busy. The boardwalk is geared toward tourists and kids and consists of many shops, pizza stands, fair games, and even rollercoaster rides at the end of the pier. I decide to try out a slice of delicious Jersey pizza. To beat the heat, Newfie Joe caves and purchases his first pair of shorts ever in his life. The $5 entry charge into the beach is a little strange, but well worth it. Tim and I jump into the ocean instantly to do some body boarding. I ask about the surf. "Right now it's a little flat, but during winter it's good," Tim replies.

The rest of the afternoon is spent lounging on the beach, catching some shut-eye. We're woken up by Tim a short while later and says he has a surprise waiting for us – his good friend Danny is coming over to take some photos of us and the van for his article. "Danny Clinch?" I ask. He confirms that it is *the* Danny Clinch, Pearl Jam's photographer!

Soon after we return to Tim's and Danny arrives with his son Max. We chat for a bit – him asking us about our trip and us asking him about his career, which includes photographing the likes of Bruce Springsteen, Radiohead, Beastie Boys, and even Jay Z – oh, and Pearl Jam! I show him my saturated video camera and he offers a few tips on trying to restore it but concedes that it's pretty much done. Max shows us the tambourine, that Eddie Vedder signed and gave to him at the last show and the two guitar picks from Stone and Mike. I run back to the van and grab the two shirts matching the very same guitar picks that he's holding up, and hand them over to Danny and Max. He prefers the Mike shirt.

Danny Clinch and his son Max in Seaside Heights, NJ.

"When Mike gave me the pick he told me I should be on his side of the stage, because he said that's where the 'rock' is!" he explains.

From there he lists all of the bands he's seen live, nearly matching the number of bands I've seen live and he's still under 10 years old. I guess that's one advantage of having a concert photographer as your father.

For the photo session, Danny suggests I pull the van out in front of Tim's house and, for the next hour and a half, he directs us through an entire photo shoot. I give Max my digital camera to play around with, and he begins making like his dad and taking photos of our photo shoot as well, as does Tim with Newfie Joe's camera. Danny's techniques are as professional as they come, asking us to wave our Canadian flag around, play with our hockey sticks, climb on the top of the van, and basically joking around with us the whole time. We prance around like models in what could have been a very intimidating process, but he makes us feel as comfortable as if our friends are taking our photos and not Pearl Jam's photographer. Without us even knowing, he constantly snaps away on his vintage camera and fills up nearly four rolls of film.

"I wanted to get the van out to the end of the pier at sunset for the photo shoot, but I couldn't swing it," Tim explains, "So this is the next best thing."

When he's finished, we thank Danny and he informs us that he'll be in Europe in September filming the Pearl Jam shows for a movie. I let him know that I'll probably be there as well, so he says he'd look for me. As the sun goes down, Danny and his son roll out and we prepare for some barbeque steaks.

Danny Clinch snapping away as we pose for a photo session.

The rest of the night is mellow, with us chilling out with Tim and his friends and neighbours. Tim shows me some of his surfing photos as well as a few other interesting items including a photo of a tour bus, which one of his friends rode on during a Grateful Dead tour. The bus just screams hippies and The Dead. Noticing my pleasant reaction to the photo, he hands it over to me. "Here, why don't you take it and hang it in the van for good luck."

He also gives me an "Eddie Would Go" sticker from the Quicksilver Big Wave competition in Hawaii that pays tribute to legendary surfer Eddie Aikau. Eddie was fearless and would take on all waves no matter the size. But he tragically sacrificed his life, while at sea, by paddling on his own for help in an attempt to save the others on board a voyage to the Polynesian Islands. He disappeared and was never seen again. The phrase was created to dismiss any doubts that one would have if they think something was unachievable because "Eddie would go."

"I can't believe I'm giving you my Eddie Would Go sticker. But you're a fellow surfer, so you know what it's all about."

The next morning we're awakened by the sun, which seems even more intense today. While Tim finishes up a few chores, I drop Rachel off at the bus station so she can bus up to JFK airport in New York, not too far away. It's rather sad to see our first passenger leave, and I thank her for coming along and helping me deliver the van down south. She tells me she had an amazing time and thanks me for bringing her along and wishes us all luck for the rest of the trip. Back at Tim's place I add the newest decoration to the van, the "Eddie Would Go" bumper sticker. Tim comments on how perfect it looks on the van and then informs me that his friend Gord will be joining us for the ride because he has an extra ticket for the show.

"It's good to have a friend with rock show connections," Gord laughs, "plus I've never seen Pearl Jam and I've heard good things. I'm excited about getting on the road. It's going to be fun."

As Jersey as it gets, Gord takes us out for breakfast to a restaurant that also doubles as a pawn shop.

"You can't leave Jersey without trying a pork roll," he insists.

Newfie Joe stays true to his vegetarian ways and orders only eggs. I, on the other hand, have to try the pork roll and it does not disappoint. After we're done we head back to the house. Tim is ready to leave so our destination is set for the nation's capitol. The van crew for this drive includes me, Newfie Joe, Tim, and Gord. Driving back down the Jersey Turnpike seems like a drive through a blast furnace. The air is dry and extremely hot. So much so that we're forced to shed our shirts.

"Why don't you have AC in this beast?" Tim wonders.

"No need for AC in BC," I laugh.

Driving through Maryland and Virginia, the prices for highway tolls begin to increase and it starts to get annoying and expensive. The temperature of 106F doesn't help either. Five hours later, the dense highway becomes a rural city maze through the confusing DC roads. We eventually get our bearings straight and are able to find Tim's hotel, where we simply drop to the floor next to the air conditioner, cranking it full blast for an hour. Feeling fully refreshed, Newfie

Joe and I tour the city, while Tim gets to work. The Capitol Building is the first stop, followed by the Washington Monument and the Lincoln Statue. The parking lot is completely full, so I double park, while we rush in for a few photos waving the Canadian flag around. Upon returning to the van, there are three officers examining the van.

"Is this your van?" one of them asks.

"Yes sir. Sorry, I just ran in for a few minutes to take some photos."

They ask for our identification and search inside the van before letting us off the hook. We then try to drive close to the White House but with every turn we seem to drift farther and farther away and so, we abandon our quick one-hour tour of America's capital and head to the venue. Neither Newfie Joe nor I have tickets to the show yet, but we meet our next passenger for the van. Within seconds of our arrival in front of the Verizon Center, we're greeted by Aussie Ben, back all the way for another tour. He rode in the van from Toronto to St. John's and is now back to ride in the van for the rest of the first leg with us. It's always great to see another Touring Van alumni. We take Ben back to his hostel, where he grabs his belongings and loads them into the van.

"Do you guys know where you're staying tonight?" he asks.

"I think so, we'll find out in a moment," I answer.

"Oh and I need a ticket for tonight," Ben informs me.

The pre-show party is taking place at a bar just across from the Verizon Center, but driving around the block a number of times produces zero parking, so I drive back toward Tim's hotel and park in an open lot for the night. A 15-minute walk brings us to the Regional Food and Drink, where Brad is already there manning his t-shirt stand with Brian. We say hello, and I'm handed a beer by Brandon from Vancouver, who's there with his girlfriend Nicole.

"Hey I've got my spare ticket for you tonight if you want it?" Brad informs me. "It's a second row seat, and you'll be sitting with me and Brian."

"Oh really? That's great. Yeah, we all need tickets, so I'll take it. Thanks."

We wander into the bar, which is a lot mellower than that of the thousands of tailgaters out screaming before the last shows, but we still have a great time. Holly, who was in Camden, arrives soon after. This time, however, we bring her the beers. I confirm with her if it's okay to stay at her place tonight, and she says it's okay. She also has a pair of spare tickets behind the stage, which Newfie Joe and Ben snatch up right away. We're all set now.

With my seats being so close, I decide to go in early with Brad and Brian to catch My Morning Jacket. For some reason, Brian has a problem with security not allowing him to bring in his eight bottles of water, which he bought from the concession stand. We try to explain to them that he will need them during the show because there's a reason why he's known as the energy man, but he's denied. After the opening act is finished, the building begins to fill and, being close up and on the floor for the first time this tour, I begin to feel the electricity building amongst the fans. I'm dead centre in the second row, merely a metre away from the stage. I hear someone yelling at me from above, and I see Newfie Joe and Ben in the first row behind the stage. I hold up the Canadian flag that I brought in, and he gives me the devil horns rock 'n' roll sign. I hear someone else calling me from my right, and it's Tim and Gord, who are just one row behind, so we all got lucky with seats tonight.

In perfect position, there's no way this can disappoint, not that the band would let that happen anyway. Halfway through the first set, McCready gives me a point and a smile, almost as if he recognizes me from other shows when I'm not sitting so close. The intimacy that this band gives you makes it feel as if they're only playing the show for you. Meanwhile, there's another 15,000 people surrounding me going crazy. Brian does not stop jumping from the opening notes of the show and he has already finished his two bottles of water allowed in by security. Beside me is Brad, who's also trying to keep up with him. But Brian is relentless. A jam-packed first set is filled with highlights and the song *Lowlight* as well.

A slower encore set allows us to recoup our energy before the band ends the set with *Alive*. During the song, I look up and my eyes lock with Newfie Joe's. Not even paying attention to the stage anymore, we rock out with each other as if we were beside one another, jumping and fist pumping in unison. He signals for me to hold up my flag, and I signal for him to wait a moment and he knew exactly when I wanted to hold it up. We go back to rocking out, until the guitar solo, when Brad helps me hoist the giant red and white maple leaf in the centre of Pearl Jam's show in America's capital city. Newfie Joe and Ben immediately begin snapping photos of the band playing to the flag, from behind the stage. When Vedder sees the Canadian flag, he points to it and then puts his hand to his heart. We go nuts at this point, and Newfie Joes notices it as well.

Another performance of *Leash*, makes it four shows in a row now after such a long wait for it. And then the show ends with one of the regulars, *Yellow Ledbetter*, only this time Mike McCready goes right into a memorable solo of the *Star Spangled Banner* to end the song and the show. When the final notes are played, we sink back into our seats to let it all settle in. Tim comes over and tells me that was one of the best shows he's ever seen and he's followed them since doing the entire Lollapalooza tour in 1992. I turn to Brad and thank him for the great ticket and he's as humble as ever. Looking over one more time, Brian is downing his bottles of water, and looks ready to continue the show. I tell him to follow us to the van, as he'll have the honour of checking off his home city.

Amongst the parade back to the parking lot, we're joined by some new friends – Michelle and Jennifer, who are twins from Long Island – but we lose Holly in the process. By phone, I give her the location of the van and she says that she'll be there shortly. As everyone gathers around the van, Brian applies the checkmark next to Washington DC.

"It's a pleasure and honour to do this Jason. Thank you," he announces.

We present Brian with a bottle of red wine as a token of our appreciation for paying for the hotel room in Philly, and for everything else he's done, and then half of the group slowly begins to disappear, as we continue to hang out and enjoy the night. With the camera still rolling I ask Ben why he's back with us.

"Last year was one of the best trips ever. Everything about it was a dream. It was perfect," he explains. "I had no money, but you guys looked after me."

"Okay but the real question is, will there be a van waiting for us in Australia?"

"We can get a van from the airport, and maybe that airport van will take us further. But so far the Aussie touring van is not looking good," he confesses.

As the clock strikes midnight, Holly still hasn't arrived, and I'm getting a little worried. Only the twins remain in the parking lot with Newfie Joe and Ben, and I've tried calling a few times but her phone seems to be off or out of battery. I decide to look for her. Leaving the others in the parking lot drinking away, I hop into the van to begin searching for Holly. I drive around the venue, circling the area over and over again but she's nowhere to be seen. I'm driving around the streets of DC looking for someone but I have no idea of her general vicinity. It's hopeless. Hearing stories about the city, I'm more worried for her safety than anything else. I begin to backtrack our route but end up back at the venue every time with the same result – no sign of Holly. I lose more hope. After nearly 45 minutes of searching, I give up and begin to drive back to the parking lot.

I try calling one more time but again her phone isn't working. As I put my phone down, I slam on the brakes because someone is on the road waving me down. It's not Holly but a guy who introduces himself as Trey. He informs me that we met with the big group of tailgaters in Kitchener last year and tells me about how he's seen our DVD and the website, and how great it is to see the van again. I ask him if he needs a ride anywhere so he hops in.

"Wow! What an honour it is to ride in the van. Thanks a lot!" Trey says, picking up my video camera.

He asks me to explain the situation, so I tell him and then he convinces me to drive around one more time, so I do. With Trey babbling away, I'm not even paying attention, as I'm thinking of what we should do when I get back to the parking lot. Trey's chattiness slowly become nonsense as I give up again and make the turn onto the final street toward the parking lot. But then, with a little over two blocks to go, I spot Holly out of the corner of my eye! At least I think it's her. I slam on the brakes and pull over, silencing Trey. As I get out of the van, my phone rings.

"Jason? It's Holly. I'm so sorry, my phone hasn't been working, and then I lost you guys, and I'm totally lost now, and I don't know what to do," she panics.

"Just turn around," I tell her.

"What?" she asks, while turning around.

And at the instant she spots me, I can spot the joy gleaming from her.

"Oh my god, I can't believe it. It's a miracle!" she says running toward me.

"I know. I was just about to leave, until I found Trey here."

"Thank god for Trey," she laughs. "Man, I was so scared. The metro closes at midnight, so I didn't know what to do. I thought you guys might have left by now."

"We wouldn't leave you behind. But it's okay. You're here now."

Returning to the parking lot, we celebrate the miracle of finding Holly. As we pack up the van, a police car pulls up into the lot and asks us to pour out all of our beer. We do what they say and they get back into their cruiser but, instead of leaving, they stay, watching us. We figure that they're just waiting for us to drive out so that they can bust us for drinking and driving. So Newfie Joe approaches them to let them know that we're hanging around a little bit longer and going to get some food. "Okay we're cool," they mysteriously reply.

Unsure of what exactly that means, we walk down a block toward Chinatown and stop in for a midnight meal. Ben tries to use chopsticks for the first time and, although hilarious, it's not that bad of an attempt. When we finish our food, we say goodbye to the twins and head back to the van, almost an hour after our police encounter. They're no longer present. Holly directs us back to her place in Silver Spring, Maryland, where there's plenty of floor space for us to pass out on. I look up at the clock – 3:30am. When I look back down my eyes shut completely. I'm done for the day.

In the morning I'm awakened early by Holly scrambling around getting ready for work. I thank her for the hospitality, and she tells me she might be coming up to East Rutherford for the shows. She leaves and I begin waking up Newfie Joe and Ben, but it's a difficult task. I have to physically lift them up off the ground and guide them toward the van, where they immediately jump to the back onto the futon and continue sleeping. As I pull back onto the I-495 to make our way back to DC, I get a call from Brad. His ride to New York fell through and he's stuck in town, so I pick him up after picking up Tim and Gord from their hotel. Leaving DC seems a little challenging, as we spend an hour driving in circles, believing we're on the right track, when in fact we're really not making any progress at all. Tim explains that the streets in DC are rumoured to have been specifically designed to be difficult for exiting the city so that if there are ever any problems with terrorists, they wouldn't be able to escape easily. Their plan certainly works on us non-terrorists. We've been making rounds for over an hour and we're still in the city!

When we're eventually out of DC, Tim announces that after the enjoyable ride down to DC and the great show last night, he has seen enough and doesn't need to go up to New York with us anymore. I offer to drive him back home, but he says he'll arrange something without sidetracking us. Driving back through Philly, we enter the New Jersey Turnpike yet again. As I pull out of the toll booth, I hear repeated honking. I glance to my left and a car pulls up beside the van, and all I see is someone holding a piece of paper up against the window. Upon further examination, I realize it's the setlist from last night's show, and the people in the car are Mandi and Eric from Savannah, who I met tailgating in Philly. Newfie Joe, who's driving, honks back, and I quickly snap a photo. They're obviously heading up north for the final shows of the first leg.

An hour onto the highway, Tim asks for us to take an exit and drop them off at the gas station. He insists that we keep driving, but we decide to hang around until his ride arrives. When it does, we thank Tim for everything and he says that he'll call me in a day or so.

Back on the highway, we continue north to our destination, New York City. Today is supposed to be a day off from the tour, but there's a show going on in New York. Just one week ago, a small intimate show was added for VH1's Storytellers series. This special one-hour show will be aired on television later in the month and the only way to get into the show was to win a lottery form the Ten Club earlier in the week. Nobody in the van won but what the heck – we decide to check it out anyway. Continuing up to the end of the I-95, the island of Manhattan appears on our right. It's exciting! We enter via the Lincoln Tunnel and Newfie Joe immediately pulls over. "I'm not driving the van in any cities, especially New York City."

Driving through New York City is a breeze. Setup in a grid, the streets are all straight and all the traffic lights are in synch with one another to work at the same time. As for the traffic, you just have to drive with the same attitude as one of the locals and keep up with their aggression – otherwise you'll be swallowed up by cars passing you left, right, and centre. Every few blocks there are warning signs that honking the horn will cost you a fine, although I hear nothing but constant honking. As we make our way down Broadway, I see a sea of yellow, as more than half the cars on the road are taxis. With a crowd formed outside, it doesn't take long for me to find The Avalon, formerly known as the Limelight and the site for tonight's special show. I park the van directly across from the venue, which looks more like a small church.

"Wow, how small is this place?" I ask Brad.

"Not sure, but I think they only gave away 200 tickets or so."

The building definitely doesn't look big enough to hold the number of people that are waiting patiently in line outside. On the other side of the street is another group of fans, those without tickets. Some are holding signs requesting tickets, some are phoning friends for help, all are anxiously waiting for a glimmer of hope. Because this was a ticket lottery system for free tickets only, there aren't even any tickets being distributed, only a guest list on which your name must be on in order to enter. We join our fellow fans across the street and I begin filming interviews with them about their thoughts.

"I really want to get in," says one guy sitting on the curb. "Seeing them in Irving Plaza spoiled me. You want to see them in a small venue."

Another fan looks like he has lost all hope but is still sitting and waiting for a miracle to happen. I cross the street to where the crowd is lined up to check the situation. Controlling the crowd is Tim Bierman, the president of the Ten Club. He sees me and asks me if the other Tim has found us yet. I tell him how everything has worked out. He looks over at the van, smiles, and then gets back to work. Back at the van, the others are just chilling out. I inform them that the head of the Ten Club is roaming around out there.

"Did you ask him for tickets?" Newfie Joe asked.

"No, I didn't ask."

"He probably thought you had tickets already."

Looking over back at the crowd I see someone waving at me, it's Danny Clinch and he's surrounded by other media, so we wave back. Another photographer walks over to the van and asks if he can take a picture of us. He works for Sony and when he discovers that we don't have tickets for the show, he offers to help. I give him my phone number, and he'll see what can be done. There's also a cameraman filming all of the action from our side of the street. As he comes closer to the van, he smiles over at us and continues filming the crowd.

"Hey, if you want, you can stand on top of our van to film," I offer.

"Sure, that would be great."

He hands me his expensive Sony professional video camera, as he climbs up on top. For a second, I consider running with the camera, as it's probably worth 10 times the value of my malfunctioning one. When he gets into position, I pass it to him. With a clear view above all of the traffic now, he begins filming everything and even films the van and interviews Brad and me afterwards. During the interview, I hear my phone ring so, as soon as we're finished, I run back into the van to answer but I'm too late. I check the call display and it's a restricted number.

"Damn, that's probably the Sony photographer," I tell the others. "Think he'll call back?"

"Don't think so man. That was our one shot." Newfie Joe reasons.

Looking over at the ticketless fans, the group has now increased. It's not looking good. A few familiar faces come by to say hi and none of them are going to the show. Brad then spots a friend of his and heads over to the crowd to say hi. He returns 10 minutes later.

"I got a ticket," he announces.

"Really?"

"Yeah, my friend hooked me up."

"Awesome. Well go get in line."

As he returns to the crowd, the lineup begins to move and it looks like they're letting people in, ending the hopes of everyone else. We sit motionless in the van, watching the crowd dissipate with each passing second, until there's no one remaining outside the venue at all. I walk over to see if there are any last minute chances but, when the doors shut, it's over and everyone else begins to make their way home. As I return to the van, a blonde girl comes up to us.

"If you guys don't get in, then it's fucked," she claims.

"Oh it's not that bad, we'll be seeing them tomorrow night," I explain.

With no show happening for us tonight, we decide to walk the streets and explore the city. On the walk, I receive a call from Gregg, who we met at a scenic overlook just outside of Thunder Bay last year. He lives across the Hudson River in New Jersey and offers his place for us to park and camp for tonight. Without any other ideas for accommodations, we accept and I write down the directions. When I get off the phone, we're feeling a little hungry so we try out a slice of New York pizza at a place appropriately named Ben's Pizzeria. By the time we head back to the van, the doors have opened up at the venue and it looks like the show is over. Brad comes out and I ask him about the show.

"It was pretty relaxed. They played a couple of songs and Ed talked about the songs," he explained. "They answered questions that fans had. Wrapped up with *Life Wasted* and that was it. That was fun!"

"They asked my question but I fucking spelled the words wrong," another fan says coming up to us. "I'm John from the Two Feet Thick website. That's why I wanted to come see you and say hello. I can't believe you guys made it."

John had conducted an interview with me through email prior to the tour. I told him to look out for us and he did.

Leaving Manhattan, I follow the directions into Secaucus, New Jersey. After a few wrong turns, I manage to find our way to a house deep in suburban New Jersey. The neighbourhood is dark but I think we have the right one. I knock on the door, and Gregg answers. We set up camp on his enormous lawn and chat for a few moments. The night is a mellow one.

CHAPTER 21: **JERSEY HOSPITALITY**

June 1 – 3, 2006 » Show 23 & 24
East Rutherford, New Jersey

MOST OF OUR TIME during the trip thus far has been in and out of the state of New Jersey, so it's only fitting that the final two shows of the first leg are held in East Rutherford, NJ. And as with all of our other camping nights, we are up early. Stopping for breakfast, I grab the morning newspaper to check up on the progress of the hockey playoffs in the NHL. And although my team, the Philadelphia Flyers, has been long out of contention, my favourite player, Rod Brind'amour, has led his Carolina Hurricanes to the verge of making the Stanley Cup finals.

"Damn! Buffalo won the other night," I react.

"How did Edmonton do?" Newfie Joe wonders.

"They won. They're in the finals."

"Oh man, we've got to go to either Buffalo or Carolina to watch the Stanley Cup finals, man," suggests Newfie Joe.

"And the schedule will put game 1 on Monday right after the tour."

"Let's do it man."

"If Carolina wins tonight, I'm in," I answer.

"Ok deal," Newfie Joe agrees.

Back on the road, we again head toward Manhattan but take a detour to visit Liberty State Park. I spot a good view of the New York skyline near the end of the dock and stop in the middle of the road to hop out of the van and take a photo. Within seconds, a police car races toward us and the cop asks what we're doing. I say that we're just taking a photo. He tells me to move on, so we find a parking lot a little further down the road. The view isn't quite as clear, but it will have to do. From there we load up on booze and head straight to the venue. A 30-pack of Miller High Life is on special for $12, so I pick up four cases for the next few shows.

Tonight's show is at the Continental Airlines Arena, which is opposite of Giant Stadium, and in-between the two venues are massive parking lots. New Jersey certainly loves their tailgating and so do we. We pull up into a prime location, and are handed beers as we step out of the van. I set up the Canadian flag on the windshield and people begin streaming over to say hi. Cali Joe makes his return and finds us instantly. He has a ticket for me tonight but Newfie Joe and Ben are still looking. So Ben heads straight to the box office to sit in line, hoping for the release of more tickets, while Newfie Joe hangs around with us and drinks beer. Mandi and Eric come by the van, after we saw them on the highway yesterday holding up the setlist.

"So you finally get to see the van in person."

"Very nice. It looks good from behind on the highway too," Mandi says.

The tailgating today is slow getting started, especially being on a Thursday. But by late afternoon, it begins to pick up. The twins from Long Island come by to hang out with us as well, bringing their friend Eli from Queens with them. I start interviewing each of them on camera and ask about their thoughts on the Pearl Jam fan base.

"All you people, that's what it's all about," Eli answers. "Alright, no more recording."

As I put down the camera, a guy comes up to me and asks if I'm Jason, so I confirm. He hands me his phone as there's apparently a call for me. It's Holly on the other end, and she tells me that she's not able to make the shows but told the person she bought her tickets from to come find me, because I'd know what to do with them.

"I didn't know if I'd find you but I guess this is the only van that matches the description she gave me," he says.

He hands me the tickets, which have already been paid for, and I give them to Newfie Joe. Even Ben's patience pays off, as he runs back to us two hours after he had left and shows us his second row ticket. Just then, the clouds begin to roll in quickly and rain begins to pour. Some run into their vehicles while some run into the building. We pack seven into the van with me, Brad, Newfie Joe, Cali Joe, and three random people and we continue working through our case of Miller High Life.

"We're killing 30-packs like they're going out of style. We're doing a Miller High Life tour down in here," Newfie states. "You can't get drunk on these beers. Hey Miller, put some alcohol in your beers would you!"

By the time the rain stops, the sky is pitch black and it's about time to go in. Cali Joe and I are sitting on the floor 30 rows back but, when the lights dim, it doesn't matter where we are, as we proceed to rock the fuck out. The show is a good mixture of old and new songs with a few rarities thrown in ranking it near the top of the best shows so far this tour. The crowd is not as boisterous as in Camden but it's close to the level from Boston. Also being a hockey arena normally, there are live hockey scores being updated all over the building. As a keen observer on the way out of the building, I find out that Carolina has beaten Buffalo tonight to advance to the final series.

"JASE!" Newfie Joe yells out, about 50 people behind me as we leave the building. "Did you hear? Carolina won!"

"I know!!" I yell back. "We're going to the Stanley Cup finals! Wooo!"

Back at the van, there's a crowd waiting for us to continue the tailgating. As most cars try leaving the parking lot, we celebrate a fantastic show as well as the Carolina victory, even though Newfie Joe will be supporting Edmonton. Every Canadian's dream is to win the Stanley Cup, and the next best thing is to be there to watch it. We're going to Carolina for sure. From further south in Fort Lauderdale, Karol informs us that she has a spare bed in her hotel and we're welcome to crash with her if we desire. Newfie Joe takes down the information but we're not sure of our plans yet.

There's a day off tomorrow in between the East Rutherford shows, and we've all decided to head back down to Philly and try to get into a Radiohead concert. I let Gregg know that we'll probably make our way down to Philly and find a place to camp for the night. After she missed her bus, Melissa from Boston finds us and asks if we could give her and her friend a lift to Secaucus, and I agree. Eli and the twins also ask for a ride into Manhattan, and perhaps another drink at a bar, and I agree to that as well. With the parking lot nearly cleared out, we pile into the van and roll out, all nine of us. I'm driving with Cali Joe up front. Melissa and her friend are in the middle two seats while Eli is sitting on the cooler between the seats. And cramped in back are Newfie Joe, Ben, Jennifer, and Michelle. Add to the fact that there are two more giant bags for empty beer cans squished in amongst my back seat passengers, and the Touring Van has never been so full in capacity.

Pulling out of the parking lot, I hear something hit the ground. It's the plastic cover that goes over the van's moon roof and it has fallen off. I make a complete loop around into the venue lot and back out onto the highway again, to try to look for it. But not knowing where it landed, I accidentally drive over the weak piece of plastic, which shatters into pieces. So without our moon roof, we move on. Melissa directs me where to go and it all goes smoothly, until I make a wrong turn at the final corner. I pull into an empty lot to make a u-turn and, as I do, I hear sirens behind me. Shit! I stop and a police officer approaches with a flashlight, peering into the van.

"License and registration please?" he asks. I hand over my license but the paperwork is in my bag, which is in the back, so I ask Newfie Joe to look for it. He leans back and begins searching for my bag in amongst a sea of luggage but is blinded by the flashing lights directly behind us.

"Can you turn off your lights please? I can't see back here," he requests.

The officer looks at me, then into the van.

"It's okay, this will do," he tells me.

Less than five minutes later, he returns and tells me that one of my brake lights is out and advises me to drive safely, before jumping into his patrol car and speeding off. Unsure of what just occurred, I drive cautiously and safely deliver Melissa and her friend home, just a block away from the lot. That was a close one. We continue our shuttle service into Manhattan, where Newfie Joe has an urge to visit the famous CBGB's bar. However, when we arrive, it's closed. Nearly 2:00am, our passengers decide to call it a night, thank us for the ride, and we drive out of Manhattan. Back onto the I-95, I'm tired and the others are too drunk to drive, so we decide to take up Karol's offer and we pull into her hotel, just across from the venue. She's happy to see us, but we're all out cold within a few minutes.

To get a head start on rush hour, we're out the door by 7:00am after thanking Karol. Everyone continues to sleep in the van as I drive back down the Turnpike into the Philadelphia area. Pulling off the highway into Upper Darby, where Tower Theatre is located, I find a parking spot on the streets and we approach the 3000-seat venue just after 10:00am. There are already six people lined up in front of the box office waiting for tickets for the sold out show, including one who saw Radiohead's show the night before at this very same building. So we grab our place in line and wait like everyone else. Hanging out with Radiohead fans proves to be a little bit slow. Perhaps it's that time of the day, perhaps it's the band's style of music, or perhaps it's just the fact that we had less than four hours of sleep last night. Being back in Philly, we just have to get another cheesesteak, so Cali Joe and I make a food run.

After reintroducing ourselves to our "poutine" of the tour, we continue to wait patiently. At 1:00pm, the box office announces they'll release eight tickets. Newfie Joe gets a front row seat, while Cali Joe gets a seat in the balcony. I'm ninth in line and Ben is tenth in line, so we continue to wait. The Joes go on to explore the area, as we're hoping to find a laundromat, if time is available. An hour later, the lady at the box office asks if I need a ticket.

"Yes, of course I need a ticket."

"Okay, this is the last ticket in the building."

I give her $40 and she hands over a ticket in row A seat 1. I compare it to the seating chart posted on the wall, and it's in fact dead centre in the first row! This only adds to the excitement of my first Radiohead concert. As I back away from the box office, a bus pulls up onto the side of the venue. It's their tour bus and, one by one, each band member steps off and into the building. When Thom Yorke comes out, I wave at a distance and he smirks back. Ben continues to wait at the box office, while I return to the van to look for the others. When I get back, I find the Joes chilling in the van with a beer in their hands. Typical.

"I got front row centre!" I announce,

"Nice! What about Ben?" Cali Joe responds.

"Still waiting."

"Shitty! Oh, there's a laundromat right across the street."

With that, I reach into the van and grab my bag of dirty clothes from the past week and a half, deposit it into the washer, and return to continue our mini tailgating inside the van. While waiting for the washer and the dryer, it doesn't take long for us to finish the remaining beers in the van. Much to our surprise, we've managed to go through four 30-packs of beer within the last two days. A lot of it was probably given away during tailgating but we also received drinks back from people as well.

"Are we alcoholics?" I ask.

"No, they just have no alcohol in these American beers. Let's get another case for the night," Newfie Joe requests.

The Joes run to the store to buy 12 more beers, while I gather up all of the empty cans into a large garbage bag and then put my clean clothes away. We have one more drink each and then head back to the theatre, where Ben is still waiting. The lineup is even longer now with Ben at the front of it, but he's not optimistic. Just to rub it in, we ask him to take a photo of us holding our tickets in front of the venue.

"Don't worry man, you'll get in," I encourage him.

While posing for our photo, someone notices my ticket and comes up to me to ask about it. I tell him that it's front row centre and then he shows me a wad of cash and offers me $1000 for the ticket. I take a minute to think about it. That money could go a long way into helping fund this tour but, then again, I've never seen Radiohead before – this is supposed to be a great little venue – and I've got the best seat in the house. So I tell him thanks but no thanks, and that I would give it to my friend before I sell it. He's stunned. Once inside, Newfie Joe and I wander down to our seats. We're unbelievably close, as there's no gap between the barrier and the stage.

"Oh yeah, you ready for this?" Newfie Joe yells out.

"You better believe it."

After the opening act performs to a half empty theatre, the seats begin to fill up, and we head outside to see if Ben has made it in. Newfie Joes goes for a smoke and Ben is still standing at the same spot for the past eight hours. Shitty! As Radiohead's scheduled start time approaches, we head inside and the venue nears capacity. Seeing the show in this intimate setting is a nice change in dynamics from the large spectacles that we've seen so far on this trip. And our view doesn't hurt either. As the lights go black, the drums begin to beat, and three of the band members are wailing away at it. Then out of the dark, Thom Yorke appears to a roaring response from the crowd. I am so close to the singer that I could reach out and shake his hand if I wanted.

Soon after Yorke's triumphant entrance, another impressive entrance is witnessed, and out of the darkness of the crowd from behind, Newfie gets a tap on the shoulder, and it's Ben. Yes, he had sneaked his way in. So all three of us are in the front row of a sold out show that none of us had tickets for just a few hours earlier. After the end of the first song, Ben explains his miraculous appearance, as someone sold him their extra ticket when their friend didn't show up. Needless to say, it has all worked out. The show is intense, and a good complement to all the shows we've been seeing lately. At around two hours, it feels a little short in duration, but that's only because we've been spoiled with the three-hour marathons that our band puts on. When the show concludes, we meet back at the van and have a drink each in celebration of a great night. Rain begins to pour and reminds me that we lost our moon roof cover, so I quickly grab a garbage bag and some cardboard to tape over the opening at the roof of the van, stopping any water from getting in. It works perfectly.

"Where are we going to stay tonight?" Ben asks.

"Not sure, we can find a place in Philly to set up camp," I suggest.

"Alright. But since we're going to stay in Philly, let's get some cheesesteak, cause I'm starving," Cali Joe recommends.

We all agree and back into the city centre I drive, toward South Street to a place called Jim's Steaks. When we arrive, the rain has stopped so we can eat in peace, and what a piece of cheesesteak it is. Our meal is had in complete silence, as everyone is busy savouring the tasty flavours. By the end of it, we all agree that Jim's Steaks has served the best Philly cheesesteaks that we've had so far. After cleaning my hands from the grease that was my late dinner, my phone rings and it's Tim.

"Hey Jase, where are you guys at?"

"We're in Philly. We just saw Radiohead."

"You guys are crazy! How was it?"

"Absolutely amazing."

"Where are you guys staying tonight?"

"Don't know. We might find somewhere to camp."

"Why don't you come here, you remember how to get here?"

"Of course," I say looking at my watch. "We'll be there around 1:00am"

This day just keeps getting luckier, as we have now found a last minute place to stay without even asking. So back up the Jersey Turnpike we go again and then onto to I-195. Newfie Joe crawls to the back for a nap, but not before shedding his soaked clothing from the rain earlier. The others follow his lead as well, and suddenly the drive is silent again, until our new roof begins blowing off and flapping around. Driving along at highway speeds, the garbage bag covering the roof begins to peel off, little by little. And as we pull onto the Garden State Parkway, the wind blowing through the gap has become increasingly annoying, so I pull over onto the shoulder.

"What's going on?" Cali Joe wonders, waking up.

"Just fixing the roof," I answer.

As I climb on top of the van to reapply more hockey tape, Cali Joe takes advantage of the pit stop and relieves himself in the bushes. When it looks to be sealed again, I jump back down from the roof, look up, and see a police trooper pulling in behind us. What now? I wait for the policemen to come out of their vehicle. There are two of them but one looks younger, as if he's being trained as a rookie.

"What are you guys doing?" one of them asks.

"I just had to pull over to fix my roof because it was leaking," I answer.

And then the van door slides open and a shirtless Newfie Joe has awakened and comes out, looking as if he hadn't slept in a week.

"What's the deal with him?" they ask.

"Oh he just woke up. He was taking a nap."

"Where did you come from?"

"We were at a concert in Philadelphia."

"And where are you guys heading tonight?"

"We're just driving to a friend's place in Seaside Heights, where we'll be spending the night."

"How many of you are there?"

"Four of us."

"Where's the fourth?"

"He's just over by the bushes taking a leak."

When Cali Joe returns, they ask us for identification and, without looking at them, they continue drilling us with questions to find out where we come from, what we do, and why we're here.

"So you're telling me that you're from BC, he's from Newfoundland, he's from California, and he's from Australia?"

"Yes sir. It says so on our IDs"

"Do you mind if we search the van?"

"No, not at all."

With the younger officer standing by watching us, the senior one enters the van and investigates our items. Ten minutes later he returns.

"Guys this van reeks of booze and there are like 100 beer cans in there."

"Those are empty cans that we're recycling. The smell is from the cans."

"You guys can't be driving around drinking inside of the van."

"The beer was drunk before concerts during the last two days when we were tailgating. We weren't drinking just now, everyone was sleeping."

The older officer asks me to walk in a straight line, touch my nose with both hands, and puts me through other tests.

"I can tell that you're not drunk but your eyes are red."

"I'm just tired."

He puts me through another series of tests and shines the flashlight into my eyes, before telling me that I passed.

"I don't know what you're on, but I can take you down to the station to put you through more tests."

"I'm not on anything, I'm just tired. And we're trying to get to our friend's place to sleep."

"Okay, we'll be right back."

We wait patiently, hoping our string of luck will continue. He returns 15 minutes later and presents me with a ticket that summons me to pay a fine for having open or unsealed alcohol in the vehicle. I ask him how much the fine is, and he tells me to call the phone number in the back to set up a time for the court hearing. I ask him if I can just pay it with cash directly to him but he says no and then he tells us to have a nice night. Court hearing? This is complete bullshit! The tiredness that had caused my eyes to look red has now gone away and it's now my anger that makes them red, even more so than before. We get back on the road, and for the next 20 minutes there's nothing but cursing and outrage inside of the van, until we reach Tim's place. I pull up into the driveway at around 3:00am and Tim, seeing our headlights, comes running out.

"I was so worried about you guys? What took so long?"

I explain to him what had transpired.

"Fucking typical Jersey cops. That is complete utter bullshit! Where did it happen?"

"On the Garden State Parkway."

"Of course it did. Were there two cops together?"

"Yes."

"Fuckers, I probably went to school with those bastards too."

"Jersey cops suck shit! They'll try to get you all the time. They're the worst."

Tim then proceeds to call the number on the ticket to find out more information and then he calls his friend who's a lawyer and deals with these cases in Jersey all the time, all this at 3:30am.

"I think you're kind of fucked. My buddy says you'll need to go to court to pay any fine. It's a stupid system."

"I can't just call in and pay, or pay online?"

"Nope, you need to go to court to plead your case, and then they'll determine the amount. It could be $500 or $600."

"What? That's ridiculous."

"Yeah, I know."

In the morning, my anger is no longer as intense and we actually manage to acquire some rest after a rough night. We decide to forget about the incident and enjoy our time while we can and then deal with it later. Today is the last show of the first leg and, with it, the end of the East Coast part of the US tour. To finish it up in style, we head back up to East Rutherford early to check out the pre-show party, organized by Chris and Mic. Another reason why we're arriving early is because none of us have tickets for this show yet, so we need to find four tickets. At the bar, I receive a call.

"Hi is this Jason?" the voice asks. I confirm. "My name is Dana, I came up to you guys at the Storytellers show and said it was all fucked that you guys didn't get in?"

"Ah right, I remember you."

"Anyway, when I heard you guys need tickets for the show I tried finding you guys and someone gave me your contact on the Pearl Jam board," she explains. "I've got my spare ticket for you if you need it."

"Really? Yes, we need like four tickets."

"Do you guys just show up at shows with no tickets or something? Is that what you guys do?"

"Sometimes," I laugh. "I believe that everything will usually work out."

With that, we have one ticket settled for the show, so we head to the venue to get a decent spot for the tailgate. As I pull in, we're greeted by a crowd and one of them asks if we need any tickets for the show, as he has three. How perfect. We arrange to purchase the tickets and everything is set for the show, so now we can just enjoy ourselves for the rest of the day. Pulling out the hockey sticks, we teach our Australian friend how to play our Canadian game.

"We're going to the Stanley Cup next week, baby!" Newfie Joe announces.

"We should pull the van up to Hockey Night in Canada," I suggest.

"Yeah! Don Cherry has to see the van."

When he's not passing the ball with the hockey stick, Ben is also jamming on his guitar with Cali Joe, reliving the moment when they first met back in Seattle last year. And much like the Camden tailgating, the party is revolving around the van with a group of about 20 hanging around us. Forgetting about the troubles from last night, I'm relaxed enough to film a number of interviews with various fans. One fan, whom I've seen at the front of every show, stops by.

"Hello, I'm Brian from Mammoth Lakes, CA."

"And you're doing the entire US Pearl Jam tour?"

"The entire tour."

He then goes on to explain that it's been too much, and they're scrapping the idea of doing 25 more Dave Matthews Bands show after the Gorge show.

"I'm tired of sleeping at Wal-Mart parking lots and getting woken up by cops."

I ask him to compare Pearl Jam fans to Dave Matthews fans and he thinks they're similar, but Pearl Jam fans are more hardcore whereas Dave Matthews fans have just joined a new craze that has swept the nation. He believes that the Pearl Jam show in Grand Rapids, MI was the best show of the tour thus far, because the energy was unmatched due to a mix up with the order of the fan club tickets causing new members to sit closer to the stage than older members.

"This is a message to Ten Club, if this ever gets to them," Brian says to my camera. "You should stop giving the low number fan club members really good seats. It's cool that they get to see the front every time. But they've lost their energy, they don't rock out anymore and there needs to be that energy. That's why you guys had so much fun at Grand Rapids. So do that at every show and you'll love it."

After our lengthy interview, he donates a No Code sticker to the van and affixes it himself. Brad arrives at this point and asks if I could call Gregg, because he wants to give his spare second row ticket to him. So I make the call and ask Gregg to come by the van before the show for a little surprise. When he does a short while later, I present him with a Mike shirt and tell him it's not the only surprise, as Brad hands over the ticket for the show. Gregg is overjoyed and thanks us for everything, then shares a few drinks with us.

As I refill our cooler in the van, someone calls out to me. It's Dana. She's wearing a Pearl Jam bucket hat. Being in the giving mood, I reach into my bag and give her my Pearl Jam bucket hat, which I hardly ever wear. She thanks me with a six-pack of Brooklyn Lager. "Are you from Brooklyn?" I ask.

"Is it that obvious?" she laughs.

When it feels about right, we enter the venue at our normal time of 8:45pm, just before the band takes the stage. Dana's seats are great, about 10 rows back side stage and the show that transpires is simply incredible. With the aisle to our side, we have enough room to rock out hard. The show includes rare performances of *Rats, Hard To Imagine*, and *Don't Give Me No Lip*. When the band comes back for their second encore they play as if they don't want the show or the tour to end, playing close to 10 more songs. After the show, Newfie Joe shows us the piece of paper he got from one of Pearl Jam's security personnel.

Dana bringing Brooklyn to us.

"I went up and told him that this might be my last show for a long time, so he reached into his pocket and gave me tonight's setlist," he explains.

Looking at the setlist, the already incredible show could have even been better as they crossed off the song *It's Ok*, an extended tag that's only rarely added for the song *Daughter*. This cover has only been played less than 15 times in their history but it's one of the favourites for many fans, so when it happens, it's special. Tonight, it didn't happen but it was still special.

Back at the van, nearly everyone we've met on this tour is waiting for us. Dana asks where we're staying tonight but I'm not sure, so she invites us over to Brooklyn to stay with her. Gregg comes up to me with a big smile and thanks me for everything. "This was a night to remember. I was sitting second row thanks to my friend Brad."

"It was an honour Gregg," Brad replies.

"Thank you. It was an honour to see you guys, in my backyard instead of in your country like last time."

"Here's the hockey tape, you've got the checkmark tonight," I inform him.

"Wow! It's an honour to do the checkmark," he states, applying the checkmark to Jersey signifying the end of the first leg, with everyone's camera flashing like paparazzi.

"Now the real honour comes. Now you get to have a shot of Newfie Screech," Newfie Joe cuts in handing over the bottle.

"Oh, that's screech baby," he describes after a taste. "I feel blessed. The circle's complete now. I hope we live to do it again."

As people leave, they say their goodbyes and wish us luck for the rest of the tour. Some of them will be back later on in the tour, as most will be at the Gorge. Brad assures me he'll see me on the West Coast, and I have no doubt of that. Still hanging around and not wanting the night to end, eventually it's just Dana, Philly Ben and the twins who remain in the parking lot with us, with Aussie Ben rummaging through the parking lot and finding a complete barbeque grill to bring back for us to start a campfire. Looking around, what was a completely full lot is now completely empty, with the exception of another van parked behind ours, with its owner sleeping in the driver seat.

"Hey we got some fans coming over to join the campfire," I say as a familiar face approaches the van. It's Bowman, who, in Ottawa last year, told us that he did the world tour in 2003.

"Oh, I'm not a fan. I just came to check it out. How's your trip going this time?" he asks.

Apparently he has been working with the merchandise staff for the tour and will be continuing on to the European tour as well. So I'll be seeing him again. Philly Ben leaves us at this point, but Aussie Ben returns from his continuing scavenger hunt through the parking lot to bring back a wealth of goods.

"Where did you find all this stuff Ben?" I ask.

"The burgers and the hot dogs I got from a bag over there," he points to a spot in the parking lot where there used to be cars a few hours ago. "The buns and the plates were in a bag over there," he says, pointing to another spot.

"Where did you get this nice bowl from?" I inquire.

"Where did the grill come from?" Cali Joe follows.

Ben also presents us with utensils and condiments for a full-on barbeque to feed our hungry stomachs, including the rather interesting hippie-looking bowl, which Dana decides to keep.

"We're set. We'll just pitch a tent and we'll feed for a week," Ben proclaims.

Ben and Dana perform for our sleeping friend after the second East Rutherford show.

After our feed, the guitar jams continue and we decide to have a little fun with the only other guy remaining in the parking lot. He's still asleep in the van behind ours. We begin playing and singing songs to him, standing beside his window. He does not even flinch. Our setlist consists of two songs, *Smile* and *In My Tree*. To show our appreciation for being such a great sport when he wakes up, Newfie Joe writes a note on a cardboard sign: "Thanks for the memories bro." At around 3:30am, we drive into Manhattan to drop off the twins, and then Dana leads us back to her place in Brooklyn, where we hang out for an hour before jumping back in the van. Cali Joe flies out at 7:00am, so it looks like I won't be getting any sleep tonight either. The others say their goodbyes and stay at the house to sleep, while Dana leads us to the airport to drop off Cali Joe. He'll be back for the West Coast, so it's a casual goodbye again. This is starting to become routine. We drive back to Dana's place, where I begin my hibernation before the next show, one month from now.

CHAPTER 22: **BETWEEN LEGS**

June 4 – 30, 2006
The South

PLANS ARE GREAT TO MAKE to give yourself a gauge of what's to come but, in order to maximally enhance your travels, you must be flexible and able to move away from plans and adjust for the unexpected. With the end of the phenomenal first leg of the US tour, my plan was to head down south to Florida to meet a friend from Vancouver on vacation, and then settle in Atlanta, GA to stay with Kyle, who has arranged some under-the-table work for me, so that I can recover some cash during the time off. But with our sudden decision to check out the Stanley Cup finals in Carolina, our plans have already slightly changed. Newfie Joe has also extended his trip and who knows what I'll have to do for that ridiculous ticket for recycling from Jersey.

After a full day of sleep at Dana's place, we decide that Raleigh, NC is too far to drive in a day, so we give the first game of the series a miss to do some sightseeing around New York City, opting to head down for the second game on June 7 instead. Dana leads the remaining members of the van (me, Newfie Joe, and Ben) down to the docks in Brooklyn for a view of the Statue of Liberty. We take the best photos we can and then hop back into the van and pull out. As I'm backing out of the parking spot, I see another car backing out and heading toward us, so I stop to wait for it to manoeuvre around me. But she doesn't stop and ends up running into the back of the van! We all get out to check if she's all right and she is, but she doesn't seem to be all there. A little woozy, she looks a bit drunk, in fact. Our van has minimal damage – only a dent on the back door, creating a small gap between the door and the top of the van – but it's still something worth noting. So I take down her insurance information and file a report of the incident with a police officer that's roaming around, but we have no witnesses.

I drop Dana off and we continue our sightseeing around the Big Apple.

Driving through Manhattan traffic, I get a honk from the car to my left. I look over and the guy is holding his laptop up against the window to show us something. Looking closer at it, I see our Touring Van website loaded up on his screen. He had seen the website domain name on the back of the van, while we were stuck in traffic, and decided to punch it into his laptop. He tells us that he drives all over the country as well and welcomes us to New York. Approaching the Empire State Building, I pull over to the side for a minute and snap a photo of the famous building up close. Within seconds of my stopping, a police officer runs toward the van and asks to see my identification before asking us to leave. Man, the enforcement is tight up here!

We drive further down the street to visit Tom's Restaurant, the famous restaurant used in the *Seinfeld* series. Their burgers, shakes and banana splits are tasty. At this point, we drop Ben off at the bus station, where he'll continue on his trip of concerts throughout America that will include Neil Young and the Foo Fighters. He plans to meet up with us at the Gorge though. Driving past the CBS studios, we stop for a photo of the van at David Letterman's marquee and then, around the corner, we pay the Hello Deli a visit. I give Rupert Gee a McCready shirt and he comes outside to see the van, even allowing us to take a photo with me and the van, holding up his new gift. "Are you guys with Pearl Jam?" he asks. I tell him no, but we are touring "with" them.

Down the road we find a parking lot and, as I pull in, I receive a call from Tim checking in on us to ask a few more questions for his article. When we finish the interview he asks what my plans are in between tour legs and I let him know that I'm heading south. He says that he'll be working at the annual Bonnaroo Music Festival in Tennessee in a few weeks and inquires about my interest in helping him out backstage for some extra cash. I tell him that I'd absolutely think about it and will let him know, pending the outcome of my court case.

On foot now, Newfie Joe and I return to the Empire State Building, only to find a one-hour lineup. Short on time, we go to the Rockefeller Plaza Building instead and are able to see the magnificent view of the city from the top. Afterwards, we walk through Central Park, which has more fence than park. We continue exploring through Times Square until nighttime and then return to Dana's place to watch the hockey game on television. Much to Newfie Joe's displeasure, Carolina wins the first game 5-4.

The next day we take the subway back into town with Dana's guidance, and head to the one place left on our list of things to see in New York, CBGB's. Entering this famous rock bar is like a dream for Newfie Joe and, with a big grin on his face, he purchases a souvenir t-shirt. This venue will be completely shut down soon, so it's exciting to see it before it goes. Pretty much every band that has ever played New York has played this place, and we stay for tonight's International Noise Conspiracy performance. The inside appears rather long in length but is quite small in size, in fact. The show is loud and seeing the stage is difficult from any vantage point, but we're watching a show at CBGB's and that's all we care about. After the show, we drop Dana off at home, thank her for her hospitality, and I tell her to expect a call from me soon. With game two of the Stanley Cup finals being held the day after tomorrow in Raleigh, NC, we decide to make a head start on the 10-hour drive tonight. But an hour into it, my drowsiness gets the best of me and I'm forced to pull into a rest stop off the Jersey Turnpike for the night.

The next morning we make a stop in South Philly for lunch, but we resist our urge for cheesesteak and instead go back to the delicious Mexican restaurant around the corner. We pick up a case of beer and continue our drive south. Driving by DC, I give Holly a call to see if she's around for a quick visit, but there's no answer so I leave a message. We visit Brian in Alexandria, VA to drop off some posters that Brad had left in the van for him, and then continue heading south into foreign territory. The fast pace of the northeast slowly mellows out and the drive becomes more relaxed. As we approach Richmond, VA, I receive a return call from Holly. She asks if we want to come back to visit and crash at her place for the night, so, without much discussion, we make the two-hour detour back to Silver Spring, MD.

When we arrive at Holly's place, she already has a full plate of shrimp cocktail setup along with a full rack of wine waiting for us. Now that's hospitality! The night is spent chilling on the deck, sipping on wine and sharing stories. It's relaxing and Newfie Joe and I are thoroughly enjoying it all, as the detour back was definitely worth the effort. Holly and I agree that we wouldn't be here right now if I hadn't miraculously found her on the streets after the DC show. Newfie Joe shows her the setlist from the last show, and her eyes just light up at the sight of *Daughter/It's Ok*. "That's my absolute favourite song! Did they play it?"

"Nope, it was crossed off."

"Why won't they just play it already? They know that's what everyone wants to hear." She heads inside to put on Pearl Jam's *Touring Band* DVD and skips through it all until the performance of *Daughter/It's Ok*. She puts it on repeat, comes back outside, and we continue our conversation.

Being a hair stylist, Holly expresses her desire to colour my hair again and reform the Mohawk for me. I accept her request immediately, so she goes inside to grab her equipment, sets up a stool in the middle of the deck and starts applying bleach to the top part of my hair until I'm completely blonde.

"You look beautiful," she laughs.

While we wait for the bleach to set in, we continue sipping wine and eating shrimp. For more than half an hour the bleach stings my scalp like needles poking into it, but my level of intoxication allows me to cope with the pain and it gets me through it. When it's time, Holly brings me into the bathtub and rinses the bleach off, to free me of my misery. With a white towel, she begins to dry my hair, covering my face in the process. Then something sparks inside of me. As she finishes and removes the towel from my face, her loving smile appears directly in front of mine and I kiss her.

"What? Where did that come from?" she asks before leaning in to return the kiss.

Continuing to lock lips, my white towel drops and with the water still running, we lose ourselves to each other. Her lips taste sweet. Maybe it's the wine I'm tasting or the cocktail sauce, or maybe it's just her. And even though I'm not wearing a shirt and the air temperature feels hot, she feels even warmer. We stop momentarily and nothing is said, only smiles, then our tongues meet again. "We have to finish your hair first," she reminds me.

She grabs my hand and leads me back to the porch, where I take my seat again. Meanwhile, a buzzed Newfie Joe is rocking out hard to *It's Ok*, which is still running on repeat on the television. He runs back to the van to grab the video camera and records my hair makeover. With her favourite song blasting, Holly pumps her fists in the air and dances around me while turning my blonde hair into red. Every minute or so, she leans in for a kiss until telling me that she's finished. Making out certainly helps kill time, while my hair absorbs the brightness of the red dye and, before I know it, we make our trip back to the bathtub for another rinse. Giving our mouths a rest, we return back to the living room to find Newfie Joe lying on the ground almost in meditation to the song that just won't end. We leave him alone and begin cleaning up everything, before heading to the bedroom.

"I can't sleep with you," she informs me.

"It's okay. We can just cuddle."

For another hour, we continue our shenanigans until we're out of energy and naturally fall asleep, with *It's Ok* still playing on the television outside. In the morning, Holly's running around again wakes me up. She's getting ready for work, but has spent some time making sandwiches and gathering snacks for us to hit the road. She hands the big black bag full of goodies over to me and gives me a kiss goodbye on her way out.

"Call me when you guys get to the game?"

"For sure."

In the living room, music is no longer playing, and Newfie Joe is sleeping peacefully. I lie on the couch, going over what happened the night before, and remember everything was perfect. As Newfie Joe awakens, we clean up and hit the road, five hours to our destination. Not much is said during the drive, as Newfie Joe continues to pound away the beers. This is his last night of the trip. I ask him what he's going to do. He says he's not sure. "I think I'll take a bus up to Toronto, get some cash, and fly to Calgary to look for work."

Arriving in Raleigh mid-afternoon, we're able to quickly find the RBC Center. The parking lot is jam-packed and we finally see some parking near the end that is surrounded by Edmonton Oilers jerseys.

"That BC plate isn't fake, is it?" one of them asks.

"Nope, we drove from Vancouver," I answer.

"Wow, that's hardcore. We drove down from Toronto," they answer.

I tell them that we didn't do the drive specifically for this, but we just happened to be in the area already. Then Newfie Joe reveals that I'm a Carolina fan and they give me shit for it, wondering how someone from Vancouver could cheer for Carolina and not a Canadian team. I explain to them about Rod Brind'amour being my favourite player and that I'm a true hockey fan who wouldn't cheer for a team just because they're from Canada. They introduce us to some fans who flew in from Edmonton for the game because the secondary market prices for the next games in Edmonton are close to $3000 a ticket, so it's actually cheaper for them to fly into Raliegh and buy a ticket for the game here than to buy one back home. The market for hockey in Carolina is regarded as one of the worst in the league, so we figured that prices would not be too expensive for us.

"What's your budget?" I ask Newfie Joe.

"I can spend about $250. That should leave me with enough for the bus ride back to Canada."

Asking around nearby we find a fan selling a pair tickets, 20 rows behind the goal, for $275 apiece. Newfie Joe gives me the okay and we've just scored ourselves Stanley Cup tickets, a dream for both of us! We celebrate by finishing off all the remaining drinks in the van. Newfie Joe admits that this will be his first time attending a live hockey game. "You ask what kind of Canadian I am for not cheering for Edmonton and here you are, never even been to a live game before? What kind of Canadian are you?" I laugh.

I call Holly to let her know that we've arrived and found tickets to the game, so she wishes my team luck for the game. Luck, however, is not required, as Carolina ends up winning 5-0 to take a commanding lead of 2 games to 0 in the best of 7 series. Newfie Joe is choked but still stoked about being at the Stanley Cup. We never did find Don Cherry from CBC but we're satisfied with how the day turned out. Well, at least I am. After the game, and not too far from the arena, we set up camp for the night in a parking lot just off the highway. Newfie Joe rummages through his belongings and discovers he is out of money and has no idea how he'll get home. I tell him to worry about it tomorrow.

In the morning, Newfie Joe still has no money, so we drive into the city to try and find his bank, the only place he'll be able to get cash. Unfortunately, there's no HSBC so I offer to pay for his ticket, but for some reason I'm unable to exchange any cash at my own bank. We return to the van wondering what to do. Newfie Joe decides to go through his stuff (once again) and this time finds a wad of cash tucked away at the bottom of his bag – his $100 emergency fund. It is just enough to purchase his bus ticket home, signalling the end of his trip.

"It's been crazy," he reflects. "Coming to America, I didn't know how it was all going to go down, but it's been a trip and a half, I've got to say."

"Highlights? Lowlights?" I continue with the interview.

"I got a couple of lowlights. Jersey cops suck ass. In general, the police in the Northeast are fucking hard. I've never had this much hassle with cops before. But we're alright. Overall, I'm glad I came down."

"Couldn't have done it without you," I tell him.

"I hope I get a chance to do this again. This is the first proper road trip I've ever done. Obviously I'm usually hitchhiking and I had a great time. I LOVE THE VAN!!! To everyone that sees this video, thank you for all the help that we've had down here. All the Pearl Jam fans are fantastic people, it goes without saying. And it's been good."

"It's been a blast having you here."

"We'll see where we meet up again, maybe West Coast, maybe England."

"It doesn't look possible but I have a funny feeling and things have worked out so far for us."

"Everything works out for a reason."

As Newfie Joe boards his bus for Canada, I'm left alone for the first time in two weeks. I take my loneliness even further south and spend the next few days making my way down to Miami. Through South Carolina into Georgia I continue to drive until I reach Florida. I spend half of a day at Daytona Beach in the ocean and also take care of some business.

I first call Kyle in Atlanta, and give him the news that I will not be in Atlanta anytime soon because I need to take care of some things. I'll let him know when I make it to his place, but for now we set our plans to leave for the second leg of the tour on June 30. He'll be bringing his friends along across the country in the van with me.

I then call the number on the police ticket from Jersey, and they give me my choice of dates for the court hearing. June 27 is the first one and actually fits into my schedule, so that's the date I choose. I again ask if it's possible to just pay online or over the phone, as I'm in Florida, but she denies my request and states that I must return to New Jersey for the hearing. Fuming from that unproductive call, I next contact my insurance company back home to report my accident from New York. They say that unless I have witnesses, it will be my word against the other driver's, so it will most likely be a 50/50 outcome due to the fact that our backs were facing each other. I'm not impressed with this assessment but I refuse to pay a single penny to fix the damage because it still opens and closes fine, so it would only be for aesthetics. It's still rather annoying though. So with that news I try to cheer myself up by calling Holly before jumping back into the ocean again.

The next few days are spent living out of the van in Miami and Key West – even reaching mile 0 at the southern most point of the United States. I explore, lounge on the beach – making use of the beach shower facilities – and then find a safe place to park the van to sleep for the night. I meet some other people but still feel lonely without everyone's presence, especially Holly's. She and I talk daily on the phone as she updates me on how the Hurricanes are doing in the Stanley Cup, even though she knows nothing about hockey. They now lead the series 3 games to 1 and are one win away from the cup.

I next head up to Orlando, where my friends from Vancouver, Sean and Susan, are flying in for vacation. They have a resort booked and have invited me to come join them while I'm in the area, so I make my way back north. On my way up, I drive through Kissimmee, FL and, intrigued by the name on the sign, I take a photo of it and send it to Holly. Even with us exploring Disney World with Sean and Susan and then lounging around at Cocoa Beach, my mind is totally out of it. I can't stop thinking about her. Whenever my friends want to go out, I'd stay back at the resort and chat to Holly online. It's almost as if my friends aren't even there with me.

During this time, Edmonton has somehow found a way to win two straight games to force a "do or die" seventh and deciding game to take place in Carolina on Monday. The winner of this sudden death game will take the Stanley Cup Championship. With that set, I let Tim know that I won't be able to help him at the Bonnaroo Festival unfortunately but thank him for his offer.

I drop off my friends at the airport Sunday afternoon and I make my way back up north to Raleigh, NC to try my luck at game 7 tickets. As I pass by Savannah, I hear a thump from the back of the van. The tire has blown. I replace it with the spare and rush out the first exit I see, hoping to find a tire shop. I finally find one just as the store is closing. After making them aware of my desires to try and make the hockey game tomorrow, the shop agrees to open up for another 15 minutes to replace and rotate the van's tires.

Arriving into Raleigh late in the night, I rest for the night in the same parking lot that we slept at after game 2. I make my way over to join the box office lineup before 9:00am the next morning and sit in line all day. The people at the box office continually tell us that there are no more tickets available, so the line that had grown up to 50 people slowly dissolves as late afternoon approaches. But this is game 7 of the Stanley Cup finals, the Mother of all hockey games, and I get a chance to watch Brind'amour hoist the cup. I'd be kicking myself if I didn't try my hardest to get in. A reporter from ABC comes by the lineup and begins interviewing us about the ticket situation, and why we're here with no tickets. Somehow, our interview turns into why I'm in the US to begin with, so I talk about the Pearl Jam tour and the van. Off air, the reporter asks if I know anything about Pearl Jam playing Southern America because his wife is a really big fan. I tell him that I'm clueless about any future shows.

As the afternoon comes to an end, the line has dwindled further, and I'm sixth in line now with the four Canadians in front of me. They begin to grow sceptical also and even contemplate leaving, but I reassure them of our chances. And at 5:00pm, an NHL official announces to us that there will be 20 more tickets released for sale. Our patience has paid off. When it's my turn at the ticket window, I'm able to buy a centre ice ticket with the four Canadians in the premiere club seats for the face value of $175, a bargain for this historic game. "These must be leftover VIP tickets!!" my brain screams. Stoked about the prospects for tonight, I buy a Hurricanes shirt at the merchandise store and then head out to enjoy the festivities that are occurring outside the arena. I check up on the van and find a group of people examining it. The tailgaters parked beside me give me food and drinks and ask about the van. I'm finally hanging out with Hurricane fans for once. As game time approaches, someone approaches and informs me that he just saw me on the ABC news before coming out. He recognizes my hair and the story about the van, which has gotten just as much attention as the game itself.

When it's game time, I head into the building and take my seat next to the Canadians, behind a group of people dressed in suits who are standing motionlessly. A few minutes later, more men in suits fill the row and in the middle of this group is none other than Gary Bettman, the commissioner of the NHL. I can't believe my eyes, and he's sitting in the row in front of me. A few minutes later, there's a bigger commotion for an entrance but he's not wearing a suit. It's actor Cuba Gooding Jr., and he's sitting in my row just four seats over. Wow! What a game already and it hasn't even started yet. I grab one of the commemorative towels given out earlier and begin waving them around madly like everyone else in the over-capacity crowd. We rise for the national anthems and remain standing for the entire game, something I've never seen before.

For over two hours, instead of sitting on the edge of our seats, we're standing on the edge of our rows, not even thinking about sitting down. But it's game 7 after all, and I'm used to standing for this length of time fairly regularly. The standing turns to jumping for joy in a rain of confetti when the game ends with Carolina winning 3-1. The commissioner, Gary Bettman, leaves his seat in front of us and proceeds onto the ice to present the Stanley Cup to the captain of the Hurricanes, my man, Rod Brind'amour. I nearly shed a tear at this point while the exuberant crowd cheers on.

Back at the parking lot, there's jubilation amongst everyone and, for a city and state that normally only supports college basketball, hockey is number one tonight.

With nothing but excitement running through my blood, I hit the road and begin to drive with no direction in mind. Off to the side I see the sign for I-95 and, within a split second, I decide to take it and head north toward more excitement. I'm going back to Silver Spring, MD to see Holly and she doesn't know it. Driving nonstop, I arrive at her place at 4:30am and sneak in. I knock on the door to her room, and she answers with no clue of what's going on.

"What?" she mumbles cluelessly.

Then she realizes it's me and freaks out. Without asking any questions, we continue what we had started last time until she has to leave for work. Later, during her hour break, Holly comes back home to see me and I'm still lying in her bed, so she lies down next to me. I'm glad to see her and I'm glad to be here, as my instincts have driven me back north. The loneliness I was feeling all week has gone away. I call Kyle to tell him that I won't be making it down to Atlanta until I'm supposed to pick them up at the end of the month. I also notify him that I've bought a new video camera on eBay that will be sent to his house for me.

At game 7 of the Stanley Cup finals to cheer on the Carolina Hurricanes against the Edmonton Oilers.

For the next week, while Holly is at work, I'm able to catch up on sleep, check emails, and service the van to get it ready for the next leg of the tour. While she's off of work, I spend every second with her and it's still not enough time. After a little convincing, Holly decides to join me on the second leg of the tour, flying to Denver to drive to Las Vegas with me. I was originally going to be driving that connection solo but I won't have to now. The week goes by swiftly with my court date fast approaching. I call Dana to let her know I'm coming back up to the area and she invites me to stay at her place again. To look as professional as possible, I borrow Holly's roommate's suit, which is a size too big for me, and Holly re-colours my hair to a dark brown, which isn't as flashy as the bright red.

The night before the court date, I arrive in Brooklyn, where Dana attempts to unjangle my nerves by taking me out to rock 'n' roll karaoke. Located at the tiny basement of a grocery store, the rock 'n' roll karaoke allows the singer to have the pleasure of singing in front of a live band, made up of local musicians performing cover music. They have an entire book of songs to chose from, where you get to feel like a rock star. Being a very popular event every Monday, the signup sheet is completely full before we even arrive. But watching their performances is still enjoyable and completely relaxes me as I prepare for court.

Early next morning, I head out to the county of Millstone in New Jersey and follow the directions through this small town. I get dressed up in the van and enter the courthouse. The building is rather small, consisting of a main court area as well as a few smaller offices. There are about 15 people holding a piece of paper resembling my ticket. Lining up for registration, I notice that everyone knows each other, including the cops.

"What did we get you on this time Jim?" I hear one of the officers asking someone. "What about you Tony?"

It's as if this is a regular occurrence amongst the locals or maybe the cops just enjoy bringing people to court. When it's my turn to register, I'm led into one of the offices where the prosecutor greets me. He reads over the file, and then explains the process to me. Apparently everyone's cases will be held in court at the same time. If I plead guilty, I'll just have to make it official in court and then pay the fine out front before I'm free to go. But if I plead not guilty, they'll put my case to the side and then run a trial for it after all the pleas are made. I plead not guilty. He asks me if I'm sure and basically says that I have no chance of winning.

"I was recycling those cans sir. No one was drinking in the van," I inform him.

"The charge is not for drinking while driving, it's for having open or unsealed alcohol in the vehicle," he explains. "Did the cans have any residue?"

"Yes probably."

"Then technically there was alcohol inside of it. This is what's going to be argued. What I can do is lower the fine to the minimum amount."

"How much is that?"

"$330."

"Okay, let's just get this over with."

I leave the office and enter the courthouse, where I wait patiently until everyone has finished registering. Then, one by one, each case is called up to be heard by the judge, and I'm eighth on the list. When it comes to my turn, I take a seat at the table facing the judge, make my plead of guilty official, and then pay the fine in cash at the registration office. They thank me for the payment and I ignore them on my way out. All I want is to rip them apart. The whole thing has been a load of shit and I just want it to be done with so that I can continue on with the trip. This was the easiest way to deal with it. A stop in South Philly for a cheesesteak to cheer me up on my way back down to Silver Spring, MD.

I arrive back at Holly's just after 9:00pm, where she has dinner ready for me. After a bottle of wine with the meal, we begin to hit the whiskey, and I teach her how to drink it "Canadian Style" by sipping it right out of the bottle. With a bottle Jack Daniels in hand, I get my hair coloured back to a more rock 'n' roll style, as Holly applies red, yellow, and green colours onto my newly bleached Mohawk. By the end of the process, our bottle of whiskey is empty, and we're both ready for bed. In the morning, I hit the road as Holly leaves for work. She restocks my supply of snacks into the same black bag as before, which I now call the Holly Bag. Hitting the highway, I begin to feel lonely again. I miss her already.

Me and Holly in Silverspring, MD in between the two legs of the tour.

A full day of driving brings me to Asheville, NC, where I give Nicole a visit. She shows me around this lovely little town in the mountains that consists of students, hippies, and artists. The night is enjoyable, as we check out most of the drinking establishments in town but all I can think about is Holly. I call her to let her know that everything is okay and that I can't wait to see her in Denver. The next morning, I thank Nicole for her hospitality and drive the remaining four hours to Atlanta to pick up my next passengers. It's Thursday June 29, and we're about to head west and rejoin the Pearl Jam tour on the other side of the country. The craziness continues.

He floated back down cause
he wanted to share his key
to the locks on the chains
he saw everywhere

Given To Fly

CHAPTER 23: **THE LONG ROAD**

July 2, 2006 » Show 25
Denver, Colorado

WHEN PEARL JAM ANNOUNCED their tour for the US, they forgot about The South, so what I plan to do is to bring The South to Pearl Jam. With an eventful month after the conclusion of the first leg, I end up in Atlanta, GA. I arrive early in the afternoon to meet up with Kyle. Still at his Taekwondo studio that he runs, Kyle gives me the keys to his place so that I can rest up for the long trip that we're about to take. At his parent's place, I find a package addressed to me sitting in his room. It's my new video camera that I bought on eBay. When Kyle returns from work, we hit the road picking up four of his friends: Mandy, Tony, Louis, and Ashley. The plan is for everyone to drive the one way with the van and then fly back to Atlanta, while I continue west with the tour. By 8:00pm, we've left Atlanta with our goal to drive 25 hours straight until we reach Denver, CO. Once there, we'll be staying with more of Kyle's friends, Jeffrey and Kelly, who I met at the Gorge along with Kyle last year. Pearl Jam will be opening two shows for Tom Petty and they will be my first shows in over a month.

Passing by Dalton and approaching the Tennessee border, we stop off for some food next to a wholesale fireworks store with its title in big bright lights. Rivalling most department stores in size, the store appears to only sell fireworks at discount prices. The bright lights and fast food wake some of us up but puts some of us to sleep as well. So feeling a bit drowsy, I let Kyle take over driving duties. He gets us through Tennessee before Tony takes over for the overnight journey through Southern Illinois into Missouri, while everyone else is sound asleep in the back. I wake up with the sun rising as we enter St. Louis. Looking out the window, I see the St. Louis Gateway Arch, with the sky glowing in the background of what would otherwise be just a very normal looking monument. The overnight drive reminds me of the last time we drove overnight in the van and ended up in a ditch in Saskatchewan.

"The key is that we still have the van after the night drive," Louis says as we stop for gas.

"Where are we?" I ask.

"I have no idea," he answers.

"We've done about 500 miles with over 800 to go," Kyle follows.

After doing most of the driving throughout the East Coast, it's nice to have my new friends give me a break from it, allowing me to migrate to the back with the futon laid out. Louis takes his turn at the wheel and guides us through a bright morning drive through Missouri. Mandy had brought her Super Nintendo along so she and Kyle pull it out, plug it into the television that's still remaining from the last tour, and begin battle on Mario Kart, while I continue to rest in the back. As we enter Kansas, the temperature jumps up another 20 degrees. Maybe it's that time of the day or maybe it's the treeless plains that allow us to absorb all of the sun but the van begins to bake us, much like the trip down to DC. As we pass Topeka, we feel as if we're on fire, so we stop off to pick up some refreshing drinks to help cool us down during the drive, but it's ineffective. Looking at the terrain reminds me again of Saskatchewan and the Canadian Prairies. Middle of America is much like middle of Canada, vast and flat with not a whole lot going on. The heat finally dies down a notch as we enter Colorado with Mandy in control of the van.

"I don't think we're in Kansas anymore," Ashley jokes.

When we finally reach Denver, it's as dark as it was when we left Atlanta, 28 hours ago. I take back control of the van for the city drive and Kyle navigates me to Jeffery and Kelly's place. A block away from the destination, we turn onto Holly Street and I'm reminded how it has been too long since I saw my Holly. She'll arrive in Denver tomorrow. By the time we arrive, we have enough time for a few drinks before retiring for the night. Everyone picks a place on the floor to crash, while I retreat back to the van.

Kyle, me, Tony, Mandy, Kelly, Louis, and Ashley at the Red Rocks Amphitheater in Morrison, CO.

The next day is July 1, Canada Day, and to celebrate it I pack seven Americans into the van and head out to see one of the most beautiful outdoor music venues in America, Red Rocks. Located in Morrison, CO on the foothills of the Rocky Mountains, this breathtaking venue is a naturally formed amphitheatre, looking over the mountains and buildings of Denver. In front of the majestic backdrop, rows of seats slope up from the stage like spacious bleacher style seating, almost as if the stage is at the bottom of a canyon. The beauty, which also reminds me of Holly, is comparable to that of the Gorge. As stage workers set up for a concert here tonight, we only wish that it would be for Pearl Jam one day. I pull out my new video camera and test it out on this amazing sight, while interviewing Kyle in front of it.

After a Mexican lunch, we head to the store to pick up some barbeque supplies for tonight at Jeffery's. Excited to see everyone, Jeffery even brings home two kegs of beer, celebrating the presence of friends from his hometown and Canada. The rest of the day is spent hanging out in the yard, grilling some food, and drinking. When it's time, I duck out of the party to go to the airport and pick up Holly. Flying high myself, I patiently watch her plane land. When she exits the gate and our eyes meet, my heart skips a beat. I jokingly pretend not to see her and continue looking around, but her beauty does not allow my eyes to stray very far. When she plants her luscious lips up against mine, I have no choice but to give her my full attention. I tell her that the four days without seeing her seemed like four years. "Oh, how I've missed you," she echoes.

Feeling a bit disoriented and not paying particular attention to the road, I end up making five loops around the airport before I'm able to find our exit. I blame her for being too distractingly beautiful. I've used a tank of gas by the time we make it out of the airport complex. Back at the house, I introduce everyone to Holly and the party continues late into the night. The only time we take a break is when VH1 is airing the Storytellers show that they filmed last month with Pearl Jam in New York. We all gather around the television to watch the intimate performance, their first on television in quite some time. At its conclusion we venture back outside to finish the first keg and, feeling a bit tipsy, Kyle begins spray painting Pearl Jam symbols onto the fence. With the night coming to a close, our friends begin dropping off one by one until only Holly and I are still awake.

"I know the perfect place to sleep," I whisper to her, leading her to the van.

"Where are we going? Are you okay to drive?" she asks as I turn on the van.

"It's only one block away."

I pull onto Holly Street and park underneath the road sign. When she sees the sign she bursts out laughing. We attempt to take photos with the sign but aren't coordinated enough to do so, so we crawl back to the futon feeling exhausted from the night. We are dead asleep within seconds. The morning is slow, but we make a decent attempt to get organized early and clean out the mess we had caused last night. Bringing our leftover food and the remaining keg along, we then head out to the city and toward the Pepsi Center, which is one of the nicest looking arenas I've seen. We pull in and try to tailgate, but the parking lot is not as exciting as it was back east. There are, however, some Tom Petty fans that cheerfully greet us, including some fans travelling around in an RV. We park the van beside them. With a gas powered barbeque already set up, they offer to let us use it and in return we share with them our keg, which is sitting pretty at the back of the van. As I'm tapping the keg, I hear someone call out to me so I respond but I don't recognize the voice.

He introduces himself as Dan. "I was supposed to join you guys for the Canadian tour in Vancouver, but never made it."

Now I know who he is. "Oh, that's right. We waited in front of your hotel for a few hours but couldn't wait any longer."

"Yeah, I'm sorry about that. I never got a chance to explain either."

"No worries man. We were concerned if you were okay more than anything else."

"Well, just wanted to come by to say hi and apologize."

I offer him a drink, but he declines and goes about his business.

With a few drinks inside of us, we head across the parking lot to Braun's Bar and Grill, hoping to find more people at the CCFA pre-party. However, inside is just as empty as outside, with just the organizers of the fundraiser in attendance so far. We say hi and buy our raffle tickets for the many interesting items up for draw, including DVDs, posters, and even a jar of raw honey. I jokingly tell Holly that I want that jar of honey and she proceeds to purchase 60 raffle tickets. I recognize the girl in charge of the fundraiser, Joy, as we've met previously at shows. She's also Canadian and flew down from Alberta for these shows.

"We love the band and we want to pay it forward to give back to the band because of all the good times they've given us," Joy says about the benefit.

It's still early in the afternoon, so instead of throwing away bags of money by drinking at the bar, we retreat to the van and continue to tailgate with the Tom Petty fans. Converging with fans of other bands has been interesting, as it's similar in some ways, but much different in most other ways. With the Radiohead fans in Philly, I could see a similar dedication to attending shows and getting bootlegs that Pearl Jam fans have, but that's about it. There seemed to be no real unity amongst them, and we formed the majority of the out-of-towners at that show. The Tom Petty fans, on the other hand, are all about travelling to the shows and the community aspects, but they aren't as dedicated to collecting all the bootlegs and posters like most Pearl Jam fans are. Seeing these differences and similarities make me feel honoured to be a part of this community that goes along with being a Pearl Jam fan — we are the complete package of hardcore dedication.

The atmosphere in the parking lot is relaxed and we finish up all of our food. When it's time for the raffle draw, we head back into the bar to listen for the numbers to be called. Kyle wins a poster from the 2003 Santa Barbara show. "It means so much to me not because I wasn't at Santa Barbara, but the fact that it's an awesome fucking poster!" Kyle gushes.

The jar of honey is up and I wait in anticipation but am unsuccessful. Holly then has her ticket called and claims her prize, a signed Quentin Tarantino DVD box set of *Pulp Fiction* and *Reservoir Dogs*. I congratulate her but she's not as pleased because she wanted to win the jar of honey for me. I grab a round of drinks and then commend Joy for her efforts on the fundraiser. Returning back to our spot in the bar, I don't see Holly anymore. I look around and still no Holly. I figure that she went to the bathroom so Kyle and I just continue chatting. A few minutes later, Holly returns and she's got the jar of honey in her hand.

"I traded the DVDs and gave the guy $10 for the honey you wanted, honey," she explains.

"What? $10 as well? Where is this guy?" I ask laughing.

"He's right there." She points, but I see no one. "Well he *was* right there."

"Don't worry. I love it! Thanks for the honey, honey," I say with a wink.

The best part is when I turn over the jar and a see a price tag of $4.99. We laugh at the irony but are glad we have the jar of honey. Back at the van, there's a small gathering of Pearl Jam fans now, including one of Tak's friends, Rose, from Seattle. Bringing her friend Konrad along, Rose had introduced herself to me at the DC show but we never had a chance to talk afterwards. They join in helping finish the keg. Jeffery then decides to pull it out of the van and perform an impressive 30-second keg stand to jump start his night. When the keg is completely dry, Kyle picks it up and brings it on top of the van, hoisting it like the Stanley Cup. After this upper we're offered a downer from the Tom Petty fans, so 10 of us pile into the van for some "herb". As we open the doors to leave the van, a big cloud of smoke exits with us. This is our cue for entering the arena, as we don't want to miss the opening band this time.

Tonight will be my first time seeing Pearl Jam as an opening band. It seems kind of strange, but if they were to open for someone, Tom Petty is as good a choice as any. Holly and I are about 20 rows up on the side stage but we have a perfect view. This is the first show that we've seen together, so it's special. And ironically, it's also the 30th Pearl Jam show for both of us individually, so it's extra special.

With Pearl Jam not being the headliners, their set is short and sweet – about 90 minutes long – but it was expected. They come back out for a short encore, but it's not quite what we Pearl Jam fans have learned to expect. Regardless, Holly and I rock out hard, so the shorter set might actually be all we have energy for. When Pearl Jam leaves the stage, our familiar feeling of satisfaction begins to pull us away from our seats and we want to make a move to the van. But hang on, there's still another band! It feels kind of odd waiting around after Pearl Jam's performance, however, Tom Petty comes out to play for about two hours, surprising me that I knew more Tom Petty songs than I thought I did. All the songs are classics and the show is top notch. Vedder even joins Petty for a performance of *American Girl* at the end the show. The second leg of the US tour, for us, is officially underway.

As we return to the van, a car pulls up to us and the people inside tell us how much they love the van, while handing over a full bottle of Grey Goose Vodka to me before driving off. I unscrew the top and take a swig of our newest gift, and it's smooth and delicious. With the hockey tape in hand, Kyle applies the largest checkmark ever done on the van and, no longer in possession of a bottle of Screech, I hand over the Grey Goose to Kyle for a shot to celebrate a great day and a fun journey to Denver. The parking lot clears out quickly and we follow shortly after. When we're back at the house, most of us are dead tired but we manage to finish the vodka before crawling back to the same sleeping spots as the night before.

The next morning feels surprisingly good. Everyone is up early and full of life, so we bring the life back to the Pepsi Center parking lot. However, Holly and I decide not to go to tonight's show and instead hit the road for an extra day of exploring through the Rocky Mountains toward our next stop of Las Vegas. I pick up my tickets for Kyle and then we hang out for another few hours, filming interviews of people in the parking lot, and enjoying a final drink with my southern friends. Everyone will be flying back to Atlanta tomorrow, but Kyle will be back at the Gorge, where we first met. I thank everyone for driving with me across the country and for the great time in Denver and then Holly and I hit the road mid-afternoon.

During the initial planning stages, I couldn't find anyone to do this leg of the tour with me, so I was expecting to drive it alone. Denver to Las Vegas is about a 12-hour drive, through the majestic Rocky Mountains and the spectacular Grand Canyon. At the other end of the drive is Las Vegas, where everyone is reconvening.

Holly had other plans. She is not going to let me do this scenic drive alone, and I'm not complaining about it. With some extra time now, we decide to take a longer more scenic route. By 4:00pm, we hit Highway 285 and begin heading south. Driving down the open road is wonderful, and being with my girl is even better. We are cheerful, singing at the top of our lungs, as the mountains in the distance draw closer. And even though we are driving south, we soon begin to climb up.

I've driven through the Rocky Mountains from Alberta down to Utah in the past, but never through Colorado. This will complete my tour of this monstrous mountain range. As we burrow through tunnels and scale the edges of the mountain, the temperature cools to a comfortable level at sunset. When the road takes us west over the mountains, the scenery turns from pleasant to spectacular with jagged edge rock formations in between forests of evergreen trees towering over the narrow highway that cuts through it all. Stopping for a rest, we explore the forests and find a river flowing freely down to the valley. We go back to the van and reach the pinnacle of the terrain just as darkness falls upon us. The path then takes us down a windy road, as we start descending from the mountain. At the bottom of the drop, we spot a campsite so we check it out.

As we check in, I purchase some firewood from the store and Holly buys a glow-in-the-dark Pagosa Valley Campgrounds t-shirt. When we pull up to our camp spot, I try to start a campfire and attempt to play some campfire songs with Cali Joe's guitar, which he had left in the van for me to bring out west. Unfortunately, my guitar skills are on par with my campfire skills and neither is very successful. After buying some starter fluid, the fire finally gets going. We give up on the guitar and resort to just drinking Jack Daniels and cuddling in front of our fire. It's peaceful and all we can hear is the crackling from the fire. Holly feels warmer than the fire itself. All of the hectic partying and run-ins with the police back east is now far off in the distance and this trip has brought me peacefully into the middle of the Rocky Mountains with Holly. It's funny how things work out. I love it.

With hardly anyone else around, we begin roasting marshmallows and telling stories and jokes. Her laughter makes me smile more than I can remember, and I don't think I've ever been as happy as I am at this moment. As the night grows long, rain begins to fall. So we retreat to the van. With water leaking through our nonexistent moon roof, together, we begin frantically taping up the opening with my special Canadian maple leaf hockey tape. Holly rips the tape and hands it to me while I seal off all holes. It's a collective effort. And even though the water dripping through basically prevents the tape from sticking, we believe that we're making progress. When the holes are all patched up, we cheer in celebration, only to watch it all fall into a soggy heap a minute later. We find it hilarious and can't stop laughing at our failed attempts. When the rain stops, almost on cue with our laughter, we leave the tape and extinguish the campfire, while the fire inside the van continues to burn, ending a magical day.

Don't you think you want to sleep?
Don't you think you oughtta
lay your head down tonight?

All Those Yesterdays

CHAPTER 24: **CITY THAT NEVER SLEEPS**

July 6, 2006 » Show 26
Las Vegas, Nevada

GETTING THE VAN from St. John's to Las Vegas was the key for Touring Van's US tour. And after winging it through the first leg by picking up both random and unexpected passengers, I'm on the verge of making the delivery to Las Vegas where the big reunion will be. It's where everyone is meeting to head up the West Coast for the home stretch. Stefan and Tak will be flying down from Vancouver, Cali Joe is flying in from Los Angeles, Tatiana is flying over from Brazil, and Tom is driving down from Wisconsin. In addition to a few new friends that I'm expecting, this will be Montreal all over again. But I still have to get there first.

Leaving Pagosa Valley early, we've officially escaped the mountains and the terrain quickly turns into a dry desolate one. Our sleep was great the previous night and we both feel re-energized for the day ahead. By 10:00am, we arrive at the Four Corners, the point where Colorado, Arizona, Utah, and New Mexico meet. We hop out to shoot a few photos with us standing in all the states at once, but a stench of something foul quickly drives us back into the van and onto the road again. Continuing westward, the dry dessert then turns into canyon regions and there's nothing but amazing red formations in every direction we look. Driving through it is surreal and the spectacular scenery eventually causes us to stop to admire and explore Antelope Canyon. Entering through a crack in the ground, we snake our way through the smoothly formed crevices, some formed in shapes of animals and some in the shapes of faces. Walking through the canyon is similar to walking through a cave, only there's an opening up top and the redness of the rock brightens up everything.

As we continue driving and pass by the Grand Canyon, I check the time and see 3:00pm. Shit! We need to be in Vegas to pick up Tak and Tatiana at the airport at 4:00pm! Their flight is due to arrive at 4:00pm and at 4:00pm we are still slowly driving through stunning Zion National Park, mesmerized by the majestic scenery. With steep cliffs of over hanging trees spanning up the hills, the drive is slow, narrow, and windy. It's simply breathtaking. We drive by a million hiking trails and are tempted to take one up, but our time is up and although rushing through this magical drive just doesn't seem right – it must be done. I get a call on my phone and it's Tak.

"Where are you?"

"Give me a few hours I'm still trying to get out of the Grand Canyon."

"A few hours?"

"Let's say 6:00pm. Did you find Tatiana?" I ask.

"Yeah, I didn't even know she was coming. That was a surprise."

By 6:00pm, I'm still halfway down the I-15, just entering Nevada. They're going to hate me, but Holly doesn't. She's amazed at my driving abilities, speeding down the highway, smoothly passing cars left and right and, with every semi-truck I pass, Holly motions to them to honk their horns. Most of them oblige. I'm making good time on the interstate highway, but too bad I was already late by the time I got on it. So it isn't until 7:00pm that I arrive at McCarran National Airport in Las Vegas. Rushing up the ramp, I pull up through the departures and see them in the distance waiting patiently. Tak and Tatiana are standing together alone, each with a suitcase in hand, but the sight of the van speeding up toward them brings a giant smile to their faces. I apologize and, as I hand them a beer, everything is forgotten. We've made it to Vegas.

"It's good to be back," Tak announces.

"How long was your flight this time?" I ask Tatiana.

"13 hours," she answers.

"Oh lord. So this beer must taste gooood," Holly follows.

The drive into the city is all talk of excitement and anticipation of what to expect from the city that never sleeps. Tak insists that he still needs his sleep though. I've been to Las Vegas a few times before, but, for the others, it's their first time. Driving onto Las Vegas Boulevard, otherwise known as The Strip, the bright lights appear and call out to us. With all the mega hotel resorts lined up in an organized fashion, The Strip is like one giant theme park of hotels acting as individual exhibits. As we cruise down the street, they go by us one by one: Luxor, Tropicana, Excalibur, New York New York, until we are stopped at a traffic light. Looking to our right is the MGM Grand, where the concert will be in a few days. Holly, filming along the way, focuses the camera onto the MGM and just as we mention Pearl Jam, the promotion for the show appears on the video screen in front of the hotel. We explode with cheers. Further down the road is Imperial Palace, the hotel where we're staying tonight.

The first thing we see entering the hotel is the casino and, as we check in, we are immediately offered free dinners and other coupons. We drop off the bags in our room, which has two queen beds, and then head back down to the casino for a few drinks. With the sound of slot machines dominating over all other noises, we feel intrigued and take up one of their promotions for a free $20 play on the slots. As expected, none of us win so we order some drinks and wait for our next Touring Van passenger to arrive, Venassa, who I met briefly in Saskatoon. An hour later, a guy asks if I'm Jason. I nod. His name is Raphael, a friend of Venassa's who lives in Vegas.

"She's somewhere around here looking for you," he trails off.

I turn around, and there she is! Being a wee bit shorter, Venassa jumps up to give me a hug. I bring them to the bar, where the rest of us are, and introduce everyone. Today is the 4th of July and with us getting into town late and trying to settle in, we realize it's 11:00pm and we somehow missed all of the fireworks celebrations, so we make our own Independence Day party in the hotel room. Venassa has brought two bottles of vodka and, along with the remaining whiskey and remaining beer, we begin to drown ourselves in alcohol, while everyone gets to know one another. Then, we hit The Strip!

Being a local, Raphael takes us to a happening joint called Margaritaville, where we share a plate of nachos and many margaritas. To work off the calories, we get out on the dance floor, which is controlled by a DJ dressed in a slick silver shirt that's brighter than the mirror ball reflecting above him. After a long travel day, Tak ducks out early, while the rest of us continue the merriment until closing. Returning to The Strip, we have to hang on to each other to keep our balance to walk straight. Raphael returns home after taking us back to our hotel, where Tak is already sleeping like a baby. We join him within seconds.

The next morning we're awakened by a false fire alarm at 6:00am, which we don't even have the energy to get up for. An hour later, our radio alarm clock goes off as set by Tatiana. She wants to go on a tour of the Grand Canyon. Again, none of us move, including Tatiana. She finally gets up another hour later and dashes out the door only to return in half an hour claiming that all of the tours have left already. The rest of us are still lying in bed, so she rejoins us. We manage to get out by the 10:00am check out time and load up the van before returning to the hotel for a quick swim in their pool. Helping out our hangover, we order a bucket of beer and sit by the pool for the next little while before leaving the hotel. Originally we had booked the Imperial Palace for two nights and then the MGM for the night of the show but, with everyone else coming in tonight as well, I thought it would be better to check into the MGM a day early and just throw away our extra night at the Imperial Palace.

"I'm excited for my first ride in the van," Venassa announces as we climb aboard. Driving down the block, I pull into the parking lot of the MGM Grand. The walk to the check-in counter is longer than our drive to the hotel, as we go through the parking lot, through the mall, past the amusement park, and through the casino. But we do finally arrive at the entrance to the casino to find a giant Pearl Jam promotion poster lighted up. The room we had booked is for a celebrity suite for two people, but by the end of the day we'll be cramming close to 10 into the room. So when we arrive at the lobby, only Holly and I get in line, with the others waiting behind. When it's our turn, we approach the counter and check in.

"Okay I've got you down for a celebrity suite," the lady says.

"That's correct."

"You guys look like a beautiful couple. I'll tell you what... I can get you a huge discount on an upgrade to one of our premiere suites. They normally go for $1500 a night but we have one left that I need to sell. For you guys I can do $300. What do you think?" she offers.

"Hmm, we might as well do this in style," I say to Holly, who readily agrees. "Okay we'll take it."

"Great, you guys will love it," the lady replies. "What are you in town for?"

"The Pearl Jam show tomorrow night."

"Oh lovely. I just checked those guys in about an hour ago."

"Really?"

"Yes. They'll be staying in one of our signature suites on the floor right above yours."

She hands us the keys and wishes us a great stay and then we return to inform the others of our upgrade. Walking to the other end of the casino, we reach the elevators. Inside, it states that we're required to swipe our key to enter any of the floors above 25. I tell everyone we're on 27.

"And Pearl Jam is staying on 28," Holly says excitedly.

As the door to our room opens, we all let out a scream of excitement over what we see. First on the right is a bathroom equipped with a telephone. Further down is the dining area which is separated from the living room by a bar counter. It is dominated by a large refrigerator and dining table and consists of two couches, a coffee table, and a large window overlooking The Strip. Turning to the left is the master bedroom with a king size bed, a large television, and an Italian marble floored bathroom that's so bright and reflective that we can all see ourselves from a distance in every direction. The bathroom includes a jacuzzi tub, a separate shower, a toilet, dual sinks, and matching white bath robes. The place is impressive and can easily fit 10, if not 20. After an hour of standing in awe of the place, we head downstairs to check out the hotel pool.

At the sight of an enormous lazy river, we immediately jump in, letting the weak jet streams push us down the water as it wraps around the entire pool area. Along the way, we go through tunnels, under bridges, and pass by waterfalls. And while some are merely sitting on inflatable tubes drifting away, we decide to swim and float our way down the lazy river. It takes nearly 20 minutes for us to complete a full cycle, which we follow up with another cycle. After our fun, we grab some margaritas and are able to find some lawn chairs to sprawl out on for a rest. When we're feeling way too comfortable, we head back to the room to get changed to see The Strip during the daytime.

Venassa
and Tatiana
enjoying the
lazy river at the
MGM Grand in
Las Vegas.

Holly and I attempt to buy tickets to Cirque du Soleil but are unsuccessful. So we start snapping photos of the many replica monuments around including the Eiffel Towel. We watch the free fountain show at the Bellagio and then meet up with Raphael – who has just finished work – before returning to the hotel, where Stefan is waiting for us in the lobby. I introduce him to everyone and lead them up to our room for some drinks. An hour later, I go back down to the lobby with Holly to find Cali Joe. With his guitar already up in the room, Cali Joe has brought his ukulele with him this time. I lead him up to the room and, as the elevator doors open, Venassa is inside with Raphael.

"HEY THAT'S CALI JOE!" she screams half buzzed already.

"Do I know you?" he answers.

"That's Venassa," I point out.

"I've seen you on the DVD," she explains. "It's great to finally meet you."

We get on the elevator as they get off. Back in the room it's a big reunion with all the boys and Tatiana, much like East Coast Canada. The drinks begin to flow and soon we're joined by more friends. Brian from Lethbridge, Alberta knocks on our door. He wanted to join us in Saskatoon, but is now going to be with us for the rest of the leg. Being a part-time poker player, he has already been in Las Vegas for a week, gearing up for the World Series of Poker later in the month. With Lethbridge being in the vicinity of Edmonton, Brian is an Oilers fan. I'm wearing my Carolina Hurricanes shirt. "Oh no! It's not going to be like this the whole time is it?" he laughs.

Venassa returns with a few more local friends to say hello before they head out for another night on The Strip, this time at the Piano Bar. She takes a final swig from her bottle of vodka to finish it off, and then they're off. As she leaves we're next joined by Jill from San Diego, who Stefan met doing some West Coast shows in 2003 and, before we know it, we're having quite the party in our suite. Cali Joe picks up his familiar guitar and starts playing some songs to pick us up even more. With music filling the room, Tatiana introduces Holly to Caiprinhas and begins mixing the Brazilian drink at a rapid pace. Brian and Stefan take advantage of the free wireless internet by jumping on my laptop and playing online poker, while we're in Vegas. The rest of us, utilizing all the mirrors in the bathroom, surround Cali Joe in the tub, as he strums away.

By the time midnight hits, we decide to head down to the casino and lose a little bit of money. Playing poker at the tables while the free drinks roll in, we last about an hour before retreating back to the room for more good times. Holly and Tatiana, who are completely blitzed at this point, somehow lose us when we leave the elevator at our floor. They continue to stay on the elevator, trying to press the button for level 28, hoping they will find the band.

"Why won't it go to 28?" Holly wonders.

"Keep trying," Tatiana encourages.

At this point, I receive a call from Raphael asking me to come down to the lobby to pick up Venassa, because she's very drunk and the security won't let them come up to the room. I head to the elevator and as the door opens, there's Holly and Tatiana still inside trying to locate the band. As they return to the room, I ride the elevator down to see Raphael waiting with Venassa. I inform the security that she's staying with me and they let her through, while Raphael goes home. "The boys are freaking out," she slurs feverishly.

Back in the room, I try to calm her down and she quickly falls asleep on the bed. As I head back to the others, I hear her mumbling something but her eyes are closed, so she's talking in her sleep. Finding it extremely funny, a few of us approach her and begin asking her questions to which she hilariously answers in French. Our laughter is so loud and drunk that we're surprised she doesn't wake up from it. Leaving her alone, we all leave the bathroom area and bring the party out to the living room, except for Tak, who closes the door when we leave and passes out on the bed next to Venassa. The rest of the night is a complete blur, as it involves many more drunk photos, more guitar music, and some self made bongo drums with our rear ends. Something funny is said that no one remembers, but Cali Joe's hysterical laugh prompts the rest of us to laugh as well. And for a good half an hour, we can't stop laughing at the top of our lungs. Out of energy, we all end up just dropping down on to the floor.

The next morning is a complete write off but, by noon, Venassa is fully recuperated and brings out some of her home made banana bread that she had brought along from Calgary. It's delicious and exactly what we need to wake up with. As a web developing, Stefan had originally planned on working online during the tour in the hotel but, after the night we had, he decides that it will be better just to take the week off and enjoy the time with everyone instead of worrying about work. We then dress for the beach and venture down to the Grand Pool once again. Walking through the Casino and then the mall, we notice that Pearl Jam music is playing throughout the entire hotel one song after another. I guess they're gearing up for the show tonight with a full day of Pearl Jam. We sing and dance our way toward our destination.

While picking up a quick sandwich, we bump into Nicole from Asheville and Jason from Philly, who decide to join us at the pool, where we proceed to parade through the lazy river with margaritas in hand and nonstop Pearl Jam playing throughout the building. Like kids at a playground, everyone is smiling, having a great time, and not even paying attention to how silly we might look. Despite the fact that we're receiving many weird looks from bystanders, it's an unforgettable moment for us. The fun continues for almost two hours, raising our excitement level for the show.

When we head back to the room to continue our pre-show party, Tom from Wisconsin arrives to complete the Montreal reunion. He had driven all the way down from Wisconsin with his girlfriend Ingrid, and they plan on driving up the West Coast as well, catching a few shows along the way. It is reminiscent of last night and the party begins to grow, as Jill brings over a few friends, Mark and Su-Ann from Los Angeles. Mark very much resembles Thurston Moore of Sonic Youth, who are opening the show tonight, and he can play a mean guitar as well. Keen to check out the legendary band, we soon make our way down to the venue early. Holly and I are dressed in matching Stone shirts, only mine is blue and hers is the classic orange.

Stefan and Tom catching up in our suite at the MGM Grand Hotel.

On the way out, Cali Joe drops his ticket from his pocket and it's left sitting on the ground at the opening of the door. He's too drunk to notice it, so Stefan picks it up and hangs on to it while we struggle to continue. And what would normally be a 10-minute walk turns into an hour-long adventure, as we stop for a drink at every opportunity along the way. By the time we arrive at the entrance, Cali Joe realizes that he has forgotten his ticket and immediately darts off back to the room, while the rest of us head in. Security surprisingly allows us to empty out our drinks into plastic cups and bring it into the venue with us and, when inside, I receive a phone call from Cali Joe. "Dude, I think I'm fucked. I don't know where I left my ticket." I suggest that he keeps looking.

Stefan tells me that he has the ticket and has purposely kept it away from him for shits and giggles. So when Cali Joe calls again 15 minutes later, I hand the phone over to Stefan. Cali Joe has given up and is outside the venue doors looking for a cash machine to buy a ticket off a scalper, so Stefan lets him in on the joke and meets him at the gate to get him in.

"You fuckers! I was going to pay double the price to get in. You got me good though," he laughs.

Waking up drunk this morning and continuously drinking throughout the day, we celebrate inside the show by drinking more beer, while watching Sonic Youth together in the standing room area before taking our own seats. As I walk down the aisle, a few people recognize me from the internet and come up to say hi: Meredith from San Diego and Lydia from San Francisco. Holly continues down and comes back up when she has found our seats.

"Oh look at that girl with the Stone shirt," Lydia says. "How cute."

"Yeah, she's with me," I reply with a smile.

"Get out! And you're wearing a Stone shirt too. That's so beautiful."

We take our seats and, as with the Canadian tour, mine are right beside Stefan's. Rocking out hard, the four of us sweat out all of the alcohol we've consumed over the day and are left completely dehydrated. But it is a great one and completely worth being thirsty for. When it's over, we meet up on the floor and Cali Joe is wrapped around in the Touring Van Canadian flag as well as a mysterious piece of pink tape. Looking further ahead, the tape continues to run along the ground, marking out the boundary lines. "I just kept pulling on this," he says, "and it just wouldn't end."

I invite everyone back to the room for an after party, where we have our very own Sonic Youth lookalike, Mark, performing a special private show for us in the suite. He's able to play all of our requests, as everyone gathers around to sing along and help finish up all of our supplies in the room. Because Holly is flying back tomorrow, we duck out for a bit to take a walk along The Strip for some time on our own.

"I didn't know what this whole van thing was about until we got here," she tells me. "I've never met so many good people in such a short amount of time. Thank you for bringing me here."

"I just wish you didn't have to go back."

When we return to the room, the party has mellowed out. There's still the same number of people around, but everyone seems a little tired from the lack of sleep from the night before. With all of our alcohol finished, the others slowly begin returning to their own rooms and, by 4:00am, we're again passed out on the floor. Vegas turns into nothing but a great party and a fun way to kick start our tour up the West Coast. These are the great people that will be joining me up along the way. I only wish Holly was coming along as well.

Hold on to the thread
the currents will shift
Glide me towards you
Oceans

CHAPTER 25: **OCEAN CALLING**

July 7, 2006 » Show 27
San Diego, California

HAVING LIVED ALL MY LIFE IN VANCOUVER, I've grown accustomed to being around the ocean. Just the sight of the massive body of water brings me comfort and gives me a feeling of freedom and hope. The sound of waves crashing calms my soul and, although I've been in and around the Atlantic Ocean, it has been over six weeks since I've seen the Pacific, my home. Our next destination will enable me to make my return. It will also complete the four corners of mainland America for the van, starting in Seattle a year ago, down from Boston to Key West in the last month, and now heading toward San Diego, before returning back up to Seattle.

With the day that we had yesterday in Las Vegas, it's a struggle to wake up in the morning. Check out time is 10:00am and everyone is still lying around at 9:00am. Holly has to catch a shuttle bus to the airport, so after a hard goodbye with her new friends, she comes down to the lobby with me for an even harder goodbye. Even though she promises to fly back for The Gorge, it's sad to see her leave. We've spent almost every second with each other for about two weeks, sharing very intimate and special moments that will be with us for a long time. And although I have a good group of friends around me now, it won't be the same without her. As we wait for the shuttle bus, we hold each other tightly, not wanting to let go. Our goodbye kiss almost prevents her from boarding the bus, as the driver has to honk to let us know that it's leaving. The bus pulls away and we smile at each other through the window until we are no longer in sight. I shed a tear and head back up to the room to gather the others.

Packing up and tidying the room, we find its condition to be not as bad as it could have been, but we still leave a decent tip for the mess we've made. As I pull the van out of the parking lot toward the front entrance, I see our next passengers waiting patiently for us – two Vancouver natives: Tamara, who we met in Saskatoon last year, and Phil. While the others load up the van, Brian pulls up in his car, as he'll be driving along with us. Before heading out on the highway, we go to the Rio Hotel Resort and its famous world buffet that consists of foods from America, Italy, France, Greece, Mexico, Japan, China, and India. It's a tasty meal and we certainly make it worth every penny. Back at the van, I pull out the video camera and choose our poker player, Brian, to do the checkmark for Las Vegas.

"How was the show last night, guys?" I ask while filming.

"Phenomenal," Cali Joe responds.

"From what you remember, you mean" Brian teases.

"Yeah I was told it was a great show," Cali Joe laughs.

The completion of the checkmark is our cue to leave Sin City. Still a little bit shaken from the departure of Holly this morning, I decide to get some quite time to myself and get away from the group by riding with Brian in his air conditioned car, while Stefan takes over the heat of the van, driving Tak, Cali Joe, Tatiana, Venassa, Tamara, and Phil.

"Alright, I haven't been in this thing in ages!" Stefan announces while starting the engine.

Our extremely tiny convoy enters the I-15 heading south at around 2:00pm and, with a five-hour drive ahead of us, we should be okay for making the show tonight. Driving with Brian, we talk about a variety of things, while *The Big Lebowski* plays on his DVD player. But my mind is somewhere far away, and everything else is merely background noise to me. As we're leaving the desert, the rain begins to pour down and traffic stacks up. Once the rain stops though, traffic speeds up again, and we're in the clear. However, this only lasts briefly as we hit rush hour entering California.

The drive is slow and, not really paying attention to my conversation with Brian or the road, I forget to navigate and we end up on the wrong highway and lose the van. So we take the next exit to turn around and get back on track. It isn't hard to catch up to the van, however. Darting in and out of the slow moving traffic, we eventually catch sight of the familiar blue beast an hour later, and we manage to roll into the San Diego area around 8:00pm together. Cox Arena is another half hour away, toward San Diego State University, which puts us into the traffic for the concert at 8:30pm.

I can see restlessness through the back window of the van in front of us. It looks like everyone is getting a bit anxious about making the show on time and we still need two tickets. Meanwhile, my phone has been going crazy, as I had made calls to friends earlier about needing tickets for the show and they're all returning my calls at the same time at the last minute, in addition to calls from inside the van from the passengers needing tickets. One after another, I'm answering the phone for 30 minutes, basically relaying information back and forth. My head is spinning, but it finally gets settled and I can now "enjoy" the horrendous traffic leading into the parking lot.

Once we're there, everyone rushes to the box office to grab their tickets. Stefan has his spare ticket for Jill tonight, but she's still on the highway stuck in the same mess that we just survived. So I wait around outside with him, while the others storm the gates of the venue. Soon Venassa insists on entering the venue too, as she's sitting with me tonight and is getting nervous about missing the beginning of the show. So leaving Stefan at the entrance, we make our way to our seats at around 9:10pm. Just as we get settled, the lights go off and we hear Vedder's voice. "One, two, three," he counts.

"OCEANS!" I scream to Venassa, as my mind suddenly snaps back to the present. The opening song is a fitting way to welcome me back to the West Coast and the Pacific Ocean. It also relaxes me and takes me away from all the worries and thoughts that have been running around through my head like a roller coaster all day. Letting it all out, I sing along to the chorus with Venassa, as we sit on the side stage about 25 rows back. This is so what I needed to get away from it all, some moving music from this special band. My escape comes to an end at the conclusion of the song, however, and my mind begins to drift again. Every song that follows reminds me of Holly in some way. And although it hasn't even been a full day since she left, I already miss her too much. Venassa is trying to get me into the show, but I can't keep up with her. Just before the performance of *Life Wasted*, Vedder mutters something to the faithful. "This one goes out to Jason, all the crew, you know who you are," I think I hear him say.

"Is that you he's talking about?" Venassa asks turning to me.

"I didn't really hear it. But I don't think so."

During the encore break, I apologize to Venassa about not being all there for the show, and she says that she's also having an emotional time as she considers San Diego her home away from home. When the band comes back on stage, Vedder begins telling a story about a teacher he once had while growing up in San Diego, and how he wrote the next song for him. The story is so beautiful that it even brings me to tears in my emotionally unstable state. The song is *Long Road*. When this is followed with *Come Back*, I can't handle it anymore. My emotions are let out. Weeping throughout the song, I cry enough to fill an ocean and I barely manage to get through it. At its conclusion, however, I feel a sense of relief and all of my feelings have opened up. By the time *Crown of Thorns* and *Alive* end the encore, I'm fully into the show again.

"I think everything is going to be okay," Venassa tells me.

"Yes, I feel good now," I agree.

The second encore is highlighted by the debut performance of *Big Wave* from their new album. Finally! The song speaks volumes to me and, when surfing king Kelly Slater joins the band for the next song, I'm rocking in my free world. The show turns out to be the most emotional show I've ever seen, and easily one of the best. Venassa agrees and rates it better than her previous favourite show,

Saskatoon, the last time she sat in the same vicinity as me at a show as well. Returning to the parking lot to meet with everyone, I notice something sitting on the windshield of the van. If it's a parking ticket, I'll freak out! But when I get closer to it, I realize that it's a one dollar bill that someone has left for the van, contributing to the cause. Cool.

Jill then comes running up to me. "You got rocked out by Ed!" she exclaims.

"You think that was me he was talking about?" not fully believing her.

"Oh gee, I don't know, some guy named Jason and some crew, duh!" she says sarcastically.

One by one, the gang returns with giant grins on their faces. While the other cars join the chaos exiting the parking garage, we hang around discussing the great show we've just witnessed. Stefan, Brian, and I even pick up the hockey sticks and start passing the ball around. I give Holly a call to let her know how much I miss her and how tough the day has been for me. She tells me the same thing and that she cried on the flight, but she's excited about coming out for the Gorge shows. I inform her that the band didn't play *Daughter/It's Ok*, but the show was one of the best I've seen. When all of the cars have cleared out, I exit the lot and stop in front of the arena, where a group of fans are waiting around, including Cali Joe and Tatiana, for the possibility of catching a glimpse of the band on their way out. I ask Venassa to do the checkmark for her home away from home and she has difficulty ripping apart the hockey tape.

"Come on, what kind of Canadian are you?" I ask jokingly.

"I'm a French Canadian."

"Even worse!" howls Stefan.

Jill had offered her place for us to crash at tonight just outside of the city, but we politely declined preferring a hotel near the centre instead. We drop off Tamara and Phil at their hotel and then begin our search through the hotel circle of the city, but are unsuccessful. We check with five or six hotels and they're all full. I look at the time and it's already 1:00am. So not wanting to waste more time driving around, Stefan gives Jill a call to see if the offer is still available. She says it is and gives us directions. We arrive 45 minutes later and thank Jill for bailing us out, and then we each choose a space on the floor to crash.

With our first real sleep within the last few days, we wake up fresh in the morning. Cali Joe needs to return home to Los Angeles today for his sister's birthday, but we're planning to spend the day in San Diego and head north tomorrow instead, so I drive him to the train station early in the morning. Watching the scheduled train approach, I give him a wave and pull back onto the road. Five minutes later my phone rings, it's Cali Joe. "I missed the train man."

"What? I saw it come."

"I know. It came but it never stopped."

I return to the station to pick him up, before heading back to Jill's place. Once there, everyone is up, except for Tak, who's still sleeping comfortably. Before the trip we had a joke about whether the "Iceman" (Tak) could handle the heat of Vegas and California and, so far, it looks like he's losing. To the surprise of everyone, Cali Joe enters with me and begins searching for car rentals online. He finds a decent one-way deal, so he says his goodbyes again and I drop him off again. When I return, we're all fully recharged and ready to head to the city with Jill's guidance. Along the highway, Jill points out the site of where the movie *Top Gun* was filmed. None of us seem too impressed, so we venture on.

I drop Venassa off at Ocean Beach to meet up with a friend and the rest of us are led to a little hole-in-the-wall type Mexican restaurant by Jill. It is absolutely delicious and a bargain as well. Meals are less than $5 with such enormous portions that only Stefan and I are able to finish. Next, we pick up Phil at his hotel and take a stroll around the San Diego Bay. Walking down the harbour reminds me a lot of Vancouver, with the vast ocean and the beautiful skyline view in the back. I look out into the water at the view of the bridge, and the sight of jet skis and sail boats roaming around.

"You guys don't seem that impressed?" Jill asks. "Isn't this beautiful?"

"Oh, it is, but you forget that we're from Vancouver and Tatiana is from Brazil," Stefan laughs.

At the entrance to the harbour, we meet up with Venassa again, before taking a walk through a park that resembles more of a carnival. With kids running around, there is a carousel in the middle of the park so, without any hesitation, we hop on it. The horses take us on a ride, up and down, while Tak and Phil film us from outside.

"You're too big to be on here," the kid next to Brian tells him.

"No I'm not. I'm a kid just like you," Brian responds. "How old are you?"

"Four," he answers.

"How old do you think I am?" Brian asks the kid.

"Four?"

After a quick bite at the food court, we jump back into the van and head over the same bridge that we were staring at earlier, out to Coronado Beach. With the others lounging around on the sand, Stefan and I sprint out into the ocean for a dip. The water is not cold but it isn't warm either, so after about 15 minutes, we've had enough and return to dry off, before taking some photos of the sunset. The sight and sounds of the Pacific are calming and relaxing, and the company that I had today has been fun, helping keep my mind off of Holly. After dropping Phil off in the city to meet with Tamara, we return to Jill's place for an early night. Today was fun and relaxing and we enjoyed it without even a single drop of alcohol.

Don't need a hand
There's always arms attached
Whippin'

CHAPTER 26: **THANK YOU ASHLEY**

July 9 – 12, 2006 » Show 28, 29, & 30
Los Angeles, California

SOUTHERN CALIFORNIA IS KNOWN FOR ITS SUNNY beaches and relaxed atmosphere, something we thoroughly enjoy while hanging out in San Diego. It's a good change of pace from the hectic East Coast of the first leg and even the beginning of the second leg. In the morning, however, we're back at it. After picking up Tamara and Phil at their hotel, we race up the I-5 trying to get Venassa to the airport, but it's the one in Los Angeles not San Diego. Her flight leaves at noon, it's 9:00am, and the LAX airport is just over two hours away. We drive as if the highway was a Formula One racetrack, with Brian and Stefan following closely behind. In the van, I'm driving with Tak, Tatiana, Venassa, Tamara, and Phil as passengers. Having missed morning rush hour, it isn't as bad as we expected it to be, and we're able to arrive just before 11:00am, allowing time for Venassa to say her goodbyes until she returns for the two Gorge shows.

Pulling out of the airport, I notice a few stares from policemen standing by and, as anticipated, a police car pulls me over. While the officer checks over my license and registration, Brian and Stefan drive by and pull into a parking to watch and take photos. After finding nothing, the officer lets us go. "Welcome to LA," he says returning to his car.

We drop Tamara and Phil off at their hotel near the airport and then we go searching for a hotel for ourselves. Ending up in the suburbs of Malibu Canyon, we're able to find the Good Nite Inn, fully decked out with a swimming pool. After checking in, Brian leaves his car at the hotel, and we go looking for a place to watch the finals of the World Cup Soccer between Italy and France. We drive around Los Angeles for an hour in search of a little Italian bar, but are unsuccessful. In the end we settle for a visit to Universal Studios, where they happen to have the game projected on a huge screen in the middle of their courtyard. We sit up on the second floor balcony of the Hard Rock café for the three-hour match, which comes to a controversial Italian win. I normally support Italy in soccer so this win pleases me greatly, as does the chilli cheese burger I order from Tommy's Burger. Driving out of Universal Studio, we hear a large commotion coming from a little building at the entrance to the highway. We notice that it's an Italian restaurant, packed with fans cheering madly. This is where we should have watched the match and what we were searching for. Oh well, such is life. At least my burger was good.

We return to our hotel for a quick dip in the pool and then head out to pick up Cali Joe from work. On the way, we pick up some tailgating supplies including a very cheap bottle of Jagermeister to go along with our expensive Red Bulls. I also find something inside the 7-Eleven store that reminds me of Holly, some Hershey's Kissables. So I purchase a large bag and throw it into the black Holly bag. Meanwhile, Tatiana decides to try a Twinkie for her first and last time ever. Coming out of the store, I ask Cali Joe if he would like to drive the van to the venue and without any hesitation, he accepts. I migrate over to the driver seat and Cali Joe has taken over the van in California.

"I'm feeling a little nervous, like when you're going to ask that girl that you like to dance with you," Cali Joe explains. "In a couple of minutes, I'm driving the van for the first time so I'm psyching myself to prepare mentally. It's an honour to roll it into my hometown show."

Arriving at the LA Forum, we take a drive around the parking lot to look for a good spot to tailgate from but, with Southern Californians preferring to be fashionably late, the area is rather uneventful so we settle for an open area in an attempt to draw other people over. As fans being to roll in, some familiar faces from the East Coast stop by the van to say hi. Then out of nowhere, Brian from DC gives me a call and informs me that he has a pair of tickets from the fan club for tonight and he's obviously not in Los Angeles. So he has already transferred them over to my name, knowing that I would be here, and asks if I could use them. Still needing two tickets for Brian from Lethbridge and Tatiana, I gladly accept and thank him profusely for the generous offer. Once inside, Brian and Tatiana take their seats in the stands and begin playing "Where's Waldo" with the rest of us on the floor, trying to pick us out in the crowd to score points from. Apparently, I'm not worth very many points because I'm easy to spot from all angles.

Sitting about 30 rows back, Stefan and I have a limited view of the stage, but we do have a lot of room to move around because we're at the front of the section. The show itself is good but nowhere near the show that we saw in San Diego. Even with nearly 20 of the songs repeated from San Diego, the flow and the energy is not as strong as the previous show. Maybe it's just the laid back Los Angeles crowd, but Stefan and I put our best efforts in and end up having a good time anyway. After the show, I call Holly to let her know how the day went. She asks if they played *Daughter/It's Ok* at the show, but they didn't.

When the parking lot has cleared out, Cali Joe brings us to the UCLA area in Westwood for some In N Out Burger, my first fast food of the trip not including Philly cheesesteaks. Once parked, Tak suddenly disappears behind a tree, where he empties his stomach before filling it with fast food and, thus, living up to his new nickname, the Yak man. Inside the burger joint, he's fine again and even orders the same Double Double burger that I do. It tastes surprisingly fresh and very savoury, even better than the yummy Tommy burger I had earlier.

Across the street, we also try some ice cream sandwiches that Cali Joe has been raving about all day. It's nearly midnight, and there's a lineup of around 50 – mainly college kids – outside of Diddy Reese. With their combination of really good ice cream in between freshly baked cookies, this better live up to the hype. I order a rocky road ice cream in between a chocolate peanut butter and a macadamia chocolate chip cookie and it's one of the best things I've ever tasted. For a low price of $1.25, it's certainly the best value snack I've ever seen. Feeling sated and tired, we deliver Cali Joe to his car and return to the hotel in Malibu Canyon.

The next day we attempt to do the grand tour of Los Angeles, because Tak is leaving tomorrow. We start off in Santa Monica for a stroll down the beach out onto the pier, before picking up Phil at his hotel and moving onto Hollywood. However, misjudging the Los Angeles traffic, we end up in Hollywood mid-afternoon. Apparently, it takes an hour to get anywhere in Los Angeles, even if it's only 10 or 20km away. Jill meets us for lunch on Sunset Boulevard where we also visit the Emek concert poster gallery. Already late in the afternoon, we decide to forgo checking out Venice Beach and instead continue exploring Hollywood, walking along all the stars on the Walk of Fame. Tak seems to be in heaven, pointing out all of the big names engraved on the sidewalk. We spend an hour browsing through Amoeba record store, and soon enough, it's time to pick Cali Joe up from work and head to the LA Forum.

With Cali Joe at the wheel again, we arrive at the entrance of the venue and there's some sort of protest happening outside. To try and get our support, they hand us beaded necklaces as we enter the parking lot. So we put on our new "bling" and set up our tailgating party and are immediately joined by some local fans. I pull out the video camera and start interviewing a few of them. "Last night was the best show I've ever seen. No pyrotechnics, no screens, they just fucking rocked. They jammed all night, it was amazing," one says

Finishing up our bottle of Jagermeister, we decide to go in early to see Sonic Youth. Tonight I'm sitting with Tatiana on the opposite end of the stage as Stefan. We are treated to a solid show – the band seems to have regained their energy as does the crowd. It's amazing how they correlate with each other. The show is great! Sitting behind us are some of the Mexicans who we met last year in Kitchener. They have traveled north for the Southern California shows and follow us back to the van afterwards, along with a few other fans, including our next passenger, Monica from Sacramento. We will be jumping on board with us tonight. At the parking lot, I get a call from Holly. We catch up on the day's events, and again she asks if they played *Daughter/It's Ok*, but the answer is still no. With a mob hanging around us, Tamara and Phil are able to find us fairly easily. Tamara puts a "Hollywood style" checkmark for Los Angeles with photographs flashing off from every direction. At the conclusion of our applause, we pile nine people in the van and drive Tamara and Phil back to their hotel.

We make a pit stop on the way at another In N Out Burger, where Cali Joe challenges me to a 4x4 competition, which basically tests who can eat their 4x4 burger the fastest. The 4x4 burger consists of four beef patties and four slices of cheese, a monstrous yet delicious feat to attempt. And although the race starts off close, Cali Joe pulls away at the end, using his wealth of In N Out experience against my virgin attempt. To wash the mouth-watering burger down, I order a chocolate milkshake to further bloat my stomach. After the feast, we finish dropping Tamara and Phil off and take Cali Joe to his car and return to our hotel.

With the back-to-back shows in the books for Los Angeles, we're rewarded with a day off. However, we're up early again to drive Tak to the airport, as he's going home before returning for the Gorge. Leaving LAX, we again get a suspicious look from a police officer, but this time we're left alone. We jump back on the I-405 and drive toward Hermosa Beach, where we're able to chill out and watch the surfers from the pier. Down by the water, we write Touring Van in the sand hoping to capture it on film being washed away. We sit and wait but the wave never comes, even after we perform a wave dance. Hoping for better luck at our next stop, we drive out to the headquarters of the radio station 106.7 KROQ.

All week we've been hearing about a secret show that the radio station is putting on in Hollywood tomorrow night, with a yet-to-be announced "secret" band. The secret is not hard for us to figure out because we have been following the tour along with the band in question. Accordingly, the Ten Club has already randomly given away 25 pairs of tickets to local fan club members for this special show at the tiny Henry Fonda Theatre. The rest of the tickets are only to be given away by the radio station, with no other way of entry. Not being able to buy or win tickets, we figure that we should pay KROQ a visit. We park outside of the station and tune in to hear the DJ, Nicole Alvarez (who we've heard is a huge Pearl Jam fan) on the air. As she tells us a phone number to reach her at on the air, Stefan makes the call.

"Hello, is this KROQ?" he asks.

"Yes," Nicole answers.

"Are you located at 5901 Van Ness Boulevard?"

"Yes."

"Look outside! You got to come see our van!" Stefan tells her.

After explaining, in a less creepy way, that we're driving the tour in a Pearl Jam van, she tells us that she'll be down in a minute to see the van.

"I think Stefan just freaked out Nicole," Brian laughs.

"Yeah we're never getting tickets," Stefan replies.

A few minutes later, a girl with dark brown hair and a headband approaches the fence between us and the station.

"Where do you guys come from?" Nicole asks.

"All over, but the van is from Vancouver, Canada," I answer holding the video camera.

"Have you been to all the shows here?"

"Yes."

"Which is your favourite so far?"

"Last night was good."

"Last night was really good cause we got *Footsteps*."

"And you guys went to San Diego and Vegas?"

"Yeah, San Diego was awesome."

"Are you going tomorrow?"

"Well that's the only show we don't have tickets to."

"I can't do anything about tickets, but I can tell you what time you should be there by," she explains. "If I were you, I'd be there by 5:30. It was a winner's only contest but, people like you, I have a feeling you'd get in."

"All right! That's great!"

"They're my favourite things in the whole world," Nicole continues. "I cried like a Michael Jackson fan at the show. It's the most positive atmosphere you'll ever be in. If I see you guys tomorrow and there's anything I can do, I'll help you out."

"Thank you."

"Pearl Jam fans rock. You guys are the best," she says walking back to the building.

With that vote of confidence we drive out to meet up with Cali Joe, as he leaves work. Heading back onto the highway, we hear Nicole back on the air talking about us. She explains that she just met these Pearl Jam fans who are driving around in a big blue van to all the shows and that we're filming a documentary, before throwing in another plug about the special show that we have no tickets for. When we see Cali Joe we inform him about our little radio station adventure with KROQ, and he gets all excited. "You guys got to meet Nicole Alvarez? That's awesome. I've been listening to her for years," he explains.

Feeling a little hungry, we're lead back onto the highway trying to find dinner. On the way there, a new set of DJs are on the air and they also mention us. "Did you hear Nicole talking about those guys driving around a van to see all the Pearl Jam shows? Now that's dedication!" they say.

After driving around in circles, Cali Joe ends up bringing us to a Polish restaurant named Warszawa in Santa Monica, and the food is delicious. Even though it's just past their hours of operation, they allow us to order just about everything on the menu for everyone to share, including stuffed cabbage, potato pancake, Polish stew, pork schnitzel, and various types of pierogies and dumplings. To go with our meal, we order a bottle of Polish vodka, which is equally as tasty, if not more, and complements the food well. Along with his recommendations of In N Out Burger and Diddy Reese, Cali Joe has really taken good care of us in the food department. After the meal, we follow Cali Joe back to his parent's place, feeling a bit tipsy and full on Polish cuisine. This is where we're spending the night. Without making any noise, we set up on the couches and fall asleep instantly.

In the morning, we wake up to our 5:30am alarm, because today we're trying to get into the secret show in Hollywood. And no, we didn't misinterpret Nicole's advice about getting to the venue at 5:30pm. We're going to spend the morning at Disneyland first. With about an hour and a half drive to Anaheim, we arrive at the "happiest place on earth" just before it opens at 8:00am. Once inside, Tatiana seems to be in heaven. "I'm a child now!" she declares.

For the next five hours we run around the theme park in excitement, taking photos, checking out all the exhibits, and trying out all of the rides including the much-loved Tea Cups. Disneyland is much better than its much larger sister version, Disneyworld, in Orlando. Seeing all the Disney characters as mascots brings back old memories and, with all the kids laughing and playing around, it's a happy way to start the day. When we leave at 1:00pm, Tatiana is sad and grabs a re-entry stamp at the exit, just in case we don't get into the Hollywood show tonight and want to come back.

Tatiana, Monica, and Brian having a ball of a time on the beloved Tea Cups at Disneyland.

Arriving at the Henry Fonda Theatre at around 3:00pm, we find a parking spot directly across from the venue and realize that we're not the only ones that want tickets. There are already 30 other ticketless people lined up. It's shades of the Storytellers secret show in New York. We head across the street to check out the situation and there's a list going around with the order of who came into the line first, so we scribble all our names on it. Back at the van, I change the writing on the side to say "Tonight we rock the Fonda?", not knowing if we're going to be attending it. The lineup begins to grow even longer. Soon Tamara arrives and then Cali Joe, taking off early from work. Brian decides to make a sign stating that the Touring Van loves KROQ, but he forgets to leave space at the bottom for requesting tickets. Regardless, he puts the sign up on the van beside our question mark.

I grab my Canadian flag and walk around to the back of the venue, where there's another group of fans hanging around. Tamara starts talking to one of the security guards, as we notice Mike McCready and Boom just hanging outside the tour trucks. When McCready notices the crowd gathered just 20 metres away, he comes over to say hi and begins signing autographs for everyone. When he approaches me, I have nothing for him to sign except for my Canadian flag so I hand it over. He looks up at me and smiles.

"So how's the van running?" he asks, while signing the flag.

"Yeah, it's running well. It's got us this far at least," I reply.

"That's great."

Tatiana has her Brazilian flag signed, Cali Joe gets his Pearl Jam hat signed but Tamara opts for a photo with McCready instead, which we inadvertently intrude upon in the background. Back out front, the line continues to build. I return to our group, while Tamara chats up another security guard. Monica then finds a friend with a spare ticket for her, but she's a little hesitant about leaving us. We tell her to go for it and we'll wait around for her afterwards if we don't get in. Getting into the line for people with tickets, Monica enters the theatre when the doors open at 7:00pm, as Stefan and I walk down the street to a café to grab some food and a couple of large lemonades to cool off with. We return to the lineup, where our situation has not changed and security maintaining that it's pointless for everyone to hang around, even advising us to leave. "Well, I still have my Disneyland stamp," Tatiana states. "So I can go back if we don't get in."

A large Hummer then pulls up to the crowd and a couple of people inside start handing out cans of a new energy drink that they're promoting. Since they are free, I grab three and slam them back to inject some energy inside me and to cool off from the heat with. I then receive a call from Monica informing me that Nicole from KROQ is standing right beside her up front. She has tickets for us but with the crowd so tightly packed already, there's no way of getting out. I tell her it's okay and that we'll get in somehow. Just then, my bladder begins to scream, so I rush back down to the café to use their facilities, but it is occupied. I wait around thinking that maybe the three energy drinks was probably a bad idea. When the bathroom door opens, I recognize the person walking out and she recognizes me as well. It's Ashley, Mike McCready's wife.

"I know you! I met you in Canada last year," she says with wide eyes. "You're the guy with the van right?"

"Yes, I'm Jason. How are you?" I answer, trying not to pee my pants.

"I'm good. Do you have to go?"

"Kind of. Yeah," I laugh.

"Go on in. I'll wait for you."

After relieving myself, I come back out and Ashley greets me again. She explains that she heard we went back to Newfoundland to retrieve the van to do the whole US tour, and how happy she is to see that we made it out west. We chat for another 10 minutes or so and then she asks if we needed tickets for tonight. I tell her that we do but I think we should be able to get in on our own, but I thank her for the offer anyway. Just then, another fan in the café comes up and tells me that he recognizes me from the Touring Van DVD. I look over at Ashley and she smiles back.

I skip back to the line and share my encounter with the others. They all wonder if I asked for tickets but, to their disappointment, I sheepishly tell them that I turned down her offer. A bit later, a screen on the outside of the theatre starts showing footage from inside and at 8:00pm they show the opening band, Sonic Youth, begin their performance. Everyone in line is getting anxious. Jill's friends Mark and Su-Ann arrive to check out the situation, as they live in the neighbourhood. We tell them that it's not looking so good, but they stay and hang out. Tatiana meets another South American in the lineup, Christian from Peru, and they begin reliving the South American tour, which they both saw. When Sonic Youth finishes, not a single person has been let in from the crowd of over 100. I look at my watch and it says 9:00pm – Pearl Jam will come on soon. But then out of the corner of my eye, I notice Ashley walking by, so I turn to Stefan and ask him if he thinks we should ask her for tickets now.

"Where is she?" he asks.

"She just walked by."

"It's up to you. If you don't want to ask her for help it's understandable."

"Fuck it! Let's just ask. It couldn't hurt right?"

We leave the line and run after Ashley, who turns the corner and is about to enter the building from the back. I call out to her and she turns around.

"Ashley! Hi! I know I said that we didn't need tickets tonight, but it's looking pretty bleak out here. Is there anything you could do for us?" I ask, hoping not to sound like I'm pleading.

"I'll talk to my husband and see what we can do," she answers as she smiles at Stefan. "How many of you are there?"

"Well, there's like seven of us, but anything would be helpful."

"Okay, I'll look for you guys out front."

"Thank you so much."

We run back to the others and as we pass through the front, Tamara calls us from inside the entrance. Her chatty ways with the security has paid off and she's in. Just as we return, we can see the band take the stage on the screen up above. The security guard then shouts to everyone to listen clearly. He tells us that he'll be calling out names off the list that was compiled earlier but, instead of calling out the names in order, he's picking them at random. Everyone then abandons the lineup and begins to gather around the entrance. In the midst of it all, Tatiana ends up following Christian from Peru into the venue. Brian is grabbed by a girl he was talking to earlier and whose name was called, so he gets in. Not too long after, I hear my name. I look around at the others, and they tell me to go for it. So I head up to security and he escorts me to the balcony, which is where the VIP and industry people are. They are all sitting down.

I run down to the front of the half empty balcony during the fifth song of the set, *Severed Hand*, and begin dancing and singing along. One of the security guards asks me to sit down because everyone is sitting, so I reluctantly do so, even though I don't really want to. Looking over the front rail, I see the floor completely jam-packed, then I look around the balcony and it's still half empty. The feeling is weird, as I'm in this 1000 capacity theatre watching Pearl Jam and I'm sitting down during *Even Flow*. The guy beside taps me on my shoulder and introduces himself as a friend of Josh from DC. I ask him if he wants to help me get everyone standing in our row because no one can really ask us to sit down if we all stand. He agrees, so we rally some people around us and soon our entire row is now standing and moving around to the music. The security guy leaves us alone after that.

After the encore, I notice some people waving at me from down on the floor. It's everyone else from the van crew. They've managed to all get in and are all up front in the general admission area. Amazing and good for them! I give them the thumbs up as the band comes back for an encore set.

The show ends up being amazing and I feel so close to the stage even being up top. Without knowing if we were all going to get in to having all of us let in within 10 minutes of the show start, an extreme adrenalin rush runs through me during the entire show, and the awesome music from the band only punctuates this excitement. The show wraps up with an unbelievably fantastic performance of *Indifference* and, spent, I watch the crowd on the floor slowly disperse.

I run back to the van and Stefan tells me that Ashley had come back out to find us and picked him out of the crowd to give him the tickets. How sweet of her. I feel the warm fuzzies. He said that she gave him four tickets for him, Cali Joe, Mark, and Su-Ann and, before they could try to thank her, she tells them to hurry up and get in the venue quickly. Apparently, everyone else who stayed waiting around outside eventually got let in after the encore as well. I can't wait to call Holly to tell her about the show and to hear her voice.

The enthusiasm over the show creates a buzz around the van, with everyone telling their story of how the show went for them. Stefan borrows my phone and gives Tak a call to gloat about how awesome the show was and how he missed out by flying home a day early. Monica is drenched in water, from both sweat from being so hot and tightly packed inside and from the litre of water she dumps on herself afterwards to cool off. She tells us how she had a taste of Vedder's wine when he passed it around during *Crazy Mary*. Tatiana tells how she had brought her Brazilian flag inside and when McCready saw it, he pointed at her. She's now very pleased that we left Disneyland early. Brian describes how he followed a girl, who was leading through the crowd with her breasts, all the way up to the front. Cali Joe says that he saw me rocking out upstairs, where not many others were in the balcony.

"The show was unreal," Cali Joe says. "But let me show you something."

"What's that?" I ask.

"It's not tonight we rocked the Fonda?" he answers, while walking around the van to the other side of the van. "It's TONIGHT WE ROCKED THE FONDA!"

He changes the question mark on the van to an exclamation mark, emphasizing how great the show was. Hoping to see Ashley and thank her in person, we walk around to the back and wait for the band to come out but there isn't much happening other than the crew loading up the tour trucks. With the prospects not looking good at the back, we return to van at the front, where there's no one left. We decide to write a thank you note on the back of Brian's sign, and take a photo of us with the van and the venue in the background for Ashley. Satisfied with the results, we are just about to pack it in, when two vans pull up to the entrance of the venue, and out of the venue walks Boom into one of the vans. Behind Boom is Ashley, walking out next. We yell out thank you to her from across the street, she notices and blows a gigantic kiss toward us and then yells "thank you" back. At the same time, McCready is walking out behind talking to someone. When he sees us, he says hi and waves with a big smile.

"Hey, there's the van," he tells someone beside him. "I signed that thing."

Ashley comes back out of the van and blows another big kiss toward us, and we wave goodbye. Satisfied with the night, Stefan and Monica leave with me in the van, while the others hang around the venue a little longer. Cali Joe hands me the keys to his parents place before he runs back to the rear of the venue in time to blatantly intrude in on Tamara's photo with Stone Gossard. He gets Gossard to sign his hat beside McCready's autograph, and then it isn't until they leave that Tamara sees Cali Joe in the background of her photo. Tonight we definitely rocked Hollywood, and to show our appreciation, I take out the hockey tape and put on the van "Thank you Ashley!"

CHAPTER 27: **CITY OF VANS**

July 13, 2006 » Show 31
Santa Barbara, California

OTHER THAN MEETING NEW PEOPLE, I've found that discovering good food to be the next most enjoyable experience when travelling to new places and, during our time in Southern California, the Touring Van crew has eaten as well as it ever has. With his can't miss recommendations, Cali Joe has brought us to some outstanding eateries for our enjoyment and his vast knowledge of good restaurants even extends up north. Today we're heading up to Santa Barbara, back to our regularly scheduled tour, to try out a Mexican joint that Cali Joe has been telling us about. "I've never tried it but it's ranked in the top five Mexican Restaurants in Western America," he claims.

After a decent sleep following a long day, we pick up Tamara in the morning at the car rental agency, where she's returning a car and upgrading to a ride in the van. With Cali Joe at work during the day, I drive Stefan, Tatiana, Brian, Tamara, and Monica up Highway 101 early to check out the coast. For the short drive, Stefan entertains us by strumming a few tunes on the ukulele, including classics such as *Baby Beluga* and *Down By the Bay*. About an hour and a half later, we arrive at our destination. We notice a few things about this small town called Santa Barbara: the city looks gorgeous, there is an abundance of wealthy people in addition to the surf bums, and there are a lot of classic vans in the city. With my head turning in all directions every five minutes at the sight of all the vans, including many Dodge Ram vans, I can hardly keep my eye on the road. To calm down my excitement and obsession with vans, I call Cali Joe to ask about places to eat, and he again mentions the Mexican place. "You guys should give it a try. It's called La Super Rica and it's on Milpas street," he says.

Since his recommendations have yet to let us down, we take his advice and head to La Super Rica, where its tiny parking lot doesn't reflect the number of people in the restaurant itself. The lineup stretches around the corner outside of the building, so we wait patiently as everyone takes their turn at cramming into this diminutive take-out stand. This is a good sign. One thing that bothers us, however, is that there isn't a single Mexican person eating here, even though the chef and the staff are very Mexican. With a large menu consisting of many combo plates of traditional Mexican dishes, the restaurant is a little pricier than the other places we've tried so far. When it finally gets to our turn in line, we order our meals, one after another, and then we have to wait another 20 minutes for it on the other side. Once we all have our meals, we get back into the van and head down the road toward the beach for a Mexican picnic.

My first taste is a little bland. Even the extra hot habanera salsa I have drenched over my sopes is tasteless and not very spicy at all. Maybe I'm just unlucky. Next, I try my beef tacos and the beef is so dry that it might as well be jerky. So I think maybe it's just my meal but, when I look around, no one is really saying much and they appear to be struggling to finish as well. Stefan elects to not eat the sides for his fish taco combo and neither does Tamara. Monica, who's Mexican herself, is not impressed either. Not eating most of our meals, we're still hungry, so we head to Trader Joes to buy some chips and salsa, a much better and more economical choice. On our way to the venue, I see another Dodge Ram van, an identical one to the Touring Van, and it's even the same colour of blue. Seeing our twin, I just have to pull over for a photo.

"It's like seeing double," I announce to the others. "I wonder if we could buy this van."

"It could be Touring Van 2," Stefan says.

With the venue located in an upscale neighbourhood, there is a strict curfew and the show is scheduled to start earlier than normal so that it can finish earlier. We arrive at the lovely open-aired Santa Barbara Bowl to find a group of fans already lined up at the gate. Instead of waiting in line, we pick up our tickets and return to the parking lot for a few pre-show drinks. Cali Joe soon arrives directly from work and, when he arrives, we give him hell for his Mexican recommendation. It's as if his other previous winners don't even matter anymore. He confesses that he has never been there and has only read about it being highly ranked.

"You guys aren't ever going to let this go are you?" he laughs.

"Never."

But because he's not arriving alone, we soften our blow a bit. With him are his boss, his boss' wife, and his mom, as he's treating them all to the show tonight. Stefan and I hand over our tickets to him so that they can all sit together, while Tamara gives her spare to Stefan, and Cali Joe gives his pair to me with the spare going to Lydia from San Francisco. With all of the exchanges, we're all set for tickets except for Tatiana, so I double check with Cali Joe, who has something arranged with Brad. Apparently Brad has a ticket promised to him from a friend, but he's not in Santa Barbara. So he called Cali Joe to let him know of the spare ticket and that he wanted it to go to Tatiana. But she doesn't know any of this. "So, uhh, where's my ticket?" she asks.

"It's coming. We have a ticket for you," I reassure her, while holding six in my hand.

Cali Joe gives Brad's friend, Amy, a call, and finds out that she's still an hour away. So in the meantime, our drinking in the parking lot continues. We continue to ridicule Cali Joe for his taste in Mexican food – even though he's half Mexican himself – but praise him for his generosity of taking his mom and boss to the show. He explains that the last time he watched Pearl Jam at the Santa Barbara Bowl he had brought his mom to her first show, so this will be her second one ever. And for his boss, he wanted to bring him into his little world outside of work and show him why he has taken so many random vacations at the last minute. As show time approaches, some of us begin to head in, leaving just me, Cali Joe and Tatiana, and she's getting anxious by this point.

"What's going on? Do you guys have a ticket for me?" she asks. "Because I saw Christian earlier and he has a spare ticket. I want to go in soon."

"Don't worry Tatiana, just give us another 10 minutes," I respond.

When Amy arrives, she delivers the ticket and, without even looking at it, Tatiana urges us to run into the venue. Holding just under 5000 seats, the amphitheatre has about five levels of seating, all with spectacular sights of the beautifully constructed stage. We lead Tatiana down to the bottom floor area and then instruct her to have a security bring her to her seat, as we take ours. She's confused and doesn't understand what her ticket says, so a security guard guides her to the seat, all the way up at the front. Pleasantly surprised, she looks back with an excited smile from the first row, as we settle into our sixth row and eighth row seats respectively. Lydia is already sitting patiently waiting for me.

"These seats are seriously amazing," she tells me. "I'm so ready for this show. Thanks a lot."

The last time Pearl Jam played this venue, a special three-hour show filled with surprise guests ensued, so there's a palpable excitement in the air for tonight. The show opens with *Oceans* and then Vedder announces that the venue looks like a miniature version of the Gorge Amphitheater, so they're going to play a mini Gorge set, referring to an all acoustic set in the daylight to start off the show. The songs are relaxing and performed as gracefully as I've ever heard them. And true to their mini Gorge reference, *Low Light* is done with the sun setting. Returning to play an energetic electric set, followed by an equally lively encore, the show consists of three full sets, almost like three acts to an opera. Matching their quality of performance is the quality of the acoustics in the venue. Being outdoors, the sound quality is top notch and the best that I've heard all tour. With *Yellow Ledbetter* ending with the *Star Spangled Banner* again, the curtain comes down on the performance to a huge applause of approval from the crowd. We all meet up in the middle of the floor, where Tatiana's eyes are glowing. "I was getting the eye from Stone all night," she explains, with what little breath she has remaining.

Cali Joe's boss gives his praise for the show and his mom seems very happy to have spent the time with her son in his environment. Back at the van, we want to do the checkmark but, with the darkness settling in and Cali Joe having to work in the morning again, we exit with the masses and make our way back to Los Angeles. Brian decides to stay behind and hang out in Santa Barbara with a friend for the night, so Cali Joe's mom takes his place in the van.

"So this is the van that Joe is always talking about," she says when getting in. "It's very comfortable and I feel honoured to be riding in it."

The drive back is filled with nothing but questions from us to Cali Joe's mom about her son, which she gladly answers to despite his embarrassment. Needless to say, the ride back is an interesting one. With Tamara flying back to Vancouver early in the morning, I drop her off at her hotel near LAX, but she'll rejoin us at the Gorge. I drop off Cali Joe's mom and then the rest of us are led to one of her spare condos for the night.

In the morning, we're able to sleep in, a feeling that's a bit unusual. We start to get antsy and feel like we're wasting the day away, so we decide to get some real Mexican food by going back to a place in Malibu Canyon that we really liked before. When we return to the condo, we make up for the missed checkmark from last night with Monica doing the honours for Santa Barbara. It's a bit anti-climatic with less press around in the daylight, but it must be done. Cali Joe leaves work early again and meets us at the condo late in the afternoon. With Brian's car parked at Cali Joe's house, we set off north on Highway 101 for Santa Barbara again to pick up Brian to add to a van crew that includes me, Stefan, Cali Joe, Tatiana, and Monica already.

The late start puts us on the highway at sunset, as we follow the coast of the Pacific Ocean in search of a spot to pitch our tents. When we approach Morro Bay State Park, I pull into a liquor store to get some directions. We follow their instructions and are led to a road that wraps around the park. As the road becomes narrower, the fog becomes thicker. Without any street lights, the eerie darkness of the drive starts to resemble a scene from a horror movie. And the deeper we get into the fog, the spookier it gets. A little further down, there's a man standing by himself being as creepy as he can be when we pass by. When the fog finally opens up, a sign appears for a campsite.

No one is around at the entrance, so we drive on in and park at the first spot we see to begin setting up. While half of us put up the tents, the other half start barbecuing some food while fighting off a pair a raccoons that are scrounging around our camp. With our hockey sticks, we eventually scare away our relentless intruders long enough for us to eat our half-cooked meal. Then we snuggle into our sleeping bags. Our final stretch up the West Coast has begun.

CHAPTER 28: **THE VAN BREAKS DOWN**

July 14 – 18, 2006 » Show 32, 33, & 34
San Francisco, California

NORTHERN AND SOUTHERN CALIFORNIA aren't only miles apart in distance, but they are worlds apart in terms of environment and landscape also. For every white sandy beach down south there are as many jaggedly edged rocky beaches up north and, as we drive up Highway 1, we witness the dramatic change. The highway becomes windier and narrower, while the elevation changes quite rapidly. As we hit a straight stretch just past San Simeon, there is a parking lot full of cars. Cali Joe is on the wheel and decides we should take a look. What we find is a seal viewing area, where a large number of elephant seals are laying on the beach. As we leave, a convoy of about 20 Porches pull in. If driving up the California coast is appealing for the Porsche club, then it's definitely good enough for the Touring Van.

With lovely scenery all the way up, we're almost forced to stop every 15 minutes for photo opportunities, not making very good progress at all. By 2:00pm we reach Monterey, giving us plenty of time to get to San Francisco. Feeling that he needs to vindicate himself, Cali Joe takes us to a seafood restaurant at the end of the lovely fisherman's wharf. It's a little pricey and the fish tastes like mud, so it's not enough to redeem Cali Joe's restaurant credibility. However, he does pick out a fine tasting Malbec for our drinking pleasure. Enjoying the view from the restaurant, we end up staying for an hour longer than expected before remembering that we have a show tonight to catch.

By 4:00pm, I take over the driving again and bring it up a notch, speeding north. Because the coastal drive has taken up more time than it should have, I'm pushing the van harder than it has ever been pushed. But it smoothly meets the uphill obstacles. When we arrive in San Francisco a rushed two hours later, we approach city hall, where I pull in to park.

"That's only temporary parking there," the parking attendant says to me.

"I know. We'll only be five minutes."

Across the street is the Bill Graham Civic Auditorium and, with the show being completely general admission, the crowd lined up outside wraps around the block with no end in sight. My watch reads 6:00pm and the doors open at 6:15pm for Ten Club members – 15 minutes before the general public. Everyone is itching to claim a spot as close to the stage as possible. Walking across the street, I see our old friend Brad near the front of the line. After a quick hello, we pick up our tickets at the box office and then half of us join the parade to get inside, while the other half return to the van. Driving down two blocks, I pull into the Embassy Hotel, where a lot of the fans are also staying. In the parking lot, I meet Anna from San Francisco, who's carrying a box of items for the CCFA fundraiser for the shows here. She tells us about the group discount rate at the hotel, which we head inside for to secure one of the few remaining rooms.

The lineup to get into the general admission shows in San Francisco.

After checking in, we rush back to the venue, where the others have reserved an entire row of seats for all of us in the third row of the balcony, a perfect location for us to all enjoy the show together and not have to fight with the crowd down below. With this being one of the first fully general admission shows that the band has done in a long time, most of the fans have taken full advantage of the opportunity to reside near the front, while we take this opportunity to have everyone sit together. Looking around, the venue is more like a high school gymnasium than a concert hall. With an open squared-shaped floor, the balcony wraps along the sides and at the ends without any overhang, a most unusual setup. Soon after taking our seat, Vedder comes out by himself to greet the fans before playing *Dead Man Walking* as a preset. "Man, I've always wanted to hear this song live," Cali Joe says with a big smile.

Sonic Youth follows with their usual set, a truly perfect way to warm the fans up for the main event. Their music is so different and raw that it can often border between great music and just noise, depending on one's mood. One thing is for sure, they're the definition of alternative rock, and it has been a treat to see them play alongside our band. Thurston Moore just shreds his guitar to pieces tonight. When Pearl Jam takes the stage, the mostly dull crowd suddenly shows signs of life and, with the floor being completely open, I see much more movement from the fans than I have at any other show.

"Looks fun," I tell Brian. "We're definitely going down there tomorrow."

"No doubt."

However, we do our best to match the intensity from down below by making the balcony shake, at least in our section. When *Present Tense* is played, all six of us are singing along together at the top of our lungs with arms wrapped around one another, swaying backing and forth. It's truly one of the best moments from any concert for me. It's one thing to enjoy the show on your own, but it can be so much more enjoyable to share the experience with somebody else – and sharing it with a group of friends is the ultimate enjoyment. Feeding off one another, our enthusiasm is through the roof, prompting someone from behind to ask us to sit down. Ignoring this ridiculous request, we continue to build our energy throughout the show until the final notes send us happily into the night.

Outside of the building, there are already fans going directly from the stage out to the entrance to begin lining up for the tomorrow night's show. That's just insane. Fully equipped with sleeping bags and mattresses, they'll brave the cold Bay Area night for the chance to be up front again. But on further thought, because there are two more shows at this 7000 capacity venue, sleeping in the lineup will save them on hotel costs all week as well. It seems like a smart idea on the surface. However, being locked down on the streets will prevent them from seeing the enchanting city of San Francisco, which is more appealing to our group. Especially for the fact that I've been feeling the symptoms of a cold coming on for the past week and, after the show tonight, I believe that I have finally caught it. Throughout the trip, I've been fighting the cold with whiskey but tonight I'll try sleeping in a warm soft bed.

The next morning, I wake up feeling a bit better and ready to drive Stefan to the airport. He has to go back home to escape the madness of the tour so that he can concentrate on work, but will be coming to Washington and the shows at the Gorge. He says his goodbyes and then we hop in to the van. As I turn on the engine and pull out of the parking spot, the van stalls. Strange. I turn the ignition on again and it seems okay, so I pull out of the lot. Driving along the streets, the engine suddenly becomes very weak, and rounding the corner to go up hill proves to be a challenge. I step on the gas more but the response is slow and then nonexistent. Overnight, the van has become gutless with no acceleration abilities at all. It was running perfectly the day before when we were racing our way up to get here but, now, it can't even make it up a small hill. The van comes to a complete stop so I back it down the hill into a parking spot on the side of the road.

"Sorry man, I don't know what's going on. It might take some time to check it out," I inform Stefan, slightly sniffling

"No problem, I'll just take the train."

We walk to the train station, where Stefan takes the much quicker BART train to the airport. When I return back to the van, I start it up again and there's enough energy to make it up the hill. As I make a turn onto even ground, the van sputters and loses power again. Coasting back down the hill on the other side, I'm able to bring the van back into the parking lot. So after putting nearly 30,000km on the van going coast to coast both ways, the van has finally broken down for the first time. I struggle to even park the van before heading back up to the room to inform the others of the problem.

"Guys, the van is fucked! I don't know what's wrong. There's no acceleration power," I complain to everyone

"It felt fine yesterday," Cali Joe responds.

"I know, but it's fucked today."

"Did Stefan make it?" Monica asks. I tell her he took the BART.

"What are we going to do?" Tatiana asks.

"Well, there's nothing open today because it's Sunday. So I'll just leave it and try it again tomorrow. If there still is a problem, I'll find a mechanic."

"Well the good thing is that we're here for a week," Cali Joe reminds me.

"Yeah, if there was any place for the van to break down, this would be the best scenario. We have enough time to sort out all the problems."

So without our means of transportation, we walk up the streets to Chinatown for lunch. With the area more touristy than anything else, we walk by many hostesses trying to lure us into their restaurant for a taste. Finally choosing a less advertised place, we enjoy a bowl of soup along with the usual dim sum items. Continuing with our walking tour of the city, we stroll down Market Street to check out the scene. Halfway there, we bump into Boom Gaspar, Pearl Jam's keyboardist. He's a really down-to-earth guy and begins chatting with us for a bit. "I'm just living the dream every day and I give lots of thanks for everything," he says.

After a warm conversation, Boom's wife, who's about half his size, takes a group photo for us. Cali Joe also gets his hat signed again, and has now collected three out of five autographs on his Pearl Jam hat. We thank him for everything and he thanks us back before continuing with the conversation again. Our chat finally ends when a street bum comes up and asks Boom for some change, a pretty comical sight for us. "I'll look for you guys in the crowd tonight," he says as we walk away.

Walking by the venue around 3:00pm, there's already about 50 people lined up. We pick up our tickets and return back to the hotel bar, where the pre-party is being held. Looking through the table of items for the fundraiser, there are the familiar guitar pick t-shirts and stickers for sale, and up for raffle are bootlegs, posters, and even a Matt Cameron drum skin from a live show. But with half the people lined up instead, the benefit's not as lively as others we've seen. Anna is doing a great job regardless, and even brings the raffle tickets out to the people in line so they can participate as well. When she returns, I pull out the video camera and ask her a few questions about what she's doing.

"Well as you know, Mike McCready has Crohn's disease," she explains. "I was really excited to hear that these fundraisers were going on and, when I found out that no one was doing it for San Francisco, I jumped on it because I love Pearl Jam and this is an important cause to me."

Going back to our table, I bring over a round of Jagerbombs for everyone, and then a round of beer. While the others are happily drinking away, I duck outside to give Holly a call. After not talking for two long days, it's great to hear her voice again. She fills me in on the details of her flight to Seattle for the Gorge and expresses her excitement for it. "I hope the van makes it up there," I laugh as I explain what happened.

The afternoon is chilled out and without needing to drive anywhere, we're all able to enjoy our time at the bar. When it's time for the doors to open at the Auditorium, we join the back of the lineup, where coincidentally, Tom and Ingrid are standing. They had camped along the coast after the show in Las Vegas and have now decided to pop in for this show and finish off the tour. Following the crowd into the building, we casually stroll onto the floor seating area, as other fans rush in to be as near to the stage as possible. Once inside, we're asked to sit down on the floor, so as a group, we claim our spot near the front. Brian leaves and returns with a round of drinks for everyone and we yap with some of the people around us including Brad, who's at his usual spot up front wearing yet another Hawaiian shirt. Sensing something is going to happen, Cali Joe and I stand up just as Vedder strolls on stage. As everyone else is making it to their feet, we slip through a few people and end up practically in the second row near the centre, beside people that have been in lineup up all day.

Vedder performs *Driftin'* by himself and then Sonic Youth takes their turn, with the crowd already pressed up against each other. There's some breathing space but very little room to move around. After Sonic Youth's performance, we look around for the others in our group and see that they've also managed to make their way up front, a few spaces down from us. Being separated from the others, Cali Joe and I begin to make new friends. The two girls in front of us, Kasie and Veronica, are from nearby Chico, California, and they express their concern about the general admission crowd. We assure them that it will be fine. "The crowd's going to move that way toward the centre," I predict. "So expect a push in that direction during the show."

When the band comes on, the push comes immediately and I ride along with it all the way to front. I'm practically dead centre, just behind the front row of fans and on the other side of Veronica now.

"Hey you brat," she laughs. "How did you get in front of me?"

Cali Joe went straight forward instead and ended up on the rail with Kasie, so we both end up on either side of the girls from Chico. With the crowd now tightly compressed, the band starts off with *Sometimes* but don't finish it because

Vedder forgets the lyrics. From there, the volume turns up and so does the pushing around in the crowd. Getting to this spot was easy but staying here proves to be a lot tougher, as fans are constantly trying to improve their positions without caring what gets in their way. Veronica asks me if we're going to make it so I slip back behind her again, as she seems to be in a little discomfort, and I begin absorbing some of the pressure coming from behind. As the show progresses, the energy of the crowd grows and we're lifted into the air at times without much choice, jumping to keep up with everyone else.

The encore gives us time to catch our breath with the usual mellow songs calming down the crowd. There's even a group swing during *Black*, as we rock back and a forth to the song until the volume is up again for the last encore that causes a final push for the front. Some are starting to get more aggressive but I'm not about to let anyone pass me and am able to hold tight to my spot. Even though it has been tough, the open floor general admission crowd definitely adds more energy into the show and the band feeds off of it quite nicely, creating a more fun overall atmosphere and a more energetic show. The sore back and sweaty shirt afterwards are only small sacrifices.

Leaving the venue, there are again people hanging around outside after the show, but they aren't lining up for the next show. At least I hope not, as there's no show tomorrow. We make a run for pizza, beer, and a bottle of whiskey for my cold, and then we return back to our hotel, inviting Tom and Ingrid to stay in our cramped room as well. Wanting to spend a full day tomorrow exploring the city, we end the night early and get some much needed rest.

The next day, the van is first on the priority list. I wake up early to try it out one more time but it's dead again. Down the street, I find a shop called Kahn and Keville just opening up, so I explain the problem to the mechanic and then I'm able to muster enough energy out of the van to bring it in. Leaving the van with the mechanic, I return to the hotel where everyone is just getting up. Our plan today is to do some sightseeing. Without a vehicle, we attempt to ride the street car down to Fisherman's Wharf but the lineup for the tram is far too massive, so we take the bus instead. However, it seems that the City of San Francisco is aware of the fact that we're without a vehicle today because, for some reason, there's free public transportation all day.

Once we arrive into Fisherman's Wharf, we bump into Brad who decides to join us for the day. Tours to Alcatraz are completely booked out, so we rent bicycles instead and take them for a casual ride through North Beach up to the Golden Gate Park and onto the Golden Gate Bridge. The sun beaming down today helps create beautiful scenery, as we follow the edge of the harbour toward the bridge. With wind blowing through my hair, I'm as relaxed as I've been at any point during this trip. The worries of the van are behind me. Tatiana had expressed some concern about having never ridden a bike before but, within minutes, she looks almost as comfortable as the rest of us. Climbing the steep windy hills as we approach the bridge, I'm reminded of the last workout I did with Brad, a marathon run through Philly. At the top, there's a clear view of the Golden Gate Bridge, which is very similar to the Lion's Gate Bridge in Vancouver. We take some photos and then ride onto the bridge. The passenger deck is crowded, mostly with tourists looking back into the San Francisco Bay. When we cross to the other side, there's a different view of the iconic bridge.

"This is the place with the most suicides in the US," Brad informs us.

Crossing back over toward the city side, we begin to make our way back to return our rentals. As we coast down the windy hill this time, we hear sirens of ambulances and fire trucks heading toward the bridge. There must be an accident or something. When we return the bikes, the shop owner informs us that someone just attempted to jump off the Golden Gate Bridge. We look at each other, making sure that we've all made it back, stunned about the fact that we were just on there no less than half an hour ago.

During our lunch of clam chowder, my phone rings, and it's the mechanic. He lets me know that he has given the van a full tune up, replacing spark plugs, belts, and fluids. So everything should be fine, they even replaced the power steering belt, which had started to loosen up again.

"It's going to cost about $500, but there are no major mechanical problems," I tell the others.

"Well that's good news," Cali Joe responds. "She needed a break. We've been pushing it hard the last few days."

We return to the hotel and I pick up the van. Driving back up the block to our parking lot, the van seems to be running fine again, so I leave it parked and we plan the rest of the day. Brian has a dream of seeing all the baseball parks in the US, so checking out the San Francisco Giants home schedule, we discover that the Milwaukee Brewers are in town tonight. And already sporting a Brewers hat, Tom is all for our suggestion to check out the game. On the way out, we take Tatiana to the train station, where she's going to the airport and fly home to Brazil. We try to convince her to skip the flight and continue on with us, but it's not possible and she'll not be returning for the Gorge. "Thank you for everything," she tells me

"Anytime. We'll see you again somewhere," I answer.

Next, we hop on the bus that will take us out to Pacific Bell Park, with Brian, who is wearing a Boston Red Sox jersey, ready to boo the hell out of Barry Bonds. We manage to find cheap seats for all of us up in the top deck, where we're able enjoy a relaxing night at the ballpark. With the visiting team, from Tom's home state, building on an already commanding lead, Cali Joe, Brian, and I decide to explore the stadium. As we roam through the hallways, practically every fan that walks by makes a comment about Brian's Red Sox jersey – most appreciative, but some are obviously obnoxious fans of the rival New York Yankees. However, it's interesting to see that almost everyone has an opinion about his jersey.

We come up to the outfield bleachers and sit just behind the outfielders, where Barry Bonds is in position. Sneaking down to where all the hecklers are, we get a clear view and a great opportunity to heckle Mr. Barry Bonds. But just as we set ourselves along an empty row, the Giants manager takes Bonds out and replaces him with a substitute for the remainder of the game because the score has become so lopsided. Dang!

When Milwaukee takes the outfield, the full time hecklers go to work. Clearly a little drunk, they have some funny comments to say if not offensive. I receive a call from Tom telling me that they see us from the upper deck and begin waving at us. Brian sees them and as a joke, pulls up his shirt, pretending to flash them his white chest. This triggers a heckler from two rows back to comment. "Hey Boston, get a tan. You're blinding us," he yells.

"What?" Brian reacts. "How did I get heckled at?"

Brad, Tom, me, Cali Joe, Ingrid, and Monica at the baseball game in San Francisco.

Laughing about it, I tell the others what section we're in and they soon join us. We watch the last few innings of the 10-1 game with the hecklers before taking the bus back to the hotel. When we get there, I turn on my laptop to check my email and am surprised to see an email from Veronica, one of the girls from Chico at yesterdays show. She found my email address on the Touring Van website and describes last night as the best show she has ever been to, thanking me for helping her through the rough crowd.

...I had no idea who you were until my friend screamed at me afterwards that I was standing and holding onto the "Touring Van Guy." Even though I'm not a hardcore fan, I know all about touring van from my friend. I just want to say you guys rock and keep doing what you are doing. My friend was actually holding onto Cali Joe and is now head over heels for him. HA HA! I have never met more nice people than I did yesterday...

I show Cali Joe, who smiles and asks to be put in touch with the other girl, so I send his email address for Kasie. Feeling good about bringing joy to two people last night, we crack open the beers and enjoy the rest of the night staying in. With the bike ride and the baseball game, today has been a perfect relaxing day in this wonderful city. Furthermore, the van is all fixed up for tomorrow.

The next morning, we wake up excited to take the van for a spin around the city and drive down Lombard Street, known as the most crooked street in the world. We all pile into the van and we're on our way. But just as I make it up the hill, the van's power cuts out again. What? How could this be? It was just fixed yesterday. I take it back to the shop, where it's put at the top of their priority list because we're leaving the city tomorrow.

So, instead, we venture over to Lombard Street by foot and street car. Walking up to the street, I don't notice anything special about it, until we reach a one-way section between Hyde Street and Leavenworth Street. The roadway all of a sudden drops along a grade that's so steep that eight sharp turns are put in to allow for driving safety. There's a speed limit of 5 miles an hour and tourists stand all along the sidewalk to watch cars crawl their way down the twisty road.

After this bit of excitement, we walked over to Little Italy for lunch, before we split up to check out different parts of the city. Cali Joe, Tom, and Ingrid head out for more exploring, while Monica and I walk back toward the hotel to meet our new passenger, Dana from Brooklyn. After I had convinced her to come out west, Dana has flown in to San Francisco and will be in the van till the end of the tour. Over the phone, we set a spot to meet on the street and, when I spot her from across the road, I decide to sneak up on her for a surprise.

"I hear footsteps," she notes, as I approach closer from behind.

She turns around just as I reach her and we hug as if we haven't seen each other in years. Wearing a straw cowboy hat, Dana hands me a bowl of homemade cookies to carry for her. I recognize that it is the strange bowl that Aussie Ben found in the parking lot during our after show barbeque in East Rutherford. Cool!

On the walk back to the hotel, Dana asks me questions from all directions, as I update her on what's been going on with the trip. She seems pretty ecstatic about joining us.

When we get back, the first thing we do is check up on the van to ensure that our trip can still continue. After replacing a few hoses and tightening some bolts, the mechanic says it should be all fine now and he doesn't charge me any more money. I'm sceptical, so I take the van for a drive around the block a few times. It seems good.

"Are you sure? I think I gave you guys nothing but bad karma back east," Dana claims, referring to all the run-ins with police and the car accident. The bad karma that she believes she caused us has now become good karma, because the van seems to run well again.

I park it back at the hotel and Dana gets settled into our room. She pulls out a bottle of Jameson whiskey, which she brought specifically to share with me, and we begin snacking on her delicious homemade cookies. The others eventually return, and tell us how they bumped into McCready while walking back. Apparently his eyes lit up when they told him that they were driving around in the van with me and Cali Joe shows us the photos. We talk for a bit and then head downstairs to the bar for the pre-show party, where Lydia is now helping Anna with the fundraiser. I notice a nice heart-shaped box raffle prize that I want to buy for Holly, so I ask Anna if I could just buy it and she accepts my cash.

Taking a break from the drinks, I run out to the concert hall to pick up my tickets, where the lineup is already fully in action. As I walk along the side of the line, it seems like a mini reunion for me because I have to stop at every third or fourth person to say hello. Back at the bar, I place my daily call to Holly and let her know that the van is fine again but I'm starting to feel very ill and I blame it on how much I miss her. She suggests trying whiskey, and I tell her I've been trying hard but it's not effective anymore. Regardless of my health, she's excited about seeing me in less than a week, which still seems like a long time to have to wait. I'm lucky to have the people that are with me, keeping me company and occupied with excitement, including the CCFA benefits.

One of the items at the fundraiser is a scrap book of fan comments that will be handed to McCready after the show. Fans can purchase a page in it and write messages, put photos, or write whatever they want. Our gang decides to buy four pages and fill it with some Touring Van love, including a special thank you message to Ashley.

By the time 6:00pm rolls around, we're geared up for the show and join the lineup for the venue. Just like the previous show, we end up near the front, with Dana even getting up to the rail. Sonic Youth plays another great set and will be missed, as this is their last show of the tour. Standing within metres of us, Thurston Moore completely trashes his guitar at the end of their performance, yet still seemingly playing notes that make up their great sound.

When Pearl Jam takes the stage, Dana already looks to be suffocating from the heat and lack of oxygen due to the close proximity of everyone in the crowd. Security people hand us some water to rehydrate, but it's only good for a few seconds. And as the show goes on, it gets hotter and sweatier. Being closer to the prime spot also makes our positions even harder to keep tonight, as the pushing around is rougher than the previous show.

The show itself is another killer one and the energy from the crowd is unbelievable. This is the third consecutive show in this city and the band has done their best to play a wide variety of songs from their repertoire, as they always seem to do. For this show Monica has a sign that says "0 for 13, where's my tambourine" referring to the fact that she's seen 13 shows this tour and

Vedder has yet to throw her one of the tambourines that he normally tosses to someone at the end of a show. Unfortunately though, because the crowd is so tightly bunched up together, she doesn't get a chance to show her sign. We're eventually able to create a little bit of room for us to move around under our own control, but that is short lived and we must move with the crowd again. My shirt is already soaked in sweat, some of it not even my own, and the show hasn't reached the encore yet. This can't be good for my cold, but it's enjoyable nonetheless. The show ends with the band just ripping it on a cover of *All Along the Watchtower,* with McCready breaking his guitar and Vedder trying to surf with it afterwards. Peeling off of each other, the crowd slowly exits, while we grasp for fresh air. Many in the crowd receive souvenirs from the band and, although Monica didn't get her tambourine, she and Brad received drum sticks from Matt Cameron, and Lydia was handed the setlist from Vedder himself. We hang around inside the venue until security finally kicks us out.

With the next show in Portland being a late addition to the tour, this is the last show for a lot of the fans we've met during this California run so we say goodbye to those that are not travelling north. Monica decides to ride back home to Sacramento with a friend, Eric, and will meet us in Portland for the final drive to the Gorge. Skipping the pizza tonight, we head straight back to our hotel, where Dana and I work on the bottle of Jameson. She claims that she doesn't drink, but she's doing a good job of keeping pace with me. The two of us are the first to fall asleep. I know that the whiskey will either stop my cold completely or make it much worse. I can't wait to find out!

In the morning, I wake up feeling sicker than ever. Cursing the bottle of whiskey that was oh so tasty just seven hours prior, I realize that it was inevitable for this on-again/off-again van cough to get the best of me and I'm surprised that I have managed to hold it off for this long. After checking out of the hotel, I have enough strength to drive the van out of the city. The van feels fine again but the driver doesn't. So crossing the Golden Gate Bridge, we stop at the viewing area to change drivers and take the opportunity to have Dana do the checkmark. Dana checks off San Francisco for us and then Cali Joe takes over the wheel, while I migrate to the back to try and rest up.

After four days, we are finally leaving San Francisco. It might not seem long but, in terms of touring time, it felt more like four months. However, the stay gave us some time to relax from all the hectic driving, it gave the van some time to rest up, and it also gave my illness time to fester. Probably sensing my plague coming on, most of the van passengers have dropped out and it's now just me, Cali Joe, Brian, and Dana. We have a long 11-hour drive to Portland ahead of us that will be an even longer one when we take the scenic coastal route, but we have a day off to do it and a clear mind for adventure. Get the fuck out of San Francisco, Touring Van!

Up here so high the sky I scrape
I'm so high I hold just one breath
Here within my chest
Just like innocence

In My Tree

CHAPTER 29: **THANK YOU GIL**

July 20, 2006 » Show 35
Portland, Oregon

SINCE TOURING IN THE VAN across Canada and now the US, I've never felt as sick as I do right now. There has always been someone not feeling well and passing around what we call the "van cough", so I've almost always been on the verge of catching something, but usually it goes away the next day. Heading out of San Francisco, I feel like I'm dying. My stomach is rolling around in circles, my throat feels like it has needles in it, and my head feels like it's being constantly struck by a hammer. I feel so weak that all I can do is lie motionless in the back. Relentlessly coughing every five minutes, I take credit from stealing the sickness away from the van, giving energy back to it so that it can keep going for everyone else. Dana calls it the "Holly sickness" and that I am missing her too much. That could very well be the case, but the daily drinking and screaming songs at the top of my lungs for the last two months probably didn't help either.

The drive along the Northern Californian coast is mostly a blur for me, as I come in and out of consciousness trying not to move a single muscle because any movement requires effort, and effort creates pain. Feeling the shivers as well, I put on three layers of clothing even though it's nearly 30 degrees Celsius outside. My ears, however, work wonders for me. While Cali Joe takes us along the edges of the cliffs, straddling the coast, as we drive at a "slowly admiring the scenery" speed. When a car, which has been following behind our snail's pace, pulls out to pass, I can hear them cursing the hell out of us. Its fuck this fuck that, motherfucker this and mother fucker that. Apparently, they don't appreciate the alluring sights of the coastline as much as we do. So after this encounter, we start adding curse words to every sentence that we say to each other as a joke.

"Hey motherfucker, how are you feeling now?" Dana asks me.

"I still feel like shit," I answer. "Thanks for asking, you fucker."

"Hey fuckhead, there's a sign that's says drive through a fucking tree," Dana says to Cali Joe. "Make a fucking right."

"What?"

"Take this fucking exit."

As we enter the California Redwoods National Forest, consisting of enormous trees that have been growing for thousands of years, Dana has somehow noticed a tiny sign pointing us to where we could drive through one of these giant trees, but we're sceptical. Looping through the narrow roads of the forest, we soon see another sign to back her up.

"There it is, there it is!" she screams in excitement.

"What does driving through a tree mean?" I ask.

"I don't know but I think you literally drive through a tree," Dana says.

Intrigued by the compelling idea, I gather all my energy to get up and switch with Dana into the front seat to film this mysterious drive through a tree. As we enter the new roadway, there's a booth at the entrance informing us that the tree has a clearance of 6 feet 9 inches high and 6 feet wide. Paying the $3 admission, we continue deeper into the woods until we see another vehicle in front us sitting inside the square opening through the trunk of the Chandelier Tree, a sight that puts smiles on our faces. "I've always wanted to drive through a tree," Dana enthuses. "I'm very excited."

"There's some question to whether or not we're going to fit," Cali Joe observes. "It's going to be pretty close but we'll try not to get stuck in the tree."

"If we get stuck, we'll just bring the tree with us," I answer.

As the vehicle in front clears away, we take our stab at it, and the closer we approach the tighter the opening seems to be. Cali Joe is not optimistic but moves forward until the nose of the van is in. We look around for clearance and there's about four inches on either side. As we slowly nudge forward, Dana begins to feel the walls enclosing and can't handle the claustrophobia anymore, so she hops out of the van. We fold in our side mirror and, inching forward slowly, we're able to get the front half of the van into the tree, just as Dana runs out in front of us to take photos. Moving further along, the top of the moon roof begins to scrape the tree a little, but not enough to stop us.

"Straighten up your wheel," Dana directs.

"Which way is it pointing right now?" Cali Joe asks.

"This way, you need to turn it left."

"How does your side look?" he asks me.

"There's an inch here but I think you're straight enough to get through so just keep it going forward," I answer.

"You're fine. You're totally fine," Dana explains.

The full van tightly inside of the tree now, but with Dana's guidance up front, we manage to slip through the tree with minimal scraping. Once cleared, we all cheer. We then check for damage, but there is none. In fact, the 2400-year-old tree standing 315 feet tall with a 21 foot diameter ends up getting most of the damage, as the moon roof was taking out chunks from below.

"It was perfect! It was beautiful! It was a dream come true!" Dana announces. "Even though I felt claustrophobic and had to get out of the van."

"That was the biggest van I've ever seen go through there," the lady working at the gift store comes out to say.

So after making history again, the Touring Van continues on its journey through the Redwoods. I get in the back to rest up but Brian has already beaten me to sleep. Later, the drive takes us back along the coast and we enter the city of Eureka, where we pull over to watch the sun set over the ocean. At this point, I'm feeling worse than I have all day. But after finishing off the bottle of Jameson, my sore throat seems to have disappeared, and my sleep becomes more peaceful. When I wake up, it's pitch dark and we're driving through the Redwood National Forest again. We decide to find a place to camp for the night, but the only campsite that we find is completely full. So, not knowing what to do, we pull over to a picnic area to cook and eat our food.

"I'm not really tired so I could just keep on driving," Cali Joe suggests, so onward we go. Not too long on the road, I fall asleep and it's just Cali Joe and Dana still up. They manage to drive us into the state of Oregon, and by then, they're also starting to feel the effects of the long day of driving and decide to pull into a beach, where they see many other vehicles camping for free. Setting up the tent, they leave me in the van to continue my sleep.

In the morning, I wake up with the sunrise and feel much better. Maybe it's the smell of the ocean, maybe it was the whiskey last night but, whatever it is, I'm a completely different person today. Walking around the campsite, I see a restaurant open for breakfast, so I order some bacon and eggs. I return to the van with a stomach full of grease and begin cleaning up the camping supplies when I notice my Holly bag open and the bag of Hershey's Kissables half eaten.

"Sorry Jason, I had to stay awake somehow to keep Joe awake on the drive last night," Dana says. "Then I realized I was taking from the Holly bag, so I stopped." I tell her not to worry about.

With my illness seemingly gone, I jump into the driver seat and we leave the beach. However, going up the hill back onto the highway, the van begins to lose power again. Cali Joe says that the van felt sluggish last night and he could hear the engine sputtering, but they made it to the beach no problem. So as soon as I get better, the van catches its sickness once again. Instead of taking the highway, I struggle through the town of Brookings, which is just over the Oregon border, and pull into a mechanic shop but they are fully booked. The mechanic suggests that we try his friend down the road at Precision Automotive. "His name is Gil," he says. "He's a good Christian man and might be able to help you out."

We drive down the street until we find Gil's shop. There are a few vehicles parked on the side with their hoods up looking like they need repairing as well. As we walk in, the mechanic already has a vehicle up on the hoist so he might be too busy for us. The Portland show, which is a special benefit show for the Northwest Chapter of the CCFA, is tonight but we might not even get out of Brookings now. The mechanic comes out from under the vehicle and greets us. I ask if he is Gill.

"Yes sir, how can I help you?"

"Our van has some problems and we were hoping you could help us out," I explain.

"We're trying to make it to Portland tonight for a benefit concert," Dana continues. "But our van has been slowly breaking down along the way."

"There's no low end power and we're having real troubles getting up the hill," Cali Joe follows.

"What year is that van? Is that an '89?" Gil asks. I tell him it is. "I used to have the same van and I know a little bit about them. Let me see what I can do," he says. Despite the obvious cluster of work he has ahead of him, he says he'll spend some time on our van first. And with him having owned a Touring Van before as well, we're in the best possible hands that we could be. This is fate! We wait patiently as he pulls the van into the shop and looks into the engine. After a quick examination, he says that there's a problem with the emissions so he replaces a valve with a spare one that he just happened to have lying around the shop. Apparently, he goes around junkyards to pick up all these parts for the Dodge Van because they're typical problems that occur. We can't believe our luck finding this guy. Dana walks across the street to the bakery, while we continue to watch Gil pick apart and fix all the small problems that he sees.

"It sounds a lot better," I tell him.

"Yeah, you'll make it to Portland no problem now. There was a clog up in the emission lines, so I sprayed into this valve to open it up again," Gil explains. "But I'm sorry to say that I think there's still something wrong and I would need the van for a full day to find it. I have other cars that need work as well."

"No you've done a lot for us. Thank you so much," we say to him.

"It's going to get you to Portland. Just keep an eye on it," Gil says.

"Thank you so much. How much do we owe you?" I ask.

"I can't charge you guys. I feel bad and don't feel like I really did anything," Gil says. "But you'll make it to your show."

"Are you kidding? Don't feel bad. You've really helped us out," Dana says, as she hands him a bagel from the bakery.

"Praise the lord. It was my honour to help you," he responds. "Good luck with everything."

"Thank you Gil."

He ended up spending a good hour and a half of his own time to help us out. We truly have the karma working for us right now. Pulling out of the shop with the van running smoothly again and sounding better than it ever has, we get back on the highway filled with new hope and optimism.

Gil saves the trip by fixing the van.

We leave the coast and get back onto I-5 heading toward Portland with our healthy van. Because it's a benefit show, the tickets for tonight's event are more expensive than usual, with the first five rows costing $1000 a ticket, the next ten rows costing $500, the rest of the floor costing $125, and the balcony costing $80. In addition, people who purchased tickets on the floor also get the chance to take part in a special pre-show meet and greet held by Mike McCready and the CCFA. We all have tickets for the balcony, with the exception of Monica who will be attending the pre-show party with her floor seats.

"So Monica's going to be able to meet Mike?" Dana asks. "And Ashley is going to be there, right?" she continues.

"Yes. We should ask Monica to give her a thank you note for us," I suggest.

Stopping at a store off the highway, I buy a thank you card that we all sign, and then Dana picks some flowers from a garden to go along with the card. I change the lettering on the van to read "Tonight we rock Portland" and, when we enter the city late in the afternoon, I call Monica and ask her what she thinks about our idea. She agrees and says that she has a hotel room checked in for us already. So I drive up to where the pre-party is and hand Monica the card and flowers. Looking inside, I can see Mike and Ashley being mobbed by everyone, who are dressed much nicer than normal. Brad is also inside and gives us a wave. Monica says that she won't be too much longer, so Cali Joe stays behind to wait for her, while I park the van right in front of the Arlene Schnitzer Concert Hall and directly underneath the marquee.

Greeting us is Philly Ben, who has flown out for the last shows of the tour. Brian recognizes him from the Edmonton show so they talk. The crowd in front of the venue is a mixture of fans and scalpers, as there are many fans still looking for tickets to the show, including Lydia and her three friends, who are really wanting to go in because it's Stone Gossard's birthday today. She asks if I've seen any spares around but I haven't. Soon Tom and Ingrid arrive and are also looking for tickets. I give Cali Joe a call, wondering what's taking so long, and he informs me that we might have an upgrade in tickets. Apparently when Ashley saw the card and flowers in Monica's hands, she was so happy about it that she gave her eight more tickets for the show. When Cali Joe returns to the van, he shows me the tickets and they're mainly in the $500 level!

So shuffling the tickets around, Cali Joe, Brian, Tom and Ingrid take the lower level tickets where Monica is already sitting, Dana and I stay with our original tickets up top, and then I give Lydia four seats together in the balcony. With four remaining tickets, I return back to the pre-party to find Ashley. She's still being mobbed by everyone but, as she walks by, she says hello. I thank her for the tickets and let her know that we don't need all of them, while trying to hand them back to her. She thanks me for the flowers but won't take back the tickets, telling me to just give them away if we don't need them. So going back to the venue we decide to sell the tickets to fans and then donate the money back to the CCFA. We are selective and try to distinguish between who are fans and who are scalpers, a task that proves to be more difficult than we thought it would be. We accidentally sell one ticket to a scalper, but end up collecting $300 for the four tickets. Cali Joe gathers the cash for the donation.

When Monica arrives at the venue, she takes us to the Travelodge hotel, where I park, and then we walk back to the theatre. We get in just as comedian David Cross finishes his performance as one of the support acts. Dana and I decide to line up for drinks, when she runs into some friends of hers. She introduces me to Jessica from Connecticut and Sophie from Rhode Island. Sophie tells me that she has met me before in Canada but she must have me mistaken for someone else who drives a van because I don't remember her. Regardless, we chat in the hallway, with her mainly asking all the questions, fascinated about me quitting my job to drive around in a van. It's apparently a conversation we had the last time we met, but I'm again clueless about it. However, I answer Sophie's questions with a smile almost as big as hers. When it's time for the supporting band, Sleater Kinney, to take the stage in front of their home crowd, we find our seats. Their performance brings back memories of the Canadian tour, but memories of Sophie from Canada still don't register in my mind.

When the lights come back on, we get a glimpse of the elegant 2700 seat theatre, which is easily the most magnificent looking venue of the tour. To fill out this marvellous building, the headliners soon take the stage and play one heck of a show for their generous friends and fans. There's a different feeling in the crowd tonight though, as most are seated during the show. It's similar to the VIP section at the Henry Fonda theatre last week. Dana and I are about 10 rows back, dead centre in the balcony, with a perfect view of the stage. We're also on the aisle, giving us ample room to rock out, while many in the balcony sit.

During the encore, Vedder alludes to tonight being someone's birthday, before singing *Happy Birthday* to Stone. A cake is brought out, which Stone grabs and places on top of his head, and then he's given the microphone to sing his song, *Don't Give Me No Lip*. I look back at Lydia's section and they're screaming with joy. Before the second encore, McCready talks about the benefit for tonight and how much it means to him. They perform a few more songs and at the conclusion of the second encore, the lights come up and people start to leave. Not believing that the show is over, we slowly walk down the steps and, then, five minutes later, McCready comes back with another guitar, so Dana and I quickly grab the nearest seats to watch the final song. As Vedder announces the song, McCready points toward our direction and blows a kiss our way. Can he really see us from down there? And then I realize who's sitting in front us, it's Ashley. What a coincidence. She blows a kiss back to Mike and is dancing along to *Yellow Ledbetter* as if she's one of us. After the song, she turns around and notices us.

"What a great show that was," she says. "That was probably my favourite show I've seen."

"It was great," I reply. "Thanks again for everything Ashley." I tell her about what we ended up doing with the spare tickets and she praises our efforts and thanks us for the support, while shaking our hands. We say goodbye and she wishes us luck before she's mobbed by some of the CCFA people again.

Outside the venue we meet up with everyone. Monica says that she almost got a tambourine tonight, but it bounced off her head to the person in front of her instead. Brad wanders over and I let him know that I want him to do the checkmark for Portland, which he's happy about, but the van is parked back at the hotel so we'll have to wait. He then hands us all passes to a CCFA after party, complete with free drinks and food until 1:00am. Perfect, we can donate the cash that we got for the tickets there in person. Being across the street from the venue, the after party lineup is massive but we manage to sneak in with our passes, claiming that we are with the charity. Once inside, we fill up on the free tapas, as we've yet to eat all day, and wash it down with numerous cocktails. By the time the free service is over, we're completely plastered.

We walk back toward the hotel, where there's a bottle of Jagermeister and a four-pack of Red Bull waiting for us. Feeling the relief of having the van run smoothly again and my health returning to normal, we continue with our own little party in the Travelodge Hotel. With the pre-party starting her day off early, Monica is more than a bit tipsy and she's curious as to how drunk she really is. So responding to her inquiry, we ask her to try walking in a straight line while balancing an empty cup on her head. Needless to say, she fails almost immediately. When she falls onto the bed, she falls into her sleep.

In the morning, Monica wakes up confused about what happened the night before. "All I remember is trying to walk in a straight line and not pushing the butterflies away during *Even Flow*," she says.

"Pushing of butterflies" refers to a hand gesture that fans do during the lines "thoughts arrive like butterflies, oh he don't know so he chases them away" in the song *Even Flow*, mimicking what Vedder does in the music video. Evidently, Monica forgot to do this, an indication to just how much fun we had.

Thank you to Gil and thank you to Ashley for a great time in Portland.

Met my Halifax Buddy Met Jason at the RedSox/Mariners Game The Friday Night before the show. Sox won and Seattle was awsome!

Made Both Shows Despite the Heat 116° at 6:00pm Crazy!

This is our chance, this is our lives
this is our planet we're standing on
Use your choice, use you voice
you can save our tomorrows now

It's Ok

CHAPTER 30: IT'S OK

July 22 – 23, 2006 » Show 36 & 37
The Gorge, Washington

THE LAST TWO SHOWS of the US tour are to be held at the amazing Gorge Amphitheater, about three hours east of Seattle. These are the band's hometown shows and their grand finale for the tour. And after the memorable performance at the Gorge last year, they've made it twice as nice by scheduling two weekend shows for a big camping party, making these the most anticipated shows of the tour. Accordingly, almost everyone who rode with us on this tour is coming back to join the Touring Van coming full circle to where it all began one year ago.

With the van running effortlessly now, we're able beat rush hour and arrive into Seattle in less than three hours. Because we have no accommodations lined up, Cali Joe makes a call along the way and says that he has a friend with an empty house for us to stay at in Seattle. When we arrive, Dana directs us toward a dock along Lake Union, where her father lives on a house boat. She surprises him with a visit and ends up staying for dinner, while the rest of us drive into town toward Safeco Field for a game between the Mariners and the Boston Red Sox. Looking for tickets, we circle the stadium and bump into some familiar looking scalpers from Portland and San Francisco.

"You guys are doing baseball as well?" I ask.

"Of course. You need any tickets?" he inquires.

"No, we'll buy them from the box office."

"Okay, we'll see you tomorrow," he laughs.

Picking up four tickets from Ticketmaster, we enter one of the most delightful stadiums in all of sports and enjoy another relaxing night at the ball park. With the rest of us cheering for the hometown Mariners, the game ends up going Brian's way with Boston winning 9 to 4.

After the game, we drive out through the city and pick up Dana at the

Crocodile Café and then toward Lake Washington, where Cali Joe's friend, Allison, has just moved into a completely empty and unfurnished condo along the lake. So we bring our sleeping bags along with some drinks and have a slumber party on the floor. Being in an upbeat mood, I have a drink with the others before leaving for the airport to pick up Holly.

It's been about two weeks since I last saw her, a time frame that's much too long for our liking. We've been able to talk on the phone quite frequently, but not being together physically has been hard. So driving out to Sea-Tac airport, my level of joy is high. I park the van and move into the terminal to wait patiently at her gate. Her flight is supposed to land at 2:30am but my watch says 2:35am, so I'm getting anxious. What if there was a problem? I see passengers coming out that look like they were on the same flight, but I don't see her. I begin to panic and walk over to check the other gates. There's still no Holly. But as the crowd clears out, one last person emerges from the gate, and it's her. We run toward each other like a love scene from a cheesy Hollywood movie, and give each other a kiss that could last an eternity. My girl has arrived and I couldn't be any happier!

"I've missed you so much," she tells me.

"I got so sick without you here," I reply. "But I'm cured now."

"Oh I'm never going to let you go," she says, while squeezing me in tight.

Holding hands, we catch up on the happenings over the past week and slowly make our way toward the van. We can't keep off of each other though, and every five steps is a five minute make-out session, even causing a car to honk at us for being in the middle of the road at one point. Resisting temptation, we hold strong until we reach the van, where I show her the half eaten bag of Hersey's Kissables and the heart-shaped box that I got for her, while she pulls out a CD containing the San Diego show that meant so much to me. Driving out of the airport parking lot, I head down the street to find a hotel parking lot.

"We're going to stay here tonight," I explain. "Venassa is arriving early in the morning, so we might as well stay near the airport."

Moving to the back of the van, we make up for lost time before eventually falling asleep peacefully. As usual, the sun wakes us up in the morning, just in time to return to the terminal for Venassa's 7:00am arrival. When we pull up to the arrival section, we're immediately greeted by Venassa and her boyfriend Tyler. They pile their camping gear into the van and then I take them back to Allison's place. During the ride, we're all chatting back and forth, clearly excited to see each other. When we arrive at Allison's place and everyone is introduced and reunited, the storytelling continues, mostly marvelling at how everything has worked out just perfectly so far and how we're in possession of an abundance of good karma. "Everything works out in the end," I preach.

We thank Allison for putting up with us for the night and drive back into Seattle to meet up with the rest of the crew at 1:00pm. Already driving Holly,

Cali Joe, Dana, Brian, Monica, Venassa, and Tyler, I have a completely full van, so Stefan has rented another van to bring down the crew from Vancouver. Along for the ride are Tak and Lester, and following closely behind in his own vehicle is another friend, Spencer, and his friends. We all meet up just off I-5 in the parking lot of Northgate Mall, where all 14 of us are introduced to one another.

"Some of you already know each other, and some of you don't," I jokingly announce like an army general. "Whether you like it or not, these are the people you'll be camping with for the next few days."

For half an hour, we blatantly loiter around in the parking lot, grouped around in a large circle, until we figure that we should probably pick up some camping supplies at the gigantic GI Joes Sports and Auto store that we're standing in front of. Entering the Wal-Mart-like store for sports and outdoors related products, we split up to locate our needs. Spending almost an hour rummaging through the aisles, we finally converge at the checkout counter with some useful items and some useless ones. When it's all said and done we are now in the possession of a new giant gazebo, some fold up chairs, another cooler, another tent, a set of barbeque utensils, and a bucket of Bats and Balls pretzels. With the Gorge still another two and a half hour drive east, we return to our vehicles to begin our convoy out to one of the best concert venues in the world.

Driving along the I-90, there's nothing but chatter going around the van, a big contrast to the atmosphere last time we drove out this way. Taking full advantage of the convoy, I gave Lester control of the video camera in the other van so that he can shoot some footage of the Touring Van in action. We smile, wave, and even attempt to moon the camera as we pass by each other on the road. By 3:30pm, we've reached the town of Ellensburg, half an hour from the venue, so we pull into a Safeway to stock up on food and booze. As we load up the van with our latest supplies, a few rain drops fall. The forecast had called for possible showers, something that wouldn't be pleasant for an outdoor show and camping situation, but the hint of rain soon fades away. With boxes of burgers and packages of hot dogs, our food supply seems to be set. However, even with an entire shopping cart full of beer, we're still not satisfied with our alcohol, so we drive into the only liquor store in town for some additions.

I'm driving the Touring Van, while Stefan passes me in the rental van.

Oozing with excitement and anticipation, we enter the store seemly drunk already – drunk on enthusiasm! I first walk in with Venassa and immediately see a section labelled "Canadian" for the Canadian alcohol. All excited about our find, we ask the store clerk to take a photo of us with the sign. She hesitantly obliges and returns to her spot at the till. Brian and Stefan then walk in and see us exploring through the Canadian vodka section, and a bottle of Pearl vodka is found, so we have to take it out and take more photos. The cashier instructs us to stop taking photos, so we oblige. Grabbing a bottle of Crown Royale and another bottle of Jameson, we return to the cashier just as Cali Joe walks in playing *Can't Keep* on the ukulele. "That's it," the cashier says, "Get out of the store, all of you. I'm not serving you guys."

After our failure to obtain more alcohol, we leave Ellensburg and continue on. The scenic drive becomes familiar again as we approach the Columbia River and are driving away from the clouds. In the van, everyone has already cracked open a beer or two and are as festive as ever. We let out a boisterous cheer that's felt in the other van as well, when we pass a sign that calls for us to take the next exit. As I concentrate back on the road, I notice a line of vehicles on the shoulder up ahead. I slow down a bit and Stefan passes me to join the lineup. When I finally realize that this is the lineup for our exit, I swerve over two lanes of traffic, after shoulder checking, and pull in just behind Stefan's van. This is insane. There's another half a mile until the exit, and all of these vehicles are slowly crawling slowly toward it. Fifteen minutes pass by until we finally reach the stop sign at the end of the exit, where there are patrol officers watching every vehicle that drives by. Turning onto the road toward the venue, the long line of cars continues with no end in sight.

Tonight is an early 7:00pm starting time so we have roughly an hour to enter, set up camp, pick up our tickets and then run in. The drive into the venue, which normally takes 10 minutes, is extremely slow and Venassa decides to walk up ahead of us waving her Canadian flag around. Over 30 minutes later, we reach the gate to purchase a camping ticket. At this point, most of the passengers make their exit and head directly to the show, while the drivers continue on through an already jam-packed campground to find an empty spot right at the very end. We claim our spot by parking our vehicles spread out in the open field, and decide to leave the setting up for after the show. Being near the back, it takes us another 20 minutes to walk through the campsite to reach the venue. Once there, we see another chaotic lineup, this one for the Ten Club tickets.

We join the lineup and see Tom and Ingrid a few spots ahead of us, so I walk up to say hi before returning to our spot. There seems to be some kind of mix up or problem at the point of pickup and the line is staring to grow behind us. When it starts to move again, someone calls my name from behind and I look back to see Kyle from Atlanta, so I walk back to say hi. I continuously move back and forth to talk to different people that I recognize, while the line moves along slowly. When we're almost there, a security guard pulls me aside and tells me that there was a complaint about me cutting in line. I tell him that I was merely going back and forth to say hello to friends and that I'm in the correct spot. He looks confused and walks over to talk to his partner. While he's gone, our turn comes up so I pick up the tickets for Holly and I, just as we hear a small roar from inside. The band has started the show! We bolt down toward the entrance when the security guard grabs me and tells us to wait while he figures out what to do with us.

"Sir, I was not cutting in line," I plead my case. "You can ask these people who were behind me."

"I don't know if I can let you in," he says.

"Talk to the people at the ticket counter. They know that I was not cutting."

He walks over to chat with the Ten Club people before returning and freeing us from our torture of hearing the performance from the outside. With the show already well under way, we run through the gate and toward the stage. When we reach the top of the hill before dropping into the bowl, we pause momentarily, as we're struck by the beauty that is The Gorge Amphitheater. Looking downwards, we see the general seating crowd in front of us, sloping toward the still half empty floor seating area, with the stage being illuminated by the gorgeous back drop of the Columbia River. With her mouth wide open, Holly is speechless. The song playing on stage is *Severed Hand*, the same song that was playing during the last time I entered a show fashionably late in Hollywood.

"We have to watch the beginning of the show from up here while there's day light," I suggest. "This is incredible."

Finding an empty spot on the hill, we sit down and take in all of the "wow factor" of the environment. Although located essentially in the middle of a desert, the lush green of the grass on the upper amphitheatre nicely compliments the sandy brown canyon and the reflective blue of the Columbia River, which it all surrounds, not to mention the red hot heat that we've immersed ourselves into. I don't remember this place being so goddamn hot. What happened to those rain drops that were felt earlier? To deal with the heat, I take off my shirt and stuff it in my left pocket, with the Canadian flag sitting in my right. Having the sweat run down my body instead of my shirt allows me to put my focus back onto the stage.

My ears are enjoying the performance every bit as much as my eyes are, and the elements are even more beautiful than I remember it to be. Being here with Holly probably has a lot to do with it. The people around us are totally chilled out, yet still fully focussed on the stage. And despite the oppressive heat, there's no other place I'd rather be. At the end of the next song, we give each other a look, knowing that we're itching to move closer down to our actual seats. Then

Handwritten margin note (right side): WITH HOLLY. FIXED IT FOR NGHT 2 THOUGH. THE OPENER. AND WE MISSED BUTTON

Handwritten note (bottom): WITNESSED JASON BEING HASSLED ABOUT CUTTING IN LINE. HE DIDN'T AND SECURITY WAS KIND OF DICKS! IOC SCREWED UP TICKET DISTRI

without a word said, we stand up simultaneously and, while holding her hand, I lead Holly down the hill skipping and dancing to the beat of *Even Flow*, which is blaring from the band. Our adrenaline slows down when Holly's leg collides with an invisible fence and the song changes to *Down*, but we quickly rise up to regain form and find our seats in row 21 next to Stefan and Lester.

"You made it." Stefan screams over the music.

"What's up with the blood?" Lester asks, pointing to Holly's leg.

We look down and blood is dripping profusely down Holly's leg, probably caused from the impact with the fence. I pull out my Canadian flag to wipe the blood dry and then our full attention returns back to the stage as the familiar opening riffs of *Daughter* are heard. How amazing would it be if the band tagged on *It's Ok*, which has become the theme song of the US tour for us? The song would not only be ideal for Holly, but for everyone else because everything has just magically worked out during this trip and the song has given us the attitude that everything will be okay no matter what. As the song nears the end and progresses into the instrumental section, the band maintains the beat and the melody waiting for Vedder to choose a tag to add on with. The crowd is silent and waiting patiently as well. But instead of singing, Vedder speaks.

"It was 104 yesterday down in Portland," he says, with the band still jamming away in the background. "And we got news that it might be 116 here today. A hundred and sixteen! Clouds have never looked so good. We've got record heat on the East Coast and the Midwest and Europe. They're bombing the shit out of each other in the Middle East. And when you go to bed at night you try to tell yourself that it's going be ok. It's going to be ok. But last night I was thinking that maybe it's not. It's getting harder and harder to say it's ok."

In anticipation of what might happen next, my body remains still because any movement causes a break in concentration, and a break from concentration wouldn't allow me to listen to every syllable of every word that Vedder is articulating. I peek over at Holly out of the corner of my eye to see her also standing frozen in the heat. With our mouths as wide open as our eyes, the sun begins to set and the chord pattern transforms into our song.

"So would you help remind me?" Vedder continues, with an eruption of cheers from the 20,000 fans. "If I say it's ok, would you say it's ok?"

They're actually playing it! They're playing our theme song of the tour! They were thinking of playing it at the final show of the first leg in East Rutherford, but it was crossed off the list because it was not meant to be. So it has taken the entire tour for the song to resurface again, but I wouldn't have it any other way than to see *It's Ok* right here at the Gorge with Holly. And with every "It's ok" that Vedder sings, we reply with an emphatic "It's ok" of our own, joining the rest of the crowd in jubilation. While everyone else insanely jumps around during the verse, Holly and I remain motionless, still in disbelief that this is actually happening. When the chorus returns, we join in and our open mouths turn into smiles. This moment has just made the entire tour for me.

"I can't speak right now," Holly says to me with the crowd applauding the end of the song.

"Wow! That's all I can say," I reply.

The rest of the first set is somewhat anti-climatic for us with most of it spent trying to recover from the shock of what had happened, but the encore allows us to cool off and get a beer at the concession. In the lineup, there's a buzz going around. I hear my name being called and turn around to see Kelly and her husband Ted from Vancouver Island. The last time I saw her, we barely got her to Winnipeg in one piece. We have a quick chat and then they even pay for our $9 beers before we make our way back to our seats in time for an excellent encore that has a good mixture of favourites and rarities. For the second encore, a spot light is all of a sudden focused on something behind us. It's shining on top of the soundboard shed, which sits in between the general lawn area and the seated area. Suddenly, Vedder appears on the roof of the shed holding a microphone. With the band still playing their instruments on stage, Vedder sings *Last Kiss* standing in the middle of the venue to the delight of everyone.

Once Vedder is back onstage, the show continues and, a few songs later, the show seems to have come to an end with the performance of regular closer, *Baba O'Riley*, but the band merely catches their breath. Vedder thanks the fans for being there from the beginning, even back in the day when they wrote some "really shitty songs" before busting out *Dirty Frank*, an unexpected song that probably hasn't been played in over ten years and maybe only a few times ever. To close the night, Vedder hands it over to McCready, who tucks us into our sleeping bags with *Yellow Ledbetter*, followed by a full band version of Jimi Hendrix's *Little Wing*, and ending with the *Star Spangled Banner*. What a show!

We wait for the crowd to dissipate, before spotting and meeting up with everyone down on the floor. Everyone is completely speechless, except for Venassa and Dana, who somehow ended up sitting together in the second row. Agreeing that *It's Ok* was the highlight of the night and possibly the tour, we try to retrace our steps back to the van. The next hour is spent wandering aimlessly around the campsite in search of the van. What seemed like a simple path that we took earlier in daylight is seriously a major challenge in the dark. We pass vehicles that I don't remember seeing and then we see them again a short while later, so basically we're walking around in circles losing all sense of direction. It isn't until we find the main pathway that we drove in on and follow it to the end that we're finally able to locate our spot at the very back of the fields. We haven't eaten all day, so we are all anxious to grill up some vegetables and burgers, and relax. Some begin setting up the tents and some start up the barbeque, but everyone has a beer in their hand.

Within a few hours, we realize that we've purchased way too much food and not enough booze. Half of our beer supply is already gone and we still have the rest of the night and all of tomorrow, but we're not too worried about it, so we continue with our partying ways. By now, most are completely hammered and some are dead tired. It's already 4:00am, so Holly and I retreat to the van and others snuggle into their tents, while a select few decide to explore the fields.

"Where are you going?" I ask.

"We're going cow tipping," Ingrid says, with an evil Wisconsin laugh.

Fully equipped with her flashy head lamp, Ingrid leads the way into the open field, determined to find cows to tip like they do in Wisconsin. But instead of cows, they find nothing. They walk back, disappointed with the results, until they come across a set of light towers. Being completely drunk, Stefan decides to climb to the top of one for everyone's entertainment. Step by step, he scales its aluminum legs until he reaches the pinnacle, where he mounts the light tower as if it were a horse. While the others take photos, "Drunk Stefan," as he is dubbed, is on top of the world. After a much more difficult task of coming down, Stefan leads the pack back to the campsite, where they crawl into their sleeping bags just past 5:00am.

The sun rises at 6:00am and the stifling heat wakes me up along with a knock on the door. Venassa can't sleep either, so she comes in and has a seat in the van. She reports some of the shenanigans that happened after our retirement last night, which makes us laugh and ultimately gets us to sit up.

Being cooked inside the van, I crawl out for some fresh air, only to find the fresh air to be just as sweltering with the sun already scorching down on my skin. I check the time and it's only 6:30am. Wearing a mask to cover her eyes, Dana is sprawled out on the grass outside of her tent, while Monica is slouched over in a chair outside also. The others are lying in their tents with their doors wide open. Everyone looks drained out and exhausted and, even though they appear to be trying hard to sleep, they're clearly awake. But there's no movement, so I grab the video camera to film the action.

"Jason, are there showers here?" Dana asks empathically.

"It's called the river. You have to walk to it," I answer

"I'll go to the river," Venassa says.

"I'll jump in a river," Dana follows, still lying face down. "I'll do it."

"Monica, did you push the butterflies away last night," I ask.

"I did because I didn't do it last time," she laughs. "Joe did you push the butterflies?"

"Mmm hmm," Cali Joe answers, trying not to use any effort.

"I came in during *Even Flow* and pushed them away," I respond.

"Thank you," Monica says.

"I did a two hand push in both directions," Cali Joe explains.

"That is nice. So we all pushed the butterflies away," Monica confirms.

"What's the atmosphere here like?" I continue.

"Hot!" Cali Joe responds before I even finish.

"Yeah," Monica agrees.

"How hot is it?"

"It's so fucking hot!" Dana mumbles immediately.

"It's really hot!" Venassa says.

"And it's only 7:30am," Dana adds. "Can we go to the river?"

Looking around the area, other folks are up and going as well and most are already leaving the campsite to beat the heat. It isn't long until we're left almost alone in the section, with only a few others remaining around us. The quietness of being isolated eventually convinces us all to give up trying to sleep and begin pacing around the site. No one has slept for more than an hour so everyone is restless. To help out with handling the blistering temperatures, Holly begins giving haircuts, doing new Mohawks for Cali Joe and Stefan, and reshaping mine. "Remember, once you go hawk, you never go back." I warn.

"I'm just going to make a minor announcement," Dana interrupts, "We're going to make an effort to recycle and clean up our garbage."

"Since this is not Jersey, we can recycle," I respond.

"Exactly! We can recycle here."

Camp Touring Van at the Gorge campgrounds.

After finishing off Stefan's hair and reworking mine, Holly puts her tools away and we dive into our next cooling off technique, beer. It's not even 10:00am yet, but it feels as if dinner time is fast approaching. Holly's leg is now showing the effects of the fence collision from the show last night so, with the help of ice and cold beer cans, we try to heal it. Our efforts, however, are only as high as our desire to move, with everyone looking completely wiped out. As time slowly passes by, the temperature continues to rise. We're soon joined at our campsite by Brian, Brad, and his friend Mike, who were all smart enough to check into a nearby air conditioned hotel last night. Fifteen minutes in the sizzling sun and they've had enough. So already dressed in our board shorts and bikinis, we leave the Touring Van parked and load up the rental van and Spencer's car to drive toward the river for our next cooling down method.

Within seconds of our arrival, I jump into the water and, even though it feels like ice, it feels so good. The others follow right behind and soon everyone is in the frigid yet refreshing water, the very same river we could see beyond the stage last night. Surrounded by rocky canyon, the setting is breathtaking and, with 16 of us all in the water together, we can't pass up this photo opportunity. After a group photo session, we leave the water completely refreshed.

Everyone in the Columbia River, cooling down from the extreme heat.

In the park area, Tak is intrigued by someone and approaches for a conversation. The guy turns around and unveils a back entirely covered with Pearl Jam tattoos. At the top of his back is the pyramid with the eye in the centre from the album *No Code*. Below it, is the Given to Fly statue from the album *Yield*, sitting in between the 5 against 1 hand from the album vs on its left and the avocado from the new album on its right. Rounding out at the very bottom is the entire Binaural solar system. It's an impressive work of art indeed and he claims, when completed, he'll have the entire catalogue of Pearl Jam albums represented on his back.

Driving back to the campsite, we stop by at the box office to pick up our tickets, so that we don't have to go through the big cluster fuck that we went through yesterday. We feel slightly cooled off, but are suddenly immersed in the feverish heat again once we return to our camp. To create some shade, we drape tarps in between our vehicles and finally set up our gazebo with two Canadian flags hanging over the sides to block the sun. This is Camp Touring Van, and in Camp Touring Van everyone is calm and happy, while fighting the heat. Adding to the warmth, we barbeque more burgers, trying to work through our large remaining food supply. We sit around a circle and reminisce about last year's experience at the Gorge, and how everyone is back with the exception of Jacinta. I suggest that Stefan, Tak, Brad, and Lester should travel for the Australian tour to bring the inaugural group back together. I then remember that we haven't checked off Portland yet, so with Brad in our presence, we give him the honour for one of the final checkmarks on the van. "Actually, this checkmark idea came from you. How did you come up with that?" I ask.

Tak with someone that has a representation of each Pearl Jam album tattooed on his back.

"At the Gorge last year you had the yield signs setup and it was just begging for a checkmark," Brad replies. "And I didn't actually see them until Kitchener and saw that it had become a custom, so it was pretty cool."

Like an experienced checkmarker, Brad applies two strips of hockey tape next to Portland at the end of the van, which matches the "Tonight we rock Portland!" phrase, still unchanged on the other side. Following the applause, I begin interviewing everyone's reactions and thoughts about the show last night. Holly excitedly reminds everyone that the band played *It's Ok*. Stefan also helps out with the interviews by continuously squirting everyone with water, as they're answering my questions on camera. By 3:00pm we've finished all of our beer and still have half of our food remaining. The amphitheatre is opening within an hour so we decide to get ready and enter early to join a pre-show party happening inside the venue. Just before we leave the campsite, Brad informs Cali Joe that he's giving his spare front row ticket to him for the show. Cali Joe is so enthused about this turn of events that he ransacks through his bag to pull out his Hawaiian shirt to match the person that he'll be sitting next to.

Learning from yesterday, I wear nothing but a pair of board shorts and my Canadian flag. On the way there, we see a medical tent and stop off to get some bandages for Holly's wounded leg. Beside the tent is a water hose, where everyone is cooling themselves down. One by one, we drench each other in the fresh cool water, only to have it evaporate within minutes of leaving. We enter the venue without any troubles today and bolt to the merchandise booth, where Holly buys a pair of Pearl Jam socks. Next, we head over to the CCFA pre-party tent, organized by David and Lisa from Seattle, who we met at a gas station on the way to the Gorge last year. Some of us win posters in the raffle draw.

With more time available today, we're able to explore around inside the gorgeous concert venue before making our way down to our seats. We enter our row and I see Mike from Lethbridge, who rode in the van from Edmonton to Thunder Bay. I point out where the others are so that he can make his rounds to reacquaint himself with everyone. With some of the campers having left this morning, we're sitting closer to the stage in row 15 but on the opposite side to where Stefan's seats are. It's been a long day, as we've been up for 12 hours already and, by the time the band comes on, I feel completely exhausted. But with the help of Holly, I'm able to use what remaining energy I do have, and join her in rocking out to every second of this final show of the tour.

The first set is solid, but something doesn't feel right to me. My body is as every bit into this as any other show, but my mind seems to be running in circles. Maybe this is just another anti-climatic moment after the amazing show last night, or maybe my mind already knows that this the end. After the main set, Vedder asks the crowd if anyone was here a year ago, to which I cheer along with more than half of the crowd. He reminds us about his plea for Tom Petty to come down, which never happened, before he launches into an acoustic cover of *I Won't Back Down*.

At the beginning of the second encore, the spotlights are again focused on the roof of the soundboard shed, as Vedder pops up on top just like last night. With all eyes pointed up upon him, he sings *Given To Fly* and, with the wind blowing through his hair, it's as if he had flown up onto the roof. When the song ends, the band goes into *Little Wing* as he runs back to the stage just in time to join in on the vocals for a full version of the song.

A few songs later, Vedder introduces the band and then makes a farewell speech before McCready leads them into *Yellow Ledbetter*, a song that I'm not sure if I actually like or not. Although it's one of my favourites and it's always a high point of any show, it also always signals the end. Tonight, I don't know what to make of it. As the song begins, everything hits me all at once, all of my emotions and all of my thoughts. This is the end of the show and this is the end of my tour, we're all going home tomorrow. This trip, which has lasted over two months bringing me to all four corners of the United States, is finished. How did I get this far? It wasn't like the Canadian tour, where Stefan and Tak played a huge part in organizing the trip. This time I was pretty much winging it most of the time, just going where fate would take me.

All of the 20 shows that I've seen this tour are now one big blur. But coming through clearly are all the faces of the people that I've met, people that have helped me out with lodging, food, tickets, van repairs, and just pure kindness. Everyone has been there for me, even through the difficult times, to help this trip become what it has become – a beautiful thing. I feel touched and a great sense of honour to have crossed paths with everyone. And as I stand as still as the chair behind me, the clearest face of them all is embracing me by my side. Her warmth is warmer than the torrid temperatures that we've endured today. What will happen with her? She's also returning home tomorrow. As the show finishes, is this finished as well?

As McCready's guitar solos carry through the song, my mind is thinking a different thought with every note being played. These thoughts are coming in and out of my head even quicker than McCready's fingers are moving on the guitar. Vedder continues on with the verse, improvising lyrics as he goes, until the chorus, which ends with the line "I don't want to stay." He repeats the line, "I don't want to stayyyyyyyy!" before McCready takes over with his final solo to end the tour. With Holly holding on to me, the only muscles that are moving on my body are my eyelids trying to stop the tears from dropping. But they're ineffective. Holly notices the liquid dripping from my eyes so she lets go of me, allowing me to take it all in. When McCready goes directly into the Star Spangled Banner, my hands come together and I begin clapping nonstop throughout the American national anthem, while I am wearing my Canadian flag like a cape and occasionally wiping my eyes dry. As the final notes are hit, my clapping becomes louder, matching the rest of the crowd.

"Thank you. Good luck to you," Vedder says. "We're going home! Sweet home Seattle! Thank you neighbours. Thank you friends. Thank you foreigners, one and all. Love you! Good night!"

I continue to let my hands show my appreciation rather than my voice and maintain it until the final clap is heard from the crowd. Wiping my face dry, I give Holly a kiss, then look back up to find an empty stage. That's it. The end of the tour.

We walk up to the front where everyone else has already gathered around Brad and Cali Joe. Brad introduces me to someone sitting in his section and, with millions of thoughts still running through my mind, I don't catch his name. But this person tells me that he's friends with Tim from Seaside Heights, and he has read the article that has been written about us from the East Coast leg.

"Jason, you're going to love the article, let me tell you," he smiles. "The issue comes out at newsstands on Tuesday."

I say my goodbyes to everyone and then head for the exit, where there are more friends to say goodbye to, while my camp mates continue walking back slowly. Running to catch up with them afterwards, I avoid any chance of getting lost again. When we get back to our camp, we gather around in a circle, where

Tak initiates a conversation sharing his thoughts on the tour and what everything has meant for him. He says that the Canadian tour was his dream, but credits my drive and dedication for allowing his dream to continue. He thanks me for bringing the van back out west for one final ride.

The discussion continues around the circle with everyone sharing their feelings and thoughts, continuing on with Stefan echoing Tak's words and explaining how these tours have become more about hanging out with good friends rather than the shows themselves. Brad describes how great it has been to meet so many interesting and great people through the van and these shows that he wouldn't have normally met under any other circumstances. Tom then tells us how inspired he was from meeting us in Canada, which urged him on to drive along side with us up the West Coast with Ingrid. Next, Holly describes how she's never met so many good people in such a short period of time and how amazing it was to see *It's Ok* played last night. And then she turns her attention to me and thanks me.

"I'm at a loss for words. I don't know what to say," I tell everyone. "It's been simply amazing and I just want to thank you all for making my dreams become a reality. I don't have too much more to say, except for the fact that everything works out in the end, you just have to believe."

I turn to Lester beside me, giving him the cue for his turn and he speaks about what a great time he's had coming down both times to the Gorge and that he's impressed with the community aspects of Pearl Jam fans, something special that he rarely sees anywhere else. Venassa follows those comments by telling us how much she loves us all and that she could not be with a better group of people. Beside her, Dana discloses how great it is to have faith in people you don't know and how karma makes the world go around. Continuing on, Cali Joe echoes my thoughts and expresses how he believes there was some magical forces pulling us through the trip, a force of love that has carried the van all the way to the end. And to close out the discussion, Monica thanks everyone for being so kind and loving to her. She describes how the music means so much to her personally and that it's a powerful force that has brought us all together.

After an intense and emotional but very rewarding round table discussion, we applaud and thank each other and drink to celebrate the tour. When our alcohol runs out, we decide to leave our camp and follow our ears toward the music that we hear in the distance. And being avid concert goers, our ears don't fail, leading us to a group from Vancouver who are banging around on bongo drums. With my Canadian flag now draped on Cali Joe, they immediately welcome us and pour us some whiskey, inviting us to join in on their drumming. Not wanting the night to end, we party with our new friends until 6:00am, when the sun rises again. Holly and I crawl back to the van to sleep for an hour, until we have to get up again to drive everyone to the airport. We clean up our camping area and pack up everything ready to go. Then I turn on the van's engine, signalling our leave. But before we leave, we have one final checkmark ceremony to do, the grand finale.

"All right, it's the end," Venassa announces.

"So this is it. This is the day after the Gorge number two," Cali Joe shouts. "The van has completed where it has started."

"All right guys let's do it," Stefan says as he drags Tak and I over to the front of the van.

"Sept 1, 2005 to July 25, 2006, the three Vancouver boys that made it possible," Cali Joe continues, as we apply the final checkmark to the Gorge.

"That's it," Stefan confirms, as I reluctantly put the last piece of hockey tape on the front bumper of the van.

"And so it was, a page in Pearl Jam history. The Touring Van is completed," Cali Joe says.

Stefan, Tak, and I applying the checkmark for the Gorge, the final one on the van.

It's hugs all around as we say our emotional goodbyes. Venassa and Tyler stay behind to leave with Stefan, Tak, and Lester, while the rest of us pile into the van for one last ride. As I pull away, the van stalls and I have to start the engine again. Even though the van quickly responds, it doesn't sound good at all.

"Uh oh," Tak says.

"You're not getting very far." Stefan jokes as I pull away. "I always hated that Touring Van. I'm finally glad to see it leave."

"Die, Touring Van! Die!" Tak laughs.

"Tonight we rock Portland?" Venassa notices. "What's that about, eh?"

"Bunch of losers didn't even change the tape," Stefan acknowledges. "If that was my Touring Van, it would say 'Tonight we stopped rocking!'"

"What if it just exploded right now?" Tak suggest as they watch me exit.

"That's the funny thing," Stefan adds. "In half an hour when we leave, we're going to pass it and it's going to be on the side of the road!"

Leaving the grass and going on to asphalt, we have officially left the Gorge and are on our way to the highway. Everyone is already asleep again, except for Dana who has her flight first at 11:00am. Driving away, I'm all of sudden overcome with emotions at the magnitude of the end and begin crying profusely, so I put on my sunglasses to hide my tears. Ten minutes later, I see sirens behind me. So I pull over and blow my nose.

"How fast were you going, sir?" the officer asks.

"Exactly 50."

"And what's the speed limit?"

"I don't know. I didn't see any signs."

"It's 35."

"Okay. Just write me ticket," I don't even care anymore.

He returns with the ticket, and I drive off at the same speed until we return to the highway. On I-90 I pick up the speed, but not too much more, as it sounds like the problems with the van are back. Without any sleep last night, I haven't had any chance to clear my mind, and it's still messy in there filled with thoughts, memories, and confusion. My emotions begin to get the best of me again, and I'm quietly crying on and off all the way to Sea-Tac airport, the whole while not knowing if the van is going to make it. Why am I so sad though? Everyone is leaving, but I'll see them again. Holly leaving probably has a lot more to do with it, and also the fact that I'm confused and clueless as to what will happen next between us. But didn't I tell everyone last night that everything always works out?

We get to the airport three hours after leaving the Gorge, and the van seems to be doing better. I pull up to the departures drop-off, where Dana says goodbye to everyone. My tears must be contagious, because her eyes are even more watery than mine. She simply thanks me. I then park the van in the lot and the rest of us walk into the terminal. Monica's flight is not too much later, so we say goodbye. Brian and Cali Joe, on the other hand, have no flight booked yet. Brian needs to fly back to Los Angeles to pick up his car at Cali Joe's place before driving back to Las Vegas in time to play in the World Series of Poker, so he quickly books the first flight at the ticket counter. Cali Joe decides to take his time and will search online from his blackberry phone but before that he follows Holly and I back to the van to say one final goodbye. Grabbing his suitcase and guitar, he gives me a hug.

"When will I see you again?" I ask.

"Soon, you can count on it."

As he leaves, I close the back of the van, a space that hasn't looked this empty since the East Coast. There are now just two bags sitting there, and it's just Holly and me remaining. Her flight leaves at midnight, so we have the whole day together in Seattle. But before we get in the van, we promise each other not to think of anything sad and to enjoy the day to the fullest. So to get us back into the joyful mood, Holly pops in the San Diego CD that she burned for me, as we pull back onto the highway. My CD player is set on random and the first song it chooses is *Come Back,* the same song that I cried through during that show when I was missing Holly. This time, she joins me in weeping through the entire song, as we hold hands.

"Maybe we should listen to something other than Pearl Jam," I suggest.

Switching CDs, I continue on the highway back toward the city, where I find a parking spot along First Avenue. We walk down to Pike Market Place for a coffee and to watch the touristic tossing of fish. Then we drive out to Queen Anne and spend the next two hours at Easy Street Records, looking through their enormous collection of vinyl and CDs, before settling down on a bench in front of the space needle. For the rest of the afternoon, we sit, holding on to each other and looking out at the 600ft tall structure that is the symbol of Seattle.

"What's going to happen to us?" I quietly ask.

"I don't know," she responds. "What do you have planned now?"

"Well, I was considering going to Europe for the tour next month but I haven't booked any flights yet, so my plans are wide open."

"I could come to Vancouver for a visit in a few weeks and then meet you in Europe," she suggests. "Do you know where you want to go?"

"I want to see Italy but I'll probably go all over. For shows, I already have tickets for a festival in England and I also have tickets for the Athens show."

"Greece? I have a client that has a villa over there and says that I'm welcome anytime. We could meet there."

"Yeah? That would be great. I was also looking at staying in London after to work for a year," I explain. "That's a short flight to DC."

"Yes, it is."

"Everything is going to work out, the way it should."

"It will. I'm so happy to have met you."

"I'm so happy you met me too."

We continue to talk, with her asking me about Vancouver and me telling her how beautiful it is. After watching the sunset from one of the piers, we find a bar to have some final drinks and enjoy our time together. When it's time, we drive back to the airport. I park the van and we walk into the terminal together. We enter the elevator and press the button for the departures floor and the door closes. It then opens again and another the person enters. I get a feeling of déjà vu. It's none other than Bobby from Rhode Island.

"Hey Jason," he greets me. "What a coincidence."

"Yeah. Didn't I see you at the airport at the end of the last tour in St. John's?" I ask.

"That's right. How funny is that?"

"Well, I'll see you at the end of the next tour," I say exiting the elevator.

Holly checks into her flight and then I escort her to the departure gates, where we hug and kiss one more time.

"Thank you for everything," she says. "I'll miss you."

"I'll miss you too," I respond. "Everything's going be okay."

Through the glass window, I watch her pass security and head down the escalator, as she waves back. I feel sad but I don't cry. I'm impressed about it. I've become stronger through the course of the day. I stand there for a few more minutes – still watching the window – for the possibility that she might come back up on the other escalator, but it doesn't happen. Feeling that it's time to go, I turn around and return to the van. I'm now alone in the van for the first time in a month. Pulling out of the airport, I see the clock on the dashboard read midnight so I'm just going to drive. It's time to go home. It's time to go back to Vancouver.

With the stereo now turned off, I get onto I-5 heading north. Passing by the space needle, I say goodbye to Seattle. But then I notice the van sputtering violently and the engine sounds as if it's dying. Dammit! The problems are back and it's quickly deteriorating. I pull into the slow lane to get away from all the vehicles tailing me, but the van is losing power fast and there's minimal acceleration available. I take the next exit and realize that I'm back at Northgate Mall. At the intersection, I check the traffic well in advance and blow right past the stop sign, knowing that the van would not go again if stopped. Pulling into the same parking lot, where we all met before driving out to the Gorge, I park the van and check under the hood but it's too dark to see anything. So I go back inside the van, pull out my sleeping bag and call it a night.

How fitting is this? The van has served its purpose. It brought joy to me and brought happiness to everyone and, now that the last passenger has left the van, it's finished with nothing left to accomplish. It's as if the magical force that was pulling us through, taking us all the way to the end, has now left with everyone else. The only problem is that I still need to get home, but the van doesn't want me to go home.

In the daylight, I attempt to diagnose the problem but everything that I can think of has been fixed along the way already. I walk up the street and I find a gas station with a garage. I ask the mechanic if he has time to look at the van and he says maybe in the afternoon, so I turn on the van and manage to slowly crawl up the block. When he finally looks at it late afternoon, he suggests that I take it to a muffler shop, as it's probably something to do with the emissions. He gives me directions to a nearby muffler shop but, when I arrive, they inform me that they're fully booked for the rest of the day and will have to look at it tomorrow. So I leave the van in their garage and call my friend Cristin, who had come up for the show in Vancouver way back at the beginning of the Canadian tour.

"Hey it's Jason," I answer.

"Are you still in Seattle?" she asks.

"Yes. I'm stuck here. Do you think I can stay with you tonight?"

"Of course."

Luckily she's driving in the area and quickly arrives at the muffler shop to pick me up. I grab my laptop and a change of clothes and head with her back to her place. I check my email and there's already a dozen thank you messages from various people. I reply to each one, giving them the bad news about the van and then I summarize what I wanted to say at our round table discussion the night before but couldn't find the words. I tell them that this whole thing was never about Pearl Jam. And although it was Pearl Jam and their music that has brought us together, it's the kindness and love from all of us that has kept us going, a bond that will last forever.

In the morning, Cristin drives me back to the muffler shop, where I spend the whole day sitting and waiting for them to work on the van. When it comes time for them to check it out, they confirm that the exhaust is clogged up, and they need to order in a new one for me that won't arrive until tomorrow. So I spend another night with Cristin and another morning at the muffler shop. When the exhaust arrives, they quickly put it together on the van, and I'm able to leave before noon, another $600 poorer. Driving it along the block, I can feel it performing and sounding better but the acceleration problem is still there, so I return to the shop. After explaining the problem, they tell me that they're just a muffler shop and can't really diagnose anything too complicated, so they direct me to a Dodge dealership down the road. At the Dodge dealership, I'm told that their maintenance department is fully booked for the next two days, but they could schedule me in on Friday. Feeling a little bit frustrated at this point, I tell them thanks but no thanks, and walk back out to the van.

I reach into my wallet and pull out my membership card for the CAA (Canadian Automobile Association) and call the toll free number on the back. I know that I have one free towing with my membership, but it's only within a certain distance. However, at this point I just want to get home and money isn't really an issue. Cristin has been great but I don't want to take up any more of her time and, even with her tremendous company, I'm feeling alone. My call is automatically directed to the AAA (American Automobile Association), where I make my request for the tow. About half an hour later, a tow truck with a flat deck arrives at the scene. With a chain grabbing onto the two towing hooks located underneath both places on the front bumper where it says "The Gorge", the van is pulled up onto the flat deck and set in position for its ride.

"Where's this going to?" the man asks.

"The Canadian border please." I answer.

"So what's the story with the van?" he asks, as we hit the road.

I try to briefly explain but, before I know it, we're already there. Taking a little over an hour, the ride up is surprisingly fast. He drops me off at the parking lot of the Duty Free shop, and then leaves without charging me anything. I drive the remaining 100m until the border and, with zero traffic around, I'm able to go as slow as I want. Thinking that the border might be a pain, I get myself ready to answer questions about why I was in the US for over two months.

"Citizenship?" the border patrol asks.

"Canadian."

"Where do you live?"

"Vancouver."

"How many concerts did you see down there?"

"Umm, about 20."

"Which one did you like the best?"

"It was probably San Diego or the Gorge."

"Ok have good day."

The van being towed home across the border after breaking down one final time.

What? That was it? Feeling kind of ripped off, I want to ask them why they didn't question me some more, but I don't, so I continue to crawl along the highway – this time on the Canadian side – until I find a pullout just before I hit White Rock. I call CAA again and a truck arrives within 40 minutes to bring me back to North Vancouver. The driver isn't as conversational as the previous driver, but he does the job by taking me to my personal mechanic in my neighbourhood. He drops the vehicle, gets me to sign his work order, and then leaves without charging me anything. After all that fucking around in Seattle, I could have towed the van back home for free? I leave a note for my mechanic to call me in the morning, and then I call my brother to pick me up.

When I finally get home, I drop off my bags in my room and call Holly. After an hour of catching up on the day's events, I give Tim from Seaside Heights a call but it goes to his voice mail, so I leave him a message.

"Hey Tim, it's Jason. Well the van made it to Seattle for the end of the tour where it promptly died. It got towed across the border today and I just made it home. Mission accomplished!"

US TOUR **BY THE NUMBERS**

68 days on the road

20 Pearl Jam shows

582 total live songs

117 unique songs

22,592km driven

8 hours in the air

28 total van passengers

8 times pulled over by the police

Longest Drive – St John's to Boston and Atlanta to Colorado both 2600km

Most played song – *Even Flow* and *World Wide Suicide* both 20 times

EXPENSES (US Dollars)
$10,853.61 TOTAL

$3,180.33 for van maintenance and insurance (total for everyone was $3,270.33)

$870.00 for new video camera purchase

$330.00 for recycling fine (Jersey Cops)

$6,473,27 tour expenses ($95.20 per day)

    $307.11 for flights

    $1,468.28 for gas (total for everyone was $2,990.00)

    $301.88 for accommodations (total for everyone was $1,584.00)

    $1,959.00 for food

    $1,221.00 for concert tickets

    $734.00 for other event tickets

    $482.00 for merchandise and souvenirs

VAN CHECKMARKS

Boston – Rachel from St John's

Camden – Jason from Philadelphia

Washington, DC – Brian from DC

East Rutherford – Gregg from New Jersey

Denver – Kyle from Atlanta

Las Vegas – Brian from Lethbridge

San Diego – Venassa from Montreal

Los Angeles – Tamara from Vancouver

Santa Barbara – Monica from Sacramento

San Francisco – Dana from Brooklyn

Portland – Brad from Vancouver

The Gorge – Jason, Stefan, and Tak from Vancouver

CHAPTER 31: **THE NEXT STEP**

August 1 – 20, 2006
Vancouver, British Columbia

SETTING OUT FOR THE US TOUR, I was anxious to get back on the road, with the main goal of retrieving the van to bring it back home. Being back to normal life, I was hungry for some excitement and adventure and, when all I wanted was merely just any adventure, the US tour was better than every adventure. It surpassed all expectations, as my intentions of meeting a few new friends and seeing some old ones instead turned into meeting hundreds of new friends and becoming closer to all of the old ones. The entire tour was one giant rollercoaster ride of emotions for me and I basically just went with it. But it has now brought me back home safely. The van, however, didn't do as well and is now in the possession of my mechanic, who I know and trust. He'll repair it in his own time and it will be back and running again soon.

My first week home is very mellow. I haven't really called any of my friends, preferring to stay home for some alone time instead. Through emails and social networks, I regularly stay in touch with my new friends and I speak with Holly on the phone twice a day but it's not the same and I feel quite sad. Riding my emotions throughout the tour brought me to the Gorge, surrounded by great friends. It was perhaps the highest point of happiness for me but, it ended as quickly as it developed. As a very positive person, I don't think I've ever been this down in my life. I miss everyone, I miss being on the road, I miss the shows, and I miss Holly. Spending most of my time looking at photos and videos to relive the good moments, I think about her all day. And then I realize that she's on the other side of the continent, and I feel distressed again.

I spend the whole day mourning, waiting for my next opportunity to talk to her, and the only thing that allows me to sleep at night is the calming sound of her voice when she calls me late. Is this love? Am I in love? Is this what happens when you miss someone so much that it hurts? I've never had these feelings before. This complication has me thinking differently and has changed my perspective on things. I had originally bought tickets for some of the shows in Europe and Australia that are coming up for Pearl Jam in the next few months, but nothing concrete. I wanted to travel the world and explore for myself, but now I'm thinking of Holly as well. I still want to venture out but I've turned my focus onto what will happen between us, during, after, and even before I go overseas. I need to find out if there's genuinely something between us.

Expressing my intentions toward her, I learn that she's also going through similar emotions as well. It's hard to have these feelings for someone that you can't see on a regular basis. To get away from it all, I tag along with some friends on a surf trip to Vancouver Island, so I can throw myself into the ocean. This is what I need. This will set me straight and calm my soul. In the ocean, I can take a step back and reflect. I don't bring my phone, so we spend the weekend without talking and upon my return to Vancouver, I feel somewhat revitalized. I start to think that this could work. I have nothing holding me down and no real plans for the future, so I can go to Europe for a few months and see what happens. She can meet me there and it will be great.

I come home to find an email from Tim informing me of the details for the release of his article. When the August issue of *Relix* Magazine hits newsstands in Canada, I pick up five copies. The well written article talks about each member of Pearl Jam on a level that I've yet to see in any other publication before. It goes deeply into their personal thoughts, a little bit about their history, a view on their political opinions, and a few sections talking about the connection with their fans and Tim's experiences on the tour. Accompanied by photos shot by Danny Clinch, the article praises Brian from DC for his proactive ideas on the guitar pick shirts and then it talks about the Touring Van, comparing it to the old days when fans used to tour around for the Grateful Dead.

"I should be interviewing you!" laughs Vedder when he catches wind of my adventure. "How was it?"

"Stinky. And they would have ended up in Cuba if I didn't navigate, but I have never met kinder, more genuinely nice people in my life," I told him.

"That makes me so happy," says Vedder, "so very happy."

Along with the article in the magazine, there's another article on the Relix website detailing Tim's adventure in the van. Excited with my 15 minutes of fame and my newly revamped attitude, I thank Tim for the article and he advises me that Danny will be in Europe to shoot a movie for the band. Being a little more assured of my plans now, I book my flight for Europe, with a one way ticket to DC for a week, followed by a round trip flight to London and then returning to

DC. Beyond that, I'll leave completely open. That night I call Holly to check up on her. However, she's not as positive as I am, as the weekend without talking was hard for her and she is a mess. Compacted by the fact that she's not able to take the time off for a Vancouver visit that she had hoped for, doubt begins to creep inside of her about how realistic we are with each other. I cheer her up and assure her that even though we don't see each other physically, we can learn to support each other emotionally and it will turn out better in the end.

"It will work out the way it should," I remind her.

I inform her of my Europe plans but don't tell her about my stop in DC, leaving that as a surprise. She expresses her excitement for me, but it's evident that she is not optimistic. Discussing the future, we plan to meet in Greece for the final show of the European tour and then see where it goes from there. A few days later, I receive a box full of goodies from Holly, filled with photos, mixed music CDs, a pair of corduroy pants, and another jar of honey. I let her know how great of a surprise the package was and for her to expect a surprise from me for the following week. When the next week comes along, my anticipation for the Europe and DC trips has me feeling happy again.

The build-up of my optimism continues all week until the day before my flight to DC. Not aware that I'm leaving the following day, Holly calls to inform me that her work won't allow any more vacation time for her, after the extra time she took off for the trips to Las Vegas and the Gorge. She begins to panic and expresses her concern of never being able to see me again. Her doubts return and she begins to cry. She wonders what we're doing and why we're doing this, and starts to think that the distance is going to be a major issue. At this point, I have to tell her that I'm coming to DC.

"What? For real?" she replies in shock. "When are you coming?"

"Tomorrow," I answer.

The sound of her tears turn into tears of joy and, just like that, all is well again. I disclose my entire itinerary and she's ecstatic to hear it. Waking up early the next morning, I begin packing for the next few months and the unknown that lies ahead. With a stuffed backpack, my laptop, and my video camera, I'm set and ready for my morning flight. At my connection in Toronto, I call Holly to let her know that my flight has been delayed, even though it hasn't, to create a new surprise. Instructing her to stay at home to wait for my call, I arrive in DC by the afternoon. Taking a taxi to a shopping mall near Holly's place, I pick up a single red rose and walk the rest of the way to the house. It's not far but my bags are starting to weigh me down, as I'm used to driving. I arrive and enter through the back with the rose in my mouth.

"Aw yeah! You made it," Holly screams when she notices me.

She fetches the rose from my mouth with hers and the kissing begins. Her lips have never tasted so good, and my bags are dropped to the ground. Still blazing hot in the Northeast, we steam up the place even more. The night is wonderful and feels as if it has been years since we've last seen each other. But to us, it has been. We end up falling asleep holding on to each other on the floor of the living room, with empty wine bottles lying beside us.

Over the next few days while Holly is at work, I would get my stuff together and start looking into and planning my Europe trip. I want to spend some time in Italy and see some of the Pearl Jam shows on the side, but more and more people begin offering me tickets for the shows that I hadn't originally planned to see. Barbara from Italy, who rode in the van in Canada, has a spare ticket for the first show in Dublin saved for me, enticing me to go. I also receive an email from Venassa and Dana inquiring if I'm going to Dublin, so I confirm with all parties that my Irish plans are a go. Next, I promise to meet Monica in Verona, after she discloses that she's going and has a hotel booked already.

While in DC, I also meet up with Josh, who rode in the van in Ottawa, and he informs me of his plans of visiting The Netherlands and checking out the show in Arnhem. He offers me his spare ticket and, without much thought, I accept. Furthermore, Cali Joe hints at the fact that he might be able to take some time off and join me somewhere in Europe as well. Even though I'm going at this alone, my friends seem keen on joining in and supporting me all the way. So after buying tickets only for the Reading Festival and the final show of the tour in Athens, Greece, it now looks as if I may be adding some more shows on top of that. But without a van, it will be interesting to see what modes of transportation I find to get around with – I'll worry about that when I get there.

The week in DC with Holly is great but on the last night, my leave is imminent and we both quickly realize it. Tomorrow I'm leaving for Europe, and nothing has changed in our relationship. We've spent the week together enjoying every moment to the fullest, but what will happen between us is still unknown. Perhaps it's even more ambiguous than before. To further keep our minds off of the issue, Holly reworks my Mohawk giving it a darker red colour, but the concern is still lingering over us.

"I'm scared," Holly confesses.

"Me too," I respond. "But we can't really control what will happen."

I suggest that I could stay in DC for a bit after my Europe trip and skip Australia, but we both come to the conclusion that this wouldn't be a good idea. She alludes to the fact that London is fairly close to DC and that she could visit me if I'm living overseas but, with working in London not being a definite plan for me, it seems farfetched. Thinking further into the future, she proposes that I stay in Vancouver and wait for her to come to me, as she has always wanted to move out west. But I discuss my desires to travel and explore the world, while she talks about having a family in the near future and that she needs some time to grow on her own before anything major happens. The more we reason with each other the more it appears as though we're at different points in our lives, and that neither of us is ready to commit to anything the other desires. "I feel like it's all or nothing with you," she tells me.

Leaving for Europe tomorrow, I want to know where our relationship stands and where it will go. I need to have a clear mind so that I can truly enjoy my travels, but we're both still unsure. So the tables begin to turn and I start to panic. I even bring up the idea of not going to Europe anymore and staying until we figure out what's going to happen, but this idea is quickly withdrawn and shot down at the same time. She expresses the fact that I have such big dreams and she would feel guilty about holding me back from them. Puddles of tears start flowing from my eyes, tears for the fact that I know what's about to happen, and tears for how much she cares about me to let me go. We conclude that we should enjoy the rest of the night and that it would be best for both of us to take some time to grow on our own and let fate decide where we go from there.

"It's like what you've taught me, it will all work out the way it should," Holly reasons. "Go enjoy Europe and then we'll see what happens."

The next day, she takes me to the airport on the metro. Without a word said we hold on to each other. At the airport, we have lunch and begin talking cheerfully about the allure of Europe and how great it's going to be. When it comes time, I check in my bag and escort Holly back to the metro station. This is it. We give each other a farewell kiss. Deep down inside, I know that this will be the last time I'll see her. Wiping away our tears, we thank each other for everything and continue hugging, not wanting to let go. She wishes me the best of luck and I promise to write and send postcards and, like that, she's gone.

I stand at the same spot for a few minutes to reflect before heading back to go through security. When I reach my gate, I grab a seat away from everyone by the window and begin staring out of it at the planes coming in and out, much like my emotions are right now. I must be strong. I'm now off to Europe with what I wanted, a clear mind. Only, it doesn't seem to be too clear at the moment. Soon I'll be in London, England, ready to explore Europe. Will I be ready? Will I be happy there?

PART THREE
THE WORLD TOUR

EUROPE

- Dublin
- Reading
- Arnhem
- Prague
- Zagreb
- Milan
- Verona
- Torino
- Bologna
- Pistoia

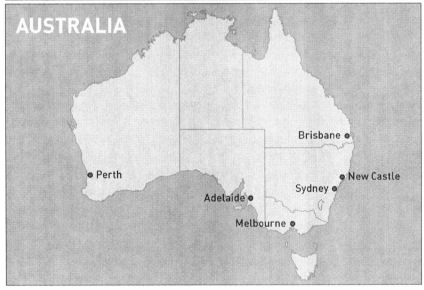

AUSTRALIA

- Brisbane
- Perth
- New Castle
- Sydney
- Adelaide
- Melbourne

How I choose to feel
is how I am
Inside Job

CHAPTER 32: **IT'S OK FOR ME**

August 23, 2006 » Show 38
Dublin, Ireland

EXACTLY ONE MONTH after the last Pearl Jam show, I've arrived in Europe for another adventure, this time in another continent. Taking the overnight flight, I arrive at Gatwick Airport in London, England in the morning feeling exhausted. I'm tired, not because of the seven-hour flight itself or for the fact that I'm changing time zones for the second time in the last week, but tired from the lack of sleep because my mind isn't let me. No matter how much wine the flight attendant would serve me, I'd only fall in and out of a daze, not fully getting the rest that I need. I might have left Holly physically in DC but, she's still with me on my mind. Having very little problems getting past UK customs, I pick up my checked in backpack and head to the ticket counter to purchase a train ticket.

"One ticket to Central London please," I ask.

"Single or return?"

"Single."

"Do you want the all day pass as well?" the man at the counter replies.

"Pardon?" I say, not understanding him or his accent.

"The all day pass allows you to travel around London all day," he explains.

"Umm, sure."

"That will be ten pound fifty."

With my all day pass in hand, I follow the crowd out through the gates and immediately notice a major influx of people within the terminal. I've heard that the London airports are some of the busiest in the world, but this is ridiculous. There are as many people here as in the last three airports that I went through to get here combined. Trying to look for signs for the train station, I'm bumped into by random people at least five times before I realize that I shouldn't stand still in the middle of nowhere. Not understanding anything going on in the airport, I ask someone where the train station is and follow his directions down the escalators. At the platform I'm confused yet again, as there are two sides to it. I ask a man dressed in a red suit, obviously working on the trains, if this train goes to Victoria Station. He confirms but, as I enter the train, he asks to see my ticket.

"Oh, this is not your train. This is the Gatwick Express."

When the next train arrives, he gives me a nod and I board a very spacious and empty train car and grab a seat with a table all to myself. Leaving the airport, the train takes me through the outskirts of London, which I find surprisingly green all around. I thought it was supposed by be grey concrete with grey skies everywhere. The seats on the train are comfortable and the room is ample, I could get used to this. Having no idea where I'm at or where I'm going, I listen to the call of the stations closely, Purley, Purley Oaks, South Croydon, East Croydon, Clapham Junction and then, finally, Victoria. Exiting the train, I follow the mob of people, who must have been hiding on the train, and make my way out of the station into what appears to be a mall. I look around for the HMV record shop where I'm supposed to meet Barbara, and I see it on the other side facing me. Getting there, however, is a more complicated task. With people rushing around in all directions, I zigzag my way through the traffic, apologizing to every fourth person who all seem to ignore me, until I reach the HMV. Ten minutes later, Barbara arrives and welcomes me to London.

"Wow, this doesn't really seem like a pleasant place," I note.

"It grows on you," she replies.

Barbara takes me down to another train system, the underground subway, which she calls the tube. We get off two stops later, only to board another train to ride on for longer. She shows me the network map for the tube system and it blinds me. There are over 10 different coloured lines going in all directions almost like a spider web. She informs me that we're on the red central line right now heading east but I'm still confused. When we reach the East Acton stop, she leads me off the train into a more rural area and we walk a few blocks to her house, where she cooks me some food from her homeland – pasta.

"So what are your plans for Europe?" she asks. "Are you going to be on that European Tour Bus or maybe a van?"

"I don't know," I reply. "No van that's for sure, but I did ask about the bus."

"You should join the bus for the trip to Arnhem."

After lunch, Barbara heads out for work, something that I'm foreign to now, while I try to rest up. Still not able to sleep, I turn on my computer to check my emails. I send one back home to let my parents know that I've arrived in Europe safely, even though it hasn't sunk in that I'm actually overseas yet, and I send a similar one to Holly. Next, I email this European Tour Bus to inquire about availability for the trip to Arnhem and receive a reply instantly confirming my spot. Good, I'm all set for the first few days. Now I can make another attempt at sleeping, but I still can't get Holly out of my mind. Have we done the right thing? How do I know what's right and what's not?

Rolling around on the bed, I decide to log back onto my computer and start typing out an email to her, expressing every single one of my thoughts and concerns. I reach deep into the back of my head and into my heart and start pouring out all of my feelings and emotions to her, good and bad. Anything and everything that crosses my mind I would type into this email, justifying to her that I really needed to let everything out and basically let her go to fully clear my mind so that I can enjoy this trip, because I'm in Europe but I don't feel that I am yet. When there's enough writing to fill a chapter of a book, I hesitantly hit the send button hoping it lands in her junk mail. It might have been too much for her to handle and might have pushed her away, but for me it must be done.

Barbara returns home in the evening and takes me back out to central London, where I walk through the famous Piccadilly Circus for the first time. Resembling a section of Times Square except with even more people, the surrounding roads loop around a massive water fountain curving in all directions, as opposed to the straight gridlock streets of New York. Because we're heading to Ireland, Barbara of course takes me to an Irish pub called Waxy O'Connor's for a pint of Guinness. With three floors and a nice wooden finish, the pub itself is bigger than any bar that I've ever been in and, being a fan of the dark beers, I'm quite impressed at the quality of taste as poured from the tap as opposed to the normal canned stout beer that I'm use to in North America.

"If you like it here, wait until you get to Dublin," Barbara notes.

At 11:30pm, the bar closes and we pay our tab. Suddenly, half of the British cash that I came with, at two and a half times the value of the Canadian dollar, are gone and I realize that this trip is going to be expensive. We return to Victoria station to catch a bus out to the airport for my first experience with Stansted Airport and Ryanair flights. Costing a total of only £40 for our return flights with the popular Irish airline, Barbara clearly chose the cheapest method of travel for us, but our flight leaves at 6:00am and the airport is almost two hours away. On the bus ride, we're able to rest up for an hour and then after checking in with only a carry-on bag each, we're able to get another valuable hour of sleep while waiting at our gate. When I wake up, I see a line of people standing restlessly by the gate, but there's still another half an hour left until boarding.

"What's going on?" I ask Barbara.

"Oh they're just queuing for their seats," she responds.

"Why?"

"Because it's general seating."

"Really? We don't have assigned seats?"

"Nope. Ryanair is all open seats."

"Is the plane going to leave earlier if we get on earlier?"

"No."

"Okay, I'm going back to sleep."

I'm awakened again later, this time by Barbara informing me that the flight is about to leave. Needing a stimulant, we buy a coffee at the stand next to the gate and then rush back just as they're about to close the door, but we're denied entry with the coffees in our hand. Apparently there will be coffee available for purchase on the plane, so we toss out our cups and board to find two seats remaining, about eight rows apart from each other. Not needing to sit next to each other because we'll be sleeping through this little-over-an-hour flight anyway, we quickly grab the remaining seats, allowing the plane to take off.

After landing, we enter through a very small and enclosed customs control, but end up on the other side in no time. Barbara has lived in Dublin before so she knows exactly where to catch the bus. Aboard a red double-decker that I thought only existed in London, we tour through suburban Dublin, with every block appearing to be the same as the previous. Just as the continuous suburbs appear to end, Barbara signals for our stop. We quickly visit one of her friends first and then we venture back onto the streets to look for the Castle Hotel, where Dana and Venassa are staying. With my mind still running in circles, I'm clearly not in tour mode yet, but as Venassa answers the door and wraps her Canadian flag around me, I'm a little closer to it. We are all together again. With the words "Eddie Would Go" embedded on her flag, Venassa explains her inspiration for pushing her to come to Dublin, when it looked like it was impossible to pull off.

"It was in memory of the van," Venassa says. "Eddie would go."

"Jason would go," Barbara follows.

I ask them how this all came about and Dana explains that she found out about getting a week off just two weeks ago and was trying to figure out somewhere to go before realizing that Pearl Jam is playing in Ireland, a place she has always wanted to visit. So she booked her flight immediately and asked Venassa to come along. With limited time, it didn't look possible for her to come but, when she heard that I would be in Dublin as well, she gave it a try.

"I had to get a passport, I had to get a lawyer, I had to get pictures done, I had to get signatures, I had to get time off from work, I had to find money," Venassa explains. "And it all came together two days before I left! So I phoned Dana and told her to have a great time in Ireland, and that I'll be there with her in mind, body, and spirit. Yep – that's right – body!"

"And we didn't even have tickets to the show yet," Dana adds.

"But it's no worries," Venassa follows. "Because in the van, Jason taught us that everything will work out."

"And it does," Dana says.

"I was telling everyone about you and the van," Venassa says to me, "And that you were touring Europe, and they said that this is inspiration."

Walking down O'Connell Street, we head toward the famous Temple Bars, where a gathering of fans are meeting up. When we enter the bar, pints of Guinness and shots of Jameson begin to flow toward us. There's a group of about 20 people gathered around with Pearl Jam shirts on that are obviously going to the show, so we join in to say hi. Many are seeing their first or second Pearl Jam show ever, so I feel embarrassed to tell them about my touring ways. But everyone is in good spirits and really looking forward to the show. One person recognizes me, however, when Barbara introduces me to him.

"This is Stian from Norway," Barbara says. "He's the one doing the tour bus for the whole tour."

"I've seen the DVD," he claims. "It's insane!"

"Well you guys will be doing the same thing," I answer.

"I sure look forward to it," he says. "When I saw what you guys did, I knew that's what I wanted to do."

We salute each other and bang our pints of Guinness together and then I take a sip, indulging myself in a little bit of heaven. The thickness of the dark roasted barley smoothly goes down my throat as its bubbly foam rests on the tips of my lips. Savouring every moment of it, I have now tasted the best porter style beer I have ever had. I quickly order the next pint with a quarter of the current one still remaining, hoping to time my finishing of the existing pint with the pouring and settling of the next. Being in the good company of Barbara, Venassa, and Dana definitely takes my mind off of everything, helping me get stoked for the show, because we're seeing Pearl Jam tonight. Dana wonders how it's going to feel for me to be on a tour bus in Europe and not be the one in charge.

"This is a little weird," I explain. "This is the first Pearl Jam show I've been to that I didn't drive to. I don't have to worry about anything. I have Barbara taking me along."

"For moral support," she adds.

"I've got Venassa here."

"For Canadian support," Venassa says.

"And I've got Dana here as well," I continue.

"You've got plenty of Guinness for support too," Barbara laughs.

"It's going to be different for me, but I'm excited to venture out to foreign territory, explore the unknown, and see where it takes me."

After a few more rounds, we walk toward the venue. When we arrive at The Point, there's already a huge crowd lining up in an orderly manner. All the shows in Europe will be general admission, so the same process as with the San Francisco shows apply – the ten club ticketholders being let in 15 minutes ahead of the general public. Unfortunately, because everything was so last minute for us, we never had a chance to purchase tickets from the Ten Club, so we join in with the other monstrous crowd. With the rain starting to pour down, the crowd begins to sing Pearl Jam songs, one after the other, and you can see just how excited these people are for the show. I forget that this will be the first real show in Europe in over six years, with most having never seen the band before. These fans have been waiting a long time to see Pearl Jam. So, not wanting to fight with all these people that are hungry to be near the front, I hang back as we enter, allowing Barbara to duke it out with them.

Inside the venue is like a long warehouse with two bars out at the front. Dana and I continue to drown ourselves in our beloved Jameson whiskey while Venassa plays around with her popcorn. It's odd to be at a show where there isn't anyone that I know hollering at me. That, of course, changes when I get a tap on the shoulder from Lethbridge Mike, who rode in the van from Edmonton to Thunder Bay. After seeing each other at the Gorge, Mike and I catch up again while the opening act, Paddy Case, is performing in the background. With Dana having a reserved seat in the stands, we begin wheeling and dealing with people in her section, switching them down to general admission until we're able to all sit together up in the stands.

Looking down at the floor, holding roughly 4000 or 5000 eager fans packed to the back, we can see how jacked up everyone is for the show. Some are already crowd surfing. When the lights finally dim and the band enters with *Inside Job*, I feel it all coming back to me. I now remember what it's like to be at these shows. The raw energy bouncing back and forth between the people on stage and the people in front of the stage is intense. The ferocious energy continues to build through the first half of the show, as it's rocker after rocker until they slow it down for *Daughter*. Starting to think about Holly, I'm reminded about the last time they played this song with *It's Ok* tagged for her. I try to fight off my emotions to enjoy the song but it's not working. As it goes into that familiar part of the song again, I stand frozen, as I did for the Gorge.

"Do you want to do a bit of singing?" Vedder asks the crowd to a reply of cheers. "I just couldn't wait to get over here and to hear people singing."

The chords change over to the distinct chords of *It's Ok*, and it happens again. My emotions win the battle over my resistance and my eyes begin to water up. And before I can pull them up to wipe my eyes dry, Venassa grabs a hold of my hand.

"This time the song is for you," she proclaims.

She's right. This song is for me. Vedder is telling me that "we've all seen better days" and that "we don't have to run and hide away" because "everything is going to be ok." He then jesters for us to say it with him and, at the top of my lungs, I scream "It's Ok" with Venassa holding on. An instant rush of electricity runs through my body and I feel rejuvenated. The cloud looming over me has been removed and all my worries are quickly disappearing. I'm in Europe watching Pearl Jam. This is a dream and I'm going to live this up the right way. Screaming out every syllable of every word of the song, I gain more and more confidence and finally feel completely myself again. My heart is still hurting but I'm in the perfect place to heal it, and I have some good friends beside me for support.

By the end of the song, the three of us are so vigorously into the show, that we nearly match the magnitude of enthusiasm that's happening on the floor, which appears to be ten times as intense as the general crowd in San Francisco. We rock so hard for the rest of the show that one fan jumps down two sections to tell us how much we're rocking. The show ends with a cover of *The Boys Are Back in Town* by Dublin's own Thin Lizzy, followed by *Leash* and then a cover of Neil Young's *Fuckin' Up*, the perfect way to close the night for a spectacular show. And even though we're all far away from home in a foreign country on a foreign continent, the feeling is definitely not foreign. On the stage tonight was something that made us all feel at home, something that brought us together in the first place, something that took us and is still taking us to many places. It's something that has now brought us back together again, and we're sharing it with the Irish and the Europeans, our new friends. Venassa and Dana get the closure that they claim they never got with the last show at the Gorge, and I am able to let loose from the power that was controlling over me.

Afterwards we decide to celebrate and explore the club scene in Dublin. With the others already inside, I find a pay phone and call Holly to detail the show for her. I tell her how much I miss her, but that I'm feeling great now because they played the song for me this time. And just like that, after a few more words are exchanged, my credits run out on the phone card I just bought. Back in the club, we continue with our Guinness binge until the wee hours of the night. We are embedded in a rotation of music that ranges from Billy Ray Cyrus to Billy Talent, with only the first few minutes of each song being played before the DJ switches over to the next. When the place closes down, we wander back to the hotel, where I thank Venassa and Dana for being here for me, wish them luck on the rest of their trip through Ireland, and say my goodbyes, before Barbara and I catch a bus back to the airport for another 6:00am flight. My Europe trip has begun, and I'm ready for it.

Venassa and Dana at the Cliffs of Moher in Ireland.

Bombs dropping down
overhead on the ground
It's instilled to want to live

Insignificance

CHAPTER 33: **THE READING FESTIVAL**

August 27, 2006 » Show 39
Reading, United Kingdom

SINCE THE TRAGIC ACCIDENT that took the lives of nine fans during the 2000 Roskilde Festival, Pearl Jam, who was on stage at the time, has shied away from festival shows and even general open floor crowds of their own. Six years later, they're back in Europe for the first time since, where general admission seating is the standard and playing festivals is what's sought after. Enter the Reading Festival, the world's oldest musical festival still in existence. Located just outside of London, the Reading Festival has become so big, that it needed to have another festival run simultaneously up in Leeds to keep the numbers manageable for the site. The lineup of bands would be almost identical, rotating their days between the two festivals. This year, both Reading and Leeds will be headlined by Pearl Jam. These festivals are a big deal in Europe, with over a hundred bands performing on multiple stages and, because of the popular demand, tickets are hard to come by. That's why I bought my weekend pass for the Reading Festival from a Pearl Jam fan six months ago, even after it had sold out.

After returning to London early in the morning with little to no sleep over the past few days, I spend the whole day and night resting at Barbara's place. So Thursday is a complete write off. Early Friday, I set off for Paddington Station to board a train for Reading. The train is full of fellow campers, packing around equipment as if they'll be gone for weeks, much more prepared than my day backpack with a change of clothes and a sleeping bag. I notice some people even wearing rubber gum boots already but, looking out the window, it appears to be fairly clear so my flip flops should do the trick.

Just half an hour into the ride, I'm at my stop. And as all the passengers depart from the train, the station is taken over by concert goers. I wasn't aware that there were so many people on this train, which now continues on north completely empty. Walking out of the station, I see that I'm in the middle of the town with no clue as to which direction to take but, judging by the parade of people turning right, I assume someone knows where they're going. There's busy traffic on the streets but, today, the traffic is from the large amount of people outweighing the number of cars on the road. Like sheep, we follow the person in front of us, and I can feel a sense of excitement going through the town. As we near the venue, a string of street vendors begin to command the sidewalks, selling everything from hotdogs and crates of beer to shirts and camping equipment.

Seeing this, I know that I'm close, so I pull out the phone that Barbara lent me and call Matt, the person holding my ticket for this weekend. He's already in the area with his friend Stewart, so I load up on supplies and we're able to meet up fairly quickly. He hands me the ticket and then invites me to camp with them on one condition – I have to help them carry back six crates of Stella Artois tall cans. Gladly accepting the offer, we continue on over a bridge and toward the festival. I ask them what to expect from the weekend and they mention checking out lots of weird and obscure bands to see what they're like.

"If they're crap we'll never hear from them again," Stewart says.

"It's 80,000 people all packed onto one field," Matt adds.

"Well the weather is cooperating, so it should be good," I note.

"Let's hope it stay dry," Matt replies.

I show my ticket at the entrance and they wrap a wristband around my right hand. Being experienced Reading Festival veterans, my fellow campers arrived yesterday to secure a good camping spot close to the concert grounds. As I enter, I see nothing but tents densely populated, with no end in sight. But despite the vast amount of campers, the area is surprisingly well organized, with sections marked off creating clear pathways. It's tent city everywhere else, however. As we arrive at our centrally located campsite, Matt's other friends Mark and Nadia are chilling inside of their nicely set up gazebo. Each of them came from either London or just outside of London and they have all been to multiple Reading Festivals, with Pearl Jam being the main attraction this time around. We place all 144 beers in the shade, even though it will all be warm in 10 minutes, and I'm introduced to British canned beans for the first time. I make my contribution to the campsite by hanging up the Canadian flag.

By mid-afternoon, we can already hear music blasting from inside, so we decided to go into the concert grounds, just a short five minute walk away. I exchange my ticket for another wristband that will allow me entry all weekend, and then we bust through the front gate along with a whole mob of other people. With tens of thousands of people roaming around already, we explore to find an entire carnival of events happening inside. You can't get anywhere without going through some of the markets that sell everything from umbrellas to artwork. Beer is flowing in every direction you look and there's enough food at the various concessions stands to feed all of Reading. Many choose to take a seat on the grass waiting for the bands they want to see, because music is why people are here. Ensuring that music is happening at all times, there's one large stage in the main area, three stages inside of tents, and a disco dance tent with a lineup of DJs. And when you want a break from the music, there's a tent for stand-up comedy and a tent with video games to keep yourself busy as well.

The camp area at Reading Festival.

We make our way to the main stage to see the singer from Panic at the Disco get struck in the head with a bottle. He's down and out for 10 minutes, while the rest of the band stops playing to check on him. Apparently it's a tradition that people throw bottles at acts that they despise and, every year, they choose one band that everyone pummels bottles at. "I reckon My Chemical Romance is going to get bottled this year," Matt says to me.

Looking through the mini schedule that hangs from a lanyard on our necks, we're not impressed with the list of bands coming up, so we return to the campsite where we already have beer. By early evening, we decide to save a few pounds and purchase food at the concessions just outside of the gate before heading back to the main stage in time for the Yeah Yeah Yeahs to perform. The crowd is already full, so we're content on being in the middle of the pack, watching the dual large screens mounted on either side of the stage. From there, we venture over to one of the smaller tents to see some of the acts that I was really excited about. The Eagles of Death Metal rock every inch of space inside and some outside of the tent. They are followed by the always amazing Mark Lanegan with the Twilight Singers. It brings back memories of our drive to Calgary when Stefan played Lanegan's entire discography in the van. The others return to the campsite satisfied, while I catch the tail end of Franz Ferdinand on the main stage with the crowd filled to the back.

As I make my way back to the camp, I notice people dancing in a tent just outside of the concert grounds, but I don't hear any music. People are moving as if it was club, but there's no DJ. I ask around and find out that this is a silent disco and upon closer look, I notice everyone wearing wireless headphones for the music. For an outsider looking in, the sight of a large group of people dancing to no music is hysterical but, for the people inside, it seems completely normal. The live music ends at midnight when the silent disco begins and lasts until 6:00am. Not too far from the silent disco is a movie tent that runs all night as well, so there's no need for sleep if it isn't required. When I'm back at the camp, some of the guys are already asleep, but I stay up for a drink with the ones that are still awake before heading off for my first good sleep of the trip.

With the amount of people camping for the weekend, there's no realistic way to put in shower facilities at the festival. But upon examining the map, we find something called the Man Wash. Curious about what the name entails, Matt and I follow the map to find that the Man Wash involves bikini-clad girls washing mostly men, who stand on a slow moving conveyor belt that pushes them along an assembly line of the girls. It's similar to a car wash, where one girl would be in charge of the hose, a couple would handle the scrubbing, another would rinse, and a final girl would do the drying. It's fun to watch but trying to get in on the Man Wash is a different story, as there are more people lined up here than the entrance to the concert grounds. We decide that it would be ok to suck it up without showering all weekend and soon head in for some music.

The first band we want to check out today is Wolfmother from Australia. Opening for Pearl Jam at a few of the upcoming shows, Wolfmother plays an energetic performance early in the afternoon. They're sort of a cross over between Black Sabbath, Led Zeppelin, and The White Stripes, and the rocking music sets a good tone for the day. We then migrate from the main stage to see a popular British band The Automatic, before watching Canadians Alexisonfire and Americans Clap Your Hands Say Yeah. It's an international day of music.

To give our ears a break, we hang out by the beer tent, which at £5 a beer, is draining our wallets quickly. I head back to the main stage to see what all the hype is about for a couple of British bands, The Streets and The Arctic Monkeys. Not as impressed as the rest of the 50,000 people in attendance are, I then return to the smaller second stage to catch the talents of The Raconteurs. As I leave the tent, rain drops begin to fall, so the others return back to the campsite, but I stay for the final act on the main stage – Muse. With incredible visuals and lighting displays, Muse put on a very pleasing show, ending a full day of music for me.

When I walk back to the camp, it begins to rain harder. Escaping into our gazebo to stay dry, I invite a few of our neighbours in as well and, with the Canadian flag still hanging, my fellow campers are mistaken for being from my country as well – but they love it. The rain continues to build along with the wind and, at one point, the monsoon is so strong that our gazebo blows over. Scrambling to retrieve it, we quickly pound a few more spikes to hold it down. When the rain finally stops, our level of tiredness and drunkenness convince us to call it a night and, for the second straight night, I have a great sleep.

Disturbing my peaceful rest, the police wake me up in the morning. They inform us that there has been a few robberies within our camping area and that some of our neighbours, who we had in our gazebo last night, are involved. When they inquire if we have anything missing, we quickly go through our stuff to find everything still intact. I emerge from the tent to see three youngsters being handcuffed, standing beside two tents that I didn't see last night. Apparently they arrived in the middle of the night and started filling their automatic fold up tents with personal belongs from around the site. I go through my bag one more time to see my passport still there. That was close. With half of our neighbours disappearing, our area opens up revealing the amount of rubbish that we've accumulated. Filling a couple of garbage bags full of trash, we bring them to the garbage bins, where we're rewarded with a cold can of Carling beer for each bag, a good system to encourage people to clean up after themselves.

I soon receive a call from Barbara, who has arrived and is already inside the concert grounds, so I leave the campsite to meet up with her. Once inside, I see her waiting patiently for me along with her friend Zita. I say hi and then quickly take them to one of the smaller tents where a Canadian band, Metric, is performing. Being familiar with the area by now, I then take them on a tour around the festival. We briefly check out another Canadian band, Broken Social Scene, before showing up at the main stage in preparation for tonight's big act.

With Bullet For My Valentine on the main stage, we're able to get fairly close to the front when we arrive. As Slayer comes on next, all carnage breaks loose and there's a huge push from behind, bringing us up even closer to the rail but also into the thick of things with all the heavy metal Slayer fans. A giant circle pit begins to form in the middle of the crowd, fuelling the constant moshing and pushing around. My body is being treated like a pretzel, with my legs being driven to the left, while my back is getting pushed forward, and a few elbows are leaning on my neck twisting it to the right. At one point, my feet aren't even touching the ground, and it's not by choice. With Barbara and Zita in front of me, I'm absorbing most of the punishment and my body is aching from it.

Surviving Slayer, I'm soon relieved of the pressure from behind and we're given some room to breathe even though no one has really left their position. Not being able to get out, the person beside me decides to relieve himself into a bottle, and he's suddenly holding a bottle of urine. But why are all the Slayer fans still hanging around up front? I find out why when the next band takes the stage. With a chorus of boos, My Chemical Romance are welcomed to the stage by flying objects, mostly the plastic bottled kind, and from all different directions. Even the guy beside me chucks his urine filled bottle at the band. The promoters had booked these guys after Slayer for a reason – to get bottled – and the crowd does not disappoint. Hundreds of bottles fly over my head landing surprisingly accurately on stage, although none ever hit the band members themselves. To their credit, the band seems to take it well, confessing that they probably don't fit in with the crowd today, but that they'll persevere and play their set. Apparently 50 Cent only lasted 15 minutes after getting a similar treatment a few years ago.

An average performance from Placebo followed, with the highlight of their performance being when their amplifiers malfunctioned and they had to stop playing for 10 minutes. The cameramen, knowing exactly what to do, start zooming in on girls that are sitting on top of people's shoulders, encouraging them to flash the camera on the big screen. It's quite entertaining and amazing to know what can keep a crowd happy. After they're finished, electricity begins to float through the air as there is extreme anticipation for the headliner and a lively force amongst everyone that I haven't seen before at most shows.

When Pearl Jam takes the stage, pressure comes from behind again – it's rough this time around – not the playful pushing around for fun during Slayer. Fans are trying to get as close to the stage as possible, not caring what or who they trample over. One fan that's able to slip her way up front recognizes me from Dublin. Her name is Pippa from London. She doesn't even reach my shoulders in height, so I'm wondering how she'll be able to see the stage. As Vedder approaches the microphone, he instructs the crowd to take care of each other and to have a safe show before the band goes into *Interstellar Overdrive*, which is subsequently followed by nonstop fast pace rockers throughout the entire show. Pippa is soon nowhere to be seen. It's perhaps the most energy filled performance I've ever seen from these guys, almost as if they wanted to bring on their heaviest and fastest songs to confront their first festival in six years head on. And if you aren't rocking along with the band, you're definitely rocking along with the crowd. Some fans that can't handle the intensity up front are pulled out by security, with a few even fainting from exhaustion.

During the encore, I manage to turn my head and get a glimpse of the crowd spanning all the way to the entrance. I've never seen a concert with this many people before, it's surreal. Even Vedder is also impressed, showing signs of emotion at various points of the two-hour plus cardio workout. The San Francisco shows were child's play compared to this. Sweating profusely, I can feel the entire crowd behind leaning on me as I'm hanging tightly onto the rail, while enjoying the intense performance immensely. Security would hand out water every few minutes to rehydrate people in the crowd. When the final notes are played, the weight of 80,000 people is lifted from my back and there's a sudden burst of the cool night time air. I look at Barbara and Zita breathing a sigh of relief and we wait for the crowd to die down. "I thought I was going to die," Zita claims.

After about half an hour, the crowd exiting looks manageable, so we head back to the campsite for one final drink with my camp mates. We talk about how great and intense the show was and then I bid farewell to them, grabbing my bags and heading back to the train station with Barbara and Zita to catch the first train back to London. When we arrive at the station, there's a large group of people waiting around. It's 2:00am and the first train is another two hours away, so like everyone else, we topple over and rest up lying on the ground outside of the station, recovering from an exhausting show and an exhausting weekend – my first festival experience.

If I don't lose control
Explore and not explode
A preternatural other plane
With the power to maintain

Severed Hand

CHAPTER 34: **THE EUROPEAN TOUR BUS**

August 29, 2006 » Show 40
Arnhem, Netherlands

As a music fan, I've always wondered what it is like to tour around show after show in one of those luxury tour buses. When we were planning for the Canadian tour, I briefly inquired about the possibility of renting a tour bus with a driver, but 30,000 reasons prevented us from following through with the idea and we chose the van route instead. Before the European tour, two Norwegian fans had similar thoughts and floated the tour bus idea around as well. But knowing the costs involved, I didn't think they were serious. In the process, there was also a handful of people who began talking about a van, with some even emailing me about advice on the situation. I was intrigued when the Norwegians announced that a bus had been secured for the entire tour. But unaware of my plans for Europe at the time, I never confirmed anything with them. However, when I met Stian in Dublin, I assured him of my plan for joining in for their initial connection, to see what the bus is all about.

With zero sleep after the Reading Festival, we return to Barbara's place in London early in the morning to rest up until the afternoon. That's when I try my first English breakfast, which apparently is served all day. The greasy plate consists of two fried eggs, two rations of bacon, two sausages, two hash browns, two mushrooms, two slices of tomato, and two heart attacks waiting to happen. Now this is a proper way to start your day up in the afternoon. Upon finishing our tasty meal, we decide to keep ourselves busy at a pub close to Kings Cross Station until 3:00pm, when the bus arrives. There are many busses in and around the area where we're supposed to meet, but we're unsure which one it is until Barbara gets a call from Stian. We're on the wrong side.

Down at the other end, we see a group people standing in a row with Stian's familiar blue hat sticking out. We greet everyone and introduce ourselves to the five others standing in front of a lineup of plastic bags full of supplies for the ride. Stian sees the bus for the first time himself and is so ecstatic that he can hardly put sentences together. I ask him about it and he tells me that it can hold and sleep 14 passengers with 60 confirmed for the tour in total. He looks relieved to finally see all his hard work pay off but credits his Norwegian partner, Pin, for doing most of the work. "Pin is the magician," he says.

Dressed in a comfortable looking green denim jacket with a matching green military hat that covers her long braided Scandinavian blonde hair, Pin comes over to make sure everyone is ready to go. She appears stressed, probably from all the work it took to put this together, but she seems anxious to get going.

"I just can't believe it's fucking here," Pin exclaims, while wiping some tears from her eyes.

"Did you have a few busses to choose between or was this the only one available?" I ask.

"It wasn't easy to rent such a thing. We contacted a lot of companies but they wouldn't do it when they realized we were private."

She reveals that it costs roughly £510 a day for the bus and another £45 a day for the driver for a total of £19,010, which they paid up front. To recuperate the costs, they're charging people £47 a day in connection fees, much like we did in the Canadian tour. But being a sleeper bus, this includes the transportation and the accommodations as well. Trying to do the math quickly in my head, I don't see the numbers adding up, so the Norwegians must have put up a lot of their own money to fund this trip. Paul, the driver greets us with his English accent and says he's ready to go, so we line up one by one to board the bus.

The European Tour Bus.

As we enter, the excited smiles on our faces are satisfied with what we see. On the first level, there's leather couch wrapped around a table – like a large booth in a diner – with a television and a microwave behind it, as well as a toilet on the side. Up the stairs, we see our main lounge area, consisting of a larger blue and yellow leather couch wrapped around the back of the bus, a larger television and stereo, and also a mini bar fridge. Down the hall on the other half of the top floor is the sleeping area, equipped with three sets of double bunks on either side of the aisle for a total of 12 beds. This thing looks posh and definitely different from the van. We each claim a bed by storing our luggage either on top of the mattress or underneath the bottom bunk, and then converge in the lounge for a toast to kick off the voyage. As the bus begins to move, Stian plays around with the stereo and puts on some Pearl Jam music, something that we'd never do in the van, and everyone gets acquainted with one another.

Stian's guitar inside of the lounge area of the European Tour Bus.

Sitting to my left is Gitta from Germany, who, along with the Norwegians, is riding the bus the entire way. She has one hand on a can of Fosters and another hand on a personally crafted box full of gifts for Pin, acknowledging her hard work for putting this tour together. She tells me that she had never seen Pearl Jam until this year but, after kicking herself for passing up a chance to see a show in Berlin six years ago, she decided to do whatever it takes to get tickets to an exclusive small show at the Astoria in London this past April. After seeing that show, she knew that doing the entire tour is what she needs to make up for lost time.

Across the table is John from Northern Ireland. Appearing to be the youngest on the bus, John seems to love the fact that I'm loaded with Irish alcohol and teaches me how to properly pour Guinness into a pint glass. With the glass tilted along a 45 degree angle, he slowly pours the thick dark liquid from the can until it reaches two thirds of the way up, when he sits the pint back down for the Guinness to settle. Once all of the white foam reaches the top and the liquid is pure black, he finishes the pour by dumping the rest in carefully and then letting it settle again. This results in half an inch of foam sitting at the top of the drink. It's delicious. Beside John is his friend Katherine, also from Northern

Ireland. Apparently they got loaded one night and thought it would be a great idea to ride a bus to Belgium to see Pearl Jam.

Stian then brings out a guitar, which he had just purchased today before boarding the bus, and explains that it will be on the bus for the trip for all the riders to play. Everyone will sign the guitar with the plan to auction it off at the conclusion of the tour, donating the money to Amnesty International. When I'm handed the guitar, I sign my name along with a maple leaf under the bridge. Stian gets it back and starts to play a variety of songs, while we rotate singers. While I'm filming along, I notice Pin also operating a video camera as well. Looks like I've got some competition now. To my surprise, she tells me that she has never seen Pearl Jam before, but is now doing roughly 20 shows in a row.

"What's your motivation for doing this tour bus?" I ask her.

"I think it's like learning to trust people all over again for me," she replies.

As our conversation gets deeper, the bus all of a sudden stops and we have arrived at the Dover ferry terminal, just over an hour out of London. Everyone leaves the bus to go through French customs, because the ferry will be landing in France, and then we wait until we're able to board. The ferry is similar in size to the enormous ferries that we traveled on for Newfoundland. As a safety precaution, we're all forced to leave the vehicle and explore the insides of the ferry. Once on board, our destination is the cafeteria. We fill our stomachs and then roam around the deck looking out into the Straight of Dover. Despite the strong winds, the warm company of my fellow passengers keeps us on the deck for the remainder of the 90-minute crossing. With Calais, France in our sights, we return to the bus to continue on where we left off, only now we are driving on the right side of the road as opposed to the left. As the night progresses, more alcohol is had and more songs are played, but one by one we begin to disappear into our beds until the lounge is completely silent.

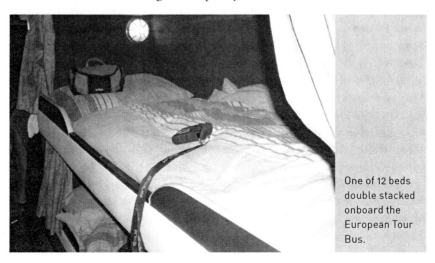

One of 12 beds double stacked onboard the European Tour Bus.

Waking up the next morning, I notice the bus is no longer moving, but everything is still dark. Opening the curtains to my bed, I step down and see light outside showing the Geldredome. This must be the venue. I head downstairs to try and thank Paul for the overnight drive, but all of his windows are covered up and there's a sign informing not to disturb him because he's asleep. So the driver takes us directly to the venue over night and then he sleeps during the day? This is too easy. Exiting the bus, I notice that we're parked beside all of the other tour busses. There's even one that looks identical to ours, with a sign that says Wolfmother on it. So we have the same tour bus as the opening band? Awesome! In the distance I see a small crowd by the gate of the venue already, so I move in closer to investigate. People are already lining up to get in and it's not even 10:00am yet, so I return to bus.

Back inside, everyone is pretty much up by now, except for Stian, who's still out cold because he finished a bottle of Jack Daniels by himself last night. I suggest that we explore the city, so some follow along. Located near Flanders Field, Arnhem is a historical town linked to World War II. But instead of historical monuments or museums, we find a modern highway and a shopping mall at the end of it. Pin and I decide to explore the mall and load up on mini DV tapes for our cameras. When we return to the bus, there are two new passengers waiting to board, Cato from Norway, and Theo from Holland. They've arrived to the venue on their own but will join the bus after the show tonight. Expressing excitement about seeing Pearl Jam for the first time, Cato can't stop smiling and hopes to get a pick thrown to him from McCready.

With the box office now open, everyone grabs their tickets, which is twice the size of any ticket I have ever seen, accompanied by a pink wristband that officially recognizes you as a fan club ticket holder for the early entry. My tickets, however, are with Josh from DC, who's supposed to find me here. The last time I contacted him was by email the day before I left for Reading, when I told him to ask around for the tour bus to find me. So while everyone migrates to the entrance gate to grab a spot in queue, I hang around in the bus with Stian and Theo, who both know their way around a guitar and a harmonica fairly well. In the middle of a song, there's a knock on the door, who I presume is Josh, so Stian goes to answer it. But, it's a girl from Vancouver, Jenn, who's joining the bus after the show as well. I flash to her my Canadian flag and she mentions that we met briefly in Edmonton. From there, Jenn and Theo both join the Ten Club queue, while Stian decides to take another nap. "You have to wake me up," he tells me. "I don't want to miss the show."

As I watch the lineup of people being let into the venue, I start looking for Josh, but he's nowhere to be found. When a public transit bus pulls up in front of the box office, a herd of people start flowing out of it, one of whom is Josh. Already with a beer in hand, he picks up his tickets and hands me a wristband. There's still time to get in before the general public, so I wake Stian up and we head into the stadium. Josh tells me that he saw Radiohead in Amsterdam last night. "It was sick," he comments. "They played some stuff I've never heard before, and I've already done some major face melting since I've gotten here."

Entering the stadium, we pick up a few beers and find a spot near the front on the field. The venue is normally used for soccer so it's enormous in size, with a 30,000 capacity. I'm thinking there's no way this place is going to be full for the show but, soon, the gates open for the general public and the place begins to fill up. Our tour bus neighbours, Wolfmother, come on to play a rocking set to warm us up, but something feels different from the last time I saw these guys at Reading – I have massive amounts of room around me. The Dutch fans seem to be very laid back as there's no pushing around or anything, so we are free to move around at our own will. But that will all certainly change once the main band comes on.

Chatting with some Dutch girls in front of us, we start to get ourselves pumped for the show. They mention that it's their first time seeing the band and they ask me what to expect, so I tell them that McCready will give them a guitar pick if they drape my Canadian flag on the rail in front of them. When the band comes on, I embrace myself expecting a huge push from behind but it's rather tame instead. I still have about a half metre of space all around me. McCready notices the Canadian flag right away and approaches to play his solo before throwing his guitar pick out to the Dutch girls in front of me. They turn around and smile. Following a high octane performance at the festival, this show continues on with that momentum, even though the crowd is not as animated and is the tamest crowd I've ever seen. But being in a dome, the noise of the crowd amplifies itself and it's loud. At the end of the set when the band leaves the stage, McCready takes his shirt off and throws it toward me, only to have a girl beside me take it away. "You know that was for you right?" Josh whispers to me.

We meet back at the bus after the show, where everyone is just glowing with happiness. Cato can hardly describe his feelings, so he shows me guitar picks from McCready and Vedder that he got from the show. The group tries to convince me to stay on the bus for at least one more show but I inform them that I need to travel on my own for a bit and that I'll be back in Italy. The trip to Arnhem was nice and easy, but it skipped out on the adventure part of getting to these shows that I enjoy so much. The bus is not the van and for me the journey is what counts. Although I had a great time, I have to follow through with my plan because this is my first time in Europe and I want to experience it. I grab my bags and say goodbye to everyone then hop on the public bus with Josh that takes us to the train station, where we follow the crowd onto a train for Amsterdam. Having just come from there, Josh is able to navigate us toward the centre of city, where we find a hotel and I get my first taste of Dutch fries all smothered in mayonnaise. We wash down our delightful snack with a few drinks at a tiny bar nearby, before calling it a night.

In the morning, Josh and I have some egg benedicts for breakfast, and he reminds me of his spare ticket for tonight's show in Antwerp, Belgium, but I'm not interested. So we say goodbye and Josh heads to the train station. I'm now by myself for the first time in Europe, and in Amsterdam of all places. But before I get ahead of myself, I pull out my trusty European guidebook to find a recommendation for a hostel. Checking into the Flying Pig, I notice a group of kids chilling out in a comfortable looking lounge area, definitely stoned out of their minds. Just inside the entrance of the hostel, the lounge area is made up of a giant couch with many pillows and cushions wrapped around a coffee table holding two massive ashtrays. I put my bags anyway, locking up my valuables, and head back onto the streets.

Like most others, my impression of Amsterdam before arriving is that it's nothing but sex and drugs, but I quickly realize that there's much more than this. The layout of the city is basically a big circle of canals and bridges winding around a big rock called the Dam. At the Dam Square, there are thousands of people roaming around during the day and almost as many white pigeons flocking in front of an impressive looking old Cathedral. In fact, the history and museums I was looking for in Arnhem is available all over Amsterdam. The lineup for the Anne Frank museum is much too long for my liking, so I opt for art over history and visit the Van Gogh and Rembrandt art museums. Choosing walking as my form of transportation, I'm able to see more of the ancient architecture and read information about historic statues, as a constant flow of bicycles speed past me. Walking around also gets me lost every 10 minutes because of all the similar looking streets and canals that I pass through. But somehow I always end up back at the Dam Square, where I reset my bearings and continue to wander around some more.

In front of a tourist shop, I see a rack of postcards trying to lure me into the store. Looking through them, I'm reminded that I had promised Holly about writing to her from every country, so I purchase some of the more beautiful ones and find a bench in a park. I first write to a few other friends before I get to Holly's, and keeping it simple like the others, all I write is "I miss you." As I write the words, I begin to feel it as well. I do really miss her. Pulling out a small photo album that she made me, I start flipping through the pictures and sadness takes over me. I should be happy looking through these, why am I so sad? I try to think of something else and escape it, but it's no use. There's no one around me now, so I'm alone with my own thoughts. I've never felt this way about a girl before, as we had so many highs together in such a short amount of time, so everything else seems like a low for me now, especially leaving her the way I did. She still has too much control over my emotions and I'm not strong enough to hold them off yet. Closing my eyes, I try not to cry and instead decide that I should take advantage of being in Amsterdam and just get fucked up on drugs.

Browsing through my guidebook, I quickly find a recommendation for a coffee shop called Dampkring not too far from where I'm at. With cushioned bar stools lined up along the counter, the place has the appearance more of a bar than a coffee shop, but the large amount of people inside convince me to follow through with this choice. The Pink Floyd blasting on the speakers coupled with the sight of many smiles around already makes me feel a little more relaxed. Everyone is drinking either a beer or a coffee and smoking reefers. I walk up to the end of the bar, where there's a separate counter for their cannabis sales. This is what I'm looking for. On the counter there's a small statue of a smiling Buddha, and behind it's a wall of drawers full of marijuana. The man behind the counter greets me and pulls out a menu. I look down the list: Dampkring Haze Delight, Buddha's Sister Haze, NYC Diesel, Kali Mist, Super Silver Haze, Alegria, AK 47, White Widow, Jack Herrer, and that's just the marijuana ranging from €5 to €10 per gram.

"What's the Dampkring Moonshine?" I ask, about the first item on the list at €20 a gram.

"That will kick your ass," he laughs. "We also have pre-rolled joints sold with or without tobacco."

"Are there any papers for me to roll on my own?" I ask.

"Of course," he replies, pointing toward a dispenser full of rolling paper, "and there are grinders as well."

"Well what do you recommend?"

"What do you want to feel?"

"I just want to be really relaxed, nothing too harsh."

"The NYC Diesel is good."

"Okay, I'll take four grams."

The man precisely measures out four grams of NYC Diesel on a scale and then hands over the supplies for me to get to work. I grab a hot chocolate at the bar and find an empty seat at a table to roll out my joints. The guy sitting beside me offers his lighter and with one puff, my mind becomes lighter. Chatting with my neighbour, I find out that he is, ironically, from Vancouver, so we proceed to discuss the weed industry in our home city amongst various enlightening topics. As our minds slowly drift away, so does the intelligence of our conversation and before we know it, we've been in the same seat for three hours. Feeling the munchies, we finally leave the coffee shop to find a chip shop nearby, where we gorge ourselves in mayonnaise covered French fries. They're every bit as tasty as anything I've ever tasted before, given the state that we're in.

From here, I attempt to find my way back to the hostel but, to my luck, stumbling around somehow leads me to the red light district. Discretely marked out by sets of red lights sitting on top of concrete pedestals that set its boundaries, the red light district is definitely an eye opener and my light head suddenly concentrates a little harder on this top tourist attraction. Herds of tourists stroll down a street that follows along a straight canal before branching off to one of the many little alleyways. There are even families walking around amongst all the drug dealers that relentlessly try to sell you cocaine and, of course, the prostitutes. On display behind giant windows that line up and down both sides of the canal in an orderly fashion, the women resemble a nicely done up doll inside of its box sitting on a shelf, while the customers stroll down the aisle for a look. The only difference is that these dolls are in your face. They would knock on their window or even try to talk to you in an attempt to lure you into their tiny rooms.

Coming in all shapes and sizes from all over the world, most of the women are very attractive and there's certainly something for everyone. A little curious, I approach one who compliments my hair. She's from the Ukraine and instantly informs me that her asking price starts at €50. Peeking behind her and the curtains, I see a room that fits nothing but the bed that sits inside of it. Although I'm tempted, I say thanks but no thanks and wish her luck in the future. Continuing down the street, I witness many excitedly entering one of these rooms, including many couples. The money that gets exchanged and the turnover rate must be ridiculous and disgusting. An hour of wandering around the normal streets again, I end up back at the Dam Square, where I know exactly what direction to take. When I return to the hostel, I notice the same people in the chill out lounge sitting in the exact same positions as they were when I left this morning. Evidently they've done nothing but smoke weed all day, so I join them with my one remaining joint before falling peacefully asleep in my room.

The next day, I wake up feeling lonely and missing Holly even more so than before, so I decide to skip the art and history and visit a few more coffee shops, quickly noticing that each one not only carries different supplies, they also have very different themes and decorations inside as well. Having a full day of marijuana and chips, I decide to have something different for dinner. While waiting in line for stir fried noodles, I strike up a conversation with the two girls standing behind me, Alaina from Sydney and Kirsten from Vancouver. After our meal, they invite me along for a drink taking me to a dingy little bar with an entrance that only consists of a tiny black door in the middle of a rock wall within a small alleyway. We follow this place up with some more drinks at a much quieter café, where we're able to chat and share stories about our travels. The night is fun and the company is exactly what I need.

In the morning, I decide that I've had my fill of Amsterdam for now and start looking around at other possible destinations. Wanting to end up in Italy fairly soon, I browse through the internet for cheap flights that would accommodate, and there's a very inexpensive one connecting Brussels, Belgium to Pisa, Italy with Ryanair. Booking the flight to leave two days from now, I head to the train station. Outside of the station, there's a parking garage that's not for vehicles but for all the bicycles that are tightly piled up against each other. I've noticed that this is the preferred mode of transportation here but this is ridiculous. For the next two hours, I gaze out the window of the train, watching the countryside of Holland turn into the countryside of Belgium. My thoughts return to Holly again but I can't escape it this time, so I just let my tears flow. I miss her laughter, I miss her smile, and I miss our feeling of invincibility when we're together. I don't feel invincible right now but very vulnerable in fact. To cover up my eyes, I slide on my sunglasses and continue staring out the window.

When I arrive in Brussels, a sense of excitement for a new city makes me feel a better. I look through my guidebook for recommendations on accommodations and, 40 minutes of walking later, I arrive at the lovely Van Gogh hostel, which could pose as a three and a half star hotel as opposed to a low budget backpackers. From there, I head to the centre of town and the wide North American style roads soon turn into narrow European brick roads. As I near the cathedral in the main square, I hear crowd noise and music growing louder. I see many tents set up in the middle of the square, sectioned off from a pathway that circles the tents. I look closer and realize that it's a Belgium Beer Festival. The large menu, showing over 100 available beers, is posted at the entrance and lures me in. I purchase my festival tokens and begin working my way down the tents. Everything tastes amazing yet very different from each other, including a coconut flavoured beer served in a coconut bowl. It's amazing how many types of fruit can be made into beer. By the time my tokens have run out, I'm fully indulged in the strong Belgium ales and my stomach brings me over to one of the many chocolate waffles stands on the streets. I struggle to make my way back to the hostel but, when I get there, I pass out without a problem.

Sleeping in well past the morning, I head straight to the beer festival with a few people from the hostel. It's more or less the same as yesterday but I'm able to try many more unique tasting beers that I wouldn't normally be able to try anywhere else. Being a Saturday, it's a little more festive. With the sound of trumpets, a parade ensues with all the major Belgium breweries being represented by horses pulling wagons full of beer barrels. There's live music, people dancing, and even a tasting contest, where blind folded people try to distinguish between different beers. We end up spending most of the day at the festival.

When I return to the hostel to grab my bags, I inquire about the airport that I'm flying out of and find out that it's not exactly in Brussels but an hour south of it in Charleroi instead. Taking the train to the south station, I hop on the last Ryanair shuttle bus of the day that takes you to the Ryanair airport. It seems like a lot of hassle, but the flight cost about €20 and I also save on the cost for one night's accommodation with my departure time of 6:00am. I arrive at the airport just after 10:00pm and find a bench to lie down on. I'm not alone, as it seems as though, many others have early flights to rest up for. With beer still running through my body, it's another easy night sleep, my first night spent at an airport.

Survived and you're amongst the fittest
Love ain't love until you give it up
Amongst The Waves

CHAPTER 35: THE ITALIAN TOUR

September 14 – 20, 2006 » Show 41, 42, 43, 44 & 45
Bologna, Verona, Milan, Torino, and Pistoia, Italy

GROWING UP IN A COUNTRY that has little to no art, history, or culture, I come to Europe looking to indulge myself in its richness of such qualities and Italy is at the top of my list of countries to see. Ever since watching the 1990 World Cup that took place in Italy, I've always been fascinated with this boot shaped Mediterranean country. I even support them in international soccer competitions because of it, including their victory at this summer's World Cup, which we watched at Universal Studios. Add to this my love for Italian food and wine and the fact that there will be a mini Pearl Jam tour in just Italy alone, I arrive into Pisa eagerly anticipating what the country has to offer.

In Pisa, I waste little time in getting straight to it. Following the instructions from my Italy guidebook, I take a public bus to Piazza dei Miracoli, site of the famous Leaning Tower of Pisa – and what a sight it is. Not that my previous stops were un-European-like, but this is more of what I had in mind coming over to the old continent. Set on top of a grassy lawn that's greener than my experience in Italy, the tower looks exactly like it does in the photos. In fact, with the equally as beautiful Romanesque cathedral beside the tower, the sight doesn't even appear to be real. The square is truly one of the most incredible things I've ever seen. But after an hour of gazing in awe, I'm hungry and make my way back to the city centre by foot. It's around 11:00am but as I walk through the main pedestrian street, I notice that nothing is really open yet except for a café at the very end. I guess it's Sunday after all. So for my first meal in Italy, I'm served pre-made microwavable pasta that's hardly edible. Nonetheless, the meal is consumed and I venture on. Seeing all I wanted to see in Pisa, I take the train half an hour east to a town called Lucca.

Lucca is a quiet medieval town hidden inside of a Renaissance brick wall, allowing very minimal vehicle traffic within its boundaries. From the train station, I walk along the top of the wall around the outside of the town toward the north, where my hostel is. After checking into the Ostello San Frediano, I check out the town. Nearby is a clock tower that offers a bird's eye view of the city where I see nothing but beautiful red roofs on every building in town, a sight well worth the 200 steps of stairs I endured to see it. The duomo is not too far in the distance, so I meander through the pedestrian roads toward it and then continue exploring within the walls. Spotting a lineup for pizza, I decide to try my first slice in Italy, but it's average tasting at best. So my first taste of pizza is not very good either. Next to the pizza, there's a gelato ice cream place. Surely they can't fuck up ice cream. I chose a mouth watering raspberry flavour. The sweet fruitiness exploding in my mouth does not disappoint at all.

With my stomach now satisfied, I return to the hostel and am able to check into my room. Previously a school for the church, the hostel is enormous, consisting of marble floors, a spiral staircase, six separate living rooms, and probably enough beds to house 100 people. Deciding not to continue my bad luck with food for the day, I stay in to eat at the hostel restaurant for a reasonable price. I share a table with a guy from Germany, who tells me that he's also travelling all over Italy, but he's doing it by foot. His next major stop is Rome, where he figures to be after a few weeks of walking. I tell him that if he ever decides to walk across Canada I would join him. We share a bottle of wine in one of the many living rooms until my eyes are too tired to stay open.

The next day, I continue for another hour and a half on the train to Florence, the city of art and music. I check into the Ostello Archi Rossi and finally have a great meal just down the street. Pleasing my taste buds with a plate of lasagna bolognaise along with a full litre of a cheap but delicious house red wine, my stomach is now content and I'm ready to walk the city. Florence has a lot to offer, with amazing architecture and historic statues scattered throughout, including an impressive duomo in the main square. The detail and work required to build this cathedral is simply incredible. Inside is an equally impressive painting that covers the underside of the dome on the roof. I climb the nearly 500 steps that spiral narrowly up to the top for a stunning panoramic view of the city, before continuing on exploring a nearby art museum that features the statue of David amongst other famous pieces of work.

Walking around town, I notice many locals staring at me and it's not just because of my red mohawk, as they seem to like staring at anyone and everyone walking by, especially females. That night I randomly stumble upon a tiny restaurant with a huge chunk of beef sitting in its display window. Hearing rave reviews about Florentine steaks, I have to try it – and it's beyond my expectations. The server refers to it as the blue steak, where the outsides are seared and the inside is almost raw but so tender that my knife cuts through it like butter. I can't recall ever eating this well on the road before. I must be in Italy.

Buying some wine and beer, I head back to the hostel and meet some people from Spain and other parts of Italy. We drink and talk about each other's country all night when the topic of music comes up. Speaking loose English, the Europeans come to the conclusion that Nirvana is the greatest band ever, so of course I have to disagree. The discussion is heated yet fun at the same time, lasting all night until some Californians joined in and side with me. By then, we're all ready to collapse and return back to our eight-bed dorm room. At breakfast in the morning, there's not a word said between us.

While in Belgium, I was able to speak some French, so Italy is my first real taste of a language barrier. Italians either speak very little English or they choose not to, so staying at hostels is certainly a benefit, as the staff is bilingual and very helpful to travelers. It's also a great spot to meet people to keep me company. I'm not actively seeking companions but, being in a hostel environment, you're almost forced to converse with others, usually over a few drinks when everyone returns back at night. Another good way of preventing loneliness is to visit friends. I have a friend in Italy, Berenice, who I met in Calgary last year. She had found out about my presence in her country and sent an email informing me that she lives in Siena, just 45 minutes away from where I am at the moment. Agreeing on a date to meet, I hop on a bus south to her lovely medieval town.

Meeting her exactly one year ago, I'm overjoyed to see Berenice again and she looks as beautiful as I had remembered. We have a few drinks at the pub and then she takes me on a tour of this enchanted little town, explaining the lovely architecture and the significance of the enormous square in the middle of the city. Apparently, there's a horse race during the summer in the middle of the square, for local bragging rights. It's a tradition and a huge event for the city, which possess all of the beauty and art of Florence with far fewer tourists and in a more compact form. We have dinner and drinks at a café overlooking the square, where I learn more about Italy and what I should see. She also updates me on how her band, Dedalo, is doing and informs me that they'll come up to Verona to see Pearl Jam. Running a bed and breakfast, Berenice offers her place for me to stay at and advises me that she'll be driving to the coast tomorrow with her family, inviting me along. I gladly accept.

Taking a two-hour drive through the alluring countryside of Tuscany, we arrive in the coastal town of Follonica, southwest of Siena. We stroll down to the beach and it's jam-packed with sunbathers lying on small pebbles instead of the fine sand that I'm accustomed to. Most of Berenice's family is there to watch her 9-year-old nephew race his first national sailing competition in the Mediterranean Sea and it's a successful one, as he finished first in his age group out of over 150 competitors. To celebrate the victory, the family takes us all out for a meal at the beach restaurant where I enjoy one of the finest pasta dishes that I've ever had. This handmade pasta, specific to the region of Tuscany, is smothered in clams and truffles, which simply melts my face. The day is relaxing and, while exposing myself to a little bit of Italian culture, I come to realize that the family aspect is very important in the country. All of Berenice's family is very close with each other and very hospitable as well. I thank them for a great stay when we return to Siena but, in turn, they thank me for visiting and wish me luck on my travels. Having the company reminds me just why I love travelling so much. It's because of the people that I meet and stay in touch with. The people make the place.

I catch the last bus back to Florence and have my sights set for Venice in the northeast. However, getting in just after 11:00pm, I miss the last train of the night to Venice, so a last minute decision puts me on a train up the northwest toward Genova instead. With no seats or rooms available on board, I'm forced to sit on a foldout chair along the sides of the aisle in one of the cars. The lonely ride is horrible and uncomfortable. In fact, I begin to feel vulnerable being out here on my own. When a room finally opens up, I head in and am able to lie down across the seats to rest up and escape the miserable hallways of the night train. The higher comfort level of my surrounds allows me to relax more and I end up falling asleep. While the train halts at its final destination, I wake up realizing that I have missed Genova completely and that I have arrived in Torino early in the morning. This is where the train has brought me and this is where I'll stay.

Walking around the city, I notice that Torino is setup completely differently as there's an abundant amount of room. The streets are as wide as they are in North America, and everything is a little more modernized than in other Italian cities I've seen thus far. The development must have come in light of the Winter Olympics that they hosted a few years back. Following the map in my guidebook, I find a hostel toward the northern part of town. Still too early to check in, I'm at least allowed to shower up in one of the private bathrooms and can leave my bags in storage so that I can explore the city. After visiting the largest Egyptian museum outside of Cairo, I grab some lunch and sit in a park with a bottle of wine. An old man sitting beside me starts talking to me in Italian. Of course I don't understand but, being complete drunk, he persists. With a large bottle of beer in hand, he continues talking to me in Italian and I try to communicate back with the limited amount of vocabulary I have, mistakenly mixing in some French at the same time. For the next hour, we're somehow able to make out what each other is talking about – it's quite amazing. He realizes that I'm a tourist when I show him my Canadian flag, so he writes down the name of a place that I must visit while in town, the Mole Antoneliana.

I follow his advice and head toward this tourist site. Inside is a neat display of articles from the movie industry, including posters, memorabilia, and even various movie sets. There's also a great view of the city on the roof. Back at the hostel, I meet two girls from Vancouver, who invite me out for dinner and more walking around town. It's funny how I keep being drawn to people from my hometown even though we're thousands of kilometres away from it. Strolling down along the river, we stumble upon a collection of bars lined up for some distance. There, avoid the obvious drug dealers along the path and bar hop for the rest of the night. The next few days are more or less the same with most of my time spent relaxing and wandering around the city until my feet are sore. At night, I enjoy a few drinks with people that I meet at the hostel. It's a considerably slowed down pace for me but enjoyable. Satisfied with my stay in Torino, I decide that I would join back up with the Pearl Jam tour when it hits Italy in a few days. When I contact Barbara, she informs me that she's on her way to Italy to visit her hometown for a few days, so she invites me to come along, realizing that I'm nearby. Having had a great time with Berenice's Italian family, I instantly head to the train station.

I scan through the schedule and find an early morning train that works out perfectly without having to book another night at the hostel. So all I need to do is kill time during the night. As I walk outside looking for a seat, I notice two Italians on a bench staring at me, as most others have done during this trip, so I stare back and they look away. I decide not to sit on the other bench but on the steps instead with my bags in front of me. I start reflecting and writing in my journal.

While in deep thought, I realize that my time in Europe has been enjoyable so far and I'm meeting lots of new people, yet I still haven't gotten Holly fully off my mind. This isn't healthy and making me sad. I miss her but recognizing that I've been able to be happy without her, I realize that it's ok to miss her. She had been a gift to me for a certain period of time and I'm grateful to have met her, as she has opened me up emotionally in ways I haven't experienced before. I reassure myself of the fact that our timing and where we both are with our lives is just not compatible, something we concluded together. My inclination is to explore the world and I shouldn't let anything hold me back from my ambitions, and that's why she didn't stop me from coming to Europe. For this I'm truly thankful for her, allowing me to pursue my dreams. I'm in Europe for fuck's sake, the perfect place to heal any miseries I might have. So I promise myself to continue enjoying everything to the fullest, while being appreciative of what Holly was in my life rather than sad that she isn't here with me. Feeling much better about myself, I continue writing my journal when I hear someone calling behind me.

"Amigo!" he yells out. "Amigo!"

Not sure who he's calling at, I ignore it at first. But he's persistent, so I turn around to find one of the guys on the bench trying to speak to me. He begins talking Italian gibberish to me so I tell him that I can't speak Italian and basically tell him to fuck off and leave me alone. Just as I turn back around, his real amigo grabs my small backpack and takes off. With my camera, my passport, and all of my money in that bag, I quickly put on my larger backpack and begin chasing after him without any hesitation. Adrenaline is running quickly through my body but not as quickly as I am running after this thief. My legs have never moved faster. Zigzagging through a number of blocks and into an alleyway, I soon approach my prey, and like a defensive back on a wide receiver in American football, I zone in on him and tackle him to the ground preventing him of his touchdown. With my right hand I yank the bag back from the kid, who can't be more than 20 years old, and load up on his gut with my right foot like in European footballer, before doing the same to his rear. As I turn back around, his accomplice takes a wild swing at me, but my boxing instincts force me to duck and slip under his arm before quickly rotating back toward his lower ribs with a left hook followed by another to his chin. Dropping the bag from my right hand, I then finish with a straight right hand that pierces through his nose. The relentless amount of training has paid off in the real world and it's as if I have never stopped boxing.

With my two opponents keeled over and lying in pain within seconds, I'm fuming and give them a mouthful before realizing just how dangerous the situation is and flee the scene in a hurry. Those kids could have been carrying knives, but I'm ok and I have my belongings back. So I return to the train station and this time, I wait inside where there's security. Still hyped up about what just occurred I feel the need to tell somebody about it, so I try talking to a security guard. Speaking very little English, the guy doesn't understand too much until I show him my bruised knuckles. He tells me I'll be safe around him and we spend the next few hours chatting and trying to understand each other. When his shift is over early in the morning, I thank him for his company and I head to a pay phone to call Holly. Not caring about how much it costs, I insert my credit card and dial the digits that I was so familiar with.

We catch up while the sun rises on my end of the phone. I tell her about my encounter with danger and how I almost lost everything and would have been stuck in Italy and she tells me about her trip to the beach trying to learn how to surf. Our conversation is very light-hearted with a lively tone. I then enlighten her about my struggles throughout the trip being without her but that I have healed from it and become better from the experience. She advises me that she has been trying to move on but is having similar problems, with the toughest aspect being not able to communicate and console one another. So we agree that we're both happy to have had each other in our lives and we'd continue on our separate ways with our heads held up. When it's time for me to go, we thank each other for the past and wish each other luck for the future, and then I board my train to freedom.

A few hours of sleep on the train refreshes me when I arrive in Borgosesia, northeast of Torino. Still a little early, I wander around town for breakfast before Barbara picks me up in a car less than half the size of the van. Being in the mountainous regions of the country, Barbara takes me for a scenic drive around a lake and then asks if I want to go to Switzerland.

"What?" I ask surprisingly.

"It's only half an hour away."

"Ok let's do it."

Driving past the Swiss border, we pull over at the first town to buy some chocolates and a postcard, and then return back to Italy less than 20 minutes later. We enter the town of Orsanvenzo to visit Barbara's family but, instead of getting the home cooked Italian meal that I was so eagerly anticipating, we move on to meet up with some of her friends for a carnival. Situated inside a large tent, it seems like everyone in town is at this dinner, with the food being as good as it is cheap. After dinner, all hell breaks loose along with Italian polka music, as half of the people bust onto the dance floor. With most of the crowd being much older than us, we merely observe from our table, but then the bottles of rum and vodka start to come. Barbara's friends all ask me about Canada and I ask them about Italy, so they start teaching me some Italian and, of course, the first phrases anyone teaches you in another language are always curse words. So being completely hammered, I don't know how many people I told to fuck off that night, but everyone seems to be enjoying my Italian.

The next day is more relaxing with Barbara taking me to Monte Rosa to hike up a mountain. It takes us a few hours up a peaceful yet steep path just to reach the midpoint of the mountain, where the darkness of the trail suddenly turns green, as grassy fields run for miles. There are even houses and ranches on this plateau. We wander around amongst the farm animals until rain begins to fall, so we descend back down to the base without continuing on any further. It's definitely nice to see the nature side of Italy, making me feel more at home. Back in town, we have a delicious dinner in the village and I'm introduced to Lemoncello, Italian lemon liquor. The night is mellow and, as we prepare for tomorrow's trip to Bologna and the first Pearl Jam show in Italy, Barbara hands me a book and insists I take it with me to read during my travels. The book is "Eddie Would Go" by Stuart Holmes Coleman.

After a few weeks away from the tour, I'm pumped for some shows again, even though I don't yet have a ticket for the show or a place to stay in Bologna yet. But that has never stopped me before. We arrive into the city the night prior to the show and meet up with Danny from England and Maria from New York, who we met in Calgary last year. She and some others have rented a van and will be driving to all the shows in Italy – sounds like a pretty good plan. At a late dinner, we're treated to some delicious tortellini, Bologna's specialty. In fact, everything we try is very pleasing to our taste buds. Seems like this is the place to be if you're a foodie. With the others retreated to their pre-booked hotel, I'm able to find one of my own to retire to for the night.

The next morning I wake up early and decide to go for a walk around the city centre, when I soon realize that I have no idea where I'm going. I attempt to locate the venue for tonight's show on a map, but all I know is the name of the place – Pala Malaguti. I ask for directions but the broken English directs me onto a train out of the city to a train station where no arena is to be found. I'm in the middle of nowhere by myself and there aren't even any locals around. As another train approaches, a few people get off, including a few kids wearing bootleg Pearl Jam shirts. They're obviously going to the show but seem to be lost themselves. Fortunately, they're able to ask for directions in Italian and board another train. So like an undercover policeman on his subject, I follow closely behind.

Following the kids out of the next station, I'm in the middle of nowhere again and miles outside of the city. The arena is nowhere to be seen and the only thing around is what appears to be a market. But they continue to walk, so I continue my pursuit on them. As I close in on the market, I recognize some of the merchandise. They're all Pearl Jam shirts and items for sale, bootleg Pearl Jam items much like the shirts worn by these kids, and there are literally hundreds of stalls selling bootleg shirts for a discounted price. I guess Italy doesn't have any copyright rules. I must be at the right place though. Behind the bootleg city, the arena suddenly appears and there's a lineup of people in front of it. That's where everyone will be. Carrying all my bags with me, I spot the bus out of the corner of my eye and approach it. Pin answers the door when I knock.

"Got any more spots for tonight?" I ask.

"Hey you made it," she replies. "Yeah, I think we have one more bed."

I enter the bus, which now has a stench far worse than anything the van has ever given off, and head up the stairs to put my bags away. At the top I find a surprise – Carlos from Mexico is on board.

"You two know each other?" Pin asks.

"We met on the Canadian tour last year."

I claim the only free bed remaining and head back down to the lounge and catch up with my Mexican amigo. He had come onboard just as I left in Arnhem and is along for the ride until the end on the bus, which apparently is now known as the Magic Bus, the Crime Bus, the Therapy Bus, as well as the Smelly Bus. Whatever it's called, the bus is now at full capacity. Some of its passengers include Danny from England and another Brit, Keith, who's freely strumming away impressively on the guitar that's now completely scribbled with autographs. I pull out my camera and start filming his creative riffs.

"Do you play in a band, Keith?" I ask.

"Yeah, it's called Hot Wax and Champagne."

As show-time approaches, we make our way to the venue where everyone else is already lined up. Stian and Gitta are near the front and greet me, as is Brian from DC who hands me his bottle of wine claiming he can't drink it anymore. He's on the bus as well. As I chat away with everyone, the wine soon disappears and the gate opens up for Ten Club members, but I suddenly realize that I don't have a ticket yet. As I turn away to walk toward the box office, a guy with shoulder length blonde hair approaches.

"Do you need ticket?" he asks.

"Yes, how much?" I reply.

"Whatever you want to pay."

"How about €30?"

"Sure. I'm Laurie from England."

"Thanks. I'm Jason from Canada."

We quickly join the remaining people in the lineup, who are still in the process of entering the building. Laurie tells me that he spent a year in Canada last year and is going to all of the remaining Pearl Jam shows in Europe before making a move to Spain to live for a year afterwards. He's been carrying around a large suitcase and a large backpack full of stuff to all the shows by himself. Once inside I meet an American who claims that he knows me from Brad but can't remember where we met. His name is Anthony and he's a fairly large and well-built individual with a thick Long Island accent. If I stick with Muscles Marinara, as he's known as in the Pearl Jam community, no one will mess with us during the show. Peering ahead a few rows I see people from the bus, leaning against the rail to claim their spots at the front. They rise to their feet almost in unison when the opening band, My Morning Jacket, takes the stage. I caught bits and pieces of their performance during some of the US tour and wasn't completely sold on them being a support band, but perhaps the energy of the general admission crowd could bring some much needed life to the opening set. However, the crowd is restless and surprisingly stagnant to what might otherwise be a decent performance. Perhaps it's because most have been lining up outside since the wee hours of the morning, or maybe nobody really cares and are only here to see the main act, but no one is really helping the cause. I enjoy certain moments but for the most part it's subpar for an act that I've enjoyed before.

When Pearl Jam takes the stage, it's a different story. A sudden push to the front, much like at Reading Festival, ensues and the pressure from the back continues to build throughout the show. Fans are leaning on each other from all angles trying to slip and slide their way closer to the front. These aren't the aggressive fans that were drunk in Ireland and England or the relaxed fans that were high in the Netherlands, these are Italians filled with emotions and an extreme passion for the music, and they're so into the moment that they disregard anything and anyone in their way. It's not something that I'm accustomed to nor is it something that I'm comfortable with. The minimal amount of breathing space that we had earlier has now been filled and is most likely overfilling. One of my arms is momentarily stuck in between two fans trying to duck underneath of me for further progression. Anthony is also feeling uneasy. Being near but not quite at the front, we may very well be in the roughest part of the crowd. And although we're able to hold our ground, it almost seems as if the fans behind us are ganging up together in an attempt to overtake our position – fans half our size. It starts to become so annoying that our focus has turned away from the show itself. To make matters worse, there's no evidence of a working air conditioner in the building. As the show progresses, the pushing increases along with the temperature and we're now steaming from the heat and from the constant elbows to the back of our necks.

"You and I could easily clock about five of them right now," Anthony yells.

"No kidding!" I reply. "I'm not going to fight them though. It's their show."

"Yeah, it's not worth it. Let's get out of here."

Drenched in sweat that does not belong to us, we aggressively push our way against the flow of traffic and eventually escape the suffocation that was employed on us, only to find that Laurie had already beat us with his departure. Now that we're standing at the very back by the entrance, I can breathe and enjoy the concert again, just as the band leaves the stage. With the luxury to freely move around now, I decide to head up to the balcony and check out how the carnage looks from above. But instead of chaos, what I see is quite a sight, as almost the entire building claps in unison during *Black*. To avoid blocking the view of anyone sitting down, I watch the first encore hanging off of the stairway railing before returning to the ground level to enjoy the conclusion of the show.

Completely dehydrated and bruised up, I'm the first to return to the bus, chugging a litre of water as if it was beer. The others soon return and I meet a few more new passengers on the bus: Barry from Northern Ireland, Anne from France, Stefan from Austria, and Thomas and Arnold from Norway. There are now 12 riders, most of who are exhausted after the gruelling show and pass out moments after boarding the bus. I stay up for a little while for a few drinks with those who are still up, but we soon turn into zombies ourselves and sleepwalk our way back to our beds.

The movement of the bus wakes most of us up in the morning, so I roll out of my bunk and crawl toward the lounge room. It looks like we have some unfinished business still sitting on the table. I empty out a couple of warm unfinished beer cans downstairs and return to find a few more people converging at the scene of the crime. Keith indicates that he must take his vitamins to start the day off right and proceeds to pull out a whole pharmacy full of drugs. I laugh and ask him what he's taking.

"This is really good for your liver. Milk Thistle is great," he explains. "And this is Omega 369. It's good for your joints and for the mind. That's what makes me so sharp and conversationable."

"Ha ha, you have to load up on this when you go on tour then," I comment.

"Yeah exactly. And this is a 1500mg slow release vitamin C."

"Why is it slow release?" Barry asks.

"Because it's so fucking big it takes your body a day to digest it."

"And what do you take it with?" I ask.

"Beer."

"Any particular type of beer?"

"Heineken is good but you can really go for any kind of domestic beer."

"What about this bottle right here?" I ask, pointing at the Johnny Walker.

"Oh the whiskey? I can take Milk Thistle with the whiskey," he ponders. "Yeah, let's do that."

"This is real rock 'n' roll right here," I comment, as Keith pops the vitamin into his mouth and washes it down with a good swig from the bottle.

"That's actually quite good," he reacts. "Ok next, what I'm going to do is break the vitamin C in half because it's actually better for your body. There's more surface area."

"You took that last vitamin and it made you smarter already," I joke, while he cracks open the beer.

Keith continues to pop a few more vitamins for his health and for our entertainment as we near the next destination of Verona. When the tour dates were announced many months ago, Verona was originally the only show that I was interested in doing in Europe. I've heard good things about the town and great things about the venue. The 2000-year-old Roman Arena, which played host to gladiator events back in the day, is now the site for operas and concerts for several modern acts including Pearl Jam. The allure was enough to convince Monica from Sacramento to fly over for this show after I advised her that this was the only show I was 100% sure of attending. As we arrive into the city, there seems to be some kind of confusion with the arena and there's no parking available for the bus, so the driver takes us a far distance outside of the city to park at a soccer stadium. We hang around trying to figure out where we are in the city, as Stian vacuums the bus and does a few cleaning chores. After an hour of lounging around we're told how to get to the city centre. I grab my bags and follow everyone else onto a public bus for a 45-minute ride.

When the arena appears, we get off the bus and are all in awe of what lies in our sights. Consisting of two levels of arches made of stones layered on top of each other all the way around, the Roman Arena is the heart of the city centre and is massive both in size and in glamour. The rough finish around the edges just screams of history. Suddenly, everyone's cameras begin flashing while Stian and I both try to capture its exterior beauty on video – and we're not alone. Most of the tourists in the area are also admiring this magnificent feat of construction, with a number of them also wearing Pearl Jam shirts.

"It's the perfect place for a Pearl Jam show," Carlos announces.

Once we're all able to take our breath back, we settle into one of the many cafés stringing along the strip that rings around the pedestrian only area in front of the arena. Pin chooses steak while it's pizzas all around for the rest of the table. The show isn't until tomorrow, so the atmosphere is relaxed and glasses of wine are enjoyed. It's the closest thing you can get to fine dining while on the road. My stomach thanks me for the meal and then I leave the group to find Monica's hotel.

Only a few blocks down the road, I approach the Hotel Siena, a cheap two star hotel fitting just within our budget. The front desk advises me of the room number and I find Monica in the midst of waking up from a nap. I drop my bags and suggest we grab a drink to catch up and cool off, as her familiar smile is warming me up inside. On the way back to the café, she tells me about her adventures when she arrived the previous day. As we join the party, the waiter asks if we want the large size beer to which we reply, "Si. Grazie!" When he returns, our eyes open in amazement at the two enormous mugs of beer that he's carrying. Each glass is one litre in size and everyone has one for themselves. This could get dangerous. So after we finish our beer close to an hour later, Monica and I decide to scope out the city.

Verona is a lovely town in an almost fairytale-like way. The streets are laid out in cobble stone and are as narrow as the city is small, with most of the paths being pedestrian only. There's definitely a romantic feel to this place, situated two hours west of its more popular neighbour, Venice, and it's not just because of its ties to Shakespeare's Romeo and Juliet. The charming architecture outlines elegant piazzas made up of delightful gardens and bold statues. Around the corner, we spot the famous Juliet's Balcony and in front of it, her statue, where tourists rub her breast for good luck. With Monica having an extra day of experience in the city, she leads me around until we eventually end up back at the arena. We are craving pizza.

"What are your plans after this show?" Monica asks.

"I'm not sure," I reply. "I might do the next few shows but I'll be in Italy regardless, and then I'll be meeting Cali Joe in Munich for Oktoberfest."

After dinner, we walk back toward the first café and the gang is still hanging out, so I give the waiter a nod for a couple more monstrous beers. Stian asks that I smell his arm pit, to which I assume that he had the opportunity to shower up. Smiling profusely, he claims that he now possesses the scent of a rose, but I guess anyone would be happy feeling clean for the first time in four days and holding a litre of beer in his hand. The crowd is now much bigger, with a number of other fans also assembling around us. As the night progresses, more and more people arrive at the scene, all of whom are Pearl Jam fans going to the show tomorrow. I guess the word got out about this place and its extravagant beverages because the population of the area expands every time I finish a drink. Soon the entire outdoor patio is completely filled with Pearl Jam fans, probably close to 100 of us in total, spilling over to the café next door as well. Pulling out my video camera, I wander around to find out who everyone is. I start with two guys from Norway.

"We walked around and it was really loud and noisy over here," one of them explains. "We saw people with Pearl Jam shirts and they were singing, so we went to get some money and came to sit down here because here is where we belong. Here we are with friends."

"It's the best fans in the world," the other adds. "No question about it."

Continuing on with the filming, I get a wave from a table from the rival Scandinavian country of Sweden. They're Johan, Petter, and Ida, all of whom don't look a day past 18 but are catching up in concert experience already, with 11 shows planned for their first Pearl Jam tour. I ask them why.

"We've seen them on DVD," Petter explains. "Seen Touring Van too, so nice meet you."

"Nice to meet you guys," I smirk.

Over at the other end of the patio is a large table hosting 12 fans from The Netherlands. I joke around with them for a bit, as they're in good spirits, before retreating back to my seat for another round of drinks, when I'm waved down by two guys in kilts who are obviously from Scotland – Neil and Fraser.

"Arena di Verona," Fraser announces. "This is it. This is the one to see."

When I return to my seat, there's a gigantic beer with my name on it, so I salute everyone at my table. This is like no other pre-party that I've been to before, where many fans would generally hang out in their own cliques. Here, there's convergence amongst everyone and the show isn't even tonight. Countless litres of beer are consumed, many stories are exchanged, and numerous songs are sung including a combined effort on a chant normally heard at soccer stadiums. "Ole, ole ole ole, Pearl Jam, Pearl Jam. Ole, ole ole ole, Pearl Jam, Pearl Jam," everyone belts out at the top of their lungs.

Stian enjoying Verona with a 1 litre stein of beer.

Amongst all of the drunkenness, Monica suggests that we do the rest of the Italian shows and then Prague, if she can find a cheap flight home to replace her already booked return flight that leaves from Milan in a few days. I assure her that she'll have no problems, so we salute the idea and finish our drinks. When the café officially closes, the bill needs to be sorted out, a task put squarely on the shoulders of Barbara and myself. We start collecting Euros by the hundreds from everyone at our table, and then I throw in a few more Euros to tip the waiter, who thanks us generously. From there, we stumble around to another bar, where more drunken shenanigans occur until Monica and I decide to leave before sunrise and climb into our beds at 6:00am.

At 10:00am we manage to check out on time. Hitting an internet café, Monica explores her options for flight changes, but any possibilities she finds cost upwards of $1500 extra. The same result is found at the actual office of her airline. I recommend just throwing the ticket away and I'll be able to find something to book for much cheaper. She trusts me and we continue on with our day. Returning to the soccer stadium, we head to the bus to see if there are any vacancies for tonight, but there isn't. No problem. We return back to our hotel to see if there are any more rooms available, but there aren't. Problem. We decide not to worry about it and head to the main strip, where we spot the 2 Norwegians from last night continuing where they left off. They offer to store our bags in their hotel room while we figure things out, so we accept.

The spectacular Arena di Verona.

Returning to the café, we see a few more hung over people reappearing in the exact same spots as before. And despite their rough lethargic state, they're back on the beers, only at a slower pace. The Scots explain that they slept outside with their kilt wrapped around themselves because apparently this is the way they use to do it in the old days on the mountains. As the afternoon goes on, almost everyone has returned to their spots from last night. In front of the arena, there's a large lineup to pick up Ten Club tickets but no movement. The tickets are late, but with tonight's show being the only reserve seating show of the tour instead of general admission, it's not a big deal. I'm supposed to be meeting someone named Karen from the US for her spare ticket, but I don't know what she looks like and we don't have phones so I hang around hoping she finds me. Meanwhile, the atmosphere around the arena is one of anticipation and excitement and it's only amplified when Pearl Jam begins the sound-check. With no roof on the amphitheatre, the songs come through clearly and it's as if we're listening to a free concert. "*Immortality* would be nice," Laurie suggests, as the band sound-checks that very song.

It sounds beautiful and upon its completion, the several hundred in attendance outside of the arena applaud in approval. Someone then comes up to me and asks if I'm Jason. It's Jess from California, the person who had hooked me up with Karen's ticket. I've not met her before either, but somehow we already know each other. She informs me that she's meeting Karen here soon and they'll wait for the tickets, so I advise her that I'll be at the café. With that settled, I return to my beer, as Berenice from Siena arrives on the scene with her band-mates. I greet them all and we join in with Monica and the Norwegians. Not much later, Jess and Karen find me easily and hand over my second row ticket for the show. And just as the party is kicking into full force, the skies open up and a down-pour like no other commences. Within minutes of the first rain drop, the street vendors, normally selling fake wallets, watches, and other accessories, instantly have umbrellas and plastic ponchos for sale. The rain is relentless and even increases in intensity, causing many to purchase a poncho, creating a rainbow of plastic standing before me.

"I've heard of safe sex but this is ridiculous," Keith comments, while he covers himself up in a poncho.

"What are you guys wearing?" I ask.

"It's the latest thing in Verona," Keith jokes, while modeling his new attire. "It's by a designer named Louis de Gamma. He does a lot of work with plastics."

With the rain continuing to fall rapidly, we're all happily covered on the patio but a little concerned whether the weather will cause any delays or, worse yet, cancellations to the concert. "No, the show must go on," Berenice insists.

Heeding her words, we all enter the arena at show-time. The hallways inside are as spectacular as the outside, so I drift around the building by myself. There's no modern finish on the inside, it's bricks and stones all the way through, and the only thing lighting up the hallways are lanterns placed along the ceiling. Liking what I see, I ask someone to take a photo for me with one of the magnificent arches that act as a gateway to the stage. He snaps two and then tells me that he recognizes me. I ask him where we met and he proceeds to take off his shirt. It's a little odd, but when he turns around I recognized the fully tattooed back that we all snapped photos of from the Columbia River at the Gorge. Off to the side is the official merchandise stand, where I notice an official yellow Pearl Jam poncho for €10, so I cave and join the poncho bandwagon.

Me and Monica in our official Pearl Jam ponchos ready to brave the rain.

Covered in a yellow plastic, I enter the venue through the red velvet curtains, unveiling an arena full of 20,000 fellow plastic-clad umbrella holding fans unleashing a roar for My Morning Jacket's final song – a roar that belongs more for a hotly contested battle than for a concert – and the main act hasn't even taken the stage yet. I feel like Russell Crowe entering the coliseum for the first time in the movie *Gladiator*. I stand speechless inside of the entrance for a while, gazing around the arena and thinking how unbelievably cool this is. The fact that I'm being soaked doesn't even matter and only adds to the experience. With the sound of thunder crackling, the crowd erupts to a deafening cheer that fills the air as much as the rain does. This is the most impressive concert building I've ever stepped foot in – and in about half an hour, Pearl Jam will be performing here. I descend down the steps toward the floor and then down the declining red-carpeted aisle toward the stage. When I arrive at the front, an usher guides me to my seat, only a few seats away from the centre aisle.

As the rain still maintains its fall, the stage looks like a mess and some doubt runs through my mind whether the show will actually happen. But they would never do that to us, the building packed to the rafters. I notice one of Pearl Jam's security guards wearing the very same yellow poncho as the one I'm sporting. He makes eye contact with me and gives a nod of acknowledgement, probably thinking, "What the hell is this crazy lunatic doing all the way over here, didn't he get enough in the US?" To my surprise, the ponchos actually do work and my clothing is actually drying on the inside, while buckets of rain drip all over me on the outside. And as its intensity picks up, the rain all of a sudden stops, cueing the stage crew to feverishly dry up the stage. There's a discussion amongst everyone on the other side of the barrier, which is about 10m away from the stage.

Then, the band comes on with *Release*. The rain returns for a few songs, but for the most part the sky has closed up for us to enjoy this magical performance. Not afraid of the puddles all over the stage, the band is as energetic as ever, and the crowd follows their lead to keep warm. Soon the poncho is no longer needed, erasing all memories of the rain. Tonight's performance is as perfect as the band could hope for, especially if they're filming for a DVD, which there has been some rumblings about. It must be the movie that Danny Clinch was mentioning about back in the US. One thing is for sure, he couldn't have picked a better venue or show to film at.

Swimming through the sea of bootleg merchandise stands outside, everyone meets up at the café for one last beer and then head off to rest up for the Milan show tomorrow night. With no accommodations arranged, Monica and I seem set on taking an overnight train to Milan to find a hotel there when we arrive. Attempting to get our bags back, however, proves to be more difficult than it should be. Entering the hotel, the guy at reception asks for our room number and when I give them the Norwegians room number he denies my entrance, stating that there are already two people in the room. I explain to him that I'm merely getting my bags back but he would have none of it.

"Impossible!" he keeps telling me stubbornly.

"But we're not staying in the room," I clarify.

"Impossible!"

"Well, can you call the room so that I can talk to them?"

"Impossible!"

"I just want to ask them to bring the bags down for us."

"Impossible!"

This is getting nowhere and getting our bags back seems to be impossible. But all the commotion must have caught the attention of Tord, one of the Norwegians, and he shows up at the lobby. I inform him of our impossible situation, so he heads back up and returns with our bags. When we arrive at the bus stop, the final bus has already left and there's a large queue for the taxis. Laurie is in the midst of it all holding onto his heavy duty luggage. He mentions that he has been waiting for an hour and that his hotel is near the train station, so we decide to move a few blocks away from the arena to try and catch cab together. Another half an hour passes and still nothing, so Monica and I decide to walk to some nearby hotels to check for vacancies instead. The first hotel down the main street is completely full and so is the second. Walking toward the next, a taxi stops in front of us, and inside is Laurie. He suggests that we join him and try to crash in his room at the Best Western, so we try and it's possible.

Despite a quality rest and a much-needed shower, we wake up feeling less than perfect. My usual mid-tour cough and sore throat has crept back and I have only myself to blame for it. Nonetheless, we join Laurie on an early morning train to Milan. Two hours later, we arrive at the central station in the middle of hotel city. There are an abundant amount of hotels here, so we bargain our way around and are able to basically name our price for a room at a one star hotel. Meeting back up with Laurie, who's also staying in the area, we walk toward the city centre – stopping only for lunch – where a very animated waiter harasses Monica for a dance. When we arrive at the main shopping arcade, we realize that we've entered fashion central with every designer label you can think of making up each of the stores. The pathway is equally impressive, as the details on the walls above the stores compliment the arched dome-like ceiling that guides us like a tunnel toward the square at the other end. At the centre of the square is the duomo, even more awe-inspiring than the one in Florence.

To say that it's impressive would be an understatement. The details of each carefully sculpted design are some of the most amazing I've ever set eyes on in this, the second largest Catholic cathedral in the world. The roofline is made up of a series of open pinnacle spires piercing into the skies. On top of the spires are statues, overlooking the city. Fighting off the thousands of white pigeons flocking along the ground in the square, we snap away on our cameras doing a full loop around this massive structure. When we've had our fill of tourist activities, we head to the metro station and follow the instructions from our hotel reception to the venue. Two hours and two bus connections later, we arrive at Forum Milan, nowhere close to Milan.

The duomo in Milan.

With tickets that Monica bought before coming overseas, we enter the massive arena and choose to stand behind the second barrier rather than the first, deciding to take it much easier for the show tonight for a recovery. To conserve our energy, we remain sitting, leaning against the barrier with our backs toward the stage for the familiar My Morning Jacket set. I'm so tired, that at one point I find myself even nodding off.

When the main attraction takes the stage, we're wide awake again and already on our feet. Feeling weak and without any energy, tonight is a night that the crowd doesn't need my contribution to the noise level. From the opening song, *Go*, to the closing, *Why Go*, the fans feed off of the band's forceful first set, creating so much energy in the air that I feel fully revitalized again. The crowd, 40,000 strong, is resounding and perhaps the loudest I've ever heard at any show. And just when the roof is about to blow, Vedder comes out of the encore by himself and dedicates a beautiful cover of Tom Wait's *Picture in a Frame* to his wife. It's performed so gracefully that the crowd is completely silent listening to every note that he plucks and word that he sings.

The elegance continues with *Parachutes* followed by one of the best performances of *Black* I've ever heard, where every soul in the building is clapping and whistling along at the end, even carrying it through for an additional minute on their own after the song's conclusion. It's so impressive that the band gives us a standing ovation and turns the energy back up for the final set. In a show where I probably spent more time watching the unbelievable crowd rather than the unbelievable band – this is arguably the best show I've seen in Europe so far. But then again, I say that at almost every show. An early night brings us a much deserved rest and sweet dreams after a dream show.

The next day is a day off from the tour, so we have an ample amount of time. The first order of business is booking something that would get Monica home to Sacramento. Otherwise, she has only a few hours to catch her return flight home. Checking my email, I receive a message from Cali Joe informing me that he'll be flying into Prague for the Pearl Jam show before heading to Munich for Oktoberfest, so I let him know that I'll see him in Prague and that Monica will be with me. He also mentions that he's now dating Kasie from Chico, CA, who we met at the San Francisco shows, and she's going to fly into Greece for the Athens show. With that settled, Monica tells me that she'd like to stay another week in Europe, either coming to Munich with us after Prague or continuing on with the tour to Berlin. Either way she'll need to leave from Germany.

"I don't really care how long it takes me to get home," Monica states. "I just need to do it as cheaply as possible."

Starting with the larger airlines and working my way down, I realize that anything into Sacramento is ridiculously expensive no matter where she flies out of in Europe. Flights to the anywhere in the US from Berlin are also fairly pricey. So I decide to look for flights between major airports in each continent and am able to find a steal of a deal flying from London to New York. That doesn't really help, except for the fact that there's also an extremely cheap flight from New York to Sacramento that works. Now we're getting somewhere. Turning to my trusty low cost European airlines for solutions, I start playing around with German trains and busses and come up with an inexpensive option.

After a bit of hesitation, she checks over all the times and prices to make sure everything works, gives her approval, and books her journey back home one by one. Her budget was $1000, but I'm getting her home for just under $600 starting with a six-hour train ride from Berlin to Cologne followed by three hours bussing from Cologne to the Frankfurt Hahn airport. From there she'll fly for two hours to Dublin on Ryanair for next to nothing, before connecting with Aerlingus to London Heathrow for an hour flight at a similar cost. In London she'll have a few hours until she boards an eight-hour flight with American Airlines to New

York. Once she lands in her country, she'll have a twelve-hour overnight layover in New York to rest up for her final six hours in the air with Jet Blue, delivering her back home to Sacramento. I've out done myself once again.

With our plans tentatively set, we hop on a two-hour train ride to Torino. Navigating through the streets around the train station, which I'm oh so familiar with, we're able to find a cheap hotel, while Laurie wanders off to his hotel. This time I play tour guide, showing Monica everything I learned about the city from just two weeks ago. It's an easy night as we merely wander around the main areas, bumping into the Swedes on two occasions, before returning to the hotel to rest up and sleep in. With the luxury of time on our hands, we have the chance to do some laundry and mail out some postcards in the morning, before setting off to Palaisozaki at the Olympic Park for the show, where bootleg merchandise booths, again, rule the area around the one lonely "official merchandise" stand that sits in the corner in front of this brand new Olympic ice hockey arena.

We hang out with the usual crew of fans, who are protecting themselves from the sun with hats made from newspapers. I inform Pin of our plans to head to Prague and ask if there are any spaces left for that bus ride and she confirms with a smile. Not too long later, we're able find a pair of seated tickets from a couple of fans, whose friends couldn't make it. We head down the road to a nearby café, where we decide to try shots of espresso. The first one feels like an instant jolt but I feel fine. The second one has me wired and I can't take any more. Rarely ever having any caffeine, I'm foreign to this feeling of wide-awakeness. Monica can't stop laughing at my quicker than regular movements, as she takes a third shot, before we're off to the show, high on caffeine.

Accordingly, the show also delivers a different performance than we're accustomed to. Half-way through, Monica and I have been jokingly but correctly predicting each and every song coming up before they're played. This amount of predictability is unheard of at a Pearl Jam show. Song after song, I take a guess at what's next, and it comes. Then I realize what's happening, the band is playing the latest self-titled album in its entirety, in the exact order as it was put together on the album. They've thrown another curve ball at us as I don't recall this ever happening in recent years. It's strange how this band can make predictability feel refreshing. The general admission crowd on the floor looks rougher than it normally does, and we feel lucky to have another easy night sitting up in the stands along the side, allowing us to return to the hotel feeling completely recovered and ready to fully rock out at tomorrow's show in Pistoia.

Feeling as fresh and healthy as ever, we board an early train and coincidentally choose the same carriage as Laurie. Sitting across the aisle is an Argentinean who I strike up a conversation with. Living in Spain at the moment, Ignasi has been to many shows himself and he starts talking about some of his experiences, as I interview him on camera. It also turns out that he has an extra ticket for this show, so Monica snatches it up. Our conversation livens up a rather dull train ride that keeps running into delays and even stops numerous times in the middle of the track. We arrive at our connecting station an hour late, causing us to miss our connecting train, and what would normally be a four-hour trip ends up taking well over seven hours before we reach the town of Pistoia.

About 50km northwest of Florence and 140km southwest of Bologna, Pistoia is by far the smallest town I've ever seen a Pearl Jam show at. It's comparable in size to Siena, maybe slightly larger, and possesses a similar charming Tuscan village feel. From the train station it's not hard to find what area the concert is at, as there's a major influx of out-of-towners that stick out more than usual. Where the stage is actually located is a different story because there's no real venue, the town *is* the venue. We soon spot a few entrances into the Duomo Square being blocked off for access, so this must be where it is. Monica gets her ticket from Ignasi and we immediately run into Pin, who seems more stressed than ever when I ask where the bus is. Apparently, it has been forced to move four times because there isn't enough room in the town for it to be properly parked. Getting directions to the parking lot by the soccer stadium to the north of the city, we drop off our bags on the bus that we'll be boarding tonight.

Coming back to the box office area, I begin searching for a spare ticket for myself, while we're treated to another free concert with the sound-check coming through even clearer than Verona. I bump into someone who I met me on the Canadian tour in Saskatoon and after we relive that memorable tour together, he asks if I know anyone looking for a ticket, so I volunteer myself. Looking for the others, I next run into a fan known only as Brynzie. He was on the bus in Bologna and one of many fans who I shared a beer with in Dublin. But the last I heard, he was on a flight back to the UK after Bologna because of work. Still, the idea of seeing Pearl Jam in a tiny open-aired square in the middle of Tuscany compelled him to skip work and fly back to Italy for one more show.

"I knew Keith had a spare ticket, so I called my boss this morning from the plane and told him that my boiler burnt down at home and I needed to wait for the repair man. So here I am," he explains, while sipping on a bottle wine.

"Ha ha, that's awesome," I reply. "Are you jumping back on the bus?"

"Yeah, but not the tour bus. I need to catch the last bus to the Pisa Airport tonight because I'm flying back home first thing in the morning for work."

Sitting on the curb, we share a few drinks and some laughs while listening to the soundcheck before we join the ten club lineup where the usual suspects are waiting patiently. This is the first show that we've joined the lineup for early entrance, so we should end up near the front. Since we'll be so close to the stage, Monica decides to make a sign, requesting for a tambourine like she did in San Francisco. With a random piece of cardboard and a sharpie from one of the fans, she pens together a sign that says "Came from Cali for a tambourine." When the ok is given for entrance, we follow Pin, Stian, and Carlos into the venue, situating ourselves along the front. Sitting down and looking around, I notice what an amazing job was done to transform this square into a concert venue. Behind us is the lovely clock tower of the cathedral, and to our sides are expensive apartment units with the owners and friends flowing out onto their balconies to enjoy the show from the comforts of their home. Literally happening in the middle of the town, it's a small show in a small square.

Pin, Carlos, and Stian waiting patiently against the rail for the show in Pistoia, Italy.

Vedder comes out shortly after to play a preset, *Throw Your Arms Around Me*, and then introduces My Morning Jacket for the last time on this tour. The performance is actually quite enjoyable this time around. As the time for the main act draws nearer, the square begins to fill to capacity. I notice Danny Clinch on stage looking out into the crowd, so I shout to him and wave. He smiles and begins snapping photos at our direction. When Pearl Jam takes the stage, the entire city erupts. The show is a marathon, mixing a good variety of fan favourites along with a few rarities including *Breath*. The overall energy from the crowd is perhaps lacking a bit, as compared to the previous shows, but the band do their best to make up for it. Near the end during *Rockin' In The Free World*, Vedder climbs the rail directly in front of us and grabs a tambourine in the process. As he spots Monica's sign, he reads it and then asks Monica if she's ready. When she nods, her long awaited tambourine is thrown to her. The show is another winner.

Returning to the bus, we say goodbye to Laurie and hello to some new friends. New on the bus, whom we haven't met yet, are Wanda from New York and Omar from Mexico, who are also joining Pin, Stian, Gitta, Carlos, Barbara, Petter, and Johan for what promises to be a great ride. Once everyone is on board, the bus starts moving right away and I'm informed that there's a new bottle of whiskey on the bus for me to help dissolve. With help from the Swedes, who still look 16, we tackle our friend Johnny Walker until our tiredness gets the best of us. Soon, we all begin to slowly fade away toward our beds, except for Petter, who passes out sitting straight up in the lounge with his mouth wide open. As we sleep peacefully through the night, our trusty bus driver takes us to our next destination, Prague. It's a long way away and in a different country.

Even flow
Thoughts arrive like butterflies
Oh he don't know
So he chases them away

Even Flow

CHAPTER 36: **OKTOBERFEST**

September 22, 2006 » Show 46
Prague, Czech Republic

ONE OF MY MAIN REASONS for visiting Europe was to have the opportunity to partake in the famous Oktoberfest beer festival in Munich, Germany. I have heard many good things about good times there, and look forward to experiencing the real thing. With Cali Joe's insistence of his attendance as well, this is shaping up to be an epic event. But first, we have to meet in Prague to see the band that has brought us to so many places together already. After a night of whiskey, I wake up to find the bus stationary and parked at a gas station.

"Where are we?" I ask.

"I don't know. The bus just stopped and the driver is asleep," Gitta replies.

Walking into the store with Wanda, there's German writing everywhere prompting me to believe that we're in Germany, but the cashier quickly corrects us and informs us that we're somewhere in Austria. As it's a truck stop, there are much needed shower facilities around, so we take the opportunity to clean up and hang out at the gas station, a drill that many of the veteran bus riders have become accustomed to by now. The only patch of grass in the area serves as our hangout zone, as we soak up the sun in total relaxation, but nobody really knows what's going. Pin presumes that the driver is resting up for the overnight drive. By law, he's not allowed to drive for more than 12 hours consecutively and with the total drive to Prague being longer, he has most likely split up the drive leaving us in the middle of nowhere for the day. We must now entertain ourselves, so I pull out the video camera and start interviewing Pin and Stian about what they've gone through these past few weeks.

"How are you feeling Stian?" I ask.

"Fucking awful! A life wasted!" he replies with a scrappy voice caused by an extensive amount of drinking, smoking, and singing. "No, I actually love it."

"What do you love about it?"

"Well first of all, I'm lazy. I don't have to do anything. Just go in to the concert and then go right back onto the bus. Second of all, all these crazy fucking people around me: a Mexican, a German, a Swede, an American, a Swede, an Italian, and a fucking Canadian behind the camera."

"What are your thoughts Pin?" I continue.

"My mind has gone kind of numb. It's been totally crazy." Pin admits. "It started out like, ok we're going on this trip to see 21 Pearl Jam shows rah rah rah, but now it's more like the people are the most important thing. It's very strange because Pearl Jam has sort of taken a back seat"

"What are the people like?" I follow.

"In general, they're just the best ever – honest, helpful, smart, intelligent."

"Crazy?"

"Yeah, crazy maybe on the surface."

"What's been the most incredible thing about this experience?"

"It's the whole thing. There are special moments every day," she answers.

"How does this trip compare to any other vacation?"

"This is no vacation," she laughs. "Instead of 3 kids I have 55 kids coming on and off. I'm the mom."

"Would you do this again?"

"Oh yeah. I just need a few days at home and then I can go again."

Meanwhile, the driver informs us that the bus can go again at 8:00pm, so we fill up with supplies at the store to prepare us for another night on a moving bus. Wanda shows some interest in my interviews of the fans, as she's a writer by profession and also thinking about writing a book about Pearl Jam fans. We share stories and ideas about our big plans for publication, while she jots down notes every few seconds and insists on interviewing me formally at some point, which I gladly agree to. She also mentions that she has a spare ticket for Berlin and lives right in Manhattan, so Monica is now set for that show and also a place to stay during her overnight layover in New York on the way home. Overnight, we finish the bottle of whiskey and continue to catch up on sleep.

When we wake up, we're at the Saska Arena in Prague. Although the Czech Republic is part of the European Union, they don't use the Euro currency yet, so we change some of our money into Czech Korunas at the first bank we see, before heading into the city. Wanda has a hostel booked by the Roxy Nightclub, so Monica and I grab our bags and follow to see if there are any vacancies, as do the Swedes, who we've nicknamed "our boys." There's room available and, even more importantly, we have a room with our boys so that we can look after them. With our accommodations sorted, our boys head back to the venue to secure a spot on the rail while Wanda, Monica, and I set out to explore the beautiful city of Prague. After getting advice from a local to "always keep straight, always," we get past the initial war zone of construction and enter the main square. In it, we find more tourists than the entire population of Pistoia, but it's for a good reason though. The architecture is different from Italy, but very impressive in its own way and there's definitely an old Russian vibe to this Eastern European capital. The city has a charming feel to it, even with all the policemen carrying rifles, something a little different and very intimidating.

"There's a clock that we're supposed to see here," Wanda suggests.

"What time is it?" I ask when we spot this clock.

"It's time to see the astronomical clock."

Sitting in front of the area where most of the tourists are gathered, the clock consist of three components – the astronomical dial representing the position of the sun and the moon in the sky, an hourly show that features figures of the Apostles and other moving sculptures, and a calendar dial with the months represented by medallions. To our luck, there's also a live show coming out from the clock tower today. Next, we visit the famous Charles Bridge featuring a parade of statues that guard the sides of the pathway, leading toward the Castle. It looks different from the photos that I've seen because there are way too many people on the bridge – too many tourists. Like sheep, we follow the crowd into the Castle and for over an hour, we hop from tour group to tour group to try and capture some information about this colossal building of royalty. After a taste of delicious Czech beer, which is so cheap that it seems like a steal, we return to the venue, as Monica and I still need to find tickets as well as Cali Joe.

Checking with the box office, we're able to score a pair of seats in the front row on the side stage. With Wanda heading in for the show, we wait around outside with the familiar Canadian flag wrapped around me, hoping to run into Cali Joe. An hour goes by and he's nowhere to be seen. We make a loop around the building but there's only one side to enter from, so he has to come through the front. When another half an hour passes and there's still no Cali Joe, I suggest that we enter the venue and see if he's inside. Making one loop around solves nothing, so we give up and try to locate our seats to check out the remaining set of the opening band Tarantula AD, who are already making some obscure sounds from the stage. Just as we are rounding the final corner to our section, he appears and is walking toward us with a beer in his hand for me.

"I knew I'd find you if I just wandered around," Cali Joe says ecstatically.

"So, another city for us," I note.

"Yeah, we're in fucking Prague seeing Pearl Jam. How awesome is that?"

Sharing quite a few more beers, which are cheap even at the venue, we soon figure that it's time to find our seats. Cali Joe is supposed to return to the floor where his friend Katie from New York is still waiting, but he decides to join us in the stands instead. As we walk down our section toward our row, I spot a few open seats. However, there's someone in what appears to be my seat. I'm about to ask the person to leave when I realize that the person is Wanda. Having seen the whole row vacant, she had snuck down earlier to see the opening band, unaware of where we'll be. So we make room for everyone and now have all four seats in the row to ourselves. This show is going to rock.

The first set is full of energy and the band seems to be letting loose, almost as if they're relieved from the imprisonment of all the DVD cameras in Italy. We enjoy every moment of it. With the Canadian flag draping over the rail and being so close to the stage, the band gives us all sorts of attention, especially Wanda, who McCready keeps eyeing and pointing to. During *Even Flow*, Cali Joe and I emphatically perform the "pushing of the butterflies" motion for Monica as an inside joke from the Portland show, when she was upset about forgetting to do so. This is the first show we've seen together since, so we overdo the action big time. Our gestures are so emphasized and so outrageous, in fact, that Vedder notices and has a chuckle. When those lyrics come up again in the chorus near the end of the song, he stops singing and allows the crowd to carry it out instead, while glancing over to push the butterflies along with us. The large smile on his face doesn't match the size of ours.

At the start of the encore, Vedder comes back out on his own to perform *Dead Man* to which Cali Joe almost shits himself. *Man of the Hour* and *Nothingman* follow and we can sense something special happening. The next song, *Leatherman*, confirms our suspicions before *Betterman* rounds out the amazing sequence of "man" songs performed for the first time in this fashion. Man, we're having a great time.

After the show, we find Katie steaming mad for being left alone in the general admission crowd, but her introduction to Wanda cheers her up as it turns out that they live within a few blocks of each other in Manhattan. We head over to the bus to say our goodbyes, not knowing if I'll see them again this tour, but everyone presumes that I will so it's very nonchalant. With the metro already shut down, everyone piles into a street-car, assuming that it would take us to the centre. Completely filled, the car has less room to manoeuvre around in than inside of the general admission crowd. However, we could still breathe and sing, so the Scots lead the crowd through a medley of songs including *The Wheels on the Bus*, much to the confusion of the odd local in attendance.

We return to the hostel and find the Swedes getting ready for bed, so we attempt to corrupt them and invite them out for a continuation of the night. But being well-taught boys, they decide to rest up for an early morning train to Berlin, which Wanda and Monica are also catching. The girls, however, have different ideas and decide to stay up to prolong the fun. Drinking and dancing all night, we return to the hostel at 6:00am sharp to see our boys getting their stuff ready to leave. They think that we're insane. I say goodbye to them, Wanda and Monica, and wish them luck with their travels, especially to brave Monica. I crash out for the next few hours and wake up by myself.

Skipping the show in Berlin as well, Cali Joe and Katie meet up with me to enjoy the beauty of Prague for one more day. After dropping off my bags at the apartment that they rented from some random local at the train station, we start walking toward the main square for the usual tourist crap. Only half an hour into it, we all confess that none of us are really interested in wandering around anymore and merely want to see how real Prague taste. So we find a restaurant with local cuisine, consisting of pork chops, cabbages, dumplings, potatoes, and sausages. Venturing out into the old town, we then find a roof top bar where we spend the rest of the day drinking pitchers of the original Budweiser and discussing everything from relationships to hygiene. When the sun begins to set, we realize how late it is and how long we've spent on top of this roof overlooking the city. We settle our bill, which costs an equivalent of €20 total for eight hours of drinking between the three of us, and then find an Italian restaurant with better potato gnocchi than anywhere I went in Italy.

The next morning, we wake up fully rested and Cali Joe makes his way to the airport to catch his flight to Munich. Not able to find a cheap flight myself, I resort to taking a five-hour train ride later in the day and setting a meeting place at the central station in Munich. During the trip, we're visited from German customs authorities at the border. The customs official gives me a serious look when I hand him my passport and then proceeds with the interrogation.

"How long are you staying in Germany?" Germany asks.

"One day," I answer.

"What's the purpose of your trip?"

"Oktoberfest!"

"Ok you can go."

Arriving at the train station in the evening, I enter a circus that consists of groups of people walking around singing and chanting with beers in their hand. Most people are dressed up in traditional German wear but you can tell the tourists from the locals. I waste little time in grabbing a drink for myself, as beer is for sale everywhere. Joe arrives moments later and leads me across the street to the hostel that he miraculously found a room in earlier today. I set down my bags and meet the other person in our room, Paolo from Italy. He had just moved to Munich and is starting his new job tomorrow, so we convince him to come celebrate with us at Oktoberfest. Cali Joe had wandered around the city during the day to get familiar with the terrain, so he leads us directly to the festival grounds.

Snapping photos with the sign at the entrance, we are as excited as kids who are about to enter Disneyland. The first thing we notice is that Oktoberfest is not just a beer festival but an entire carnival filled with rollercoaster rides, fair games, shops, concessions stands and, of course, beer tents. The carnival is a mess of people coming from all directions, so we must keep a good eye on each other in order to stay together. With bright lights showcasing the many rides available, we're in disbelief of these brave souls who come to ride these roller coasters at a beer festival. "So I guess the idea is to get really drunk and then you go on these rides and get really sick," Cali Joe comments.

Walking through the park and past a dozen beer tents, we soon enter the Spatenbrau festival hall. As we open the doors and enter, the echo of cheering, singing, and laughter magnifies and hits us immediately. The place is jam-packed on two levels full of beer swinging jubilance. It's like a semi-organized party, where everyone has a designated table, which many are standing on top of, and it involves people of all ages and all nationalities. We stand in awe and are wondering how it all works until one of the lovely barmaids, dressed in a very sexy traditional German dirndl, escorts us to a table and brings us a large beer each. The size of the steins equal those in Verona – one litre in volume – but what's inside of them is what sets it apart. It's my first taste of German beer in Germany and I like it very much. With no preservatives or chemicals added, the natural taste is refreshing and I can see how they're so consumable.

For the next few hours we slowly attempt to catch up with the others on their enjoyment, one beer at a time. With a band playing traditional Bavarian tunes on top of an elevated stage, many are singing along and everyone is dancing on top of tables, in the aisle, and all around. It's kind of surreal to be in such an environment and taking in a little bit of foreign culture that offers a lot of enjoyment along with it. There are many families here participating with their children and their grandparents. Doesn't anyone in Munich need to work tomorrow? However, our friend Paolo does, so we leave when the music stops at around 11:00pm, but Cali Joe and I aren't ready to head back just yet. Wandering around the city, there's still a festive buzz in the air so we try out a few bars, but they seem a little more tame than the beer hall. We ask a local for advice on where to go at this time of the night and he tells us to follow him. Being chaperoned to a few more bars, Cali Joe and I share more drinks and watch our fearless leader's failed attempts to pick up every girl he sees. Amused by the situation, we thank him for his time and return to the hostel.

In the morning, we head to the train station to find out what our options are and decide to purchase a ticket for an overnight train to Zagreb, Croatia, the location for the next Pearl Jam show. This will allow us to do a full day of Oktoberfest and then sleep on the train afterwards. Storing our bags at the hostel, we begin to take in some of the tourist sites, including a rather disappointing show at the Glockenspiele clock tower, where mechanical figures appear out of the window for a dance every hour. The city has a great vibe going on and there are people everywhere on the streets hanging out and, of course, drinking steins of beer. Knowing that the locals already have a head start on us, we return to the festival grounds by 1:00pm and there's an even larger crowd roaming around, so we waste little time in entering a tent for our first drink. Inside, we find some empty spots next to a group of Australians and instantly make friends. When a barmaid comes by with a breathalyzer, one of them is keen to measure the amount of alcohol in his breath. But being that it is also his first drink of the day, the result is not that exciting, but he still purchases an official certificate stating his Oktoberfest alcohol percentage anyway.

Next, we meet a group of German girls from nearby in the Bavaria region and they decide to take us to the Hippodrome tent, where apparently there's a younger crowd. Normally, most of tables have reservations on them at set times, which are booked many months in advance, but there's also a section for non reservations and we're lucky enough to find a table for all of us. From here it's nothing but steins of beer and good times. As the hours go by, our area becomes even more festive and fills up more and more with young people. We meet many locals dressed in official dirndls and lederhosen, all of which are interested in our countries, and with our level of intoxication slowly rising, so does our level of understanding German. Hopping from table to table, we meet mostly Germans and our conversations consist of random gibberish mixed between English and German dialects, but we couldn't be happier and enjoying the moment any more. Any random spiel would all be settled with a group "Prost" at the end and everyone's spirit's taken up another notch. Cali Joe and I have enjoyed a lot of great moments together, but I don't think we've enjoyed this amount of fun lasting for this sustained amount of time. We're in the tents going strong for nearly 10 hours, and he's even responsible for breaking two or three glass steins for being too enthusiastic when we "Prost!"

Cali Joe with a local, enjoying Oktoberfest in Munich, Germany.

Before we know it, the alarm on my watch goes off and it's 10:30pm, time for us to leave for the train station. I notify Cali Joe and he says okay, so we say goodbye to everyone, who all try to convince us to stay longer, and then climb down from the table. I bend down to grab my bag, located underneath the table, and turn back around, but Cali Joe is gone. I look around the area and up the aisle but there's no Cali Joe. I assume that he went to the bathroom, however, 20 minutes goes by and still no sign. I take a walk around the very busy festival hall, but it's like trying to find Waldo. Searching outside of the tent, he's nowhere to be seen either. So I return back to the hostel and grab my bag, but his suitcase is still sitting in the storage room. The receptionist at the front desk hasn't seen him either and it's all a mystery. He can't be going anywhere though, as I have the train tickets for both of us, so I head to the internet café and send him an email to let him know that I'll be waiting at the train station, hoping he receives it on his blackberry.

Standing on the platform of our train, the clock ticks past midnight and he doesn't show up. Our train leaves without either of us on it. Back to the hostel and there's still no sign of him, so I email him again letting him know that I'll be catching the morning train to Croatia and hope that everything is ok and that I'll see him at the show. I purchase a new train ticket and hang around inside of Burger King, as it's the only place open at this time of the night and it also has a good overhead view of the station, keeping an eye out for any Cali Joe appearances. Every now and then, I would return to the main floor for a search around the station without any success. When it's time for the morning train, I head down to the platform half an hour early hoping he'd show up, but he doesn't. So I board the train by myself and pass out immediately.

I'm awakened by a stoppage, when an announcement is being made on the train. Not understanding the message, I notice that the entire train begins to empty, so I ask someone about what's going on and discover that there's construction on the tracks ahead and we need to take a shuttle bus to another station to catch another train from there. We are somewhere in Austria again and, again, I have no clue. But following the lead of everyone else, I line up for one of the eight shuttle busses waiting for us. Entering the bus from the front, I make my way toward the back and as I approach the rear entrance, I see Cali Joe entering the bus from the back.

"Oh hey, how are you doing?" I greet as I notice him.

"Oh hey, yeah good," he answers. "Where did you get the hat?"

"Hat?" I answer with confusion, then realizing that I'm wearing an Oktoberfest hat. "I don't know."

We grab a seat at the very back. A few minutes go by and then we look at each other.

"So what the hell happened last night?" Cali Joe wonders.

"Ha ha, I don't know," I respond. "We were leaving the tent. I grabbed my bag and when I turned around you were gone. Where did you go?"

"That's a good question. I blacked out at some point during the night and the next thing I remember is waking up at a subway station around 2:00am on the other side of the city."

"Did you get my emails?"

"No. I lost my phone, I lost my hat, and I lost you."

"Crazy. So you lost a hat and I gained one," I laugh.

It turns out that he had made his way to the hostel just minutes after I had checked back there for a second time and then he also waited at the Burger King overnight, but he sat outside of the station instead of inside. He then went to wait at the platform just before I arrived but further down, and he caught the exact same train as me. And even with all of the shuttle buses present, we somehow ended up on the same one. On board our next train, we look through the photos on our cameras and some of the story begins to tell itself. With every photo we toggle through, our faces look drunker and drunker. We can tell at what point the night became a blur. And then I find out where my hat came from. There's a photo of me kissing a girl, who's wearing the hat, and then the next photo has us again, only I'm wearing the hat now. What a mess, but so much fun.

"Here we are on the road again, on our way to Croatia," I laugh.

"Yeah, we rocked Oktoberfest! It was good time from what I remember. Put it on the list!" Cali Joe tells my camera.

The mystery of where I got my hat from is solved from this photo.

They said timing was everything
Made him want to be everywhere
There's a lot to be said for right here

MFC

CHAPTER 37: **GOODBYE EUROPE**

September 26 » Show 47
Zagreb, Croatia

AT THE BEGINNING, the only ticket that I had actually purchased for Pearl Jam's European tour was for the final show in Athens, Greece. Many months and many shows later, I've come to my final European show but it's not Athens. Having seen nearly half of the tour already, I feel that it has been enough and I need to explore the old continent some more. So instead, I've given my Athens tickets to Cali Joe and Kasie, who is flying in to meet him in Greece, allowing Zagreb, Croatia to be my final European show. With Italian and Eastern European influences, Croatia is near the top of my list of countries to visit, as it is for Cali Joe as well, so we're excited to go. It's a shame that our great night in Munich has limited our time in this Balkan country.

Going through Austria and then Slovenia, with multiple customs checks, our train brings us into Croatia early in the afternoon and we enter Zagreb soon after. Not wasting any time, we immediately begin walking the city upon arriving at the central station. The city is definitely different from any of the other European cities I've visited so far. Leading into the city, the rough streets and rundown buildings with random bullet holes confirm the city's involvement in previous wars. Walking through the main square, we can see the rich history that Zagreb possesses. The buildings are old and, although not as refined as Prague or as modern as Munich, Zagreb has its own enchanting look. The vibrant colours of the buildings are very pleasing to the eyes, as are all the beautiful people walking by. For an hour we slowly stroll down one of the main streets, turning our heads and doing double takes of every second woman that passes by.

"What's going on here?" Cali Joe asks. "Is it me or is every woman here really gorgeous?"

"It's me too," I reply. "This is ridiculous. It's even better than Prague."

"I know. I'm starting to get a sore neck."

Unable to navigate properly anymore without being distracted, we start talking to some of the locals, asking them where the location of the concert is. We soon get the answer and begin following a group of kids, who are also heading to their first Pearl Jam show. They stop off at an ATM machine to take out some cash and we do the same, obtaining a large amount of Croatian Kunas. Around the corner is the Dom Sportova. It's the site of tonight's show and there's already a huge lineup to get in. We are confronted by scalpers almost instantly, but most of them don't speak English. One that does, however, negotiates a price for us and then takes us to the actual scalper to purchase the tickets. He then insists on a fee for his services to which both the scalper and I refuse to pay. But for a fair price, we now have two tickets.

Walking up the stairs toward the entrance of the venue, we spot a significantly smaller lineup. It's the Ten Club lineup. Still wearing my Oktoberfest hat, I'm immediately approached by Marit, a German girl that has been travelling on the bus, who starts snapping photos of me wearing the hat from her country, much to her delight. The core group is there waiting patiently for what will be the final show for most of them and the European Tour Bus as well. Pin, wearing a name tag like everyone else in the queue, informs me that the bus will be leaving for London immediately after the show if I needed to get back there. This gives me an extra option, as I'm unsure of my plan yet. She also offers us her hotel room across the street to clean up and to store our bags in, so we accept and then I start mulling over my options on the internet. My preference is to return to Italy to further my explorations of the country, but it seems like any flight from Zagreb to anywhere in Italy is rather expensive. I do, however, find something from London to Naples for next to nothing, so I book it. With the bus ride, it's actually much cheaper to return to London and fly to Italy rather than fly or train there from Zagreb. My plans are now set but Cali Joe gives up on trying to figure out a good way to get to Athens from Zagreb and will instead try to reach it by taking a 30-hour train ride on four connections. Ouch! With that all sorted, we enter the venue.

Feeling a little bit under the weather from last night, we decide to grab a couple of seats on the side stage, instead of battling it out with the general admission crowd, hoping for a similar result as from Prague. There's no supporting band tonight, so Pearl Jam takes the stage immediately at the usual time. Both Cali Joe and I are definitely in a weakened state, but the music brings some life back into us and we enjoy a very gratifying show. Keeping with the tone of the other European shows, it's nonstop energy from the band from start to finish, leaving us even more exhausted by the end of it. But it's a great way to end the Euro tour for me.

Back at the bus there's a gathering of new and old faces, most of who are picking up their luggage, as they'll be flying home from Zagreb rather than riding back to London with the bus. Gitta is the only one taking up the difficult task of travelling to Athens to complete the entire tour for her. The shortest distance traveled will be Sidonija, who's from Croatia. She tells me that I don't know her but she knows me from a photo that she took a year ago at the Ottawa show, when apparently I was sitting behind her. Stian is both happy and relieved that the tour is over for him, with 22 shows under his belt, touring like a rock star. He even flew his younger brother out for this final show to give him a little taste of what he's been up to this past month. Pin is glad not to be taking care of the extended family anymore but will treasure the memories and new friendships she has made in the process. Carlos is decked out in Pearl Jam wrist bands, one from each of his 16 shows in total. They cover almost every inch on both of his arms, replacing the series of Pearl Jam tattoos that he normally wears. There is, however, a message tattooed on his arm that's still visible and it says "See you in Australia," the next stop on Pearl Jam's world tour. I inform him that I need to figure out a few things and check flights, but that I'll try to see him there.

Just one of Carlos' arms, both tattooed in wristbands from every show.

Cali Joe and I hug goodbye and I wish him safe travels and a good time in Greece. We refrain from getting emotional as we both know that we'll be seeing each other again very soon. With everyone else staying for one final party in Zagreb, I thank them all once again and then board the bus one last time along with Rob from England, and Niall and Maggie from Ireland. Our destination is London. The ride is somewhat mellow, as everyone is a little sad that the tour is over and a little worn out from it. But there are some good conversations and music to keep us entertained. Shot gunning it through Austria, Germany, and Belgium, we arrive at Calais ferry terminal in France 12 hours later. The ferry ride back to the UK is symbolic of the end, as this is how we entered onto mainland Europe to begin with. When we reach the other side in Dover, the driver informs us that he can no longer continue because his 12-hour maximum is up, so we end up finishing the journey on a train. Back in London, I have a day to rest up at Barbara's place before heading to the airport and flying back to

Italy to finish off what I started a few weeks ago.

Having only covered the northern part of Italy, I return to explore more toward the south, starting in Naples. Arriving at a small airport, I arrive with much excitement only to have it taken away when my backpack never shows up at the baggage claim. Alitalia has mishandled my luggage. Checking with the lost luggage office, which is essentially the size of a closet, they discover that my bag has been left in Rome and will be on the first flight out in the morning, so they take down my information.

"What's your temporary address?" Alitalia asks.

"I don't have one," I answer.

"What's the name of your hotel?"

"I don't have one."

"Do you have a contact number?"

"No."

"Is there anyone we can contact to reach you?"

"No, I don't know anyone here."

"When will you have contact information?"

"I don't know. I have no plan. Can I just come back tomorrow to claim it?"

"We can't tell you exactly when it will be here, but I assume before noon."

Bussing toward the train station, I enter what appears to be the seediest area I have encountered yet, with the hustlers and hookers out in full force. I retract from making eye contact with any of the sketchiness that's staring me down and quickly find a cheap hotel. I drop my bag off and then pick one of the many street restaurants to sit down for some food in the city where pizza was invented. But I don't just order any normal pizza, instead, my broken Italian helps me order a deep fried pizza that's absolutely delicious and costs only €5. I have an easy night drinking alone in my cheap hotel and then return to the airport in the morning to pick up my bag, which has just arrived. Reluctantly, I return to the same cheap hotel after failing to find a hostel with any vacancy before I wander around the city of filth. For some reason, people here just use the streets as their own wasteland, dumping garbage all over the place. There are piles of rubbish at every corner. Furthermore, the motorists on cars and scooters are the rudest I've ever seen, contributing to the chaos that is the traffic in Naples. No traffic laws are obeyed here with some scooters even using the pedestrian sidewalks as a passing lane on their red light. At least the food is incredible.

To get away from all of this nonsense, I take a day trip to nearby Pompeii, site of the famous ruins caused by a two day volcanic eruption from neighbouring Mount Vesuvius. Being uncovered from the layer of ashes, the rediscovery of this ancient city from the Roman Empire has allowed tourists to get a glimpse of what life was like over two thousand years ago. The ruins are a surreal sight. With everything made and carefully carved out of stone, it's amazing how sophisticated simple life was back then. Now a world heritage site, Pompeii is one of the most visited tourist attractions in the country and it's easy to see why. The cobble stone walkway leads swarms of tourists through the different styles of houses for different classes of people, as well as their theatre and sports venues. The fascination of this village is well deserved and I spend the entire day roaming around history before returning back to Naples at night.

By now, the traffic has all of a sudden died down for some reason, and the streets have become pedestrian streets in the central area. There must be a festival going on this weekend, as crowds begin to form around live music at almost every corner of the main street where piles of garbage used to be. And this runs for more that 20 blocks in length. I take in numerous live acts, while purchasing cheap beer from kids running self-made concession stands. The whole atmosphere is very lively and brings out the character of the city. Maybe Naples isn't all that bad after all. It just takes a few days to really get it. I close the night out with another mighty tasty pizza. This one simply consists of tomato sauce with basil and a big ball of buffalo mozzarella cheese, but the thick-crusted pizza margherita is better than any of the thinner crusted pizzas I had up north.

After the city experience of Naples, I decide to spend a few days further south on the beautiful Amalfi Coast. Choosing the destination of Positano, I book a hostel in the morning and arrive by early afternoon via a bus that first goes through the city of Sorrento before straddling the amazing coastline of cliffs over hanging the sea. Winding our way down the cliffs, the sight of Positano appears and it's beautiful. With houses stacked on top of each other hanging onto the cliffs and looking as vulnerable to falling off as it probably did when it was first built, Positano is very small. The bus stops in the middle of the street and announces that we've arrived. I get off and am able to find my hostel very quickly, the Hostel Brikette. When I check in, I can't help but notice the unbelievable balcony spanning half the entire hostel itself. I grab a mojito at the bar and sit down to gaze out at the amazing sight down below. Wow.

"It's pretty incredible," a guy says, while sitting down at my table.

He's Mike from Sydney, Australia and we immediately chat about travelling and share stories with each other. He tells me about his exhilarating experience at the Running of The Bulls festival in Pamplona, Spain, while I mention my Pearl Jam tours to which his eyes open wide up. He loves the band but has never seen them live before, so of course I mention that they're touring Australia next, and there's a chance that I'll go with an extra ticket in my hand. So he accepts my offer and we continue on meeting others at the hostel, who we head out to explore Positano with. From the minute we step down the stairs of the hostel, the stairs continue onto the streets, and no matter where you go you must take stairs. Situated on an extremely steep slope of the cliff, the steps are necessary to make commuting around easier. Needless to say, it's a workout to go anywhere in the city, which makes everything more enjoyable and worthwhile once we reach it.

The next few days are spent hanging out with my new friends on the beach, hiking the breathtaking cliffs, eating kilograms of buffalo mozzarella balls and, of course, walking up and down thousands of steps. For our hike, we wander around aimlessly and take random routes on random sets of steps. Some would lead to great scenic views, while others would lead to people's houses or dead ends, including one that seems to be an endless set of stairs only to finish with disappointment half an hour later. However, we persist and eventually find a worthwhile path that leads to a small village with a restaurant. The restaurant has a great view of everything from its balcony, including the beach that we swam in early in the morning. With this sight, we realize just how far we've walked and decide to return to our hostel by bus instead. But the stair-master workout has allowed us to explore the amazing area and see very rewarding views from different angles in the process. Each night we attempt to find some affordable nightlife in the town – but there's none – so we resort to the customary hostel drinking games on the balcony instead.

Positano, Italy on the Amalfi Coast.

When it's time for everyone to continue on with their own trips, we all head our separate directions. I decide to make my way to Rome, along with a couple of guys from Arizona, Anthony and AJ, who have been telling me about this hostel that they're returning to because they loved their stay there the last time. Located close to the train station, Freestyle is an extremely tiny hostel run by a friendly group from India. The place is very grungy and there are only two bathrooms to be shared by a capacity of over 30, so I'm not too sure what they're talking about. However, the tiny common area acts as a reception, internet room, dining room, and a meeting place for similar backpackers who are on a budget. Along with the free internet, the hostel offers free dinner as well, serving up salad, pasta, and wine, so most travelers are encouraged to return back and snuggle up against each other in the cozy environment. The result is that everyone gets closer to one another, creating a vibrant atmosphere. It's not a hostel to stay at if you want to sleep.

Wandering around the streets the first night with Arizona (Anthony) and an Australian, Damien, we find our way into a square consisting of many cafés. Having already consumed quite a few beers at the hostel before coming out, we continue on with the flow of beverages, until a soccer game all of a sudden breaks out in the middle of the square. Of course we have to join in. So the tables are set – it's me, Arizona, and Damien against three Italians and we end up beating the World Cup champions at their own game 6-0, leaving them embarrassed. Their girlfriends, who they were trying to impress earlier, have now mysteriously disappeared as well. We return to the hostel feeling like we've conquered Rome.

The next day starts off a little more tamed as I decide to do the tourist thing and see the overcrowded Spanish Steps, which are nothing special at all, before cutting in line for the Vatican to save on an hour of waiting around. At €14 admission per person and an average of 40,000 visitors a day, the Catholic Church must be doing quite well for themselves. Luckily, I still have my student card from university to get a 40% student-discount. Displaying many very impressive and equally as detailed works of art, the hallways of the Vatican act mainly as a deterrent and time delayer to keep tourists happy before they're actually able to see the Sistine Chapel. After getting through all the paintings, sculptures, and artifacts quickly, I finally reach the Sistine Chapel, which is simply an art masterpiece. So much so, that taking photographs and even talking is not allowed inside. I sneak a few photos in but they don't turn out at all. Next is the Roman Coliseum and, in continuing with my theme of not willingly contributing to the Roman tourism industry, I sneak in from the exit to see this ancient sports venue that's more impressive looking from outside than inside.

That night at dinner time, Arizona and I decide to gather up the troops from the hostel and lead a proper pub crawl. Covering large distances, because Rome doesn't seem to have many bars close together or even many proper bars at all, we manage to hit five or six bars with over 20 of us going at it hard. I've been somewhat disappointed with Rome, mainly due to the sweltering heat (even in October), the swarms of tourists around, the lack of respect from locals, and the amount of filth on the streets that would even rival Naples, but we go out in style on our last night tearing apart the city with drunken madness. Miraculously we're able to lead everyone back to the hostel safely, despite the fact that most of the night is not remembered. All that I remember is that we enjoyed it immensely and that's all that counts.

Waking up woozy the next morning I continue sleeping aboard a train back up to Florence. My plan is to visit Paris in a few days, before which I have some time to play around with in Italy. My reason for returning to Florence is none other than the blue steak. It was so tender and delicious the first time around that I must have it again before leaving the country. After chatting to numerous other people about it, I decide on a restaurant called Aqua al 2. Arriving at the familiar scenery, I locate an internet café to figure out my flights to Paris. Not being able to find a decent price, I turn to my good friend Ryanair and find a flight out of Milan to Paris for dirt cheap. I have nowhere to stay in Florence, as everything is fully booked, but I could take a train to Cinque Terre and meet up with Arizona there for a night before heading to Milan the following day. This will work out perfectly.

Excited about my new plan, I head toward the restaurant just as it's opening for the night, but they inform me that reservations are full for the next four hours with the next available time being at 11:00pm. I feel disappointed, walking away, and begin to look for alternatives but, as it's Thanksgiving weekend in Canada, I decide that I must have the steak and will wait it out if I have to. Wearing both of my backpacks, I roam around the city and catch some of the many live musicians on the streets until it's time for my treat. When I return, there's a tiny table in the corner waiting for me. I'm seated and I go all out. For my first course, I order the assorted pasta sampler which includes half portions of five different gourmet pastas of my choice – a broccoli sauce, an eggplant sauce, a pumpkin sauce, a mushroom sauce, and a tomato sauce. Along with the house red to wash it all down, all are delicious in their own way and a perfect way to prepare me for the main dish, the blue steak. It does not disappoint. As I gingerly cut through it, the juices come out mixing with the savoury blueberry sauce that it's accompanied by. It simply melts my face. The steak is as tender as any piece of meat I've ever had. Every bite is like a hit of narcotics and leaves me wanting more, making the trip back to Florence totally worthwhile.

I return to the train station ready for my 2:00am train to Cinque Terre, but the train station is locked. There seems to be some fire prevention maintenance being performed inside and the station doesn't reopen until 4:00am, at which time, I enter to discover that there are no more trains to Cinque Terre for another six hours. I walk away disappointed and begin to regroup. Looking up at the train schedule, I see that the next train to depart is for Venice. That could work. I missed out on Venice last time so maybe this will make up for it. Arriving at 10:00am, I come out of the train with a large crowd that does not go away and only increases in size as I exit the station. Peeking through some gaps in between the crowd, I see the Grand Canal and elements of a beautiful city. But with the ridiculous amount of tourists around, I can hardly see it. I walk through the narrow streets that straddle around mini canals by the hundreds, and decide that this density of people is too overwhelming for me and I can't handle it anymore, so I return to the train station an hour into my stay and leave Venice for a more calm and relaxed place, Verona.

Returning to the site of some great memories from just a few weeks ago, I roam around the city reminiscing. The Arena di Verona stands as beautiful as I remember and I still can't believe that we saw a concert in there, let alone a Pearl Jam concert. Sitting down at the same café where we partied into the wee hours, I order one more stein of beer for old time's sake. The waiter recognizes me and my red mohawk and wonders where all of my friends are. I tell him that Pearl Jam isn't playing tonight so they aren't here, but I returned because I enjoyed the city so much last time. He smiles and doesn't charge me for the beer. It's a nice way to spend my last day in Italy in probably my favourite city of the country. Finding a hostel a little further away from the centre, I spend the night in Verona before training to Milan the next day for my flight. Only, it isn't Milan that I'm flying out of but a town called Bergamo, about an hour away, instead. With what appears to be an extension of the city on top of a mountain, which also acts as the back drop for the town, Bergamo seems alright. But with my limited knowledge of the city and location of the airport, I spend minimal time there before hopping on a public bus to my flight.

I arrive into Paris Beauvais on the final flight of the night and somehow miss the final shuttle bus into the city, two hours away from the airport. The schedule shows an early bus leaving in the morning, so I find a bench inside to lie down on, only to be awakened by security a short while later, informing me that the airport is now closed for the night. Shit! Now what? I exit the airport and look around and I'm in the middle of nowhere. I'm not in Paris, I'm in Beauvais and there aren't many people or even parked cars around. Walking out a bit further, I see a dark corner at the end of the parking lot that's fenced off and looks somewhat safe and unnoticeable. With a large patch of grass and a few trees around, I lay down my sleeping bag and decide to sleep underneath the trees in the open air, concealing myself from the rest of the parking lot. In the morning, I wake up to the noise of traffic, alive and ready to catch my bus into the city.

In Paris I visit a friend, Romain, who I used to surf with back in Vancouver. He's from France and we had originally planned to meet in the Southwest Coast to do a surf session before going to Paris, but the timing didn't work out. It's ironic that the last time I saw Romain was for his going away party in Vancouver, just two days before I jumped in a van heading east toward Newfoundland and beginning this all encompassing trip. On the first day, we do nothing but share stories, me of my travels and he of his working life. By the end of the day, he feels inspired and is determined to explore more adventures for himself. He also teaches me how to make a proper crêpe. The next few days I spend countless hours walking around the enormous city of Paris, eight to nine hours a day on average. I find that walking a city is the best way to discover it, and Paris is a pleasant city to walk in. The city is full of monuments and statues everywhere – I visit the Notre Dame Basilica, The Arc de Triomphe, and I walk up the

Eiffel Tower. A few days later, when my feet become too sore to walk anymore, I thank Romain for his hospitality and hop on a train crossing under the English Channel back to London.

Staying with my good friend Barbara once again, I spend the next few days figuring out my plan. There have been talks about meeting up with my Californian friends at the Bridge School Festival in San Francisco. Originally, my flight was an open-ended ticket with a return flight back to DC, where Holly is and where I was not sure where I'd go from. But since we've now moved on from each other, I accommodate by changing my return flight to avoid the hassle of DC. However, the airline does not allow me to change the city of departure or arrival so I'm forced to book a new flight into New York instead and then another flight back to Vancouver with a weekend stopover in San Francisco for the festival. With more time on my hands, I take the opportunity to pay off my credit card bills and notice a few outrageous charges from phone calls that I made to Holly at pay phones, including a ridiculous $260 single call for our last conversation. I just don't have any luck when it comes to phone costs. Hell, I could have flown to DC and talked to her in person. Needless to say, a long distance relationship isn't cheap at all, and I'm glad that I don't have to fork out that kind of money to maintain one anymore.

I thank Barbara for everything she has done for me, helping me adapt easily in my first trip to Europe – a memorable few months indeed. I inform her that I have been thinking about moving here to live and work for a year after New Year's and, in any case, this is definitely not the last time I'll be in Europe. This trip has been merely an introduction to new places and new friends, giving me just a little taste of what the old continent has to offer. And I have only just scratched the surface of it all. Italy was the only country that I really spent a significant amount of time in and, even at that, I saw no more than a quarter of it. There's certainly much more to explore, so I'll be back in the near future.

Can't find the candle of thought
to light your name
Lifetimes are catching up with me

Elderly Woman Behind The Counter In A Small Town

CHAPTER 38: BRIDGE SCHOOL FESTIVAL

October 21 – 22, 2006 » Show 48 & 49
Mountain View, California

WHEN SPENDING A GOOD AMOUNT OF TIME on foreign soil, there's something comforting about hearing the sound of your own language being spoken in a familiar accent. Although exciting and educational, exploring new cultures on a new continent can be exhausting and frustrating at the same time. As I return back to North America, I feel as if I've been away for much longer than the actual two months that it was. As the sound of the English language, from the new world, travels into my ear for the first time again, I feel relieved and very much at home, even though I'm in New York City far away from home.

In New York, I stay with Dana, who is both a great host and a great friend, one of the many great people that I've been lucky enough to have met through this band. She's busy with everyday life, so I spend most of my time relaxing and doing my own thing. I visit Cristin from Seattle, who is now studying in New York. A whole lot has happened since we last saw each other so we spend a good amount of time catching up. I also inform Tim from Seaside Heights that I'm in town and he tells me that the rumoured Pearl Jam Italy movie that Danny is working on looks amazing. He squeezes me into his busy schedule for a quick interview on camera for my documentary and we catch up. He asks about Newfie Joe, but the last time that I saw him was in Raleigh, NC and he was getting on a bus to Toronto, with no money in his pockets. "He said that he might try to make the Gorge or the Reading festival, but he never did," I explain. "He'll turn up somewhere though. Hell, he might even be in Australia."

"They'll never let him into that country," Tim laughs. "You're going?"

"Yes, I think so."

"Gosh, you're an animal."

We discuss music, Pearl Jam, and surfing. By the end of it, I realize that I'm missing the waves. With nothing really planned beyond San Francisco, I

THIS ALL ENCOMPASSING TRIP | 331

return back to Dana's place and jump online to check flights. As I'm browsing, a notification pops up advising me of a new message from Ten Club. They've officially announced the dates for the long rumoured shows in Hawaii. Without hesitation, I book my flight from Vancouver to Australia, coming back through Hawaii for the final Pearl Jam show of the year. I had already bought some of the tickets before, and a month in Australia along with a week in Hawaii will provide me with my surf fix. I email a couple of friends back home asking if they'd like to join in on a week of fun in the sun in Hawaii, and the response is positive as expected. Dana hates me but also loves me at the same time, so we celebrate over our usual bottle of Jameson on my last night in New York, before I fly back to the West Coast.

The site of three memorable shows just three months ago, San Francisco is where my Californian friends and Tak are converging to meet up. Through the rough general admission conditions at those amazing shows, Cali Joe and I were inadvertently introduced to Kasie and Veronica from Chico, CA, who have since become close friends of ours. At the completely disorganized San Francisco airport, we all arrive at relatively the same time and are escorted to the legendary Phoenix hotel in downtown by the Nor Cal girls, with a bottle of Grey Goose vodka ready to go. Being reunited again calls for celebrations at the hotel and, even though we're all jet lagged, there's not much sleep to be had. "It's good to have Jason back on the mainland again," Cali Joe announces.

In the morning, we struggle to wake up and get going. But with the motivation of a great festival lying ahead for us, we eventually gather our energy to leave the hotel. Heading south down highway 101 for 45 minutes, we enter the town of Mountain View, site of Neil Young's Bridge School Benefit Concert, headlined by the man himself, Neil Young. The annual concert runs for two days and all proceeds go to Bridge School, a school for children with disabilities and learning disorders. The lineup for is always the same both days and performers are generally friends of Neil's that play for free to help out the cause. Pearl Jam is a regular performer and will be on stage this year as well.

There's free parking just outside of the Shoreline Amphitheatre, where a shuttle bus takes us to the gates for the venue. Having attended the festival before, Kasie and Veronica have come prepared, complete with warm blankets and pot brownies. Along the grassy hill, we find a nice open area to set up our station for the day, just as Neil Young welcomes everyone with a song. He introduces the first performer of the day, Gillian Welch, who mixes traditional country folk style music on the piano with hymn-like melodies that are very attractive to the ears. Kasie approves. Death Cab for Cutie then pleases the crowd musically with a short set before Trent Reznor takes the stage on a piano, backed by a string quartet.

These bridge school festivals have traditionally been fully acoustic sets, so seeing Reznor perform solo is going to be interesting. It's the performance that

I'm most looking forward and he does not disappoint. Pulling together the quartet just a few weeks prior, Reznor plays a few Nine Inch Nails songs to a more mellow and jazzy style that accompanies the strings very nicely and simply blows me away. The arrangements of the songs were put together by Martin St Pierre of Cirque du Soleil fame and really reveals what Reznor's musical talents is capable of producing beyond hard rock industrial music. Kasie approves again and starts feeding us her pot brownies, home made from Chico, CA. To go with the brownies, we take turns making concession runs for gigantic cups of Sierra Nevada beer on tap and orders of garlic fries that contain more garlic than fries.

After Neil Young performs another song, the Foo Fighters come on for their mini set, before Brian Wilson performs classic Beach Boys hits in what's arguably the most crowd pleasing performance of the night. Fans on the lawn, old and young, are brought to their feet, dancing along to surf songs from the 1980s. He even has the security guards shaking their asses. By the end of the fun section of the show, we realize that the full bag of brownies that we started with has now been diminished quite drastically and there has been no affect yet. We resist from eating more when Pearl Jam takes the stage.

As with the other mini sets, Pearl Jam only performs eight acoustic songs while sitting down, contrary to the energy filled European marathons that I have just returned from. However, it's a relaxing performance to go with the theme of the festival and, near the end of it, I've become even more relaxed as the brownies have officially taken affect. Feeling woozy and light on my feet, I almost tumble over during the final song of the set, while attempting stay standing. My eyes open and close occasionally and laziness has taken over. Cali Joe is also feeling the consequences. Tak, on the other hand, seems to have gotten a jump start with the brownies. Having been napping on the grass during most of the earlier performances, as usual, he's now as lively as I've ever seen him. I notice this even with my suddenly slow attention span. The Dave Matthews band is next, and I lie down on my back and completely fall asleep as they take the stage. Arising from my pleasant dreams, I now see Neil Young performing a 13 minute version of *Cortez The Killer*. I feel refreshed and not sleepy anymore. Still slightly happy, I'm able to enjoy the rest of the final performance of the night from the headliner.

After a much needed pit stop at In N Out Burger, I'm now wide awake. Cali Joe and I go for the 4x4 burgers again and the quadruple patty and cheese combo not only cures our hunger, but it also puts us back into drowsy mode. We check into our hotel near Mountain View, which the Nor Cal girls booked for us, and all pass out from exhaustion and the brownie effects. The next day is an even later start, but we arrive at the venue at 2:00pm. Having gone through the exact same show the day before, we know what to expect now, and we don't touch the pot brownies, yet. Joined by some friends of Kasie and Veronica's, we chill out and relax for most of the show, lying on the grass along the hill. With a laid back and very Californian atmosphere, it's a good change in pace from some of the hectic moving around that I've been doing of late. The lineup is the same as the first day, and the sets only have some alterations from the night before. Pearl Jam, on the other hand, plays a completely different set, as usual. By the end of their performance, we begin to tackle the brownies once again. In fact, we're more interested in finishing up the brownies than listening to The Dave Matthew's Band performance. Neil Young closes the night by playing some of his favourites, but once again, Trent Reznor's performance stands out the most for me.

With Cali Joe flying out early in the morning, we head straight back to the hotel to rest up. Tak and I, however, have one more night in San Francisco, so the girls take us on a tour of North Beach and Fisherman's Wharf. Then Kasie allows me to drive her car down the curvy Lombard Street, something that I wanted to do in the van last time only to miss out because of mechanical problems. It's a joy turning those corners at 15km/hr nonstop. We thank our Nor Cal friends for their hospitality, organizing the whole weekend for us, and even finding us a hotel to check into for tonight. It's a nice way to end our weekend in San Francisco. The music was great but the company was even better. It reminds me, once again, of what great people I've met throughout the year. Travelling is too much fun and addictive. We board our plane the next morning and head home to Vancouver, but I won't be staying for very long.

I got myself a mansion then I gave it away
It's not the world that's heavy
just the things that you save
And I'm drifting, drifting away

Driftin'

CHAPTER 39: OLD FACES IN NEW PLACES

November 7 – 8, 2006 » Show 50 & 51
Sydney, Australia

BEFORE THIS YEAR OF MADNESS began, the only real place that I had traveled
to on my own was Australia. Three years later, I return to the land down under,
looking forward to visiting friends, riding some waves, and seeing a few Pearl
Jam concerts. After unpacking and washing all my clothing just a week earlier,
I repack my bags on the morning of my flight about an hour before I leave. I
find that packing at the last minute prevents me from over thinking, keeping me
from bringing unnecessary items along that will never be used. With my luggage
sorted, I head out to Vancouver International Airport filled with anticipation of
another great trip.

My level of excitement comes crashing down shortly afterwards, when I'm
told that there's no Australian tourist visa on my records at check-in time. That's
impossible though, because I registered for it when I booked my flight in New
York and even have a confirmation email. The check-in lady asks if I have the
confirmation with me, which I don't, so she isn't sure what to do but doesn't
recommend that I board the flight because I may be turned away in Australia.
Frustrated, I insist on boarding the flight and I ask her to call the Australian
consulate to look into it some more, so she coordinates. Upon giving them my
details, she's forwarded to the government offices in Australia and put on hold
for what feels like ages.

Maybe this is a sign for me not to go through with this trip. I was hesitant
about it before, but decided to continue travelling because I wasn't ready to go
home yet. Even Carlos from Mexico, who was supposed to meet me in Australia,
had to cancel his trip at the last minute. I have tickets to one show for each city
except for the last one in Perth, but most of the cities had multiple shows added
on from the public sale without any Ten Club tickets available, so I didn't bother
with tickets for the extra shows. I figured that I would be doing my own thing

like I had done in Europe. Do I really need to go down there? It's an awfully long way to fly and get denied. As I ponder the decision of turning around and heading home, the lady returns and tells me that they have my application on record but there was an error in the processing that she won't elaborate on. She says everything is fine but I just have to pay the $30 visa fee again. Fearing that I might miss my flight if I argue, I pay the additional fee and board my plane.

The flight is rather uneventful other than the unlimited wine and the personal movie screen in front of me with multiple movies for my choosing. With airplanes seemingly being the only place where I'm able to watch movies nowadays, I gladly browse through the selection. Eight hours later, I land in Honolulu and transfer to my connecting flight through the completely open-aired Honolulu airport. The temperature is rather warm for being late in the night, a small preview of what to expect when I return at the end of the trip. From here, the flight to Sydney is another eleven hours of movies and wine, as the excitement of flying somewhere never allows me to sleep on planes. Grabbing a rather expensive shuttle van into the city, I find the Wake Up Hostel, a place that I stayed the last time I was in town. I check in, but it's only 9:30am so I can't go into the room yet. Instead I lie down on the couch in the common area on my floor, and relax peacefully for no more than 10 minutes, when I hear someone calling my name.

"Jason?" the unfamiliar voice yells. "Are you Jason from Touring Van?" I confirm. "I have your DVD, man. I contributed to the cause."

His name is Dennis from Toronto and he appears to know quite a bit about me, which is a little unnerving at first, but he seems like a nice person. He tells me that this is the first trip he has ever done and is probably going to do the entire tour so I advise him that since we're so far away from home, it's probably a good idea to see more of Australia rather than worrying about doing all the shows. At least this is what my intentions are for this trip. We continue our conversation until we're able to enter our rooms and drop off our bags. Having not slept at all during my 20-hour flight, I'm enticed into going for a drink before resting up since I'm in fucking Australia. Dennis reveals that he has Newfoundland blood in him, which comes into play when we step out of the hostel onto the main street of the city, George Street.

"This is a sign, let's do a pub crawl on George Street," Dennis suggests.

"Do you know how long this street is? How about we get to the first one and see how we feel from there."

Having not slept, I'm just running on adrenaline when we get to the first bar. And as always, it's never just one drink. Once I get the taste, the juices start flowing again and suddenly, I'm not exhausted anymore. We proceed to the next bar and then to the next, covering all of two blocks thus far and it isn't even noon yet. Entering Chinatown, we grab lunch and I decide that the pub crawl must go on. So for the rest of the day we slowly inch our way toward the Sydney

Opera House, over 15 blocks away, hitting every bar along the way. Needless to say, we never make it to the Opera House. By 10:00pm we've been on it for close to 12 hours, desperately needing sleep, so we allow a cab to take us back to the hostel for a well deserved rest.

Fully rejuvenated in the morning, we walk in the same direction along George Street, refraining from entering any bars to accomplish what we couldn't yesterday. We finally reach the harbour, site of the famous Sydney Opera House and Sydney Harbour Bridge. Like the tourists that we claim we are not, we snap away with our cameras and soak in the warm rays from the sun. We explore around the area known as The Rocks and inquire about the opportunity to climb the Harbour Bridge, but it's far too expensive. All of the sights are as beautiful as any city can offer, and the breathtaking ocean and city views remind me of Vancouver, minus the mountains. Taking the same way back on the other side of the road, we decide to hit the bars this time. But to ensure that we make it back to the hostel in stable conditions, we only enter every second one. Two days into my Australian trip and I've already spent nearly $200 on booze and I haven't even seen any shows yet.

Monitoring my costs more closely, I check out of the hostel the next day to walk up a few blocks toward the University of Technology, where a friend of Venassa's, Max, has invited me to stay at his place. I've never met or even talked to the guy before, but he says that any friend of Venassa is a friend of his, so he graciously welcomes me into his student residency – even though he's not a student. To return the favour, I bring him two bottles of Bombay Sapphire Gin and some maple syrup, much to his appreciation. The day is more relaxing as we hang out at the flat, while his roommate, Elana, cooks us dinner.

The next day is the first show of the tour. It's also the day for the Melbourne Cup, a massive horse race in Melbourne and one of the biggest events in Australia. So Elana invites me to come along with her to join her friends for their Melbourne Cup party. With women decked out in elaborate dresses and hats, everyone takes this horse race seriously. It's a gathering of friends and family to watch two minutes of racing excitement that has been much hyped and speculated on for weeks. But it's much more than this. Fashion at the race track, as well as the bars, is almost as important as the race itself. People are judged on their outfits and awards are given out to the best and most extravagantly dressed people. They even crown a Miss Melbourne Cup. In other words, the event is mainly an excuse for everyone to drink and have a good time.

As with any horse race, there are all sorts of gambling involved from sports betting outlets readily available at every corner of the city. Trying to make myself feel included, I take part in the gambling as well, taking the two Japanese horses in the field, even though they're underdogs. About two hours of partying later, the race finally begins and there's a hush amongst the crowd at the bar. As the starter's gun blasts, signalling the horses to start galloping, the cheers begin to escalate in the bar. I have no idea which horse is which and all I hear is the noise of the crowd and then a big let down when the race is over. The results come on the screen a minute later, and the underdogs have won, the Japanese horses finished first and second. I won $30, enough to make up for the extra $30 I had to pay for entering this country. It's funny how things often balance out in life.

With my newfound wealth, I return back to the city centre to meet up with Mike, who I met in Positano, Italy. We've been keeping in contact and I had promised him my spare ticket if I was in Sydney, so with my attendance confirmed, he is now going to his first Pearl Jam concert. From the main station, we take the train out to Olympic Park, site of the Acer Arena and the opening show of the Australian tour. I head directly to the box office to pick up my tickets, which are in the fifth row. Wow! It looks like Australia is the place to be to get good seats. Mike is super stoked now. I turn around and see Aussie Ben approach, so I ask him again if he has a van ready for me to do this tour with. He does not. A few moment later, I see Philly Ben, what a big surprise to see him here. We chat and wander over toward the merchandise stand, which is outside of the arena. Along the way I spot Gitta from Germany. Apparently doing the whole European tour wasn't enough for her either, and she booked a last minute flight here and was able to get all the tickets. I won't get sucked into this though because I have an agenda for my time in Australia that I want to stick to without allowing these distractions lure me into doing more shows than I really want. At the merchandise stand, most of the items look very familiar and similar to the stuff on sale at the other tours, so I don't bother. But Mike and I both purchase a poster. Then, I get a tap on the shoulder.

"Let me see your passport," a mysteriously familiar voice says to me.

"What?" I answer.

I turn around and see someone wrapped in a white hoodie concealing his face. I know this hoodie, I know this voice and, as he slowly reveals his face, I know this face. It's Newfie Joe.

"What the fuck?!" I exclaim.

"How do you like that?" he says in excitement

"They let just about anyone into this country don't they? How are you?"

"I'm good, a little tired, but I'm here."

For the next 20 minutes, we remain standing in front of the merchandise stand with total disregard of anything around us, and catch up on what has been happening. He tells me that after he got to Toronto from Raleigh, NC, the last time I saw him, he got a loan from his brother to fly out to Calgary, where he has been working on the oil rigs ever since. He quit his job a few days ago, got his shit together and before he knew it, he was on a plane to Sydney, with a 12-hour visit in Los Angeles to surprise Cali Joe as well. Arriving this morning, he had a hunch that I would be here. This tour just got a little more hardcore.

"It was pure craziness," he explains. "I decided to come at the last minute. I had no passport I had no flight, and within 26 hours it all came together."

Moving our conversation toward the pre-party across the street at The Brewery, Newfie Joe asks me if I have a van on the go. To his disappointment I tell him that I have flights booked already and I plan on visiting friends along the way so I don't know if I'll be doing that many shows. But with his miraculous appearance now, I agree to meet him at each of the cities and do at least the shows that I have tickets for. He calls bullshit. A few moments later, my travelling partner for the tour sneaks up behind me and surprises me as well. It's Annette from Melbourne, who we met at the London, ON show on the Canada tour. She had done a great job twisting my arm to convince me to come down for this tour, helping me book flights and even offering me her spare ticket for the Newcastle show, which was added later but I wasn't sure about going to yet. She still has it saved for me and will need to know about it soon, as there are many that need a ticket. So I tell her that I'll go and that I have a surprise for her. When Newfie Joe returns with a couple of beers in his hand, she freaks out.

Over the next few hours, more familiar faces appear before me. Eric from Sacramento is here with his wife and will be putting on a Wishlist Foundation fundraiser at some of the shows. Next, Christian from Peru comes by to say hi. We met briefly in California when he gave his extra ticket to Tatiana for the Henry Fonda show in Hollywood. I don't know him too well, but he remembers me and he seems like a good guy. Here I am, halfway around the world, and I'm running into all these familiar faces. Mike is amazed at how everyone seems to know each other in an almost small town kind of way – or a community, as I point out to him. He thanks me for bringing him to the show and is really looking forward to it. So not to delay the excitement any longer, we head into the building to watch the opening act Kings of Leon, a great band from southern America. Their performance is great and very uplifting and energetic. I might actually come in early for more shows to see them again.

When the lights come up, Mike heads to the bathroom and I start chatting to the person just arriving at the seat on the other side of me. His name is Julian from New Zealand, but he lives in Melbourne. He asks if this is my first concert, and I chuckle and say no. We continue chatting and, slowly, he gets my story out of me. By the end of our conversation, he offers his place in Melbourne for me to stay at, which I accept and take down his contact info. Then, I hear someone from behind heckling at me. "This show would be better if there weren't any Canadians here," he says.

I turn around and the face looks familiar, but I know I haven't met him before. His name is Nathan, also from Melbourne, and he explains that he's a friend of Stefan's and he knows all about me. Apparently, he did a video with Stefan for a Pearl Jam show in Seattle a few years ago, that I've probably seen before, which would be why he looks familiar. He also offers his place for me to crash at while I'm in Melbourne. So the show hasn't even begun and already I have two options for places to stay in Melbourne. I grab his contact just before the lights dim and the band takes the stage with the classic opener of *Release*. Mike is already going nuts, as our seats are perfect. All throughout the show, he's singing along with the rest of us and pumping his fist fiercely into the air. I can tell he's enjoying the show, especially at the masterful guitar performance by McCready. As McCready's fingers frantically move back and forth between notes on the guitar that he strategically places behind his head, Mike is out of his mind and turns to thank me for the tickets. He does this many times throughout the show, just shaking his head in disbelief of what he's seeing and thanking me time after time. I feel happy to bring him along.

As *Rockin' in the Free World* ends a powerful opening show, we all rush out of the venue to try and catch the last train into the city. I spot Newfie Joe a few rows behind, and he's passed out sitting on his chair. Apparently he had fallen asleep during the encore due to exhaustion from the flights and layovers and probably from too many beers before the show. I wake him up so he can meet up with Philly Ben, while Mike and Annette follow me to the train station where everybody packs into one train. The Olympic park is in the middle of nowhere and no one lives near the area, so thousands of people from the show jam into the train, as it's the only means of public transport back into the city. When we reach Central station, Mike once again thanks me for the tickets for the best show he has ever seen and then wishes me luck with my travels and with the tour. He, too, believes that I'll be doing all the shows.

Before leaving the venue, Newfie Joe and I set a meeting spot in front of Annette's hostel at 11:00am in the morning. By noon, there's still no sign of him, so Annette and I take a walk down to the harbour thinking that we might find him there. After no more than 10 minutes of admiring the Opera House, we spot Newfie Joe, who'd had similar thoughts about finding us down here. It's funny how we're always on the same train of thought. We take the opportunity to snap a few photos of us as evidence that we were in Australia and then go for lunch. Heading back to the venue, I insist that I may not attend the show and will base my decision on how nice the poster is. Why? I don't know. But I need to have some kind of control over this addiction.

"Uh oh, it's a nice one today," Newfie Joe describes.

For a moment, I examine the kangaroo dressed in a suit and tie. It looks kind of cool, but it's not great. I look into my wallet to see what my money situation is, look around at everyone and walk away to ponder my decision before coming back to the merchandise stand. "Alright, give me a poster."

We walk over to the box office to see if there are any tickets available and there is an entire row free in the balcony, so we jump at the opportunity to sit together: me, Newfie Joe, and Philly Ben. This show, along with all other second and third shows for each city, didn't have any tickets available for sale through the fan club, only tickets through the general public sales, meaning that most of the floor seats have been allocated to promoters, industry personnel, scalpers, and people who were lucky at sale time. The regular fan club members will be scattered throughout the venue, away from our normal priority seats on the floor. But as always, there are sometimes good seats being released on the day of the show, so there are two fans lurking around the box office hoping to upgrade their ticket situation and we introduce ourselves. Both of them I remember seeing in the front row at the first show because they can't be missed. One is about 6 foot 8 inches tall, named Mick, while the other, Gus, is also a big guy with long red hair flowing down below his shoulders.

The trip just got more hardcore. Newfie Joe surprises me in Australia.

We start talking about the shows and they seem to be veterans of the Australian Pearl Jam tours, having seen them at each of the tours and planning to do everything this time around. The conversation continues at the bar over a few drinks. Talking about past tours and albums, Gus reveals that he wouldn't have decided to do this whole tour had the new album not been this good. Mick shares a story from an Australian show in 1998 where the seats on the floor were all taken out by everyone in the crowd during the show, each passing them one by one toward the back to create a general standing area instead of the restrictions of seats. Over the next little while, we share stories from our tours and a few drinks to go with them. Suddenly, Gus pauses and stares at us.

"Wait a minute. You're not that van freak, are you?" he wonders.

"Yes, that would be him," Newfie laughs.

"I bought your DVD," Gus follows.

"I did send a couple down this way," I laugh. "It looks like we'll be seeing lots of each other during this tour."

They suddenly seem more comfortable around us and talk more and more about their experiences with Australian tours of the past and what to expect this time around, as I interview them on camera. Newfie Joe asks about the hitchhiking laws in Australia, and the response is negative. We do, however, find someone who's driving up to Brisbane for the next show, setting up a ride for Newfie Joe. They also further denounce our idea of ever driving the tour in a van because the distances are too great and Aussies tend to prefer flying, so everyone has all of their flights booked already, including myself.

As the show approaches, our excitement level rises. Our seats are in the rafters, but it doesn't matter because we'll all be together and I don't remember the last time I saw a show sitting with Newfie Joe. Getting in after Kings of Leon finishes, we climb up to our section, the highest level that I have sat for a Pearl Jam show in a long time but I'm ecstatic about it. The view is a bit different, but it's nice to have a variety of angles from show to show. For this one, I can clearly see the entire crowd, many who are dressed far too nicely to be at a rock concert, including some in suits. They must be the industry people or the promoters who took away these seats from the fan club.

The show begins and we immediately try our best to make our section bounce coinciding with *Do The Evolution*. Feeding off the energy of each other, we're simply going nuts. But everyone else in our section is sitting down and casually watching the stage from their ass. This might be normal for the balcony I guess, but everyone down below is also sitting down as well. It's an unfamiliar sight for us – we're normally closer to the action – but it's not stopping us from having a good time. Browsing the venue, lower level and balcony, I can pick out other people that should have gotten fan club tickets as they're the only other ones in the crowd standing up. These are the fans that should be closer to the stage. The crowd on the floor is on their feet, but there's little to no motion or any excitement coming from them at all. Is this what the crowd normally looks like and I just don't know about it because I'm usually up closer and can't see behind me? Or is this just because the majority of the ticket holders, down below, aren't really fans and only obtain tickets through the promoters and industry people? The latter is what seems more likely. "It wouldn't hurt for you to move a bit," Vedder tells the crowd jokingly.

We feel the same way. This is the worst crowd I've ever seen at any show in my life. The arena doesn't seem to be interested at all. What a disgrace. It's not as if they aren't paying attention because they are. The crowd is just not showing that they're into the show and I can only wonder how that reflects back on the performers on stage, who are trying to play to a stationary sold out crowd. They might as well be performing to an arena full of mannequins. It's not very motivating at all, even though Pearl Jam is putting on a heck of a performance. As a result, the band cuts short on the show by a few songs, obviously disappointed with the crowd. I guess there's bound to be some duds in there and thanks to the crowd, this show is definitely one of them. On the positive, a disappointing Pearl Jam show is still better than most other concerts and we had a blast rocking out together, which is all that really matters. With no one really in a festive mood afterwards, we all return to our accommodations and regroup for the next show in the next city.

CHAPTER 40: BACK ON FULL TOUR MODE

November 10 – 11, 2006 » Show 52 & 53
Brisbane, Australia

AUSTRALIA IS A LONG WAY AWAY from anywhere else in the world and, much like Canada, the distances between cities are great. Some of us out-of-towners have been feeling the jet lag upon arrival and, even though I had a few days to get over it, the real test will come as we begin to travel within the tour. After an uneventful crowd at the last show, we're all happy to be leaving Sydney and moving on to Brisbane in hopes of a better showing. The trek is a long one and even the experienced Newfie Joe decides against his preferred mode of hitchhiking to take up the offer for a ride with David from Colorado. I, on the other hand, fly up with Annette on flights that she had already booked for me months in advance. She asks me again whether I'll be taking her spare ticket to the Newcastle show and I reconfirm that my attendance is 100%. Why not?

Today is a day off, so upon landing, we board a shuttle bus taking us two hours north to the lovely Sunshine Coast and the town of Coolum, where we'll be staying with Annette's brother, Simon. The Sunshine Coast doesn't offer much sunshine however, as hail the size of golf balls has been falling and destroying properties and vehicles over the last few days. We arrive at Simon's place and rush into the house to escape the weather, passing by vehicles with heavy dents on their hoods because of it. The damages are so severe on one car that the owner's insurance has recommended the car be written off completely rather than repaired. With the conditions outside, there isn't much to do other than have an indoor Aussie barbecue. It's too bad, because looking out on the porch of Simon's place situated on top of the hill, Coolum seems to have a lovely beach when the sun is out. Taking it easy today, we crash out quite early and also wake up bright and early when the sun finally makes an appearance.

To take advantage, we head up to the more popular Noosa Heads, where flocks of tourists gather and where Olivia Newton John has a house on the beach.

Today, however, there aren't as many people as usual and we're able to roam around the beach freely on our own. By noon, we head back to the more quiet town of Coolum and I try my first ever Aussie meat pie, which is immediately followed by my second ever Aussie meat pie. It's just a normal pie with your choice of meat inside, but it's very tasty. To my surprise though, condiments aren't provided and you must purchase ketchup, or as they refer to it here, "sauce", to go along with your pastry. This is apparently common throughout the country everywhere, including places such as McDonalds. Filled up with meat and grease, we prepare for the journey down to Brisbane for the show. Tonight I have my spare ticket still available and without much convincing, Simon's friend, also named Simon, decides to take it after I guarantee them to be excellent seats. We hop into Simon's "ute" (short for utility vehicle, which is Australian for truck), which is all decked out in Eddie Would Go stickers, and make our journey down to Brisbane for the show. Simon is big into his surfing and I mention to him that my next stop is Hawaii, hopefully in time for the Eddie Aikau competition. He's immensely jealous.

We get to the venue, which is in the middle of a forest, at around 7:00pm and have a few drinks at the truck before a few more at the beer garden that surrounds the Brisbane Entertainment Centre. A good vibe is felt almost immediately, so we walk up to our third row seats. Inside, I bump into Michelle and Rob from Philadelphia. They are here for a vacation, using Pearl Jam as an excuse to finally visit Australia and the Great Barrier Reef. We chat until Kings Of Leon brings some more energy into the place. When they're finished and the wait for Pearl Jam begins, I look around behind me to see what the crowd looks like and they're doing the Mexican wave. It's completely opposite to Sydney. The fans here are anxious and excited about this show, and this momentum only continues to build as the band takes the stage. It's deafening in here. This is more like it!

The band feeds off of this energy to put on their best performance of the tour yet. Vedder commends the crowd for their enthusiasm and slanders Sydney in the process. With everyone on a high afterwards, we head downtown for a few drinks. One of Annette's friends meets us there and is nice enough to invite us to crash at her place during our time in Brisbane. The girls head back first, while the boys remain for a few more drinks over conversations about travelling and surfing, before grabbing a taxi back.

Some of us are hurting the next morning, but the sun is scorching hot so we walk along the river toward South Bank to take advantage. The route is a scenic one, as across the river is one of the most beautiful skylines anywhere. Along the way, a jogger runs by us in the opposite direction, and Annette believes it's Stone Gossard. But with her reaction coming a little late, we'll never find out if it was. Down at South Bank, we grab lunch at one of the many concession stands in the area, explore the markets selling hippie paraphernalia, and then hang out at the man-made beach comprising of many children playing joyfully in the water. When the sun becomes too much, we head back to get ready for the show but I'm not sure if I'll be attending tonight. I've already made plans with an old high school friend, Anderson, who now studies in Brisbane, so I tell Annette that I'll call her later when I figure out my plan. Anderson picks me up and takes me for a seafood dinner, having Moreton Bay Bugs, which are bay lobsters specifically found in the north coast of Australia. It's good food with a good friend. Catching up, Anderson tells me of his torturous study routines for Medical School, with almost three more years remaining. On the other hand, I enlighten him about my travels and he is envious and really appreciates my adventurous ways.

"Why aren't you going to the show tonight?" he asks me.

"I wanted to meet up with you," I answer.

"Are there tickets left? I'd like to see why you keep going to these shows."

"Of course, we could get tickets when we arrive if you want to go."

"Alright let's go."

So my plan to stay away from the tour has failed, as even my non Pearl Jam friend is bringing me back to the show. Of course, I gladly take him along. When we get back to the forest again, I head up to the box office to see if there are any tickets left, but there isn't. I tell Anderson not to worry, we'll go to the beer garden and a ticket will come to us. He seems sceptical but follows along anyway. At the beer garden, I find Newfie Joe, Angus and Mick sharing a laugh, so we join in to share a drink and a laugh or two. With the show approaching, Anderson is starting to wonder whether we'll be enjoying the show inside the arena or enjoying the beer garden outside of it. As I reassure him that we'll be inside, a friend of Aussie Ben's, Leigh, walks by and says hi. We had been introduced in Sydney so I recognize him and offer him a drink, but he tell us that he just needs to sell his two spare tickets before going in.

"You have two tickets together?" I ask.

"Yes, they're not great though," he responds. "You want them?"

"Definitely, I don't care where we sit. Thank you."

Anderson can't believe it. It was that easy. We grab one more round of drinks and then head in. Our seats are on the floor about 30 rows back, but we're at the front of the section so there's no one standing in front of us to block our view. It's perfect. The show is another amazing one, including a beautiful cover of *Picture In a Frame* by Tom Waits and a hard core punk cover of *Kick Out The Jams* by MC5 that blows the roof off. And despite being in the same circumstances as the second Sydney show, where no fan club tickets were available for the fans, the crowd is electrifying and the Sydney experience is in the past. Anderson really enjoys the show and thanks me for bringing him, even though I insist that it was him that brought me to the show. However, he does question the logic behind seeing a band so many times in a row. I explain to him that the friends

I've made are the reason why I keep going to all these concerts because they're some of the best people I've ever met. On the other hand, the shows are, in fact, a small reason why I relentlessly travel to see this band. And then I realize what I'm saying and begin to question my hesitation about going to some of these shows. If I'm not going to the shows for the shows, why am I trying to stay away from the shows? My reason was to spend extra time with friends, but I seem to be able to find time for them and still make it to the concerts, where most of my friends will be.

Newfie Joe applauds in appreciation of the music that he hears in Brisbane, Australia.

"Ok I'm in," I turn to Newfie Joe to say.

"In for what?" he asks.

"The whole tour," I reply. "Let's get a van and drive to Perth."

"That's my boy!"

Because I have an early flight in the morning, Anderson drives me directly to the airport. I thank him for his company and hope to see him again. It's 2:00am and my flight is in four hours, so I find a nice corner to set my sleeping bag and lie down on but, just like in European airports, I'm not the only one. The floor is covered with many travelers resting on the floor, waiting for their early flight as well. It takes me a little while to get to sleep, as I'm filled with excitement. It's excitement over the fact that I have now entered into full tour mode and we're going to get a van. The Australian tour will now be done properly.

Feel the sky blanket you
With gems and rhinestones
See the path cut by the moon
For you to walk on

Unthought Known

CHAPTER 41: **TOURING FANS UNITE**

November 13 – 16, 2006 » Show 54, 55, & 56
Melbourne, Australia

FLYING IS QUICK AND EXPENSIVE but driving is slow and fun. So far in Australia, there has only been one mode of transportation during the tour and that has been by air. But with my decision to enter into full tour mode, I'm determined to change this trend. There will be a van put together and we'll drive across the country, the way the tour is meant to be done. As of right now, it's only Newfie Joe and I vanning the final leg of the tour to Perth but, before we leave Melbourne, we hope to find a van and fill it up.

Flying early into my favourite Australian city, I find my way around rather easily and am able to check into my hostel, which I booked a week ago. The booking is only for one night, so my flexibility will return tomorrow when the first of three shows in the city takes place. The hostel reception staff goes over the rules and information for me and then mentions that it's free pancake breakfast Sunday and asks if I want to get in on it. I accept the offer and reach into my bag to pull out one of two remaining bottles of maple syrup that I had brought over to share with a bunch of strangers. Within ten minutes, the bottle is empty and I'm the most popular person in the hostel. As with any hostel, there's a mix of international travelers from everywhere, so we swap travel stories with each other. Amongst the conversation, a good looking couple from Ireland mentions that they just finished a road trip around Australia in a camper van they rented one-way from Perth. Intrigued by the van aspect of it, I inquire more about it, so they hand me the card for Wicked Campers, a company that specializes in one way van rentals for budget travelers. This sounds perfect. I write down the name and website in my daily planner – yes, there *is* some sort of organization to my travelling madness – and thank them for the information.

Escaping my newfound friends, I venture out into the city in search of the one thing that I need to do today and that is to purchase a cheap mobile phone.

Now that I'm doing the whole tour, I figure that it would be best to have some inexpensive means of contact for all of the people I'm meeting, something I should have done on the other tours instead of paying outrageous phone bills. Down the main shopping district on Bourke Street, I find a Vodafone store and pick up the cheapest possible phone they carry and fill it up with enough credit for the time I'm here. All this for less than $100, which is a bargain compared to all the charges that I accumulated on the other tours. I grab a seat on a bench on a street that is only shared by pedestrians and street cars, and start sending text messages of my new phone number to the only contacts that I have – Annette, Gus, Julian, Mick, and Nathan. As I finish, I hear a voice calling me. "What the hell are you doing here?"

I look up and don't recognize the face at first, but then it registers. It's one of the guys I did the infamous pub crawl with in Rome. My memory is faded and I don't remember his name but he reintroduces himself as Darren, so we decide to grab a beer to catch up on each other's travels. Apparently, he stayed at the Freestyle Hostel in Rome for another week and they tried to do the pub crawl once again, only to have it fail miserably. No one knew where to go, people were getting lost along the way, and some didn't even make it back to the hostel that night. "We needed you and Arizona to lead the charge, man," he claims.

Our catch up is short and sweet but it shows how exciting and unpredictable travelling can be. When you can just randomly run into people you met on the other side of the world, you know that the world is much smaller than people think. I return back to the hostel to quickly check my email and notice a reply from Jacinta, who I emailed a few days ago. Jacinta has always been my travelling hero and inspiration to see the world, and she even took part on the very first Touring Van trip to see Pearl Jam at the Gorge over a year ago. Excited to hear that she's in her hometown while I'm around, I give her a call and she's able to meet up with me right away. She tells me that she's off for her next adventure in just two days, India.

"Wow, you don't stop do you?" I ask.

"You're catching up though," she counters.

We talk about good times in Vancouver and other travel prospects and then she asks about the shows. I mention that I have a spare ticket for the show the following day and would love for her to come with me, but she hesitates before declining, alluding to everything she needs to get done before leaving for six months. But a few more drinks and laughs later, she changes her mind and begins working through the logistics of making the show work. She would need to head to the airport a few hours after its conclusion, which is very doable. "I better head home to start packing and get my stuff together now," she concludes.

As we part ways, I receive a call from Julian to inquire if Newfie Joe and I are still staying with him starting tomorrow. I confirm and he gives me directions. As I'm chatting on the phone, a text message arrives from Nathan, who wants to meet up. So I conclude my day with a few more drinks. We chat about his time in Canada and his bizarre quest to find someone who he calls "Happy Guy." Apparently, Nathan felt a bit down while working at a resort in Banff, Alberta until one day, when cleaning out one of the rooms, he found a photo in the garbage can of a man smiling in such a big way that it brought a smile to his face and made him feel better. He kept the photo, bringing it back home to Melbourne, and decided to start a campaign trying to find out who's the man in the photo, thus, his quest to find out who is "Happy Guy." It's an intriguing mission for a truly funny person. In the morning, I check out of the hostel and head out to the streets, where Julian is already waiting for me.

"You want to go for a drive?" he asks.

"Sure. Where are we going?" I reply.

"Bells Beach and Torquay."

Bells Beach is a world famous surf beach that was also featured in the Keanu Reeves movie *Point Break*. I've been before, but am not complaining about the destination by any means. Unfortunately, the weather turns sour as we approach the south coast, bringing with it a strong hailstorm along with a thick fog, so any hope of viewing some surf action disappears. However, the drive is a good one and the delicious "burger with the lot" at a small burger shack in Torquay makes up for the disappointment. Consisting of a slice of pineapple, a beet, and a fried egg that sits on top of an Aussie beef patty that's smothered with bacon and onions as well as lettuce and tomatoes, this Aussie style burger simply melts in my mouth and gets my juices flowing for the show tonight.

On our way back into the city, I receive a call from Gus informing me that he has a spare front row ticket for me tonight. Already having my own tickets, I politely decline, but mentioned that I think Annette wouldn't mind having it for her hometown show. Gus gives me the ok to ask about her interest in upgrading seats, and she happily accepts but has concerns about having to sell both of her tickets now. This is no problem though, as Newfie Joe is in need of a ticket and she is able to sell the other shortly after. Sorting out the ticket situation in front of Rod Laver Arena, I pull out the video camera and start talking to people and gauging their interested about joining the van for the drive to Perth.

"I don't know what the word on the street is, but I'm keen," Gus says. "But not if you're overbooked."

"We're not overbooked," I answer. "You're the man. You're from Adelaide."

"Well, when you say you want to do the van thing, are you hiring a van?"

"Yes, we're hiring a van and driving from Adelaide to Perth."

I continue to talk to people about the van idea, with the only definite being a fellow Vancouver resident, Clayton. Ben is happy to end the show in his hometown of Adelaide citing that if the touring van was present, he'd be first in. Upon hearing the fact that I brought along the hockey tape for the trip, however, he indicates that there could be a possibility of his involvement.

"I think Joe is waiting for you at the pub," Gus laughs.

I meet up with Newfie Joe at Bridie O'Reilly's, where the pre-party is taking place. But it's rather uneventful and fairly pricey to top it off. Newfie Joe introduces me to a couple that he has been chatting with all afternoon, Brett and Diane from Sydney, who are very impressed with our travels. When it's time for the show, we head back to the venue, but not before they offer their place in Sydney for us to stay when we return for a third show this weekend.

Jacinta, looking exhausted, meets me in front of the box. Our seats are amazing yet again, row four in the centre. She's thoroughly impressed at how close we are to the stage, almost as much as she's impressed with the show itself. For two and a half hours, the band puts on their usual incredible performance, which is accompanied by an equally energetic crowd in attendance, led by Annette and Gus in the front row. The highlight of the night comes in the second encore during *State Of Love And Trust*. Near the end of the song, Vedder comes out to the edge of the stage, directly in front of Gus and simply tosses him the microphone. The next thing we hear is Gus belting out the remaining lines of the song with Pearl Jam backing up his extreme karaoke. "Eh o eh o ehh oooooo!"

Did that just happen? I'm ecstatic and the moment sends shivers down my body. I can only imagine how Gus is feeling. The band maintains this energy throughout the next couple of songs, finishing off the show with a bang. After the show, we jump up to the front row to see Gus and Annette, and they look as if they've been struck by lightning. There's a glow around them, more so on Annette, as she gives me a giant hug. Jacinta thanks me for the tickets and runs off to catch her flight, while we all gather around, still inside the arena and still in awe of what just transpired. There's a whole group of fans just hanging around wondering what we should do and, since this is the first venue on the tour that's within the city limits, we decide to find a bar.

Annette suggests the Crown Casino because it's just across the river and is open late. So onto the casino bar we go for a few celebratory drinks, all twenty of us. Once there, we begin to get more acquainted with all the familiar faces that we've seen at the other shows so far. It appears that there is a large number of people that will be travelling to most, if not all, of the shows on this tour. It's very exciting. I meet Ivan from Mexico for the first time. Carlos had mentioned that he couldn't make it to Australia, but has given all of his tickets for the entire tour to his friend, Ivan. He informs me that he has a spare ticket for me to any of the shows I need, so I request a ticket for the last show in Perth, which I have now decided to drive toward. Christian from Peru also mentions that he has a spare ticket for tomorrow's show and asks if I know anyone needing one.

"I need a ticket for tomorrow," I respond.

"It's yours."

After a few drinks, Julian says that he has some errands to run in the morning and needs to go home but encourages us to stay out as long as we want, handing over a set of spare keys. We end up sticking around until closing time, and by the end of the night, my mobile phone is filled with a hand full of new phone numbers. It's already 5:00am and seemingly too late to return back to Julian's place, especially in the condition we're in, but Nathan graciously offers his couch for Newfie Joe and me. So I send Julian a message notifying him of our plans not to disrupt his household.

In the morning, Nathan offers us toast for breakfast and grabs the one jar of peanut butter in a cupboard full of vegemite. It's another day and another show. Instead of spending a fortune on drinks before the show at the bar again, we decide to buy some drinks at the store and have a little picnic in the park. At the store, we scour through the cases of Victoria Bitter and Toohey's beers to find out what the best value would be. Both are rather inexpensive along with other light and probably tasteless beverages, but something else catches my eye just as we're about to check out. The price of box wine seems to be even cheaper, with four litres of wine going for under $10. That's the winner. Newfie Joe immediately switches his two cases of beer for eight litres of box wine. To go with the wine, we decide to grab a stack of plastic cups and a wheel of brie cheese. With our picnic supplies all set, we hop on a tram and head back toward the venue. I start sending off text messages to all my new contacts about our plan for a picnic in the park at the Sidney Myer Music Bowl, an outdoor music venue, where Pearl Jam played almost 10 years previously, in the Botanical Gardens that sits directly across from the venue.

With the city in clear view in the background, the amphitheatre has a nice grassy hill to sit on for our wine and cheese picnic. I do the honours and try out the cheap wine first. It's surprisingly very drinkable and might I say, even tasty. We have a chuckle over it and continue pouring out of the box as the troops begin to arrive, Gus being the first. Glancing over at our box of wine, he simply burst into laughter. He claims that he hasn't drank "goon", as they call cheap box wine, since he was in college, but he gladly accepts a full glass from me after showing us the proper way to drink it – directly from the tap.

As the glasses of goon are polished off one by one, our picnic begins to grow exponentially with many new friends joining in, so I start introducing people to the camera for their comment on the tour thus far. Clayton from Vancouver is enjoying his time in Australia but criticizes the Australian crowds at the shows, especially in Sydney. A response comes from Hinn, who does not try to defend his home city but, rather, apologizes for Sydneysiders, claiming that they have a reputation of being too good for everyone. Gitta from Germany and Einat from Israel declare that nothing will match the energy of a European crowd. Tom from Tasmania, says that since his home state is not cool enough for a show, he's doing the whole tour. The atmosphere is relaxed and fun, the perfect way to lead up to a show. With Newfie Joe skulling the goon, I turn the camera onto Gus to ask him about last night.

"Oh man, I knew you'd do this to me," he jokes.

"It's ok to brag about it," Clayton follows.

"You had no choice, he threw the mic at you," Nathan follows.

"Well, Ed had been eyeballing me a bit," Gus answers. "He saw me singing along all night and during *State of Love and Trust* he was watching me sing every verse line for line. He clearly remembered back in Adelaide in 2003, when he forgot the words to *State of Love and Trust* and he looked down and saw me singing it, so me and him obviously have a connection when it comes to that song," he jokes.

"Relive that moment," I continue.

"I can't remember a thing. I couldn't hear anything," he reminisces. "It was cool. It was amazing. It's one of those things that you hear about and dream of and you never even know someone that it happens to, let alone it being you. And it was over like that."

"So is that the highlight of your Pearl Jam career?" I inquire.

"Yeah, but the tour isn't over," he laughs. "Clearly, we're working our way to a full blown duet."

The picnic in the park at Sidney Myer Bowl before the second Melbourne show.

The picnic in the park turns out to be a huge success and is a hit with all involved, so much so that there's a request to do it all again before the next one. As the show nears, the crowd slowly diminishes until it's just Newfie Joe and I. We finish the remainder of the drinks and clean up the area to remove all evidence of our existence in the venue. As we exit the park, I glance at the watch and it's 8:45pm, the show is about to start any minute now. Feeling a bit tipsy, we sprint down the hill, across the street, and then across the bridge over the river to get to Rod Laver Arena.

As we enter the building, there's an odd feeling. The hallways are completely empty but a large roar is heard from within as the first notes of the concert are struck. The band is already on the stage and we can certainly feel the electricity running through the air with the building completely shaking, as the great rock spectacle is happening inside of it. So we run as fast as we can through the deserted path and then through the entrance to the seating area, where we are hit with a powerful force exerting from the concert that's already steam rolling on momentum. The band is well into their set and the crowd is at full volume as well. The feeling is unreal and we stand still momentarily in amazement before realizing that we should get to our seats, so we go our separate ways. I find my spot rather quickly as Christian is already jumping a metre up in the air to the beat of *Go*. This is only a sign of things to come. Feeding off of each other's energy, we fully capture the hard rocking show that's presented before us. Christian and I relentlessly rock the fuck out.

To build on the camaraderie that was built from the night before, we decide to gather everyone together for another night out after the show. The group has now expanded even more. This time a local suggests we hit a backpacker's bar called The Joint because it's open very late. It's Tuesday night and The Joint is not the busiest of places but we're about to give them some business with nearly 50 of us entering at once. This is my type of bar. It's a bit of a dive, but it has pool tables at one end, a balcony at the other, two large projection screens pumping out music videos, and couches all around. The only thing wrong with the place is the cheesy pop music videos on display. I approach the bar to order the first round of Jagerbombs and the barmaid asks what's going on. I inform her that we just come from the Pearl Jam concert and are all looking to drink. "Right on," she replies.

As the drinks are being made, she whispers something to her fellow bartender, who then disappears into the back room. We get our drinks and then, all of a sudden, the music videos on the screen turn from Pink into Pearl Jam. He must have made the switch. For the rest of the night it's nothing but alternative and grunge music videos on rotation, and we're all just having a ball. There's a day off from the tour tomorrow, so everyone is definitely making the most of it. It's beer after Jagerbomb after beer, with not a single sober person in sight. As the morning begins to creep in, people start to depart for their beds, while Newfie Joe, Mick, and I hold strong until closing time. When we exit the bar, we see nothing but blue skies because it's 7:30am already. To say that time flies when you're having fun is an understatement. I'm still somewhat coherent, so I guide Newfie Joe back to Julian's place, where we still haven't been to yet.

Following the directions from his text message, we ride a street tram down south, and then stumble a few blocks to hop onto another tram. When we enter the second tram, we're immediately approached by four undercover transit police, asking for our tickets. We don't have any, although we didn't technically have enough time to purchase any when we boarded before they approached.

"We gave you 30 seconds to purchase a ticket and you didn't make an attempt to do so," they claim.

They ask for our identification, but we don't have any on us. They ask for our address, but we tell them that we don't live in Melbourne. The four of them begin to look befuddled as to what to do. At the next tram stop, some of the passengers getting off begin mouthing off at the undercover cops, resulting in a shouting match between one of them. "Don't you guys have anything else better to do," one person yells at the cops. "Leave them alone."

The cops look frustrated now and simply tell us to leave the tram on the next stop, so we oblige. Coincidentally, this is our tram stop anyway. We enter the house at nearly 9:00am to find two mattresses neatly setup for us in Julian's room. He greets us good morning and asks if we need some sleep, to which we respond with an unenthusiastic nod. I try to stay awake a bit longer and chat with Julian but, before I know it, my eyes begin to shut and I pass out on the mattress. A call from Mick a few hours later wakes me up. He informs me that he's waiting for us at a bar called the Espy in St Kilda. Apparently, last night, I had invited everyone to meet at this bar today, events that I don't recall. I tell him that we'll be a few hours as Newfie Joe is still completely passed out, so he tells us to take our time because no one else has arrived yet.

While waiting for Newfie Joe to wake up, I bust out my last remaining bottle of maple syrup for Julian and his flatmates, Beck and Janet. They decide to make pancakes and the maple syrup is quickly devoured. Around mid-afternoon, Newfie Joe enters the kitchen still drunk, with a bottle of Kahlua in one hand and a bottle of vodka in the other. He wants to make a White Russian to cure his hangover. But one White Russian turns into eight and, before we know it, the entire afternoon is gone. I call Mick to find out what the status is at the Espy and he confirms that everyone is there but some are starting to leave. We finally make our way down to the bar to see only Gus, Mick, and a few others remaining. With a minimal amount of drinks, at least compared to the other nights, we're able to watch a couple of local bands play and have a rather relaxing night before getting some much needed rest.

We're able to sleep in the next morning again, but this time we wake up more revitalized. Because the picnic was such a success the other day, we decide to head back to the park for another pre-show gathering, picking up some goon and cheese along the way of course. Unfortunately, the Sidney Myer bowl is closed because they're setting up for a special benefit concert for Make Poverty History that will take place tomorrow, a show that both Pearl Jam and U2, who are also touring Australia at the same time, have been rumoured to be in attendance for. Instead, we merely gather along the river, which even provides proper picnic benches for us. The picnic is another goon fest, setting the tone for another great show, the final one in Melbourne. Another gathering afterwards, this time at the Queensberry Hotel bar, caps off a fantastic week of shows.

The next day is another day off with most of us staying in Melbourne. I've been meaning to meet up with a friend of a friend since arriving into town, so finally with some free time, we go for lunch. On our way there, I receive a call from Gus informing me that he's by the river with some cheese and a box of goon waiting for us. Gus has a ticket for the Make Poverty History concert, a radio contest winner's only show, so he's having his own little pre-show party for it. I let Newfie Joe know where he is and, within an hour, he shows up. Mick has also arrived at this point, hoping that the rumoured bands will come. Meanwhile, I'm still out to lunch and clueless of what's going on. While he's gingerly sipping away at the goon, Gus receives a call from Tom from Tasmania. "I'm inside the venue. The show is about to start and Jeff and Stone's guitars are on the stage," he observes.

"Fuck off!" Gus replies.

"Seriously, they're coming on."

"Fuck off!"

"Get in here quick."

Gus feverishly hangs up, tells the others what he was told and proceeds to chug up the hills of the Botanical Garden to the venue. Mick and Joe follow behind with the goon but, without a ticket, they only get as far as the fence. What they see and hear through the fence is Bono and the Edge on stage introducing Pearl Jam for a collaborative performance of *Rockin' in the Free World*, kick starting the benefit concert. After the song, the rock 'n' roll superstars leave the stage and the venue and Gus follows along to meet up with Newfie Joe and Mick. They call me to fill me in on what they had just witnessed and how incredible it was, then proceed to ridicule me for not being there with them.

By this point, I've returned back to Julian's place, where we are discussing the plans to hire a van from Wicked Campers. Julian is now set on joining us and will be my co-driver for the trip. Things are looking up in the van department. We meet up with the others for dinner before returning back for an early and relaxing night. What a week it has been. With three consecutive shows, Melbourne gave all the fans an opportunity to converge and now a large group of touring fans have been formed down under and a plan for a van is on the go. The Australian tour is starting to become my kind of tour.

I'll be hanging upside down
And there I will swing
for all eternity

Comatose

CHAPTER 42: **BEST SHOW OF THE TOUR**

November 18 – 19, 2006 » Show 57 & 58
Sydney and Newcastle, Australia

THE AUSTRALIAN TOUR OPENED with back to back lacklustre shows in the most populated city in the country, Sydney. This is solely attributed to the motionless and underwhelming crowd put before the band. After a string of powerful and uplifting shows in Brissy and Melbs, the tour returns back to Sydney for a third show and a chance for redemption. We thank Julian and his lovely flatmates for their hospitality and head to the airport for our flight. Julian will take care of the van and meet us in Adelaide. Adelaide to Perth will be a little bit of a different story.

"No planes, it'll be straight hardcore." Newfie proclaims.

We arrive into Sydney late in the morning to catch a train out to the suburb of West Ryde, where Brett is picking us up. Dropping our bags off at his apartment, we chill out for a few hours listening to music and sharing a conversation, before driving out to Acer Arena at Olympic Park. Upon arrival, we bump into Nathan and Clayton instantly. Nathan has no accommodations for tonight and asks where we're staying, so Brett also invites him over to crash at his place. He is appreciative and thanks Brett for the offer. Clayton, on the other hand, appears to be exhausted. "It's show eight, I'm fucking beat," Clayton complains. "I didn't sleep last night. I'm running on fucking Red Bull, man."

Walking toward the venue, we see Gus and Mick already sitting underneath a tree with a box of goon. What have we started? We sit down for a few glasses, lying out in the sun for a while, before I realize that I still don't have a ticket for tonight yet, so I continue on toward the venue. In front of the box office, Aussie Ben is sitting in a circle with a group of fans and, after I announce that I need a ticket, Gitta informs me that she has a single in the balcony that she'll sell for half price. I snap it up. As I'm about to walk back to the tree, I catch a glimpse of something out of the corner of my eye. In the middle of their circle is a tambourine, with a list of songs written on it and entitled "Newcastle Setlist" at the top. With Newcastle being a last minute add on to the tour, most are predicting it to be special. So to help aid the band in preparation for it, these fans have decided to collaborate and write down a list of songs they'd like to see be performed. Gen from Sydney hopes to throw the tambourine on stage tonight for the band to see. Browsing through it quickly, I see mostly rarities and obscure songs that the band probably won't play. We might get one of these, if we're lucky. "Good luck," I wish them, as we near show time.

Based on the previous shows in this arena, we enter with absolutely no expectations. I head upstairs, while most of the others remain on the ground floor. Sitting up in the balcony is never a problem for me but sitting up there by myself this time seems a bit strange. As the show starts, almost the entire balcony remains seated. Perfect, another disappointing crowd in Sydney. But as I stand alone in my section, I notice signs of some life down below. The floor looks as if it's bumping with activity, so Vedder thanks the crowd for showing up this time. The show is substantially better than the other Sydney shows purely based on the fact that the crowd is much more animated. As a treat, the band performs a cover of *I Got You* by a popular New Zealand band, Split Enz, which even gets the crowd in the balcony on their feet. Near the end of the show, I notice the Newcastle tambourine get thrown on stage. But instead of reading it, Vedder proceeds to play with it as he would normally do, smashing it through his fist, signifying that Sydney three has been a smashing success. Sydney has redeemed itself and everyone leaves the building fully satisfied.

Back at Brett's place, it's a calm evening until I receive a call from Julian notifying us that he has worked out the deal with Wicked Campers for a week long van rental to be picked up and dropped off in Adelaide. It's now set, we have the van. With that all sorted, our enthusiasm convinces Brett and Diane to do a mini road trip of their own and suddenly decide that they would drive us up to Newcastle without any tickets for tomorrow night. Nathan, however, will be heading back to Melbourne because this is his last show of the tour.

The rest of the night is spent watching Pearl Jam's *Single Video Theory* DVD, which features the making of the album Yield, showcasing Jack Irons as the drummer. Nathan enlightens us on his drumming experience and how Irons is his favourite drummer of all time. Almost on cue, Brett runs into his room and pulls out a smashed up drum stick that he got during a show thrown out to him by none other than Jack Irons. He hands it over to Nathan, who holds onto it in admiration for the rest of the DVD. His appreciation of Irons continues into our conversation afterwards, still holding the drum stick.

"You know what?" Brett says. "It's yours. You can have it."

"Oh wow. I don't even know what this means," Nathan explains. "Thank you so much. I love this karma thing."

Dropping Nathan off at the train station on our way out the next morning, we hit the road in excitement. A mini road trip is better than no road trip, and it will gear us up for the big road trip that lies ahead. Newcastle is roughly two and a half hours away along the coast, so it's a lovely ride up. This is a show that was added after the fact, in response to a petition that was put together by a group of fans from the area. It's also taking place in the smallest venue of the tour, making this a much anticipated show, even though the Newcastle Entertainment Centre looks more like a warehouse than anything else. After sorting Brett and Diane out with tickets at the box office, we head down to the beach to dip our feet in the ocean before heading to the bar for the pre-party.

Attempting to recruit more van riders, we receive confirmation from Ivan about his participation in the adventure, bringing our total to five at the moment, with Tom and Gus showing interest as well. It's another gathering of the usual suspects at the bar along with the addition of a local celebrity, former world surfing champion, Mark Richards. Being a fellow avid surfer himself, Mick is almost shaking in nerves as he approaches the legend for an autograph. Mark mentions that he's a friend of Vedder's and was supposed to take the boys out for a surf this morning, but the idea was vetoed by tour management to prevent exhaustion. However, he has been invited to the concert and is looking forward to it with much anticipation. "It's going to be a good one," he boldly predicts.

Brett and I dipping into the ocean in Newcastle.

With that vote of confidence, our expectations are raised to the roof, as we walk across the train tracks back to the venue. Entering the venue, we notice just how small it actually is. The place resembles a barn inside, more narrow and long, and very similar to The Point in Dublin. Annette leads me to our seats, dead centre in row eight, beside Joel and Megan from Perth, who are newlyweds on their honeymoon going across the country with the tour. I mention our plans to drive out west, so they advise me to bring lots of water and to watch out for kangaroos. They've done the drive back and forth many times but, when asked if they were doing it this time around, they cite time constraints as being the main deterrent against the drive.

As the lights come down, the roar of the crowd rises and the band, unexpectedly, comes out with *Alive*, one of their main staples usually played near the end of the night. This is either going to be one of those greatest hits shows that most Pearl Jam fans seem to despise, or it will be a show filled with surprises. It turns out to be the latter. Vedder even informs us that they'll play songs tonight that they normally don't play, such as *Brain of J, Red Mosquito, Whipping, Leatherman, Down, Undone*, and this is just the 20 song opening set. When the encore starts off with *Thumbing My Way*, I glance over at Newfie Joe, who's standing a section over with his eyes closed, taking in the song that relates to him the most. The encore continues with *Masters Of War, Footsteps, Crown of Thorns, Alone,* and *Even Flow,* all of which you'd be lucky to see on its own on any given night. It looks like the setlist on the tambourine in Sydney was more accurate than we first thought.

Before the second encore, Vedder explains the reasoning behind the unconventional show by bringing the friend that was responsible for writing tonight's setlist onto the stage. It's none other than Mark Richards, the same surfer who was at the bar earlier. Concluding with McCready scorching his guitar on Jimi Hendrix's *Little Wing*, the show is easily the best show of this tour thus far and quite possibly one of the best all year. Often when these shows are overhyped or the expectations are extremely high, the standards are never quite met. However, tonight far exceeded all predictions for a memorable show.

"It's the best concert that I've ever seen. I think every song was a fucking moment tonight," Newfie Joe proclaims. "It was just one song after another going 'Wow, I can't believe they would play that' and then they'd go to the next song and it's 'Oh my god, I can't believe they're playing that.'"

"Had I known that Mark Richards was doing the setlist tonight, I would have gone to town on him at the bar earlier," Gus jokes.

"I mean, I could possibly never see a show again maybe, and I would feel quite content because this was that good," Newfie Joe explains.

Brett and Diane thank us for convincing them to come up for the show and bid us farewell before heading back to their car for the drive back to Sydney. Riding high from the show, we decide to pick up a box of goon and head to our hotel to celebrate because there aren't any bars open at this time. So everyone that's staying at the Ibis Hotel packs into our room that Annette had booked for me, her friend, and herself. It's here that, after four glasses of goon, Big Mick decides that he'll now go to Perth for the final show, which was not in his original plans because he's getting married only a few days afterwards. Perth is completely isolated on the West Coast of Australia and far away from any of the other cities on the tour. So many fans have purposely left the final show off their travel plans. But after a show like tonight and with Newfie Joe and I talking up the van trip, essentially telling him that he needs to join us, Mick figures that he'll try to make this work before his wedding.

"Yes, you need to do this before it's all over," Newfie Joe laughs. "Before you get completely whipped and broken and crushed."

"Pass me the goon, now!" Mick insists. "I'm doing this, because I want to drink goon with Newfie Joe."

From Mick, I then turn my attention to Aussie Ben, who was also content on ending his tour in Adelaide, his hometown. And although the initial idea of driving through the Nullarbor desert, the most desolate place in the country, in both directions does not exactly appeal to him, Ben decides that flying to Perth and driving back in the van could work. With all the rash decisions, Annette also commits to the final show of the tour, but any requests for her to join a van full of sweaty guys are immediately rejected. We now have six passengers for the van trip, so we call Gus to notify him of our latest recruitment in an attempt to add one more, but he doesn't commit. However, he does suggest that we have a proper keg party at his place after the first Adelaide show to celebrate Mick's wedding. It will essentially be a bachelor party and also an official send off for the van trip. Newcastle won't be forgotten and will be hard to top, but things are looking good for Adelaide.

If he can't sleep
how will he ever dream?
Unemployable

CHAPTER 43: **THE BUCKS SHOW**

November 21 – 22, 2006 » Show 59 & 60
Adelaide, Australia

A BUCK IS A MALE DEER and in Australia a group of macho men are often referred to as bucks. From this came the term bucks show, which refers to a bachelor party featuring a group of young bucks. At the conclusion of the tour, Mick will be marrying his fiancée Karla, so to celebrate this occasion, we've decided to put on a bucks show party at Gus' house to be followed by a bucks show on the road when we stuff him in our van for the drive to Perth, after he officially got the ok from Karla to join us for the additional four days. To get to Adelaide, Annette and I would have to train back to Sydney to catch our flight. We arrive in Adelaide late in the afternoon and head straight to Ben's house, where we're staying tonight. With Annette not feeling well, we have a very easy night, drink free, and are able to catch up on some much needed rest.

The next day, I head over to Gus' house and help set up for the party. Picking up some snacks, plastic cups, and two kegs of beer, we're fully prepared for something good tonight, in case the show doesn't turn out to be. But the chances of that happening are slim to none. In his classic 1970 Holden HG station wagon, Gus takes us all to the show in style. He had originally offered his car for us to drive to Perth if we weren't successful with finding a van. Apparently, he wouldn't have been too concerned about getting it back, suggesting that we could merely dump the vehicle off a cliff when we get to Perth. Seeing the station wagon in person, I don't blame him. The doors on one side don't appear to be operating properly despite Gus' claim that it's not broken.

"They open," Gus maintains. "But there's a special technique to do it."

We are the first to arrive at the Adelaide Entertainment Centre and the only ones in the parking lot thus far, so we have our pick of spots. Taking up pole position near the exit, so that we're able to leave quickly afterwards, Gus walks around to the other side, opens the door, and lets us out, as we can't figure out the technique he was referring to. At the box office, I pick up my tickets, which are in the third row. Happy with my score, I inquire about tickets for tomorrow night's non Ten Club show, because I'm still in need of one. They do have tickets, including a front row ticket at the very end, so I gladly snatch it up. Across the street, we meet up with everyone at the bar for some drinks and I start asking people what we should expect and see on the drive to Perth.

"Nothing," Aaron from New South Wales answers. "Dirt and 'roos."

"I think you guys are insane," Emily from Melbourne follows. "You have no idea. It's going to be so hot."

Megan and Joel reiterate the need for good music and snacks along with lots of water, while another couple from Perth, Avin and Leah, describe it as being crazy but awesome at the same time. When asked if they're doing the drive as well, their answer is a resounding no but maybe next time. Sonia from Adelaide predicts that the trip will be filled with a lot of boredom, a lot of road kill and a lot of dirt, but wishes us luck on the dream holiday, as she sarcastically calls it. My van talk is interrupted when Julian calls to inform me that his flight has been cancelled due to a lightning storm. He'll now be arriving bright and early tomorrow morning from Melbourne, when we can pick up the van from Wicked Campers. Ben arrives to the venue shortly after, and is taking my spare ticket for tonight's show, his hometown show. His previous best seats have been in Halifax, where he had tickets in the sixth row, which was also my spare ticket. Tonight, he'll be in the third row and he's stoked.

Before the show starts, we hand out invitations for the after party to fans that we recognize. We're on Stone's side tonight and decide to give him some love during the show. So at the end of the first few songs, Ben and I merely point at him constantly, making him feel a little uncomfortable. Then halfway through the set, someone from behind mumbles to us that Stone might sing tonight, to which I respond by chanting "let Stone sing" continuously. Ben immediately backs me up followed by Tom, who's standing on my other side. Soon everyone else in our section joins in as well and, before we know it, our chant has taken a life on its own, interrupting Vedder's speech to the crowd. "We're a democracy here," Vedder looks over in acknowledgement. "We'll discuss that on the next session."

Satisfied with our recognition, we continue pointing at Stone randomly throughout the show, with the occasional "Stone" chant to further decrease his comfort level, even though we all know he loves it. When it comes time for the final encore, Vedder backs away from the microphone to let Stone take centre stage. The ever-humble rhythm guitarist diverts his spot light back toward Vedder, calling him an amazing person and thanking him for everything he has done for the band including singing tonight, even though he's as sick as a dog.

"And I'll sing for you guys, if you want." Stone offers, looking over at us.

Grabbing the microphone with full force, he delivers an energetic rendition of *Don't Give Me No Lip*, a fun song that only adds to the boisterousness of the crowd, much to the appreciation of our section. Ben, Tom, and I are jumping so high during the song that our feet barely touch the ground. It's perhaps the most enjoyable moment on the tour to date. Following the song, Vedder points to Ivan, who's holding up a shirt with a song request written on it. The request is for Carlos, who couldn't make it down here, and the song is for *Sad*. Ivan chucks the shirt on stage for Vedder to read up close. Vedder sees it and dedicates the desired song to Carlos. These highlights contribute to a very pleasing performance. Expecting a large turnout for the party, we all pile into Gus' car immediately after the show and return back to the house for Mick's bucks show party.

Trying to capture some of the moments on film, I go around the house filming and talking to fans with Ben getting his old cameraman position back from St. John's. There's still a buzz over Stone's performance and Clayton even suggests that we start a "let Gus sing" chant at the next show. Talking to people about the tour, the majority of the fans are very impressed at how well everyone has gotten along. Warwick, from Newcastle, enthusiastically describes the people he has met as being amazing.

"I knew I'd meet people on the tour," he explains, "but I didn't think that I'd meet you guys. You guys have all been great."

"I've been blown away for the most part," Gus comments. "To me, the most amazing thing has been the social side and the community thing that we've never seen on an Australian tour before. And most people I've spoken to haven't seen this level of interaction between the fans before."

"So you never expected it," I inquire.

"No, not at all. I expected spending two weeks on the road by myself."

"And what has it become?"

"It's just become a two or three week party, nonstop. But I'm loving it."

Just about everyone who we've met throughout the tour is here celebrating with us, including a large contingent of Melbournians making the short trip. Brad and Dawn are from Melbourne and Darren is from nearby Geelong, but there are a number of fans from elsewhere who are living in Melbourne including Leigh from Sydney, Nadeen from Jordan, Sarah from Toronto, and Joni from Tasmania. The party lasts late into the morning, with those still in attendance merely passing out on the floor one by one. Thanks to our repeated injection of alcohol into his system, Mick has been blitzed all night, barely able to walk or talk near the end. The night eventually becomes a blur and exactly when the party officially ends is unknown.

When I gain consciousness again, it's time to pick up Julian from the airport and head directly to the Wicked Campers depot to pick up the van. Approaching the industrial area of the city, we wait in anticipation. Our first reaction to the van is that of laughter. Sitting in the garage by its lonesome, the Toyota Town

Ace van is smaller than I could imagine, as it's perhaps two thirds the size of the Dodge Ram. But surprisingly funnier is what's freshly painted on the body. All Wicked Camper vans have a different theme designed and spray painted on it every time it's hired out. The theme for our van is the Bratz Dolls, with two badass looking dolls painted on one side and a third doll on the other side next to the label "Rock Angels." On the back lies the phrase "Be a man not a fool, pull the chain not your tool" with the "wicked" logo on the front of the van. It looks more like the Kylie Minogue Touring Van than the Pearl Jam touring van. After the initial hysteria, we accept the fact that this is our van and we're going to drive it proudly. "It's wicked man," Julian proclaims.

We sign the van under my name and Julian as a second driver, providing our driver's license and credit card info. I'm only driving the one way to Perth, while Julian will stay on and return it back to Adelaide. With all the paper work settled, we bring the van back to the house for the others to scrutinize. Their first reaction is also of laughter. Gus examines the insides of the van, with three seats in the front, a mattress on top of some compartments in the back, and a sink and kitchen setup in the trunk. Clayton seems to love it, while Newfie Joe is a little concerned about the size of it.

"Yeah, this is going to be a problem for Mick," Newfie Joe claims.

"He wouldn't even fit in the front seat," Gus follows.

"How many people do we have?" Newfie Joe asks.

"Six for sure, maybe as many as eight," I answer.

"This will fit eight easily," Clayton states.

"I think Annette is going to love it," Gus replies.

"There needs to be some hockey tape," Newfie Joe suggests, "but I like it."

The Aussie Touring Van from Wicked Campers.

After further inspecting the van, we conclude that the kitchen cabinet in the trunk is not necessary and its removal would provide much needed free space. Accordingly, we unbolt their attachments to relieve the trunk of its clutter and bring the sink into the house, where it will be reattached prior to the van being returned. We now have some space to put our bags and luggage in and the van is ready for the road. Despite the large grin on his face, Gus denies the fact that he now wants to join the van. On the way to the venue, we pick up a couple of large pizzas and some beer for some tailgating prior to the show.

When we meet Mick and Ivan at the venue, we declare ourselves the Rock Angels. Mick reckons it will be a tight fit, but it shouldn't be a problem for him to squeeze in the back. I suggest that the Canadian flag be draped over the windshield of the van for old time sakes, but Julian alerts us that he has something better by pulling out a cloth banner that he made yesterday, when he was stranded at home. On the banner is a painting of the van driving off through the desert into the horizon with kangaroos on the side of the road and the title "Driving to Perth" at the top. The banner is for me to hold up while I'm at the front row tonight but, before that, it's draped over the van. Ben and Annette arrive soon to inform us that their flights to Perth have been booked and won't be joining us in the van. Ben, however, will take the ride back while Mick and I depart by air. So the only other possible person to join the van now is Gus.

"I've been told by many people that going one way is good," Ben justifies. "But going both ways is not so good."

When show time comes along, we take down our tailgating setup and I stuff the banner into my pocket ready for my front row seat. Walking past every row of chairs in the building, I arrive at my seat near the end of the row. Security checks my ticket and then issues a wristband for me, signifying my pit status. I peek over to the middle and see Gus standing at his usual spot. He offers to slide me in between him and his brother and I accept. So for the next two and a half hours, we rock our hairs off, Gus with his long wavy red hair and me with my spiky green mohican like hair.

Still clutching onto the banner, I see an opportunity to throw it on stage at the end of the first encore. When the band is jamming through the final notes of *Alive* and Vedder takes a leap into the air, I toss the banner up over the rail toward him. As his feet are grounded again, he notices the banner in front of him and grabs it before fleeing the stage with the rest of the band. Upon his return, Vedder has the banner in his hand and lays it down by the drum kit to perform a song. At the conclusion of the song, he snaps up the banner and walks over to the microphone. "Someone here is driving to Perth," he announces to the crowd. "I wish them luck. Be safe, thank you."

Vedder throws the banner back at me and I'm leaping with joy, hearing nothing else other than the cheers erupting from various spots behind me that are guaranteed to be the rest of my van crew. Gus gives me a pat on the back. At the end of the show, when Vedder finishes and gives the stage to McCready to close out with *Yellow Ledbetter*, he turns over to me and starts mouthing something that I can barely make out except for the end of it. "Thank you and good luck," he says with a smile. "See you in Perth."

With a smile and a nod, I thank him back. Next, Stone leans over and wishes me luck as well. He then turns to Gus and asks if he's going to Perth as well. "Of course," he replies, as they both laugh about the rhetorical question.

Everyone gathers around the van afterwards to wish us luck for the long drive ahead. Clutching onto a freshly caught tambourine from the show, Megan describes the feeling about going home for the final show as being bitter-sweet because going home also kind of feels like it's already the end. For another hour in the parking lot, we say some final words and goodbyes to some, while rejoicing over the adventure ahead for the final show with others. Many photos are snapped of all the smiles that are present, including a group photo session of the entire van crew standing in front of the van. This is the send off for our journey through the desert. Finally, we have a van and we're driving it to the next city for the next show. Newfie Joe and I can not be any happier.

The banner that I toss on stage at the second Adelaide show for the band to see.

I'm a lucky man
to count on both hands
the ones I love

Just Breathe

CHAPTER 44: **THE AUSSIE TOURING VAN**

November 25, 2006 » Show 61
Perth, Australia

PRIOR TO THE AUSTRALIAN TOUR, I had made an attempt to gather interest over doing a touring van for the entire tour. With little feedback, I decided not to pursue this tour as rigorously and would instead enjoy what this isolated country has to offer, not worrying about going to too many shows. When Newfie Joe surprisingly appeared at the first show, my agenda changed and getting a van together eventually became the priority. This goal has now been met. We now have a van and are driving the final leg of the Australian tour, Adelaide to Perth. Google maps tells us that it's roughly 32 hours of continuous driving – covering nearly 3000km – but others have warned that it's much longer than that, calling us insane for even attempting it in the short amount of time that we have. There are two full days in between the shows. Can we do it?

An early night after the last show allows us to get an early start on the long drive ahead. The entire van crew stays over at Gus' place, so it's only natural that we try one more time to lure him into the van, but he declines again. As everyone piles into the back, we realize that Gus not coming with us is probably for the better. It's rather cozy back there; at least that's what it looks like from the driver's seat. Our luggage fits perfectly into the compartments below the bed and in the trunk. This maximizes the amount of space for the back seat passengers to lie down if they wish to nap. I add some last minute decorations to the van with my trusty roll of hockey tape imported from Canada, and then we're ready to roll. With Julian on the passenger side, I start the engine and we bid farewell to Gus. He wishes us luck and a safe trip.

"You reckon I'd reach Perth before you guys?" he laughs.

And with that challenge thrown out to us, our mission has been set. With our team of Rock Angels including Mick from Cairns, Australia, Julian from Christchurch, New Zealand, Ivan from Mexico City, Mexico, Newfie Joe from

St. John's, Canada, and Clayton and me from Vancouver, Canada, we must beat Gus to Perth. At 6:00am, it's the crack of dawn and the streets are completely empty. Getting out of the city is rather simple, but driving on the other side of the road is not. I might have overlooked the fact that Australians drive right hand drive vehicles in the left lane. Nonetheless, I adapt quickly and soon reach the highway, which is even more deserted. With everyone passed out in the back almost immediately, the activity level inside the van is just as disinteresting as the drive itself. To try and liven things up, we pretend that we're already not on speaking terms with one another just an hour into the drive.

"Ivan, can you please tell Clayton to go fuck himself," I jokingly yell out.

"Mick, tell Jason that he can kiss my ass," Clayton responds.

It's all in good fun and exactly what's needed for a trip like this. With six guys cramped inside of a tiny van for a drive that will last two days straight, we must have a good sense of humour to keep us going strong. Otherwise, it will be a miserable experience and there will literally be no escape from each other. This is human bonding at its best, as we hit the open road, taking on the adventure and the unknown together. With the windows rolled down and wind in my hair, this is what I've grown accustomed to this past year. It's simply a phenomenal feeling. I glance back and the only person not passed out, Newfie Joe, gives me a nod of concurrence. We've done it again.

Two and a half hours into the drive and my eyes are already starting to shut. Music is pumping from the iPod but the terrain hasn't been too enchanting. With the occasional bush or tree, a slight ditch on either sides of the road, and a flat dirt terrain beyond that, the views have been less than plain. The A1 freeway would dip toward the coast every now and then for glimpses of the ocean, but our hopes are always let down when we are steered back inland away from any scenery. To prevent a similar episode to the one in Saskatoon, I pull over at the first gas station we see since leaving and fill up the tank, not knowing when there will be another one again. I pick up a can of baked beans for breakfast and quickly scarf it down. Everyone is now awake after a good power nap, and has a comment on the van's comfort level in the back, enticing me to join them.

"I was totally fine," Clayton remarks.

"Not bad, how many more hours is it?" Mick wonders. "30?"

Ivan mentions that he has never done a road trip like this before and is sure that it will meet his lofty expectations. But as much as I want to sit cross legged with the boys in the back, I stay upfront in the passenger seat allowing them to make adjustments to the seating layout while Julian takes control of the wheel. Rearranging the luggage in the trunk, they're able to set the top of our bags level with the bed and, in doing so, extend the bed all the way to the back. This expands the amount of room for everyone, including Mick, allowing us to lie down completely stretched on our backs for a more comfortable ride.

"We're fucking rocking the van now," Clayton responds.

"This is better," Mick excitedly explains.

"Okay, wake me up when we get to Perth," Newfie Joe instructs, as he prepares for hibernation.

The drive from the passenger seat is almost as exciting as from the driver's, but at least I can stare aimlessly out my window into this excitement and not worry about controlling the wheel. There's something about watching landscape pass by continuously through a window that's relaxing and soothing. Time doesn't even become a factor anymore because the more you look at it the slower it seems to be moving, so you might as well forget about keeping track. With the clock neglected, time begins to fly and before we know it we have reached Kimba, halfway across Australia with a sign to prove it as well. Being only on the road for five hours, we're making great time and ahead of schedule.

We stop for a stretch and a photo opportunity with the extravagant sign that consists of a map of the country, showing Kimba in the middle and a whole lot of nothing between Kimba and Perth. The title "Halfway across Australia" sits atop of the map, with some additional information listed along the side. Here we discover that the name for one of the world's most unique tracks of unspoiled wilderness, the Nullarbor Plain, does not originate from the aboriginal language as most, including us, would think. Instead, it's derived from the Latin words Nullus Arbor, meaning no tree. It's also the world's largest single piece of limestone, with an area close to 200,000 square kilometres stretching over 1000km wide. Looking at the side of the road, a sign tells us that Perth is 2280km away. The prospects of driving through this dry part of the country have only become more enticing. Once everyone is seemingly ready to leave, we pile back into the van with Mick taking over driving duties.

"Uh, where's Ivan?" Clayton asks, as the engine is started.

We look around and he's nowhere to be seen. He finally appears, emerging from behind a bush where he was relieving himself, and begins to take photos. We shout out encouragements for him to return to the van, so he comes rushing backing claiming he didn't have enough time to take photos. Nonetheless, we pull into the gas station across the street to fill up, waiting for Ivan to accompany us. Once he jumps back in the van, we take off.

With Clayton, the little one, taking shotgun position next to Mick, the big one, Julian and I take a much needed break and join the back seat party. What I find in the back is a comfortable ride, resting on a three inch thick mattress over top of wooden compartments. The music from the front speakers travels to the back, but it's somewhat faint. Newfie Joe is reading a newspaper and Julian is reading a book. This, along with some Mexican magazines that Ivan brought, is the only reading material we have onboard. While Ivan is playing with his camera, I fall onto my back, feeling defeated by the heat which rivals the drive to Washington DC in May. The outside air temperature is moderate, but inside it's like an oven. The heat is soon victorious and I pass out.

Ivan, Newfie Joe, and Clayton sprawled out in the back of the Aussie Touring Van during our drive to Perth.

As I wake up three hours later, there's a sense of urgency going around. Our gas tank is running low because there hasn't been a gas station since Kimba. From my calculations prior to the trip, I figured that the van could do roughly 300km on a full tank, right now we're at 305km and the light has been on for the last 10km already. The next town is coming up, but we might not make it. This has been our biggest fear; breaking down in the middle of the desert with no one around, which wouldn't be fun at all. Fortunately, the frantic moment comes to a close 315km after Kimba, as we find a gas station entering the town of Ceduna. We've been pushing the speed a little bit trying to make good time and, thus, the van has been less fuel-efficient. So a collective decision is made for us to drive at a slower speed, closer to the speed limit of 110km/hr. This will give us better gas mileage and reduce the chances of the van running out of gas. Knowing the driving limits will also help. "I reckon I could have gotten another 20km," Mick advises. "So that would be 330km on a full tank."

"Wait, Ivan's not here." Newfie Joe advises, as we're about to leave.

"Where the fuck is Ivan?" I ask.

A few minutes later, Ivan returns from the washroom, he was the only one to vacate the van. In Ceduna, we see the ocean for the first time in seven hours. Who would've thought that we would be in Australia and be away from the ocean for that length of time? The pleasant sight is alluring, so we park the van and walk down the pier. Situated nearly 2000km from Perth, Ceduna would seem like a fishing village, but there's little evidence to prove this. It seems like a nice town though. Before leaving, we hit the grocery store along with a drive-through beer store to load up on supplies. It's just past 3:00pm, so we decide to make a stop at an upcoming surf beach for lunch. Cactus Beach takes us half an hour off the A1 freeway but, having driven over 10 hours consecutively, we're in need of a lunch break. The beers, however, are already distributed throughout the van before we leave town.

The detour takes us around Blue Lake, which is clear and still enough to reflect the blue skies above, and then through a vast set of white sand dunes. It's a refreshing sight to say the least. A sign is spotted up ahead, with the name

Cactus Beach scribbled over top of its former name of Point Sinclair. Following the arrow, we drive past a campsite and arrive at the parking lot of this remote surf beach, which is known to have some of the best breaks in the country. We gather together our sandwich supplies and a couple of beers each from the cooler, or esky as the Aussies call it, and make our way down to the ocean. Walking along the man-made pathway over the rugged terrain that can be inhabited by snakes and scorpions, we approach the lookout deck to find two surfers in the shark-infested water. The waves are medium in size, but constant. It looks like fun.

Continuing down on the dense, fine sand, we fight off the copious amount of flies to allow our feet to dip in the water, where the sand turns into rock. It's warm but not as warm as the heat in the air, which is only moderate due to the circulating wind. We scale a few of the larger rocks to climb up high above the water for a better view and a place to settle for our picnic, which consists of sandwiches with a heavy dose of ham and a little bit of sand. The afternoon is chilled out, as we spend a good solid hour gazing into the ocean, knowing that the next closest body of land is Antarctica.

"You know, I have to go there one day," Newfie Joe tells me.

"Antarctica is my ultimate travel dream," I reply. "Think we can get a van down there?"

Feeling recharged, we return to the van with Ivan arriving there first this time. He asks if he can drive, so we all take turns making fun of Mexican drivers before I hand him the keys. I get back into the passenger seat and get handed a beer. The two cases of Emu Export and Coopers Dark Ales aren't going to last the night. Re-entering the freeway, we see a sign advising us to watch out for kangaroos and wombats for the next 79km. This could be exciting. But 79km passes by and there has been no sign of life. With everyone wide awake for once, the conversations in the van are at an all time high.

Clayton and Ben at a common highway sign on the way back to Adelaide.

Another 79km later, we hit a roadhouse. These roadhouses are all we're going to get from here on out. They act as a gas station, mechanic shop, restaurant, and general store all in one building – and a small one at that. It's also the only thing in sight since the last town, basically representing a town all on its own. With a sign advising that the next roadhouse is over 200km away, we fill up the tank here. As I pump the van up with fuel, I watch everyone leave the van for their toilet and smoke breaks, everyone except for Ivan. He's still in the driver's seat staring at the mirror. After a few minutes, he makes his way back to the trunk to grab a bottle of water but, instead of drinking it he removes his hat and soaks his hair inch by inch. After slicking it back with a comb, he looks quite glamourous. With his hair freshly greased back, he then refits his hat back on, to cover up the artistry that he had just created. I can't help but laugh.

"What so funny?" he asks with a smile. "I feel dirty."

The others return just as the fill up is complete. I run inside to pay for the petrol, return to turn on the engine, and take over as the driver.

"Ready to go?" I ask.

"Nope, we're missing one," Mick says.

"We're not going to make it on time because of him," Clayton jokes.

"Where the fuck is Ivan?" Newfie Joe asks.

It's now just past 7:00pm and the sun has already begun to set. And because we're situated in the middle of a stretch of flatness that stretches thousands of kilometres, we probably have at least another hour or two of daylight. The dirty Mexican is finally spotted standing across the road and taking a photo of a giant whale statue that sits in front of the roadhouse. We sit and watch him slowly walk back toward the van, admiring the photos that he had just taken on his camera. Looking proud of his photography skills, he climbs back in.

"Ivan, you're fucking hilarious." Clayton laughs.

For the next hour, I chase the sun toward the west, with my visor down to block the brightness of the rays beaming from the only object in the sky. The blue skies rapidly begin to change colour, with light blue fading into a faint grey before a solid yellow and orange combination takes over. The vividness is in full effect over the plains for a good half hour and it's a pretty spectacular sight. When the sun fully eclipses the horizon, orange begins to dominate the yellow; and just as this climax is beginning, we hit the start of the Nullarbor Plains. A sign that reads "Nullarbor Plain, Eastern End of Treeless Plain" sits by its lonesome on the side of the road, so I pull over for this magical photo opportunity. What great timing.

"Look Ivan, we've officially entered the Nullarbor Plains, buddy," Clayton encourages Ivan, still lying down in the van. "Come check it out."

We all observe in awe, snapping away on each of our cameras. It's nothing but flat weed fields and dirt in every which way we look. The wind is constant but not too strong, the temperature is moderate and not too hot, and the flies are hovering around and not too friendly. None of them bite, however, they're just a little annoying. We stand gazing at the majestic view for half an hour before the skies turn purple and then toward dark blue, with black certainly on the horizon. To wake us up from our utopian state, Julian jumps into the van and starts doing donuts on the dirt with it, before speeding up and down the highway for our viewing pleasure. With Julian's happy feet, we let Mick take back control of the vehicle for the next stretch, as the sky grows darker.

At the entrance of the Nullarbor Plains during sunset.

By the time we hit the next roadhouse an hour and a half later, the sky is completely black but lit up by the glowing stars. The clearness of the sky really emphasizes the stars in detail, and it's probably the best I've ever seen them. Not knowing whether other roadhouses are open over the night, we fill up the tank here and change drivers again. The sky may be glittering but, without street lights, the freeway is still very dreary, so we'll switch it up as often as we can and drive much slower than before. This is the advice from the guy at the roadhouse anyway. He cautions that animals on the road will be difficult to see at night. If we hit one, we're told not to try and swerve away from it but hit it dead on instead. This will ensure that we don't flip. But if it jumps, it may go through the windshield and, apparently, if we do hit a kangaroo, the vehicle will stink of kangaroo carcass for a long time. We don't have one of those kangaroo bars that we see at the front of some vehicles to deflect the road kill away from the engine. The bottom line is that we don't want to hit any animals.

So Julian takes over the van and within minutes, we hit an animal. The only noise we hear is a crunch, and nobody knows exactly what happened, other than Julian. He knows exactly what happened and stops to tell us all about it. Luckily it's only a rabbit about the size of his foot but, for good measure, he reverses back over the rabbit then drives over it again to put us back on track. By his explanation of the situation, it sounds as if he doesn't like rabbits very much. Nonetheless, he assures us that there will be no more road kill inflicted by the van and he stays true to his word. Our speed slows down to 80km/hr so another hour and a half passes until we hit the next roadhouse, just prior to the border for Western Australia. It's just before midnight and we've been on the road for almost 18 hours but, apparently, we're about to enter the most heavily kangaroo infested area of the trip.

"The lady inside said that we'll see kangaroos the size of Mick by the fucking hundreds," Clayton reports. "And she said it's a six and a half hour drive to Norseman, but if we do it at night it'll take ten and a half hour and we can only do 40km/hr."

"And no high beams, otherwise you'll startle them and they'll just jump toward you," Mick follows.

"Drive in the middle of the road and, if we hit a kangaroo, just pull over and put your high beams and your hazards on," Clayton continues.

"Now we're in for an Oz experience," I comment.

"I don't want to see one kangaroo," Mick hopes.

Julian jumps back to the driver's seat with these instructions laid upon us, while I'm on roo watch sitting to his left. After a quick quarantine check at the border for any organics entering the state, we enter Western Australia and instantly spot two kangaroos standing on the side of the road next to a sign that warns us about the presence of stray animals for the next 340km. We continue to drive very carefully around 30km/hr in the middle of the lane, and I continue to spot these popular marsupials every couple of minutes, yelling out "ROO" every time I see one, including many lying dead on the side of the road. Newfie Joe also begins to develop an eye for the roos, spotting one in the middle of the road before me and even before the driver does. Julian slows down even more, coming to a complete stop just several metres in front of the big red. It stands still, straight up, looking directly at us, much like a deer would in this situation. However, Julian ends the staring contest by flashing the high beams at him, signalling him to leap away.

I ask Newfie Joe how he's able to spot the kangaroos so quickly, so he enlightens us. Apparently, you should look for the eyes, because the headlights from a car or any light, for that matter, causes a reflection in the eyes that makes it glow or sparkle in the dark. The situation keeps us wide awake at least. We hit the next roadhouse three hours later but because we've been driving slowly, our tank is still half full. Nevertheless, we make a pit stop and top it up. A sign on the entrance door says that Perth is still another 1300km away. It's coming up on 21 hours on the road and fatigue is starting to set in. Looking more tired than he's been all tour, Clayton asks if we're going to stay and setup camp or continue on. I laugh at the thought, bringing him back into the program, and then taking over the van for the overnight drive.

With Mick on roo watch now, I'm able to calmly steer the ship away from its icebergs for another three hours until we get to the next roadhouse. We've been driving for 24 hours now and everyone looks depleted and exhausted. I'm not feeling that bad, but pick up a couple of cans of Red Bull anyway to re-energize myself. Clayton commends the setup of the van, saying that being able to fully lie down throughout the drive has prevented any chance of being all cramped up like he would in other vehicles. As we take off again, Clayton falls to the mattress and is out cold within seconds. The others follow shortly after, with even Mick, my roo watcher, dozing off into peacefulness, until it's just me awake in the van. It's almost as if I'm driving myself through the Nullarbor during dusk, the worst time of the day in terms of animal visibility.

The sun is about to return, but my nerves only begin to pick up. I've seen this before, driving into a ditch after the Saskatoon show. We were lucky that time but would we be as fortunate if something were to happen today? Five of my new closest friend's lives are at risk here, and I hold control over anything happening to them: control that I don't actually have control over. If I fall asleep the van could veer off the road, and we may or may not hit anything before I'm startled enough to realize. If my attention span is not good enough to spot animals on the road, I could hit them and cause major damage to the vehicle and to everyone in it. If we flip, we're all at risk, considering how close we're sitting to the windshield in the front and the nonexistence of seatbelts in the back. Of course, I can always just pull over, but I don't feel all that tired despite our lack of tantalizing surroundings.

We've been driving for a day now and the scenery has remained relatively unchanged. It's amazing how such a large country can have so much empty space and such a vast area of nothing. I guess it's kind of similar to the prairies in Canada or the US. But there's no green here; everything is just brown and dirt, probably more like northern Canada. We haven't even seen another car yet, only a couple of large transport trucks, which are incredibly long. I counted 18 sets of wheels on the last one that went by. All these things running through my head actually keep me focussed on the task at hand.

A sign in Eucla to help us out in the right direction.

With the sun fully up and visibility back to hundred percent, I realize just how many kangaroos are in the area. There are troops of them everywhere. Some are closer to the road, some are further away, but most are moving around in mobs. And then there's the occasional carcass on the side of the road, including one lying near a sign indicating that we're entering Australia's longest straight road, 146.6km without even a kink or the slightest curve in it. It's certainly one of the longest in the world. I pull over to snap a photo, while the others are too weak to make an effort. Returning to the van, I see a few unusually large vultures perching on top of the only tree in sight. They're waiting for me to leave so that they can have a go at the carcass. Sure enough, as I pull away in the van, the vicious birds swoop down to the road and begin ripping this casualty of the trucks to shreds.

As I pull into the next roadhouse at around 9:00am, the glowing sun wakes everyone up. A few of us feed on a large bacon and egg breakfast at the diner section of the place, while some merely smoke and stretch out. Ivan decides to organize the trunk, putting any jackets and clothing on top of the bags in a nice orderly fashion to increase the comfort level of laying our heads down on top of them. His work is like magic and we let him know about it too. Clayton pulls out a hand full of change, roughly $3, and claims that it's all of his remaining cash available to fund the rest of his trip.

"It's called Perth or broke," he proclaims.

"Looks like we're pimping you out," I suggest.

"You'll be standing on the side of the road with your leg out," Julian adds.

"Fuck that, I'm pimping Ivan out," Clayton responds.

With my overnight shift completed, I've been relieved of my driving duties, handing off the reins to Julian with roughly 1000km to go. With everyone fully awake and relaxed, we bring out the freshly purchased box of goon, and all sing along to Johnny Cash's *I've Been Everywhere*, with Mick changing one of the lyrics from "across the desert sand" to "across the Nullarbor man, I've been everywhere." The sun is warm, the goon is tasty, and the company is good, so the next few hours just fly by. We finally reach the town of Norseman just before noon, where we stock up on food and drink supplies for the rest of the day. Being in the first town we've come across since Ceduna, our mobile phones finally have some reception. Mick and I both receive text messages from Gus. In mine, he simply hopes we "haven't gooned ourselves to death yet," and on Mick's he mentions that a lot of fans have been contacting him and wondering how we're making out on the drive. People care about us.

Norseman marks the end of the Nullarbor plains and, with it, the roadhouses as well. There will be proper towns from here on out. It's also a crossroads for us, where we can either go north inland straight across to Perth or we can go south along the coast before cutting back up. As with yesterday, we want the sight of water while having lunch, so we head south. Nearly three hours later, we arrive in the coastal town of Esperance. Picking up some fries (or "hot chips", as they call them), we head straight to West Beach along the bottom coast to set up our picnic in a parking lot that overlooks the rough waters of the ocean. Mick shows us the art of eating hot chip sandwiches consisting only of bread, fries, and ketchup. It's a common Aussie snack and a tasty one at that.

Having a nice relaxing lunch by ourselves, we're almost ready to pack up and go when this other van pulls into the parking lot and parks a few stalls down from us. It's also a Wicked Camper van, but this one has jungle animals and the name "Madagascar" painted on it. We watch very closely as four girls crawl out of it. It's our sister van. Within seconds, Ivan, Julian, Clayton and I begin walking toward them, almost on cue, to greet our fellow wicked van mates. The girls are from Germany and are travelling the opposite direct as us, going from Perth to Sydney but, judging by our conversation, they don't appear to have the slightest clue where they're going or a sense of direction on top of that. Clayton asks if we could switch vans.

Satisfied with finally seeing someone else on the road other than ourselves, we motor on with our goal of making Perth tonight to defeat the odds and the doubts of others. The drive takes us back inland before we cut up through areas that are as empty as we've seen yet, but with one difference – it's green. Although still seemingly dry, acres of fields dominate this area along with some trees and bushes as well. It's certainly a welcomed sight after all the red and brown dirt we've endured. Almost five hours of driving and two gas stations later, we arrive at the town of Hyden and its famous wave rock. Curious about this attraction, we decide to do something touristy for a change since we're making good time. However, as we creep closer to 9:00pm, daylight is starting to run out and we're barely able to see the characteristics that make this giant 14m high 110m long rock look like a breaking wave. Nonetheless, we're able to read the information about it, learning that the unique formation was formed by erosion over time.

When we leave the national park, the sky has gone completely dark and I'm back in the driver seat ready for the final stretch of our adventure. We're roughly 350km and five hours away from our destination so we should be on track with arriving in Perth tonight, something we're all looking forward to. A caution sign for animals appears again, but this time it's only for 12km. Still, I'm alert and drive with care, as we don't want to hit anything at this stage of the trip.

As the distance remaining decreases, so does the number of gas stations that are still open. Because we're no longer in the Nullarbor plains anymore, there are probably no more 24-hour gas stations coming up. Most of them, in fact, seem to close before 10:00pm. We filled up the tank before the wave rock, but that doesn't give us enough gas to make it to Perth. With just over 100km left, we approach a town called Brookton, which appears sizeable enough to possibly have a 24-hour gas station. It does not. We pass the next town, Westdale, and their gas station is also closed. Without enough fuel, we have little choice but to stop and wait for the morning. Mick, who's driving at this point, mentions that he saw a park in Westdale, so he pulls a u-turn and heads back the way we came from. Within seconds of his actions, we hear and see sirens behind us.

"Shit! It's the cops," Mick shouts out. "Put down your drinks."

"Driver's license please," one of the two approaching policemen asks.

"How many in the van?" the other cop wonders.

"There are six of us," Mick answers.

There are empty beer cans clearly visible everywhere and no one in the back has any sort of seatbelts because the van can only legally hold three passengers. Newfie Joe and I glance at each other and memories of Jersey come to mind. The cop asks Mick to blow into a breathalyzer, which he blows into confidently, while the other peeks into the back with his flashlight. After a few anxious moments, the cops return, handing the used breathalyzer to Mick and informing him that he scored a big zero on the test. He advises us to drive safely and lets us off the hook. That was easy, and Mick even gets a souvenir out of it. Apparently, in Australia, you're allowed to drink in moving vehicles if you aren't the driver. We drive off, feeling relieved that it was one of the Australians driving at that point and not a Canadian or a Mexican.

Now that we're home free, we drive back to the park that Mick had pointed out earlier and set up camp. There are a few vehicles parked on the street, which gives Julian the brilliant idea of siphoning gas so that we can keep on going. But after thinking it over, reaching Perth tonight wouldn't do us any good, as we'd need to find a place to camp out there anyway. With picnic tables and trees around, this is as good as any place to camp. Newfie Joe sets up his own tent, while Mick, Julian, and I set up the large tent that came with the van, leaving Ivan and Clayton to snuggle up in the van. Gazing up into the sky in wonder, I see the stars even clearer tonight than last night. With only a few beers remaining, my tent mates and I, the drivers, stay up a little longer to finish off our drink supply and congratulate each other for a job well done. We're just over an hour away from Perth now, after almost making it tonight, and we're damn proud of our achievement of being on the road for 44 hours straight.

In the morning, we wake up well rested from a much needed six hours of sleep. I haven't felt this good since arriving to Australia. We take down the camping gear and, when I open the van door, I find Ivan scrunched up in his sleeping bag and lying not on but inside of the mattress. He's literally sandwiched in between the two layers of foam. He's shivering and starts complaining about how cold it was last night. Meanwhile, Clayton is next to him in a t-shirt with no sleeping bag and I'm wearing only a tank top and we both feel quite comfortable with the weather.

"That's because you're from the North Pole," Ivan suggests.

When the van is all loaded up and we're ready to go, Ivan starts stripping down as he's feeling the heat again. He's right though, the night does get a bit breezy and, compared to the daytime, it may be considered cold. We pull into the town's gas station, not too far from the park, and fill up on petrol and sausage rolls. Everyone takes turns with the washroom, cleaning up and preparing for civilization again. This is the last small hick town that we'll see. Next stop, really big hick town. As we get closer to the city, the scenery is still very empty and yellow fields still dominate the terrain. You wouldn't know that we're near a major metropolis. This explains why it's one of the most laid back and isolated cities in the world, with most of its residents having never left Perth.

At 11:00am, about 53 hours after we started this journey, we officially arrive in Perth and head straight to the Subiaco Oval, home of the West Coast Eagles of the Australian Football League. We are the first to the venue, beating Gus in the process. With no one around, I pull the van onto the sidewalk and park it directly in front of the stadium for a group photo of the van, the crew, and our destination that we reached. Walking around the venue, I see that the tour buses have beaten us here and equipment is being setup. We drive around the area to find some real food for lunch and then pick up some Emu Export and other tailgating supplies for the show. As we head back to the largest venue of the tour, Julian stays behind to get a special photo developed and a frame for it.

With the banner hanging on the windshield, and various flags out on display, our tailgating party is the meeting point for all. There are snacks, music, and plenty of goon. Hinn from Sydney thinks he's at a Halloween party, wearing an orange Pearl Jam tour beach towel as a cape along with a black mullet wig on his head to give us a good laugh. Gitta and Einat explain their encounter with members of the band at a local beach yesterday, as they arrived a day earlier. When Gus arrives, just before 3:00pm, he describes his flight as being "fucking boring" so we fill him in on our exciting adventure. Annette and Ben show up shortly after as well, so we tease them about flying out here instead of riding in the van when they had a chance.

"At least I did the complete journey in a plane," Gus justifies. "You didn't do the complete journey in your van."

Newfie Joe and I glance at each other and agree with Gus. But although this tour has been a combination of planes, trains, cars, and vans, the final mode of transport is our preferred method. This is even illustrated in tonight's show poster, the crowning piece in the series of 12 for the tour, done by Australian rock poster artist Daymon Greulich. The poster features a car, plastered with Pearl Jam stickers, driving on the highway into the distance toward Perth, much like the banner that we created and threw on stage in Adelaide. If this isn't the quintessential representation of the Touring Van, I don't know what is. There are more than enough copies to go around, so I purchase 10 posters for myself and for some of my Touring Van crew back home. Keeping two copies for myself, I have everyone in the Aussie van crew sign one of my posters for memory sake.

Ecstatic about the artwork, I call Cali Joe to inform him that I'll be bringing a present for him when we meet in Hawaii. He's up in Chico, CA with Kasie and Veronica, who will also meet me in Hawaii. They request that I call them back if *Throw Your Arms Around Me* is played. This is a cover song from the Australian band Hunters and Collectors that Vedder sometimes plays during the pre-set before the opening band takes the stage. So knowing that I won't even be inside the building until the main act, I agree to make the call if it happens. I also take the opportunity to confirm with him that our accommodations have been booked before handing over the phone to Newfie Joe for them to catch up.

"Let's give Timmy a call," Newfie suggests, when he hangs up.

So, again with my cheap Australian long distance calling card, I ring up Tim from the Jersey Shore. He picks up and is surprised to hear from me. I fill him in on what has been happening with the tour down under and then he fills me in on what's going to happen in Hawaii. When I tell him that I get in on the Friday, the day before the show, he sounds disappointed.

"Dude, didn't you hear about Thursday?" he asks.

"No I didn't," I reply. "I haven't kept up to date on anything."

"They're playing the Eddie," he says with excitement. "It's a private show, but I can get you in."

"The Eddie" is the Big Wave Invitational surf competition that happens every year at Waimea Bay on the North Shores of Oahu, celebrating the memory of the legendary Hawaiian big wave surfer Eddie Aikau. It's also the origin of the phrase "Eddie Would Go," which is cemented on the Touring Van in bumper sticker format. Apparently, Pearl Jam will be playing a secret private show at the opening ceremonies, one day before my flight arrives. I'm stunned, as this seems to have the makings of being my dream show, so I notify Tim that I'll look into it and try my best to change my flight. I wish him all the best and then lay a surprise on him with Newfie Joe taking over the conversation. I inform Mick of the latest news and his eyes light up about a possible Hawaii trip, before reality sinks in when he remembers that he's getting married next week. But to help salute his special occasion, we put on a little ceremony for him.

"So here we are," Newfie Joe begins. "Where are we?"

"Perth," Julian answers.

"Subiaco," Mick corrects him.

"It makes no difference," Newfie Joe follows. "It's the journey that counts. It's the goon that's been the time in Australia."

"The goon's been keeping us going," Mick reiterates.

"It's been two and half weeks of just craziness," Newfie Joe echoes. "One of the reasons for that craziness is because of someone who happens to be one of the tallest people I've ever met and he goes by the name of Big Mick."

"You guys dragged me along the whole way," Mick claims.

"We got him drunk one night and he decided to come along," I verify.

"The silliest decision of my life," he jokes.

"As it happens, this crazy fuck is also getting married," Newfie Joe continues. "So this has been the adventure of the bachelor party continuing from Adelaide, and he finishes the buck's show in the van in Perth. So we had to do something to commemorate this special occasion."

"So we got him a little something," I add in.

"Because he'll probably forget about us next week," Newfie Joe says.

"How?" he laughs.

"It's a little souvenir, a little reminder that this was all real. And that this actually happened."

Julian presents Mick with a card and a picture frame containing the photo of all of us with the van in front of the Subiaco Oval taken just a few hours prior. The card reads: "Hey Karla, thanks heaps for letting Mick do the tour with us. You must be a top chick and hope we all meet up soon. We all love the boys." A very exuberant Mick thanks us all with handshakes and hugs before we force him to scull the goon out of the bag without spilling a drop.

"It's been an unbelievable two and a half weeks," Mick declares. "I'll never ever forget it. Met some awesome people, some crazy Canadians. Let's just top it up with a fucking awesome show."

The Aussie Touring Van crew in front of Subiaco Oval in Perth: Mick, Newfie Joe, Ivan, Julian, me, and Clayton. This is the photo given to Mick as a present.

A few moments later, the parking lot attendants approach and ask us to move our vehicle over to the grass field across the street, because they need the parking lot space for stage equipment trucks arriving tonight for tomorrow night's Robbie Williams concert. We reluctantly oblige, but find our new surroundings even better. Sitting on nice comfortable grass, we continue the tailgating up until show time. Tonight I'm on Carlos' spare with Ivan, but he does not accept my money when I offer to pay for it, noting that Carlos wants to give me the ticket. How nice of him.

We enter the massive stadium of 40,000 capacity and walk straight to the rail for our seats at the end of the front row. Looking around I see all of the familiar faces in the first few rows, kind of like Newcastle. Mick somehow scored a last minute ticket that put him at his normal spot in the middle, so we move down to say hi. There are a few empty seats beside him dead centre on the rail, so we decide to occupy them while their owners aren't present. As the show begins, they're still empty and we remain in them. Although the stage is set up higher and farther from the rail than normal and the fact that there's a fairly strong echo in the acoustics, we're very close to the band and they're so on that it doesn't matter. With this being the conclusion of the Australian tour, the feeling throughout the show is a little bit strange. Nonetheless, Ivan has his Mexican flag draped next to my Canadian flag on the rail, and we rock out hard.

"Is the van here?" McCready mouths to me.

"No. But we're all here," I answer, pointing to everyone around us.

At the start of the encore, Vedder comes out on his own with a guitar and, to the surprise of everyone, especially myself, he plays Kasie and Veronica's request *Throw Your Arms Around Me* in the middle of the show. Scrambling around in excitement, I quickly dial Cali Joe's number directly from my phone hoping that there's enough credit for the long distance call. When I hear an answer, I simply hold the phone up for them to listen and the only thing I hear coming from their end of the phone are screams. I'm not sure how clearly they can hear it, but I'm sure they can make out what it is. As the song ends, I see that the call has ended a few seconds earlier and that I'm now out of credit on my phone as well, but it was worth it. As the second set closes, we still have ownership of our amazing seats, as we watch Vedder dedicate the Split Enz cover, *I Got You*, to all of us. "This is for everybody that has been travelling around," he announces. "All these people have been travelling around. We don't even know what to say. Thanks so much."

The show and tour ends with *Rockin' in the Free World*, when an Australian flag finally makes it onto the stage. Vedder grabs it and puts it over himself like a cape, much like Hinn and his beach towel, and then he jumps down to the floor and proceeds to run along the railing, giving everyone up front high fives. My hand is met by Vedder's with a forceful purpose. When he jumps back onto the stage, he begins smashing a tambourine along with the beat as he normally does and then singles out Ivan as the recipient of the souvenir. However, as he launches the musical instrument toward us, someone from behind jumps over Ivan and the rail and steals it away from him, before fleeing the scene of the crime. Vedder looks pissed but tells Ivan to wait one moment. When the song ends, he thanks everyone for a great tour and then hands the bottle of wine that he has been sipping on to security and points to Ivan. The security guard obliges and hands over the bottle to Ivan, still three quarters full.

The band returns to give one final bow to the crowd and then they start kicking Aussie Rules footballs into the crowd. One by one each band member punts one out and, with all of us being so close to the stage, it seems hopeless for anyone we know to end up with the unique souvenir. Newfie Joe, who's sitting further back, comes very close though, having a ball bounce right off of his hands, while not being able to hold on to it. So if he played American football he'd be a defensive back not a wide receiver. When it comes to Stone's turn, he knocks the ball straight up into the air and hits a spot light, causing the ball to return back near the front. There's a scramble for it just behind us, with half a dozen people each seemingly having ownership of it. But out of nowhere, I see the ball slip in between everyone's hands and Clayton emerging from underneath the pile with the ball. Like a running back hopping over tacklers, he immediately leaps over rows of chairs until he reaches the front row where the rest of us are. He shows us the ball, which is signed by everyone in the band, so I hand him the Canadian flag to wrap around the ball, keeping it concealed while we exit the venue.

Back at the van, there's a huge group of people waiting around with enormous smiles on their faces. With everyone gathered in the area, we decide to remain at the grass field until they kick us out, as we really have no desire to leave. As other cars begin to leave, our free space begins to grow and, before we know it, the entire grass field across from the stadium is completely empty with the exception of all the travelling Pearl Jam fans still on location. There are nearly 30 of us still chilling on the grass, chatting amongst one another, not wanting it all to end. We have no place to stay tonight, so we might as well just set up camp here. The stars are shining as clear as ever and, when our drink supply appears to run out, it's immediately filled up again by Krystie from Perth. She even decides to order 10 pizzas for everyone and, sure enough, they're delivered directly to us in the middle of the field. The food is quickly consumed and the drinks follow, until we're left with nothing but ourselves.

Goodbyes are said and tears are shed. Gus thanks us for everything and guarantees that we'll see him again. He also declares that we have to van the whole country next time. Annette, my travel partner for most of the tour, can't keep her eyes dry, as she gives me a hug and a final goodbye. I assure her that I'll see her soon again as well. In fact, at this very moment, lying on the grass with all my newfound friends, I decide that it would be a good idea to move down here and live in Melbourne for a year. I'll stay on course, going through Hawaii, and then go back home, but I will return in the new year. Newfie Joe has already decided to stay down under and hang out until he's no longer welcome by the Australian government. The trip has just been incredible and as with other tours, it has been all about the new friendships created, even when I was seemingly trying to avoid it to be on my own at the early stages. The loving kindness of the people I've met through these tours are infectious, almost like an addictive drug. Once I get a hit, I want more, and I keep coming back for more because it only gets better and better. My rash decision is a popular one, as everyone is looking forward to seeing me sooner rather than later.

With the exception of Mick, who's flying home the next day, everyone in the van, along with Ben, is staying a few more days in Perth before some of them begin the long drive back to Adelaide. So we spend the day relaxing at Scarborough Beach to soak in some sun and swim in the ocean. Ivan pulls out his bottle of wine, given by Vedder, and wants to share it with everyone. It's a bottle of 1997 Vasse Felix Heytesbury Cabernet from Margaret River, a few hours south of Perth. The bottle is almost full and a great souvenir from the show, so we reconfirm that he's certain that he wants to drink it.

"Of course, wine is always meant to be drunk," he explains. "Besides, Eddie would have wanted us to drink it."

With these instructions, we take turns sipping the wine directly from the bottle on the beach. It's not the classiest thing to do but the fact that it's in a bottle already makes it classier than all the boxes of goon we've consumed this trip. Besides, this is how Vedder would want us to do it. The wine is very flavourful and delicious, going down as smoothly as any wine I've tasted. None of us are wine connoisseurs but we're very impressed. So much so, that we all agree to take a drive down to Margaret River the next day and visit the winery. The five-hour drive, covering 300km seems like a piece of cake for us now.

The 1997 Vasse Felix Heytesbury Cabernet given to Ivan from Vedder.

At the vineyard, we see the 2002 Heytesbury on display in amongst all the awards it has won. We taste test several of the new releases and notice the price for the 2006 Heytesbury available for $70 a bottle. Wow, if the new release costs this much, what's the 1997 vintage worth? To answer our curiously, Ivan pulls out the empty bottle for the wine tasters to examine and their jaws just drop. One of them hasn't even seen this vintage before, while the other claims it to be so rare, that she didn't know even know where someone would be able to obtain it. Their estimated value of the wine is approximately $1000. So we've been consuming $10 boxes of goon all throughout the tour and we end up finishing the trip with a $1000 bottle of wine on the beach. We each pick up a bottle of the new vintage Heytesbury before we leave and happily make our way back to

Perth to drop off Ivan at the airport. He's flying to New Zealand.

With no place to stay, we decide to simply park in the parking lot of a hostel and sleep in the van for the night. Just as we're getting settled in, I receive a call from Ivan. Apparently, he was not allowed on the plane because he doesn't have a return ticket booked yet. So we make our way back to the airport to get him. Ivan will now ride back to Adelaide with the van along with Newfie Joe, Clayton, Julian, and Ben. In the morning, the boys drop me off at the airport for my flight. As much as I want to drive back with everyone in the van, I need to visit a friend in Brisbane, whom I missed last time, before leaving for Hawaii. I thank everybody for the great time and the memories and wish them all luck for another long drive, back the same way we came. At least they won't be shot gunning it this time and actually have a few extra days to play with. Julian is the only real driver remaining, with Mick and me departing, but he reckons he'll be able to hold the fort. I leave my ship, not knowing whether it will sail or sink, but I have faith in the guys to make it in one piece.

"The van is yours," I inform Newfie Joe.

"This could get interesting," he replies.

"Let's do it again," Ben and Ivan both echo.

In Brisbane, I catch up with Gordon, an old friend from Vancouver. We were really good friends back home and I've visited him in Brisbane before, so we naturally pick up right where we left off. However, as much fun as we have reminiscing, all I can think about is the trip that I had just completed and Hawaii coming up. The plan is to spend a week in Maui after the show but I haven't booked any accommodations yet. So I do a quick search and book something reasonable and within everyone's budget, as I had promised that I would take care of it. I look into changing my flight to arrive in Honolulu a day earlier for the private show but, having booked the cheapest possible fare already, changes to the original booking aren't permitted. With the cost of booking a brand new flight being close to $1000, I decide that it's not worth the money or the trouble. It is, after all, only one show and, even if it's my dream show, my friends won't be there to enjoy it with me.

In the past, I would have probably made more of an effort to make it to a secret Pearl Jam show but, since it's also a secret to my friends, it is not as relevant anymore. I've realized that the shows aren't what are important to me. Rather, it's the sharing of this common interest with good people and the adventures that we take on together that keeps me going to these shows. Newfie Joe said it best, "It's the journey that counts." That's exactly what I strive for and have been striving for this whole time. I'm hungry for adventure and Pearl Jam have just been providing me with opportunities to fill that hunger. Challenges are what intrigue me, and the harder the challenge, the more rewarding the results are. The next adventure is Hawaii, the easiest adventure yet.

I escaped it
a life wasted
I'm never going back again
Life Wasted

CHAPTER 45: **ENDING IN PARADISE**

December 2, 2006 » Show 62
Honolulu, Hawaii

FIFTEEN MONTHS, 14 COUNTRIES, 3 CONTINENTS, 61 PEARL JAM CONCERTS, and hundreds of new friends, it all comes to an end in Hawaii. Considered by many, including myself, to be paradise, Hawaii has some of the most beautiful and isolated tropical islands in the world. With the Australian tour injecting new blood into my system, I'm feeling happier and better than ever. I'm rejuvenated and ready to meet up with my friends in paradise. Flying through Honolulu on the way down to Australia, I see a glimpse of the island of Oahu from the plane, and it looks tiny. Flying back from Australia, I first make a stopover in Auckland, New Zealand for a night. It's very uneventful. I can take a trip into the city, but arriving early in the evening doesn't allow me a lot of time to do Auckland justice. So I stay only at the complimentary hotel near the airport courtesy of Air New Zealand for the layover. On arrival, I have to go through the hassle of applying and paying for a visitor's visa, which I can claim a refund for when I leave the country less than 24 hours later. I'm sure I'll lose something somewhere in the exchange rates.

Boarding my flight to Honolulu, I find my usual aisle seat near the rear of the plane. A few moments later, I get up to allow a man to take his window seat next to me, noticing that he's wearing a jacket that says "U2 Vertigo World Tour" on the back. Pearl Jam will be opening for U2's final show of their world tour in Honolulu next week, a show that is technically Pearl Jam's final show of the year, not the one that we're seeing tomorrow night. After seeing Pearl Jam open for Tom Petty, I have no interest in them as an opening band again so I won't be attending that show. I don't ask but I wonder if he's going. We soon receive our meals and it's surprisingly decent. The chicken penne actually tastes fresh. My neighbour isn't hungry though, so he offers me his meal, which I gladly accept.

"So what were you down in New Zealand for?" he asks me, as I'm eating his pasta.

"It was just a quick stop over from Australia," I answer.

"What was in Australia?" he follows.

"I was following this rock band on tour."

"Oh? Which one?" he asks with intrigue.

"Pearl Jam. I followed the band for the whole tour with a bunch of friends."

"Oh wow. I'm seeing them with U2 next week. I was just on U2's Australian tour, which ended last night in Auckland. My name is David."

We continue to chat about bands and gigs and it turns out that he runs a company called OTX (Ovation Travel Experiences) that caters to fans through organizing travel packages for concert tours, putting on pre-show meet ups for the fans, and arranging accommodations and transportation to and from shows. It sounds oddly familiar. Basically, his company model is to provide fans with their entertainment experience of a lifetime. So you can actually turn this into a job? I fill him in on what I've been up to and my experiences with the Pearl Jam tours and he seems genuinely interested in everything I've done, especially with the Touring Van, so he hands over a business card.

He tells me that he's putting on a Hawaiian luau for U2 fans the day before the concert in Honolulu. There will be dinner, dancing, hula and fire dancing, as well as a tribute band playing all night, and he describes it to be the largest fan gathering of the tour, inviting me to come along as well. I thank him for the offer but politely decline because I'll have left Hawaii by that point. My answer is disappointing to him and he finds it surprising that I'm not even going to the show. He even offers to get me tickets.

"It's two of the biggest bands ending their world tour together," he describes. "It will be an unbelievable show."

Still, I don't commit but we continue chatting and I find out more about his experiences from working with big name artists such as the Rolling Stones, Cher, Madonna, Paul McCartney, Red Hot Chili Peppers, and Stone Temple Pilots. Starting the company from the grass roots level in the 1970's, David expresses that he has tried reaching out to Pearl Jam before to get involved with their fan base, but has been unsuccessful thus far. So I give him my take on Pearl Jam fans and show him some of my photos from the tour this year and he's impressed. Our conversation is both enriching and educational at the same time, as the 10-hour flight passes by quickly and we land in Honolulu in no time. As we depart the plane, David expresses his interest in collaborating with me on a future Pearl Jam tour and asks me to contact him when the next one comes about. We wish each other luck at the baggage claim and go our separate ways.

As I enter through the arrival gates, I immediately get lei'd by Kasie. The scent of the lovely flowers is almost as nice as the scent of my lovely friend. Kasie and

Veronica from Chico, Monica from Sacramento, and Lydia from San Francisco were all on the same flight out of San Francisco, but none of them were aware of this until they were actually on the plane. Cali Joe arrived a little bit afterwards, as did Brian, Lydia's friend from Monterrey. Team California has been waiting patiently at the cocktail lounge for my arrival but they're now "popping off". It's always good to see old faces again, as it's always a big reunion each time. The girls from Chico thank me for my phone call from the Perth show and begin describing the event as it took place in their household. A few moments later, Sarah from Toronto arrives, coming in from Melbourne, bringing our group to a total of eight. With this many of us, it's actually cheaper to get a limo rather than hailing a cab to our hotel. So we decide to enter Honolulu in style.

Barbara and Rob had already arrived earlier in the day from the UK and are waiting for us at the Queen Kapiolani Hotel, where we have two rooms booked directly across from Waikiki Beach. After a quick introduction for everyone, we drop our bags off and immediately jump in the ocean with our clothes still on. And even though it's late in the evening, the water is warm and welcoming, exactly what we had expected. Treading water in the open ocean, I look up into the sky and the moon is bright and round. I'm amongst friends in Hawaii and it doesn't get much better than this. We dry off at the hotel before heading down the street to a jam-packed bar called Lu Lu's. It's filled with more of a college crowd, but we're able to get a spot on the balcony and rip through a few rounds of drinks.

When the bar closes at 3:30am, the natural next step is to head straight to the beach. Walking along the water, which we were just swimming in only a few hours earlier, we reach the end of the pier where a man is mysteriously laying, passed out on his back. A few joke photos are taken with him, as he lays motionless but breathes very loudly. Everyone hovers around this enigmatic person, while Cali Joe decides to jump back into the water again. As he comes back up, another man approaches and asks us how his friend is doing. We inform him that he's just sleeping. But when he calls out his name, Cloberson, the man, once peacefully resting away, instantly pops up and looks around utterly confused, completely surrounded by strangers who suddenly high five him.

"Let's go to the Hideaway," Cloberson proclaims, after his initial disorientation.

"What's the Hideaway?" Cali Joe asks.

"It's a bar," Cloberson's friend replies. "You guys want to join us?"

"There's a bar still open?" I follow.

"No, but it opens at 6:00am."

I peek down at my watch and it reads 4:30am. Still thirsty for one more drink, we decide to tag along, thinking it's nearby. We head down Kalakaua Ave toward this magical Hideaway Bar, following two strangers reassuring us that it's just up ahead every 10 minutes. With minimal amount of sleep amongst all of us, the walk seems longer than our flights. Cloberson was smart to rest up before this excursion. As the minutes tick away, we begin to become sceptical of this mythical bar that opens at 6:00am. Accordingly, the girls decide to pull out and cab it back to the hotel to call it a night, while the guys are still interested to see where this ends up. So onward we march, Cali Joe, Brian, Rob, and I.

A 24-hour breakfast place is spotted shortly afterwards, so at least we have a backup plan in case the Hideaway doesn't pan out. But as we round the corner of the restaurant, low and behold, the Hideaway appears before us nearly 40 minutes into the walk and there's a lineup outside of it, solidifying the bar as a happening place. Apparently, all the people are in the same situation as us and are waiting for it to open to continue on drinking. There's still 20 minutes until opening time, so we leave our new friends to get some breakfast first before the Hideaway opens. Back at the bar, Cloberson and his friend are already wasted by the time we return. They also have six pitchers of draft beer sitting in front of them with empty glasses waiting for us, so we help ourselves. The first pint goes down like water but the second one is a struggle, except for Rob who, coming from England, probably doesn't feel like he's drinking in the morning. Completely fatigued now, we decide that it's probably time to go back to the hotel and actually get some rest.

A short nap does me a world of good, as I wake up fresh and ready to take in Hawaii in the sunlight. First, we gather around for our second breakfast of the day. The menu at the hotel restaurant features spam in many of the dishes. Intrigued by this Hawaiian obsession with spam, I order the traditional spam and eggs with a side of hash. It's very tasty, similar to corn beef and hash. Over breakfast we discuss our plans for the following week, as we have a condo booked for a week in Maui but no flights sorted yet. Barbara, Rob, Lydia, and Monica will be joining me on the second largest island in Hawaii, and the general consensus is for us to get the fuck out of Honolulu as quickly as we can, so we proceed with booking the very first flight tomorrow morning with one of the local island airlines and also a rental van in the process. Now we're ready to soak in the sun.

To assimilate myself with the culture, I pick up a Hawaiian shirt from one of the many ABC general stores and immediately put it on. It's also a tribute to Brad, who will no doubt be wearing one of his many Hawaiian shirts when we meet up before the show. With my new attire, we roam around Waikiki. Being a weekend in December, the streets are busy and the beach is packed with tourists. It's not exactly our scene, but the scenery is still lovely. From what I gather from walking along the main strip, Honolulu has an abundant amount of shops (especially surf shops and ABC stores), Hawaiian barbeque takeout restaurants, bars, and shaved ice. Office buildings peer out from the background, making Honolulu seem very much like any other city in America, except that it's situated on the coast of an island. Guess we'll just have to wait for Maui to get the secluded paradise feeling. The warm temperature is always good though.

As the afternoon (and our desire to further explore this major tourist port) winds down, it's time to meet up with other fans at the pre-show party. A vast amount of mainland Americans have come over to partake in the tour's finale, bringing along the CCFA fundraiser once again, this time held in a private function room at a bar called Dave and Buster's. Laura and Eric from the Wishlist Foundation are both on hand to facilitate the fundraiser benefiting both the CCFA and a local charity called the Hui Malama I Ke Kai Foundation. It's a gathering of many old friends, whom I haven't seen since the US tour in the summer. Brian from Lethbridge is present and he fills me in on his experience at the World Series of Poker just after the Gorge shows and says how excited he is about spending a week at a resort here. Also in attendance is Brad, sporting his flashiest Hawaiian shirt yet. To go with the shirt, he's also wearing an authentic Scottish kilt, which is part of his heritage.

"Dude, why didn't you fly in a few days earlier?" the Hawaiian Scot wonders. "That show at Waimea was unreal."

"I couldn't change my flight man," I reply. "I would have had to book a completely new flight and that was just too pricey for me."

Brad fills me in on the details of the private show for all the people involved with the Big Wave Surf Competition. He was on the beach for the opening ceremonies where all the surfers paddled out into the ocean and joined hands in a sacred circle to pay tribute to the legendary Eddie Aikau. Apparently, Vedder even paddled out with them, a surreal moment as Brad describes it. He also bumped into Tim from the Jersey Shore who offered to get him into the concert later in the night, but Brad didn't want to leave his friends behind. Instead, they hiked around Waimea Park and found an entrance on their own into this exclusive show.

"There were maybe five actual fans in attendance," he explains. "I could tell I was standing next to some famous surfers, but I had no clue who they were."

"Oh man, that sounds like my dream show," I respond.

"Yeah J, I was thinking of you the whole time."

Even with Brad continuing to glorify what could have been my most ideal way to end an incredible year, I don't feel too concerned about missing it. I merely smile and express my happiness for Brad being there, but I'm not choked about my absence. Maybe it's the toll that all these shows in such a short period of time have taken on me and maybe I'm not as keen about the shows as I was when this whole thing first started. People go through phases and perhaps my phase of religiously following Pearl Jam has peaked. This is the end of a lengthy world tour, and the momentum that I once had in this marathon could be running out of steam. At the pre-party, I'm simply going through the motions of greeting old friends without really making the effort to meet new ones as I once would enthusiastically do. Yet, as Brad hands me a souvenir from the surf competition, I still feel that I belong and there's no other place that I could imagine being right now other than where I am.

"The green is the only colour they had left, but I figured that you'll like it regardless," he says, as he hands me an official Quicksilver "Eddie Would Go" shirt with this year's event dates on the back. I love it and try it on immediately. Brad also unveils two new shirts that he arranged to get designed for the Wishlist Foundation. The shirts feature Matt Cameron and Boom Gasper, the two remaining members to which he hadn't done a shirt for yet, and he wants Cali Joe and I to model it for a couple of photos. They look great and the designs are far more in depth than the previous guitar pick shirts, which were awfully popular, all helping to raise money for Wishlist Foundation charities. We donate some money to the benefit by buying a page in the scrapbook that will be submitted to the band at the show, fill it up with comments and photos from all of us, basically thanking the band for the great year and everything they've provided for us.

Me, Brad, and Cali Joe modelling the new shirts.

The Blaisdell Centre Arena is not too far from the bar. We arrive shortly after the doors open with plenty of time to spare, carrying the infamous Canadian flag that has been with me the whole way. It's signed by McCready and also by some of the guys in Australia, so we figured that it would be a good idea for everyone here to add to it and somehow give it to the band. Walking around the venue, I approach everyone that I recognize with a black sharpie and kindly ask if they want to write some words for the band on the flag. Up in the stands and around the floor I go, making the rounds, until I reach Brad in the front row. He adds his words of wisdom and then offers to throw the flag on stage for us due to his proximity during the show. I accept the offer and put the finishing touches to the flag, which is now half filled with thank you's from my friends.

Kings of Leon are opening again tonight. They've been one of the best supporting acts I've seen, at least when I manage to get in early enough for them. I sit 15 rows back on the tiny floor of this 8,000 capacity venue with Veronica next to me – she's on my spare. We notice Cali Joe, Kasie, and Monica all sitting together just a few rows ahead beside a couple of unfilled seats, so we make the jump to join our friends for the opening band. When these seats are still not accounted for by the time Pearl Jam takes the stage, we remain in them until further notice. Having my friends around definitely helps enhance the experience for me, one that I've endured 61 times in the last 15 months. As the first set comes to a close, it's probably safe to say that our seats are secure and we'll be able to stay together.

"Alright, if you could join your energy with us for just a bit of a prayer here," Vedder announces, as Boom accompanies on the organ.

What follows is one of the most captivating moments in a show that I've encountered during this tour.

"Ua mau, ke ea o ka aina, i ka pono, o Hawaii!" Vedder sings.

The volume of the crowd gets louder and louder as more and more of the locals begin to recognize the song with each word belted out one after the other by the surfing singer, who is rumoured to have a place of his own in Hawaii. The noise and cheers grow exponentially until the roof is blown off of the place by end of the first line, "O Hawaii!" The atmosphere sends chills down my body, giving me goose bumps all over. Wow. This is the loudest I've heard any crowd anywhere during this tour. The song is *Hawaii 78*, a political love song by Hawaiian ukulele artist Israel Kamakawiwo'ole, and it's sort of an anthem around these parts. It's utterly magnificent. I look over at the others and they aren't even sure what's happening on stage. No one can really put words to it so we revert to actions and hold each other's hands with smiles all around for the ritual. I haven't grown tired of these shows yet. I love them as much as I always have. There's a reason why I chose to follow this band at the beginning, before I even met anyone. They're that good and consistently one of the best live shows you'll ever see. And now that I have so many friends in the community, the shows have merely taken a backseat to everything else. I just look to have a good time now because the shows are always good.

At the end of the first encore, I see the Canadian flag get tossed onto the stage. It drapes itself over one of the speakers for the rest of the song until it's swept away by a stage crew to add to their collection. It has been with me for the whole journey but it's now with them. When the stage is set for the second encore, Vedder begins thanking his crew and then he refers to another family. "This year we've seen a lot of people that have shown an incredible amount of dedication by travelling around to see this group play live," he addresses the crowd. "We've seen this in Australia, in Europe, back on the mainland. And they've been really good to us and, perhaps even more importantly, good to each other. We're proud of you for that and we really appreciate it."

His words really don't tell us anything new, other than the fact that the generosity of all the incredible people that I've met within this community hasn't gone unnoticed by the band. We truly are a unique breed and I'm also so thankful for all of my new friends. As the band finishes up the final set of their final show of the tour, I absorb the music in and stand proud of my accomplishments, happy for everything that I've gone through. This isn't the Gorge, where emotions got the best of me and blinded my sight of what this is all about. It's the end, but it's only the end of the tour. There will be more shows in the future. But more importantly, this is just the beginning of the good times I'll share with my new acquaintances for many years to come. *Yellow Ledbetter* signals a close to the show and is also a cue for us to exit the venue. We hang around outside the venue for a bit to figure out what everyone is doing for the after party, but it all appears to be too much hassle to deal with. Our flight to Maui is early in the morning, 5:45am to be exact, and we didn't exactly sleep at all the night before. So we decide to head back toward the hotel.

On the walk across the parking lot, I see a familiar face approaching us in the opposite direction. She makes eye contact and smiles at me as we cross paths, so I say hi. I know I've met her before, but I can't quite put my finger on exactly where or when but most importantly what her name is. We both turn our heads as we pass each other and I smile back at her, while we both continue on.

"How's it going?" I yell back at her.

"Good," the mysterious girl replies, with an engaging smile.

"Good seeing you again," I follow and continue marching on.

I just can't figure out who it is and it's killing me. As we approach the main road, Brad hails a taxi and suggests that we grab some food at the Denny's by his hotel, since none of us have really eaten yet. You know you're back in America when you're going to Denny's for breakfast at one in the morning. These are my last few moments with some of my friends, as half of us are flying out to Maui in a few hours, while the rest are staying put for another day before returning home to their jobs. Instead of a sentimental goodbye, everyone is dead tired but happy to have spent as much time together as we could within the short time period. We know that we'll see each other again because we are friends for life now. "I'll see you guys soon," I tell Cali Joe, Kasie, Veronica, and Sarah.

I pry Rob, Barbara, Monica, and Lydia out of their beds, while it's still dark outside. A taxi takes us back to the airport where we board a small jet headed for Wailuku, Maui. The flight only lasts half an hour, but the sight of the sunrise from the plane is nothing short of spectacular. We pick up our rental van, which was my choice of course, and hit the road by 7:30am with our destination being the resort town of Kihei. On the map it appears to be hours away, but in reality, the trip takes less than 20 minutes. Two of my friends from back home, Andrew and Rachel, are also joining us on this vacation. They flew in last night from Vancouver and are scheduled to meet us at the resort at around 8:00am. Being away from home so much this year has sort of taken me away from my friends back home. They don't understand what it is that drives me to do what I do, but they're missed every step of the way. Seeing them in any situation is a treat, especially in Maui.

"It took you guys long enough," Andrew greets us with his usual sarcasm.

I look down at my watch and it says 8:15am.

"Yeah, we were in a crack house last night," Rachel follows up. "We almost died."

Getting in just after midnight, the two hung out at the beach to wait for our arrival until they were offered a place to stay by a local walking by, ironically, named Eddie. Apparently, he left Andrew and Rachel alone at a mysterious apartment when the real owners returned with a score of crack. It was quite a heart pumping situation indeed. As the story goes, the owners of the apartment started interrogating my friends but, due to some clever responses under fire by Andrew, they were able to escape before anything alarming occurred. Andrew pretended to answer his phone and noted that they had to leave to come meet me. The ploy worked to perfection. Obviously feeling a bit startled, they jokingly hold me responsible for this bizarre start to their vacation.

"Thanks, Jason!" Andrew and Rachel say in unison.

The manager's office at the condo is not open yet and we can't pick up the keys, so we drive back into town, only 30 seconds away, and hit up a bar for some fruity cocktails. Hawaii is two hours behind the time of the mainland, so there are a slew of NFL games already being shown. By 10:00am, we're a bit tipsy already and what started out as a sketchy beginning to the Maui vacation is all forgotten. We return to the condo before noon to get the keys and claim our beds. For $150 a night, we're getting a place with two bedrooms and two bathrooms directly across from the beach in Kihei. Not bad for seven of us. Barbara, Lydia, and Monica grab the master bedroom with a triple sized bed, while Andrew and Rachel occupy the kid's room consisting of two singles, leaving the sofa bed in the decent-sized living room for me to share with Rob. Once all settled, we cross the street and hit the beach.

With the combination of good company and good weather, the next few days are some of the most relaxing and enjoyable moments. If I thought Perth was laid back to an extreme, we're on Maui time now, which basically means that time isn't even an issue here. Things are taken slowly for it all to be fully absorbed. In fact, nothing is really a big deal on Maui. The stunning sunsets, alluring white sand beaches, consistently pleasant weather, and delicious seafood will take your mind off of any worries you may have back home. Add to it the exotic nature of its location in the South Pacific, with English as the spoken language, how could Hawaii not be loved? It's even part of North America and my American friends don't even need a passport to visit. This is the perfect place to end the year. This is paradise.

The days are spent exploring the plentiful amount of beautiful beaches and, although the surf isn't particularly going off on this island, the body boarding is ideal. Up the West Coast of the island, we visit the more touristy town of Lahaina, where there are many shops for us to pick up a few souvenirs, a cheesy Bubba Gump chain restaurant to fill our seafood and Forest Gump trivia needs, a Cold Stone Creamery to satisfy our craving for ice cream, and an enormous banyan Tree that nests what sounds to be hundreds of birds. We bump into Nicole from Asheville, NC on the street, apparently having the same taste in vacation locations as us.

On another day, we go for a drive out east to Hana on the ever-exciting Hana highway. The windy sharp turns on this narrow single lane highway give you the perception that you're driving through a forest, which, in fact, you are. We stop to explore some of the many waterfalls along the way, situated within tropical trees that remind you of Jurassic Park. I never knew Hawaii was so green. Closer to Hana are some black sand beaches home to some of the roughest waves I have ever seen. The rock formations show the amount of wear and tear caused by the enormously crashing waves. Maui is definitely a wonderful site during the days. With the exception of the daily one-hour tropical rainfall, the sun shines so bright and long that even my naturally tanned skin begins to get some colour.

As for nightlife, there really isn't a lot provided for us here. On one night, we walk down to the local pub, the only pub in town, and get absolutely trashed thanks to some crafty pre-drinking at the condo, where Andrew wows us with his margarita making skills. And there must be a hole in my glass because the bottle of whiskey is demolished in no time. The effects are apparent when I pour beer from a pitcher directly onto our table, completely missing Rachel's cup, much to the laughter of the others.

Another night, thanks to Andrew's willingness to sit in on a time share presentation, we receive discount tickets to the most touristy activity of them all, a Hawaiian luau. With fire throwing grass skirt dancing entertainment before us, we chow down on a buffet featuring a full roast pig amongst other local delights. Most in the crowd are newlyweds, honeymooners, or couples on wedding anniversaries. To say that we stick out would be an understatement. Looking around I can safely conclude that the average age of vacationers in Hawaii is much older than us. Nonetheless, the party is fun and seeing the amount of joy in some of their faces, many who'll have this as their one vacation of the year, brings a smile to my face. So what if they're doing the cheesy touristy things, wearing shirts with flowers on them that they'll probably never wear again at home. Hell, I bought and wore one of those shirts and we're participating in the same touristy events. Hawaii is one of the top tourist places in the world, whether we like it or not, and this is the type of entertainment that allows people to let go of their everyday lives. Here, they can feel free of any worries and just enjoy themselves and I think that's fantastic.

Rob, Rachel, Lydia, Andrew, me, and Barbara at the Hawaiian Luau.

Our five days in Maui pass by quickly. Isn't it ironic that when time isn't a concern at all, you end up not having enough time? This is exactly how this past year has gone for me. On our last day in Maui, we'll need to fly back to Honolulu to catch our corresponding return flights back home. However, we feel the need to hit the beach just one more time before leaving, so we jump in the van and drive to nearby Baby Beach. Without any clue of the time, we stay in the water, which is so calm that it is completely transparent, until we feel that we're reluctantly ready to go. I turn on the ignition in the van and the clock reveals that we have only an hour until our flight leaves. Shit! I gun it out of the parking lot and then step on the gas, as if I was a racing in Formula 1. We still have to return the van, so we arrive at the car rental lot 20 long minutes later. How fitting is it that the year ends with an adventure to the airport. Everyone has the inclination that there's a possibility that we might miss our flight, but no one seems to be overly concerned about it. If we make it then we make it. If not we'll be fine. It's not the worst thing in the world to be stuck in Maui.

With everything checking out okay, we hop on the shuttle bus, dropping us off just outside of the departures terminal with 20 minutes left until takeoff. Luckily for us, the Maui airport is open air and outdoors like every other airport in Hawaii, so stepping off the bus, we're already at our check-in desk with no lineup, probably because everyone is on board already. The airline staff quickly checks us in, using valet baggage services, and instructs us to hurry to the plane. Like track stars we sprint through the tiny airport, being slowed down only at the security check, and arrive at our gate where the plane is waiting for us. As we step on, the door shuts behind us immediately. We've just barely made it, symbolic of how the year has gone. Everything has just worked out.

There are few words said on the short flight, as no one wants to talk about leaving. We make it to Honolulu as scheduled but our luggage doesn't. Our late check-in didn't allow enough time for the valet baggage service to deposit them, but they'll arrive on the next flight. And as we stand around wondering what the next step is, reality hits and we all realize that our home is calling, apart from Barbara and Monica, who are sticking around for the U2 and Pearl Jam show the following day. As it turns out, Rob ends up staying for the show as well, after missing his flight home the next morning and having to re-book. Goodbyes are said but there's little doubt that we'll all see each other again soon, even though we all have different flights back on different airlines to different places. This is not the end; it's only the beginning. This all encompassing trip has brought me more new friends than I could ever have imagined, all who are very special in their own unique way. We've shared so many magical moments together and created enough memories to write a book.

As I leave my friends and wait for my flight back to Vancouver I sit alone at my gate feeling proud of all my accomplishments in such a short time. What started out as an innocent drive to see my favourite band has turned into something much bigger than anyone could have dreamed. The people I've met have truly touched me and inspired me to continue to do bigger and better things. It was never about Pearl Jam – it was about so much more.

It's about losing your friend in a crowd in Munich, Germany and then running into him the next day at a random train station in Austria. It's about believing that you've overslept and left too late, but, in fact, you've inadvertently arrived at the perfect moment to pick up an unexpected hitchhiker that you would become very close with. It's about getting your bag stolen in Italy and running after it to get it back. It's about relentlessly drinking box wine worth $10 throughout the tour and then drinking a bottle of wine worth $1000 for free. It's about the fan that treats someone different at every show to a front row experience. It's about thinking you've thrown out a full bottle of vodka only to find it in the dumpster still in drinkable condition. It's about finding the best cheesesteak in Philly. It's about flying halfway around the world only to have an old friend surprise you with his appearance. It's about the Norwegians, who put the money up front to get the tour bus on the go. It's about sitting around a camp fire and telling your friends how much they mean to you. It's about coming together as a community to raise money for good causes.

It's about meeting up with people all over the world. It's about surfing the Pacific and then driving across Canada to surf the Atlantic. It's about the fan that's too gracious to brag about his brush with fame, singing with Pearl Jam. It's about meeting your heroes, who are just as thrilled to meet you. It's about camping at your first music festival with a group of strangers and getting along like you've known them for a long time. It's about driving over 50 consecutive hours across Australia with five friends in a van that seats three. It's about driving to game 7 of the Stanley Cup Finals and scoring tickets behind the commissioner. It's about running your tank dry in the middle of the night, then continuing on when some strangers go an hour out of their way to bring you back some gas, then falling asleep and driving into a ditch, before blowing a flat tire all in one night, but still making your destination without any animosity. It's about converging together in Verona with a hundred new friends from fifteen different countries. It's about bonding with people over a wine and cheese picnic in the park. It's about throwing your prepaid bus ticket away to ride in a van full of strangers instead. It's about breaking down in the van after it has delivered its final passenger. It's about trusting people whom you've just met.

This is what living is all about: following your dreams, having faith in people, believing that everything will work out. I've enjoyed unbelievable luck throughout the year, but is it just luck? No one is really this lucky, are they? To have met the people that I've met, to have seen the places that I've seen, and to have experienced the lifetime's worth of experiences that I've experienced, I credit this luck to my positive outlook on life and to everything that encompasses it. Negativity is very easy to dwell on but, if you look at the bright side of things, it's amazing how much of a difference it can make. As I look back at my trip, I remember all the good times and smile. And then I went home.

Feeling incredible at the end of the tour in Maui.

WORLD TOUR **BY THE NUMBERS**

104 days on the road
69 days in Europe
35 days in Australia
25 Pearl Jam shows
652 total live songs
110 unique songs
3,916km driven
3,560km by bus
87 hours in the air
80.5 hours by train
70 total Euro Bus passengers
6 total Aussie Van passengers
Longest drive – Adelaide to Perth 52 hours
Longest flight – Vancouver to Sydney 18 hours
Most played song – *Alive* and *Do The Evolution* both 23 times

EXPENSES (US Dollars)
$12,969.08 TOTAL WORLD TOUR EXPENSE ($124.70 per day)
$7,421.70 total Europe tour expense ($107.56 per day)
    $1,859.00 for flights
    $679.90 for trains
    $1,305.20 for accommodations
    $2,237.30 for food and drinks
    $923.00 for concert tickets
    $417.30 for merchandise and souvenirs
$5,547.38 total Australia tour expense ($158.50 per day)
    $2,891.00 for flights
    $188.33 for trains
    $95.24 for van rentals (total for everyone was $600)
    $91.90 for gas (total for everyone was $580)
    $289.24 for accommodations
    $855.00 for food and drinks
    $880.00 for concert tickets
    $256.67 for merchandise and souvenirs

THIS ALL ENCOMPASSING TRIP
BY THE NUMBERS

197 days on the road
13 countries
62 Pearl Jam shows
1,705 total live songs
148 unique songs
40,494km driven
3,560km by bus
103 hours in the air
80.5 hours by train
100s of friends
1000s of memories

EXPENSES (US Dollars)
$27,342.59 TOTAL EXPENSE
$4,050.38 for van maintenance and insurance (total for everyone was $5,920.46)
$1,245.00 for new video camera purchases
$330.00 for recycling fine (Jersey Cops)
$21,717.22 total tour expense ($110.24 per day)

　　$5,355.73 for flights
　　$868.23 for trains
　　$95.24 for van rentals (total for everyone was $600)
　　$1,800.77 for gas (total for everyone was $5,013.33)
　　$2,039.48 for accommodations (total for everyone was $5,149.20)
　　$5,409.30 for food and drinks
　　$3,916.50 for concert tickets
　　$734.00 for other event tickets
　　$1,497.97 for merchandise and souvenirs

EPILOGUE

THIS all encompassing trip was a lifetime of memories for me to experience in just over a year.

Here I am, four years older but forty years wiser, still on this high.

I don't think I will be coming down from it anytime in the near future.

Sure, security and stability would be safe, but I will be just fine.

ALL my education and work experiences cannot match the life lessons that I am receiving.

Leaving at the prime of my prospective career was not a mistake, it was relieving.

Living without daily routines and letting go of material possessions was a much needed releasing.

ENCOMPASSING the world to visit friends and to explore new cultures is my passion now.

Now that I have lived and worked all over, I look back with appreciation of that first trip across Canada.

Canada is still my home but I have not limited myself to just one.

One of the most amazing things is how everything works out, with one particular coincidence that just blows my mind.

Mind you, I was not aware of it at the time, but I had met the girl of my dreams on the tour, and she is pretty.

Pretty much clueless, I talked to her as her friends climbed the van for a photo after the second St John's show I was at.

At the Ottawa show, she was with her mom, unintentionally flaunting their newly purchased limited edition hoodies in front of me as I fled the scene.

Seen with her friend at the Portland show, she was introduced to me by Dana as Sophie.

Sophie was the familiar looking girl who I didn't recognize after the Honolulu show even though she said hi, as did I.

I now live happily with Sophie and we are taking it as it comes, not planning what is next.

Next to enjoying life together, there is nothing that can be as good.

Good riddance normal life and welcome fulfilling life.

TRIP of a lifetime can continue, as I describe.

Ride whatever wave comes and wherever it takes me, that's what I'm living by.

I am loving life and living it to the fullest with my girl,

Pearl Jam, thank you for being the catalyst to this all encompassing trip.

CPSIA information can be obtained at www.ICGtesting.com

263726BV00004B/244/P